Praise for Applied Software Project Management

"The challenges in effectively managing software development projects are well known. Books on software project management tend to focus on the tools and techniques for managing projects. There are two problems with this: 1) not every project needs to use every technique, but it is not clear which techniques to use for particular projects; and 2) projects are frequently derailed by social and organizational concerns, not technical problems. *Applied Software Project Management* by Stellman and Greene offers a fresh perspective by providing practical advice to project leaders on project management. It offers a way for project managers to select the specific techniques that will benefit a particular project.

"This book provides practical advice on how to convince stakeholders that quality activities are worth the investment, how to determine what are the most important quality practices to implement, given limited time and budget, and how to work with others and motivate them to improve the development process."

—SANDRA SLAUGHTER, PROFESSOR, TEPPER SCHOOL OF BUSINESS, CARNEGIE MELLON UNIVERSITY

"The stepping-stone for missed expectations is set when the decision to fund a project is based on investment assumptions that are not shared with the project manager. Shareholder value is equally undermined when business leaders cannot easily determine the true status of their projects. Stellman and Greene open the door to greater profitability by making the case for top-down and bottom-up transparency, from project conception through closeout. Read this book for some practical guidance you can start applying right away."

—RICHARD TOLEDO, EXECUTIVE DIRECTOR/EASTERN U.S. FOR PROGRAM PLANNING PROFESSIONALS, INC., ALSO KNOWN AS PCUBED

"Whether your software team is centrally located or geographically distributed, *Applied Software Project Management* provides practical advice on how to effectively manage the efforts of your team."

—SANJAY PODDER, PMP, CSQA, ACCENTURE IDC—AVANADE AG, AVANADE MUMBAI CENTER LEAD

"To be honest, I wanted to write this book. There are a fair number of books that discuss project management from a philosophical or theoretical point of view, but few that address it in real, practical terms. *Applied Software Project Management* does just that and does it well. Stellman and Greene walk through the aspects of software development, including defining a project vision, choosing a development process, configuration management, requirements tracking, and testing, with real examples and discussions of tools used in the wild.

"I've chosen this book for my graduate software engineering class aand will make it part of any client project. It's honest, practical, and full of real experience."

—DAN PILONE, SENIOR SOFTWARE ARCHITECT WITH BLUEPRINT TECHNOLOGIES AND LECTURER AT THE CATHOLIC UNIVERSITY OF AMERICA IN WASHINGTON, D.C.

Applied Software
Project Management

Other resources from O'Reilly

Related titles

The Art of Project Management

Essential Business Process Modeling

Practical Development Environments

Prefactoring

UML 2.0 in a Nutshell

oreilly.com

oreilly.com is more than a complete catalog of O'Reilly books. You'll also find links to news, events, articles, weblogs, sample chapters, and code examples.

oreillynet.com is the essential portal for developers interested in open and emerging technologies, including new platforms, programming languages, and operating systems.

Conferences

O'Reilly brings diverse innovators together to nurture the ideas that spark revolutionary industries. We specialize in documenting the latest tools and systems, translating the innovator's knowledge into useful skills for those in the trenches. Visit *conferences.oreilly.com* for our upcoming events.

Safari Bookshelf (*safari.oreilly.com*) is the premier online reference library for programmers and IT professionals. Conduct searches across more than 1,000 books. Subscribers can zero in on answers to time-critical questions in a matter of seconds. Read the books on your Bookshelf from cover to cover or simply flip to the page you need. Try it today for free.

Applied Software
Project Management

Andrew Stellman and Jennifer Greene

O'REILLY®

Beijing • Cambridge • Farnham • Köln • Paris • Sebastopol • Taipei • Tokyo

Applied Software Project Management
Andrew Stellman and Jennifer Greene

Copyright © 2006 O'Reilly Media, Inc.

All rights reserved.

Printed in the United States of America.

Published by O'Reilly Media, Inc.

1005 Gravenstein Highway North

Sebastopol, CA 95472.

O'Reilly books may be purchased for educational, business, or sales promotional use. Online editions are also available for most titles (*safari.oreilly.com*). For more information, contact our corporate/institutional sales department: (800) 998-9938 or *corporate@oreilly.com*.

Publishing Editors:	Mary T. O'Brien and Andrew Odewahn
Production Editor:	Jamie Peppard
Cover Designer:	MendeDesign
Interior Designer:	Marcia Friedman

Printing History:	November 2005: First Edition.

The O'Reilly logo is a registered trademark of O'Reilly Media, Inc. The *Theory in Practice* series designations, *Applied Software Project Management*, and related trade dress are trademarks of O'Reilly Media, Inc.

Clear Case, ClearQuest, Rational Robot, Rational Rose, Rational Unified Process, Requisite Pro, and TestManager are registered trademarks of IBM. Microsoft Project, C#, and Visual SourceSafe are registered trademarks of Microsoft. Six Sigma is a registered trademark of Motorola, Inc. UNIX is a registered trademark of The Open Group. Perforce is a registered trademark of Perforce Software, Inc. Java is a registered trademark of Sun Microsystems.

Many of the designations used by manufacturers and sellers to distinguish their products are claimed as trademarks. Where those designations appear in this book, and O'Reilly Media, Inc. was aware of a trademark claim, the designations have been printed in caps or initial caps.

While every precaution has been taken in the preparation of this book, the publisher and authors assume no responsibility for errors or omissions, or for damages resulting from the use of the information contained herein.

RepKover. This book uses RepKover™, a durable and flexible lay-flat binding.

ISBN: 0-596-00948-8

[M]

TABLE OF CONTENTS

Preface

SOFTWARE PROJECT MANAGEMENT is the art and science of planning and leading software projects. It requires knowledge of the entire software development lifecycle: defining the vision, planning the tasks, gathering the people who will do the work, estimating the effort, creating the schedule, overseeing the work, gathering the requirements, designing and programming the software, and testing the end product. Throughout the process, there are many team members who are responsible for these tasks; the project manager needs to have enough knowledge of their work to make sure the project is staying on track.

To be effective, a project manager must have a wide range of expertise. In this book, we provide an introduction to all of these areas so that you can guide the rest of your team on their tasks. We help you run successful software projects, and we help you diagnose and fix the ones that have gone off track.

Goals of the Book

This is a practical book. This book describes the specific tools, techniques, and practices that a project manager needs to put in place in order to run a software project or fix an ailing one. A project manager can use this book to diagnose and fix the most serious problems that plague software projects. It contains essential project management tools, techniques, and practices, which have been optimized to be as straightforward and easy to implement as possible. It also contains advice for avoiding the problems that a project manager will typically encounter when bringing these tools into an organization.

By the time you have read this book, you should be able to:

- Define the scope of your project
- Estimate the effort required to do the work and schedule your project
- Conduct thorough reviews of documents and code
- Gather software requirements and create specifications
- Effectively manage the design, programming, and testing of the software
- Provide guidance if your project runs into quality problems
- Manage an outsourced project
- Make effective changes to the way projects are run in your organization

We have been researching and implementing these tools, techniques, and practices throughout our combined careers. Each of them is the culmination of years of trial and error in many different organizations across multiple industries. Every one of these practices is the solution to a specific, chronic problem. Many people opt to live with the problem, because the solution seems too complicated. Our ultimate goal in writing this book is to help you build better software.

Often, the original idea (before we optimized it) came from a book that we read to solve a specific problem that we encountered on a software project (just like you are doing right now!). References to some of the books that we found most helpful appear in the text in order to help you learn more.

Who Should Read This Book

Many software organizations have trouble delivering high-quality software on time. Most of them have talented team members; almost all of them realize that there is a problem. People in these organizations may have already read books about management, quality, and programming. What all of these people have in common is a need to change the way a software organization works. They may not always recognize the nature of the problem, or what is causing delays or bugs. What they do know is that something needs to change.

We wrote this book for anyone in a software organization where there are chronic problems producing software on schedule and without defects. The intended readers of this book include:

- A project manager responsible for a software development project and/or team
- A programmer, designer, business analyst, architect, tester, or other member of a software team looking to improve the product he is working on

- A quality assurance manager or team member who is attempting to implement defect prevention, or is responsible for establishing or improving an organization's software process

- A consultant hired to improve project management practices, software process, or overall software quality in an organization

- A project manager who has been put in charge of a project that has been outsourced

Comments and Questions

Please address comments and questions concerning this book to the publisher:

O'Reilly Media, Inc.
1005 Gravenstein Highway North
Sebastopol, CA 95472
(800) 998-9938 (in the United States or Canada)
(707) 829-0515 (international or local)
(707) 829-0104 (fax)

We have a web page for this book, where we list errata, examples, and any additional information. You can access this page at:

http://www.oreilly.com/catalog/appliedprojectmgmt

We also have a companion site featuring additional information for project managers, trainers, educators, and practitioners here:

http://www.stellman-greene.com

To comment or ask technical questions about this book, send email to:

bookquestions@oreilly.com

For more information about our books, conferences, Resource Centers, and the O'Reilly Network, see our web site at:

http://www.oreilly.com

Safari Enabled

When you see a Safari® Enabled icon on the cover of your favorite technology book, that means the book is available online through the O'Reilly Network Safari Bookshelf.

Safari offers a solution that's better than e-books. It's a virtual library that lets you easily search thousands of top technology books, cut and paste code samples, download chapters, and find quick answers when you need the most accurate, current information. Try it for free at *http://safari.oreilly.com*.

Acknowledgments

This book would not have been possible without the efforts of many people. First and foremost, we would like to thank our friends at O'Reilly Media: Andrew Odewahn, Mike Hendrickson, and Andy Oram. They have provided us with invaluable guidance and support throughout the entire process. And special thanks to Mary O'Brien, for guiding us from the first draft to the completed version that you are holding.

We are indebted to our reviewers for the time and effort they put into helping this book be successful. Without them, this book would contain many factual and conceptual errors. So, thanks to:

- Scott Berkun
- Gnaneshwar Dayanand
- Oleg Fishel
- Tarun Ganguly
- Sam Kass
- Dave Murdock
- Neil Potter
- Eric Renkey
- Virginia Smith
- Chris Winters
- Heather Day
- Matt Doar
- Karl Fogel
- Faisal Jawdat
- Marc Kellner
- Jayne Oh
- DVS Raju
- Rob Rothman
- Lana Sze

We would also like to thank our friends at Carnegie Mellon University: Sandra Slaughter at the Tepper School of Business and Anthony Lattanza at the School of Computer Science, who helped us with our initial proposal.

And special thanks go to Lisa Kellner, without whom this would be a much more difficult book to read, and to Nisha Sondhe for taking the photographs that capture each chapter's main concepts (except for Chapter 7, which was taken by Steven Stellman. Thanks Dad!).

Andrew would like to thank Mark Stehlik, Catherine Copetas, Klaus Sutner, and Robert Harper at the CMU School of Computer Science. Jenny would like to thank Robert Horton, who exposed her to many of the ideas that later became the practices in this book. And we would both like to thank Jim Over, Tim Olson, and the rest of the folks from the Software Engineering Institute who have answered our questions over the years.

And finally, we would like to thank our families and friends for putting up with our incessant babble about all of the things you're about to read.

Good luck!

—Andrew Stellman and Jennifer Greene
November, 2005

CHAPTER ONE

Introduction

SAY A PROJECT THAT STARTED OUT AS A SMALL, STOPGAP UTILITY has turned into a raging behemoth, sucking seemingly unlimited time from your programmers. Or the president of your company announced that your project will be done this week, even though you know that it still has an enormous number of bugs. Or your team delivered the software, only to have users complain that an entire feature is missing. Or every time the team fixes a bug, they seem to uncover a dozen more—including ones that you *know* were fixed six months ago. If you are a software project manager, you may recognize these problems (or similar ones) from your own career.

Many software organizations have problems delivering quality software that is finished on time and meets the users' needs. Luckily, most software project problems have surprisingly few root causes, and these causes are well understood. Solutions to these problems have been discovered, explained, and tested in thousands of software organizations around the world. These solutions are generally straightforward and easy to implement. However, they are not always intuitive to people who do not understand project management, and that makes them difficult to introduce. The goal of this book is to teach you about these solutions and help you integrate them into your own organization.

But this book is about more than just solutions to typical project problems. Every single technique, practice, and tool also helps establish an environment of trust, openness, and honesty among the project team, the management of the organization, and the people who will use or benefit from the software. By sharing all of your project information, both your team and your managers can understand your decisions, and they can see exactly why you made them.

It's easy to forget that project management is more than just a technical engineering skill. Good project management really boils down to a few basic principles that, if you keep them in mind, will help guide you through any software project:

- Make sure all decisions are based on openly shared information.
- Don't second-guess your team members' expertise.
- Introduce software quality from the very beginning of the project.
- Don't impose an artificial hierarchy on the project team.
- Remember that the fastest way through the project is to use good engineering practices.

A project manager needs to understand every facet of software development in order to make good judgements. You don't need to be a programmer, software tester, requirements analyst, or architect in order to be a good project manager. But you do need to know what these people do, why they are on your team, the common pitfalls they succumb to, and how to fix them. You need to be able to read and understand the documents that they create and provide intelligent feedback. And by relying on objective analysis (rather than gut feelings, personal preferences, or a perceived hierarchy within your team), you can use this knowledge in order to make decisions based on the best interests of the project.

Tell Everyone the Truth All the Time

The most important principle in this book is transparency. A project manager constantly makes decisions about the project. If those decisions are based on real information that's gathered by the team and trusted by management, that's the most likely way to make sure the project succeeds. Creating a transparent environment means making all of that information public and explaining the rationale behind your decisions. No software project goes exactly as planned; the only way to deal with obstacles is by sharing the true nature of each problem with everyone involved in the project and by allowing the best solution to come from the most qualified people.

But while anyone would agree with this in principle, it's much harder to keep yourself and your project honest in practice. Say you're a project manager, and your project is running late. What do you do if your boss—much to your surprise—announces to the world that your project will be done on time? Unfortunately, when faced with this situation, most project managers try to change reality rather than deal with the truth. It's not hard to see why that approach is appealing. Most people in software engineering are very positive, and it's not hard to convince them that an unrealistic deadline is just another technical challenge to be met. But the passage of time is not a technical challenge, and if the expectations are unrealistic, then even the most talented team will fail to meet them. The only real solution to this problem is to be open and honest about the real status of the project—and that's going make your boss unhappy.

And so, instead of telling the truth, many project managers faced with a deadline that's clearly unrealistic will put pressure on their team to work late and make up the time. They silently trim the scope, gut quality tasks, start eliminating reviews, inspections, and pretty much any documentation, and just stop updating the schedule entirely. And, above all, they wait until the very last minute to tell everyone that the project is late.., hoping against hope that luck, long hours, and a whole lot of coffee will correct the situation.

And sometimes it works... sort of, until the users have to work around bugs or missing features, until programmers have to start patching the software, and until managers have to go on a charm offensive in order to smooth over rough relations among everyone involved. Even if the deadline was met, the software was clearly not *really* ready for release. (And that's assuming the team even managed to squeeze it out on time!)

That's why the most important part of building better software is establishing transparency. It's about making sure that, from the very beginning of the project, everyone agrees on what needs to be built, how long it will take to build it, what steps will be taken in order to complete the project, and how they will know that it's been done properly. Every tool, technique, and practice in this book is based on the principles of freely sharing information and keeping the entire project team "in the loop" on every important decision.

Trust Your Team

If you are a project manager, it's your job to be responsible for the project. That means that you have to do whatever it takes to get the project out the door. But it does not necessarily mean that you know more about the project than everyone else on the team. Yet many project managers act in exactly this way. They arbitrarily cut down or inflate any estimates that they don't understand, or that give them a bad gut feeling. They base their schedules on numbers that they simply made up. And, most importantly, they make every project decision based on how it will affect the schedule, instead of considering how it will affect the software.

Managing a project is all about forming a team and making sure that it is productive. The best way to do that is to rely on the expertise of the team members. Any project manager who tries to micromanage his team will immediately get overwhelmed, and the project will come screeching to a halt.

Every single role in a software project requires expertise, skill, training, and experience. There is no way that one person can fill all of those different roles—she would need several lifetimes just to gain enough knowledge of each discipline! Luckily, nobody has to do it alone: that's why you have a team full of qualified people. It's up to them to recommend the best course of action at each stage of the project; it's up to you to make informed decisions based on their recommendations.

If you don't have a good reason to veto an idea, don't do it. Usually, the people on your team know best what it takes to do their job. The most important thing that you can do to support them is to trust them and listen to them.

However, you cannot blindly trust your team. You need to evaluate their ideas in relation to solid engineering principles. This is why the first part of this book goes beyond "traditional" project management (creating project plans, developing estimates, building schedules, etc.) to cover *all* parts of a software project. Every project manager needs to understand at least the basic principles of software requirements engineering, design and architecture, programming, and software testing in order to guide a software project through all of the phases of development.

Review Everything, Test Everything

Reviews get a bad rap. Many people see them as frivolous. "In a perfect world," many project managers say, "we would review all of our documents. But we live in the real world, and we just don't have time." Others feel that the only reason for a review is to force various people to sign off on a document—as if a signature on a page somehow guarantees that they agree with everything that it's stapled to.

The purpose of a review is not to make a perfect document or to generate a page of signatures. Rather, a review does two things: it prevents defects in the software and it helps the project manager gain a real, informed commitment from the team. What's more, it's important to recognize that no review is perfect—and that's just fine. It may not be possible to catch 100% of the defects before coding has started, but a good review will catch enough defects to more than pay for the time it took to hold the review.

It is *always* faster and cheaper to hold a review meeting than it is to skip it, simply because it's much easier to fix something on paper than it is to build it first and fix it later. When a review turns up an error that takes a few minutes to fix in a document, it saves the team the hours, days, or weeks that it would take to fix the error once it has been built into the software. But even more importantly, reviews frequently uncover errors in documents whose resolution requires a lot of discussion and decision-making. Errors like this can completely destroy a software project if they make it all the way into the code.

Many project managers try to schedule reviews, only to meet with an enormous amount of resistance from everyone around them. Peers, project team members, and senior managers all seem to resist the idea of "yet another meeting." Oddly, the same project managers who are unable to scrape together an hour and a half to review a scope document at the beginning of the project generally have no difficulty whatsoever scheduling lengthy, tedious weekly status meetings with no agenda, goal, or purpose. (Of course, not all project status meetings have to be run that way!)

The truth is that there is no such thing as wasted time in a review. On average, every hour spent reviewing and repairing documents saves well over an hour later in the project. This is true because it catches costly errors early on in the project, when they are cheap to fix. But reviews have other valuable benefits as well. By bringing team members into a room to evaluate each others' work, reviews foster respect among the team members for everyone's contributions. And, most importantly, a review results in a real commitment to the work that is produced by the team, not just a signature.

Testing—whether it is unit testing, functional testing, performance testing or regression testing—is just as important, and just as likely to be dismissed as unaffordable or "idealistic." Yet software testing activities are just as cost-effective as reviews. The team can't "test in" quality at the end of a project just by tacking on some testing tasks. Testing must be planned from the beginning and then supported throughout the entire project. To come up with a quality product, the entire team needs to actively look for defects at every stage, in every document, and in the software. It's the project manager's responsibility to make sure that this happens.

All Software Engineers Are Created Equal

A software project requires much more than just writing code. There are all sorts of work products that are produced along the way: documents, schedules, plans, source code, bug reports, and builds are all created by many different team members. No single work product is more important than any other; if any one of them has a serious error, that error will have an impact on the end product. That means each team member responsible for any of these work products plays an important role in the project, and all of those people can make or break the final build that is delivered to the users.

There are many project managers who, when faced with a disagreement between a programmer and a tester, will always trust the programmer. This same project manager might always trust a requirements analyst or a business analyst over a programmer, if and when they disagree. Many people have some sort of a hierarchy in their heads in which certain engineering team members are more valuable or more skilled than others. This is a dangerous idea, and it is one that has no place on an effective project team.

One key to building better software is treating each idea objectively, no matter who suggests it or whether or not it's immediately intuitive to you. That's another reason the practices, techniques, and tools in this book cover all areas of the software project. Every one of these practices is based on an objective evaluation of all of the important activities in software development. Every discipline is equally important, and everyone on the team contributes equally to the project. A software requirements specification (SRS), for example, is no more important than the code: the code could not be created without the SRS, and the SRS would have no purpose if it weren't the basis of the software. It is in the best interest of everyone on the team to make sure that both of them have as few defects as possible, and that the authors of both work products have equal say in project decisions.

The project manager must respect all team members, and should not second-guess their expertise. This is an important principle because it is the basis of real commitments. It's easy for a senior manager to simply issue an edict that everyone must build software without defects and do a good job; however, this rarely works well in practice. The best way to make sure that the software is built well is to make sure that everyone on the team feels respected and valued, and to gain a true commitment from each person to make the software the best it can be.

Doing the Project Right Is Most Efficient

The first part of this book is a presentation of techniques, tools, and practices for every phase of a software project. They are designed to be implemented one at a time and in any order (with a few restrictions). This means that you have a lot of freedom to choose the approach that is best for your project.

But no matter which one you choose to implement first, you can be sure that your project will be better off with the practice than it would be without it. This is because building the software correctly the first time is always preferable to doing it wrong and having to go back and fix it.

Every practice in this book is designed to help you build software efficiently and accurately. What's more, there are many ways to implement every single one of these practices. We put a great deal of effort into developing the most efficient version of each tool, technique, or practice we present in this book. We did this by stripping out as many of the "bells and whistles" as possible from each practice without compromising its basic integrity.

There are more complex and involved ways to implement every single idea in this book. Wherever possible, there are references that will point you to more in-depth reading that contains advanced applications of these tools and techniques. The goal of this book is to help a project manager put the basic versions of these practices in place quickly, in order to see immediate improvement in the efficiency of a project.

Software engineers are a very practical bunch. They do not like adopting practices unless they believe they will see a net gain from them. A practice must save more time than it costs to implement. Every single tool, technique, and practice in this book is time-tested. These practices (or similar ones) have been used in many successful projects around the world and in organizations of all sizes. These practices would not have found such widespread adoption if they were not efficient.

All of the effort that goes into reviews, unit testing, requirements engineering—everything that does not directly produce code—positively affects the bottom line of your project. If it looks like a lot of work, you should think about the effort you are saving by not having to fix the problems later when they show up as defects in your software. What's more, you can be confident that we optimized the techniques that you are putting in place in order to make them as easy to adopt as possible. But most importantly, you can be sure that your project will go more smoothly with them in place than it would without them.

This principle is most important when a project starts to slip and a deadline looms nearer (or when one is blown altogether). It may be tempting to start cutting out these practices and concentrate all of the effort into pumping out code. That's one of the most common mistakes that project managers make. Cutting out good project management practices will make the project take longer, not make it go faster.

Part I: Tools and Techniques

If you're a project manager and you're reading this book, you probably can think of chronic problems on your projects that you need to solve. What's more, you probably want to do it without trying to change the entire culture of your organization. You want to build better software; you don't necessarily want to undertake a major process improvement initiative, or try to change the way everyone in your organization thinks about building software. This book is written to treat a number of common problems separately by providing self-contained tools and techniques that address them.

Most people think of a tool as a piece of software that can be used to manage a project schedule, track defects, or automate other tasks, in order to increase productivity on a project. While there are certainly software tools like these discussed in this book, we support a wider definition of the term. Here, "tool" is used to mean any self-contained concept, practice, technique, or software package that can be applied independently to a software project, in order to improve the way it is performed. Risk management, for example, is as much of a tool as Microsoft Project or Subversion. To make this distinction clear, the term "tools and techniques" will be used throughout the book to indicate this concept.

The idea behind these tools and techniques is to allow a project manager to pick and choose only those practices that solve the specific problems she is having with her own projects. When a software project is in trouble, a disproportionate amount of the trouble is usually caused by a small number of problems. The tools and techniques in this book are meant to address those specific problems. An organization that implements all of these tools and techniques will see an enormous gain in both productivity and user satisfaction for minimal cost. A project manager who targets the specific problems that he has found in his organization can address only his most pressing problems and still see a very noticeable gain—and at a much lower cost than trying to tackle every possible project problem!

Because the tools and techniques can be applied independently, one useful way to use this book is to take a "toolbox" approach to building better software. Consider the tools, techniques, practices, software packages, and other ideas in this book as individual tools in a toolbox. You can select the right tool depending on the specific problems and challenges that you face in your projects.

While these tools have been developed to be used by project teams, most of them can be implemented by a single person, either working alone or in a team environment. Using this book, even a single team member working alone can have a significant effect on both the quality of the software being produced and the effectiveness of the organization to which he belongs.

Each chapter in Part I of this book is based on a specific phase or area of a software project. It contains specific tools and techniques a project manager can use to help address problems, as well as information that most project managers should know about what goes on during that phase of the project. Part I covers the following tools and techniques, divided into different areas of project management:

Chapter 2, *Software Project Planning*
  Vision and Scope Document

  Software Project Plan

Chapter 3, *Estimation*
  Wideband Delphi Estimation Process

Chapter 4, *Project Schedules*
  Project Schedules

  Earned Value Metrics

  Project Scheduling Software (such as Microsoft Project and Open Workbench)

Chapter 5, *Reviews*
  Inspections

  Deskchecks

  Walkthroughs

  Code Reviews

  Pair Programming

Chapter 6, *Software Requirements*

Use Cases

Functional and Nonfunctional Requirements

Software Requirements Specifications

Change Control

Chapter 7, *Design and Programming*

Configuration Management

Subversion

Refactoring

Unit Tests

Project Automation Software

Chapter 8, *Software Testing*

Test Plans

Test Cases

Test Automation

Defect Tracking System

Postmortem Meetings

Metrics

Most of these tools and techniques can be applied independently of one another. However, there are a few that rely on tools in other parts of the book. (For example, it is very difficult to build a test plan and test cases without a software requirements specification.) When this is the case, it is always because the software project will be better off with the other tool in place first, and the project will see a greater gain by implementing the other tool instead.

Many of the practices in this book are described using a *process script* that contains step-by-step instructions to help guide the team through the practice. "Script" should bring to mind a script read by an actor, rather than a script run by a computer. All scripts follow the same format (which is based on the template used for use cases, defined in Chapter 6) that contains:

• A name, one-line description of the purpose, and a brief summary.

• A list of work products that are used in the script. Work products are labeled as "input" if they already exist and are used in the script; they are labeled as "output" if they are generated or updated by the script.

• Entry criteria that must be satisfied before the script can begin.

• A basic course of events, which consists of step-by-step instructions to lead the team through the script activities.

• Alternate paths that the team members may follow to deviate from the basic course of events.

• Exit criteria that should be satisfied when the script ends.

There's an old saying: "There's only one way to be right, but a million ways to be wrong." This is *not* necessarily the case with sofware projects! In practice, the vast majority of projects go wrong in one of a small number of ways. At the end of each chapter in Part I, there is a section aimed at helping you diagnose the symptoms in your organization in order to determine if that chapter's tools, techniques, and practices will help fix the specific problems. This section contains several scenarios that should describe the way this problem typically looks from the outside. The "Diagnosing" scenarios in the chapters in Part I describe these problems in a way that should seem very familiar to project managers suffering from them. If one of these scenarios seems eerily familiar to you, there is a good chance that the tools in its chapter will help.

Part II: Using Project Management Effectively

It's not enough for a project manager to understand practices that are used by all of the team members. A good project manager also needs to know how to lead the team. The second part of this book is focused on learning how to use the five basic principles listed above in order to work with people, teams, and organizations. Each chapter in Part II takes on specific areas of project management:

Chapter 9, *Understanding Change*
> Introducing practices, tools, and techniques to your organization's culture
>
> Avoiding the most common pitfalls in selling your ideas
>
> Planning for your changes and making them succeed

Chapter 10, *Management and Leadership*
> Understanding responsibility, authority, and accountability
>
> Creating a culture of transparency in your organization
>
> Working with your organization and your team

Chapter 11, *Managing an Outsourced Project*
> Preventing the most common sources of failure in outsourced projects
>
> Forming a relationship with the team and management at an outsourcing vendor
>
> Reviewing and collaborating between organizations

Chapter 12, *Process Improvement*
> Understanding when process improvement is useful (and when it isn't)
>
> Utilizing process improvement models and certifications
>
> Working with third-party processes and methodologies

Our goal in writing this book is to help you build better software. If you implement all, some, or even one of these practices, we think you will see a noticeable improvement in the efficiency of your projects—and that it will make your job easier. We have tried to make it clear throughout this book exactly why we think these things are important. We use them every day in our own work, and we hope you find them as helpful and satisfying as we do.

PART ONE

Tools and Techniques

CHAPTER TWO

Software Project Planning

AN URGENT NEED CAN BE A GOOD MOTIVATOR. Software is usually built to address an urgent need. For the stakeholders—meaning everyone who has a concern or real interest in the success of the project—the fact that the need is urgent helps to convince the organization to dedicate time and energy to addressing it. For the software engineers, an urgent need means that their work will be appreciated and used in the foreseeable future. And for the management of the organization, it means that there is a clear direction in how they need to run things.

But urgency can also be the source of a project's most difficult problems. Urgency causes people to panic, and to potentially gloss over important parts of the project. People will rush into gathering requirements (or, even worse, rush into building the code!) without thoroughly understanding the needs of the people who want the software built.

If a project manager does not really understand the context in which the software is being built, then the only thing that the project team sees is the urgency; they lose track of the needs. They can see the individual problems that they are working to solve, but they may lose track of the big picture.

Unless the team understands the needs that drive the project, they may end up with a narrow focus, causing them to waste time addressing problems that are of little importance to the stakeholders. It's easy to build great software that solves the wrong problems, but the only way to build the appropriate software is for everyone in the project to understand and agree on both why and how that software will be built before the work begins. That's the purpose of project planning.

Understand the Project Needs

When a stakeholder does not feel that his needs are being met, he usually puts pressure on the project manager to provide an early version of the software, so that he can personally verify that the team really understands why the software is being built. This is a big source of communication failure between the people who need the software and the team members who are building it. When the stakeholder asks for an early version or a prototype of the software, he is usually asking for evidence that his needs are understood and being addressed. When programmers hear this request, however, they interpret it to mean that the person is interested in the details of what they are doing, and that he wants to be given a tour of the solution as it is being developed.

This may sound funny to some seasoned software engineers. Such a basic lack of communication couldn't really be that widespread…right? But most software professionals have had to sit through uncomfortable meetings where a designer or programmer gives a demo or walkthrough of all of the great work he did, only to be surprised that nobody seems to care.

The reason nontechnical people seem so bored in demos and walkthroughs is because they came to see confirmation that the technology team understands their needs. Instead, they got a lecture in software design, which they did not want. This situation can be frustrating for everyone involved: the software engineers feel unappreciated and condescended to, while the stakeholders feel like their needs are not being taken seriously.

A project that starts out like this is likely to experience scope creep, delays, and even out-right failure. What's worse, nobody in the organization will really even understand why the project had so many problems. All they will see is a team that built software that didn't work properly and had to be repaired or even rewritten. This is a very bad situation for a software engineering team to end up in. Even when a team is technically proficient and capable of delivering high-quality, well-written software, when faced with a problematic project, most managers will intuitively feel that the team is incapable of delivering software without major quality problems.

What usually stalls a project is a lack of good project management. To prevent problems, the project manager must identify the people who are making decisions that affect the project and understand why they need the software built. By talking to them and writing down their needs, the project manager can set the project on its proper course—and give the stakeholders the feeling from the very beginning that the team is taking their needs seriously.

Drive the Scope of the Project

When the project begins, the project manager has a unique role to play. The start of the project is the time when the scope of the project is defined; only the project manager is equipped to make sure that it's defined properly. Everyone else has a role to play later on: users and stakeholders will provide expertise, requirements analysts will write specifications, programmers will build the code, etc. Everyone involved in the project has some input into the scope, but only the project manager is solely dedicated to it.

Defining the scope is the most productive thing a project manager can do to get the project underway. It is usually counterproductive to do any other project activity before everybody agrees on the scope, because that activity could fall outside of the scope without anyone realizing it. For example, many programmers will immediately begin coding proof-of-concept prototypes before even talking to the users or stakeholders; many stakeholders will encourage this because they intuitively feel that they cannot make decisions without seeing something in front of them. But building a working model is a very time-consuming way to figure out that a feature is not needed. If time is a concern, this is definitely not an efficient way to build software.

By focusing on discussing the scope and writing a vision and scope document, the project manager can ensure that the team starts out moving in the right direction. This should not be hard—when the project begins, everyone is highly suggestible. Nobody is really in her area of expertise yet: the code is not ready to be built, requirements are not known well enough to be gathered, and designs and test plans cannot even be approached yet.

Instead, there is a great deal of knowledge floating around in peoples' heads. To make sure that knowledge is captured, there must be a single person responsible for gathering it. This is the main role for the project manager at the start of the project. Once he starts talking to individual people about what they expect to see in the project and writing down their thoughts, the scope will start to coalesce and people will start feeling comfortable with the direction in which it is going. This can happen very quickly once the project manager starts asking questions and writing down the answers.

This is why the project manager is the driving force at the start of the project. It may not always feel like it, but the most important project decisions are made at the project's outset. This is when the broad strokes are laid down, when the major features of the software are defined. If there is a misunderstanding at this point, the team can be sent down an entirely wrong path, which can cause them to lose all of their momentum.

When a project team is first assembled, there is almost always a sense of anticipation and excitement among the project team and the stakeholders. The project manager can take advantage of this energy to drive the project in the right direction.

Talk to the Main Stakeholder

The project manager's first task in any software project is to talk to the main stakeholder. Unfortunately, it's not always immediately obvious who that stakeholder is. The project manager should find the person who will be most impacted by the project, either because he plans on using it or because he is somehow responsible for it being developed. In other words, the project manager needs to find the person who will be in trouble if the software is not developed. (There are often several people who are in this situation. The project manager should talk to each one, starting with the person who he feels will provide the most useful information.)

When a project first starts, a project manager's job is not unlike that of a tailor fitting someone for a custom suit or dress. The tailor's customers will pay a premium for tailored clothes, rather than paying less for an outfit off the rack. But this customization also means that they will need to spend time with the tailor choosing the patterns, going through fabric swatches, taking measurements, and giving some of the precise instructions necessary to customize the clothing. The customer does not see this as a chore, but rather as a perk. By giving exact specifications, the customer can get exactly what he wants. The project manager should try to form the same sort of relationship with each stakeholder that the tailor does with his customers. He can do this by working to understand exactly what it is that the stakeholder will need from the software, and then by helping the project team to deliver software that is tailored to those needs.

Unfortunately for most project managers, the typical relationship with the stakeholder is more like the relationship between a car mechanic and his customer. The customer does not see that the mechanic is using specialized skills to fix a potentially difficult problem. He just can't use his car until the mechanic says it's fixed. He wants the fix to be as fast and cheap as possible, and he doesn't fully understand why it costs so much. What's more, he's always a little suspicious that the mechanic is doing more work than necessary or ordering a part that's too expensive. The customer never knows what's wrong until the mechanic examines the car, and the cost is always an unpleasant surprise. As far as the customer is concerned, the mechanic is simply removing an annoyance, and the customer resents having to pay any money at all for it. This is exactly how many stakeholders think about their software projects and the teams that build them.

For this reason, it's important for the project manager to take responsibility for the delivery of the project from its very beginning. Each stakeholder should feel like the project manager is his main point of contact for any problem or issue with the project. He should feel that the project manager understands his needs, and that he will work to make sure that those needs are addressed in the software. He should be comfortable going to the project manager with any problems or changes at any point during the project's duration.

This sort of goodwill from a stakeholder can often be established in a single conversation or an initial meeting at the beginning of the project. The project manager can do this by blocking out time to meet with the stakeholder, leading him through a conversation about his specific needs, and then showing that he really understood those needs. The way the project manager shows the stakeholder that his needs are understood is by writing a vision and scope document, and then having the stakeholder review it.

Write the Vision and Scope Document

The *vision and scope* document is one of the most important tools that a project manager has; it is also one of the easiest to implement. A good vision and scope document will help a project avoid some of the costliest problems that a project can face. By writing the document and circulating it among everyone involved in the project, the project manager can ensure that each of the stakeholders and engineers shares a common understanding of the needs being addressed—and that the software must address them.

Some of the most common (and expensive) problems that a project can experience are caused by miscommunication about the basic goals of the project and about the scope of the work to be done. (The *scope* of a project usually refers to the features that will be developed and the work that will be done to implement those features. It often also includes an understanding of the features that will be excluded from the project.) By controlling the scope, the project manager can make sure that all of the software engineers' activities are directed toward building software that will fulfill the needs of the stakeholders.

The "vision" part of the vision and scope document refers to a description of the goal of the software. All software is built to fulfill needs of certain users and stakeholders. The project manager must identify those needs and write down a vision statement (a general statement describing how those needs will be filled).

Many software engineers will recognize the sinking, pit-of-the-stomach feeling when, upon seeing the software for the first time, a stakeholder or customer says, "But I needed the software to do this other thing, and I don't see that anywhere." The vision and scope document helps project managers avoid that problem by catching misunderstandings early on in the project, before they have a chance to influence the code and send the project down the wrong path.

When a project is initiated, the project manager should take the lead, talking to the stakeholders and creating a vision and scope document before the first line of code has been written. However, sometimes project managers must take over projects on which the programming has already been started. This is never an easy situation—senior managers don't usually change project managers unless the project is already in trouble. But even when a project manager has to take over a project that has already been started, it's still a good idea to go back to the stakeholders and build a new vision and scope document. This is the project manager's best chance at catching scope problems as early as possible. If the project has started to go off track, the best way to repair the damage is to assess the current needs of the stakeholders, and then to create a plan to change the software in order to meet those needs.

Table 2-1 shows a typical outline for a vision and scope document. When talking to each stakeholder, the project manager should direct the conversation so that all of the topics in the vision and scope document are discussed. Typically, stakeholders will be happy to talk about all of this. They know their own needs very well, they understand who will be using the software, and they generally have many opinions about what features should go into it. The project manager should take lots of notes during this conversation—enough so that writing the vision and scope document is mostly a matter of transcribing those notes. (Stakeholders will often appreciate lots of note-taking, because it shows that the project manager is listening to them and taking what they say seriously.)

TABLE 2-1. Vision and scope document outline

1. Problem Statement
a. Project background
b. Stakeholders
c. Users
d. Risks
e. Assumptions
2. Vision of the Solution
a. Vision statement
b. List of features
c. Scope of phased release (optional)
d. Features that will not be developed

The outline itself provides a good guide for the discussion with each stakeholder. It can be used as an agenda for the meetings that the project manager uses to gather the information about stakeholder needs. It's a common mistake for a project manager to approach the writing of a vision and scope document as little more than a bureaucratic exercise. The project manager's goal should be to learn what each user, stakeholder, and project team member thinks about the software in order to develop a single, unified vision and ensure that everyone shares that vision. He should treat the document as a tool to build consensus among the stakeholders and project team members. In other words, the important part is the discussion of the vision and scope; the document is simply a record of that discussion.

Project background

This section contains a summary of the problem that the project will solve. It should provide a brief history of the problem and an explanation of how the organization justified the decision to build software to address it. This section should cover the reasons why the problem exists, the organization's history with this problem, any previous projects that were undertaken to try to address it, and the way that the decision to begin this project was reached.

Stakeholders

This is a bulleted list of the stakeholders. Each stakeholder may be referred to by name, title, or role ("support group manager," "CTO," "senior manager"). The needs of each stakeholder are described in a few sentences.

Users

This is a bulleted list of the users. As with the stakeholders, each user can either be referred to by name or role ("support rep," "call quality auditor," "home web site user")—however, if there are many users, it is usually inefficient to try to name each one. The needs of each user are described.

Risks

This section lists any potential risks to the project. It should be generated by a project team's brainstorming session. It could include external factors that may impact the project, or issues or problems that could potentially cause project delays or raise issues. (The process for assessing and mitigating risk below can be used to generate the risks for this section.)

Assumptions

This is the list of assumptions that the stakeholders, users, or project team have made. Often, these assumptions are generated during a Wideband Delphi estimation session (see Chapter 3). If Wideband Delphi is being used, the rest of the vision and scope document should be ready before the Delphi meeting and used as the basis for estimation. The assumptions generated during the estimation kickoff meeting should then be reviewed, and any nontechnical assumptions should be copied into this section. (Technical assumptions—meaning assumptions that affect the design and development but not the scope of the project—should not be included in this document. The estimate results will still contain a record of these assumptions, but they are not useful for this particular audience.)

If Wideband Delphi is not being used to generate the assumptions, the project manager should hold a brainstorming session with the team to come up with a list of assumptions instead. (See Chapter 3 for more information on assumptions.)

Vision statement

The goal of the vision statement is to describe what the project is expected to accomplish. It should explain what the purpose of the project is. This should be a compelling reason, a solid justification for spending time, money, and resources on the project. The best time to write the vision statement is after talking to the stakeholders and users and writing down their needs; by this time, a concrete understanding of the project should be starting to jell.

List of features

This section contains a list of features. A *feature* is as a cohesive area of the software that fulfills a specific need by providing a set of services or capabilities. Any software package—in fact, any engineered product—can be broken down into features. The project manager can choose the number of features in the vision and scope document by changing the level of detail or granularity of each feature, and by combining multiple features into a single one. Sometimes those features are small ("screw-top cap," "holds one liter of liquid"); sometimes they are big ("four-wheel drive," "seats seven passengers"). It is useful to describe a product in about 10 features in the vision and scope document, because this usually yields a level of complexity that most people reading it are comfortable with. Adding too many features will overwhelm most readers.

Each feature should be listed in a separate paragraph or bullet point. It should be given a name, followed by a description of the functionality that it provides. This description does not need to be detailed; it can simply be a few sentences that give a general explanation of the feature. However, if there is more information that a stakeholder or project team member feels should be included, it is important to include that information. For example, it is sometimes useful to include a use case (see Chapter 6), as long as it is written in such a way that all of the stakeholders can read and understand it.

Scope of phased release (optional)

Sometimes software projects are released in phases: a version of the software with some subset of the features is released first, and a newer, more complete version is released later. This section describes the plan for a phased release, if that approach is to be taken.

This is useful when there is an important deadline for the software, but developing the entire software project by that deadline would be unrealistic. The most common way to compromise on this release date is to divide the features into two or more releases. In that case, this section should identify specifically when those versions will be released, and which features will be included in each version. It's reasonable to divide one feature up between two releases, as long as it is made clear exactly how that will happen.

If a project manager needs to release a project in phases, it is critical that the project team be consulted. Some features are much more difficult to divide than others, and the engineers might see dependencies between features that are not clear to the stakeholders and project manager. After the phased release plan is written down and agreed upon, the project team should always be asked to re-estimate the effort and a new project plan should be generated (see below). This will ensure that the phased release is feasible and compatible with the organization's priorities.

Features that will not be developed

Features are often left out of a project on purpose. When a feature is explicitly left out of the software, it should be added to this section to tell the reader that a decision was made to exclude it. For example, one way to handle an unrealistic deadline is by removing one or more features from the software, in which case the removed features should be moved into this section. The reason these features should be moved rather than deleted from the document is that otherwise, readers might assume that they were overlooked and bring them up in a review. This is especially important during the review of the document because it allows everyone to agree on the exclusion of the feature (or object to it).

Review the vision and scope document

Once the vision and scope document has been written, it should be reviewed by every stakeholder, by the members of the project team, and, ideally, by at least a few people who will actually be using the software (if they are available). Performing this review can be as simple as emailing the document around and asking for comments. The document can also be inspected (see Chapter 5). However the document is reviewed, it is important that the project manager follow up with each individual person and work to understand any issues that the reviewer brings up. The project manager should make sure that everyone agrees that the final document really reflects the needs of the stakeholders and the users, and that if they build the software described in the second half of the document, then all of the needs in the first half will be met. Once the document has been reviewed and everyone agrees that it is complete, the team is unified toward a single goal and the project can be planned.

> **NOTE**
>
> More information on understanding user and stakeholder needs can be found in *Managing Software Requirements: A Use Case Approach* by Dean Leffingwell and Don Widrig (Addison Wesley, 2003). More information on defining features and creating a vision and scope document can be found in *The Art of Project Management* by Scott Berkun (O'Reilly, 2005). A more detailed template for a vision and scope document is described in *Software Requirements* by Karl Wiegers (Microsoft Press, 1999).

Create the Project Plan

The *project plan* defines the work that will be done on the project and who will do it. A typical project plan consists of:

- A statement of work that describes all work products (specifications, test plans, code, defect reports, and any other product of work performed over the course of the project) that will be produced and a list of people who will perform that work

- A resource list that contains a list of all resources that will be needed for the product, and their availability

- A work breakdown structure and a set of effort estimates (described in Chapter 3)

- A project schedule (described in Chapter 4)

- A risk plan that identifies any risks that might be encountered and indicates how those risks would be handled, should they occur

The project plan is used by many people in the organization. The project manager uses it to communicate the project's status to the stakeholders and senior managers, and to plan the team's activities. The team members use it to understand the context for the work they are doing. The senior managers use it to verify that the project's cost and schedule are reasonable and under control, and that the project is being done in an efficient and cost-effective manner. The stakeholders use it to make sure that the project is on track, and that their needs are being addressed.

It is important that the organization reach consensus on the project plan. To accomplish this, the plan should be inspected by the representatives of the project team, senior management, and stakeholders. Many project plans are stored simply as a folder containing a set of word processor and spreadsheet files, or are printed and stored in a binder. It is important that the project plan is periodically reviewed, and that any deviations from the plan are tracked at the review sessions. Frequent reviews are what can keep the plan from going stale and becoming a work of fiction.

It's difficult, if not impossible, to build a project plan without a vision and scope document. Without it, the actions that a project manager would have to take in order to create a project plan are almost identical to those required to create the vision and scope document. For this reason, the project manager should begin the planning process by first writing a vision and scope document; all other planning activities depend on it, and the time required for the project manager to create it will pay for itself when the project plan is created.

Statement of Work

The first component of the project plan is a *statement of work* (SOW). This is a detailed description of all of the work products that will be created over the course of the project, including who is responsible for creating each work product. The description of each work product should contain a reference to any tasks in the project schedule (see Chapter 4) in which it is involved. The vision and scope document is a useful starting point for the SOW. But the SOW serves a different purpose—while the vision and scope document talks about the rationale for the project (the needs that must be met, the list of users and stakeholders who need it built, etc.) the SOW simply contains a detailed list of the work that must be done and all of the work products that will be produced.

The SOW is included as part of the project plan, but it should be a separate document that can stand on its own. It should contain each of the following:

- The list of features being developed. If the software is being released in phases, the features should be divided into those phases as well.

- A description of the intermediate deliverable or work product that will be built. This is a list that covers (but is not limited to): software requirements specifications, design and architecture specifications, class or UML diagrams, code or software packages (divided into separate libraries or modules, if necessary), test plans and test cases, user acceptance plans, and any other document, source code or other work product that will be created. A brief description—no more than a paragraph—is usually sufficient for each one. The SOW also should list any standards or templates that will be used to create the work product.

- The estimated effort involved for each work product to be delivered (possibly based on the results of the Wideband Delphi estimation session), if known.

Resource List

The project plan should contain a list of all resources that will be used on the project. This list should go beyond what's covered by the project schedule by including a description of each resource, as well as any limits on that resource's availability.

Most project management software packages provide a feature to maintain a resource list. If this is not available, the resource list can either be a spreadsheet or a word processor document containing a simple list, with one line per resource. The list should give each resource a name, a brief one-line description, and the availability and cost (if applicable) of the resource. All resources should be handled in the same way, regardless of type.

Estimates and Project Schedule

Once the statement of work and the resource list have been created, the project manager should build a project schedule. This is usually done in several steps:

- A work breakdown structure (WBS) is defined. This is a list of tasks that, if performed, will generate all of the work products needed to build the software.
- An estimate of the effort required for each task in the WBS is generated.
- A project schedule is created by assigning resources and determining the calendar time required for each task.

The project plan should include the complete revision history of the WBS—it should contain a list of any tasks that are added, changed, or removed, and when those changes occurred. It should also include estimates and a project schedule, including any revisions that were made during the review meetings. (Chapter 3 contains a repeatable process for generating a WBS and estimates. Chapter 4 describes how to create a project schedule.)

Risk Plan

A *risk plan* is a list of all risks that threaten the project, along with a plan to mitigate some or all of those risks. Some people say that uncertainty is the enemy of planning. If there were no uncertainty, then every project plan would be accurate and every project would go off without a hitch. Unfortunately, real life intervenes, usually at the most inconvenient times. The risk plan is an insurance policy against uncertainty.

Each of the risks in the plan must be assessed by the project manager and the team. Risk assessment is an important part of planning a software project because it allows the project manager to predict potential problems that will threaten the project and take steps to mitigate those problems. Adding a risk plan to a software project plan is an effective way to keep the project from being derailed by surprises or emergencies. Many people are thrown off by the word "assessment"—it's a word that is usually associated with finances or accounting, not with project management. But in this case, it's appropriate. A good project manager will assess the risk of her projects in much the same way that a good stock trader will assess the risk of his portfolio. In both cases, potential problems should be identified, and the relative probability and impact of each risk should be estimated. Certain risks will be much more likely to occur and, if they do occur, they might cause much more damage than others. In those cases, steps should be taken to hedge the project (or portfolio) against the risk; this is usually referred to as "mitigation" when it is done in the context of project planning.

Risk planning for most projects can be done in one meeting, usually in less than two hours. The meeting is led by the project manager, who should select a team similar (or identical) to that of the Wideband Delphi session (see Chapter 3), with the exception that there is no moderator. Table 2-2 contains a script for creating the risk plan.

TABLE 2-2. Risk planning script

Name	Risk planning script
Purpose	To assess risks and create a risk plan.
Summary	The risk planning meeting happens in three parts: a brainstorming session to identify risks; a discussion in which the probability and impact of each risk is estimated; and a discussion to identify actions that can mitigate risks. The end result is a risk management plan, which should be included verbatim in the final project plan.

Work Products	*Input*
	    Any project documentation that has been developed so far.
	Output
	    Risk plan.
	    Assumptions generated by the Delphi process.
	    Assumptions in the vision and scope document.

Entry Criteria	The project manager has gathered the project team for a two-hour meeting to assess the project's risks.
Basic Course of Events	1. *Brainstorm potential risks.* The project manager leads a brainstorming session to identify risks. Team members suggest every risk they can think of; the project manager writes the risks on a whiteboard as they come up. Brainstorming should be reminiscent of microwave popcorn: a few ideas should "pop" at first, followed by a large number being fired rapidly, slowing down to a final few "pops." The team will generally be able to judge when the risk identification is over. 2. *Estimate the impact of each risk.* The team assigns a number from 1 (highly unlikely) to 5 (very likely to occur) to represent the estimated probability of each risk. Similarly, impact should be estimated by assigning a number from 1 (for a risk with low impact) to 5 (for a risk which, if it occurs, will require an enormous effort to clean up). 3. *Build the risk plan.* The team identifies actions to be taken to mitigate high-priority risks and creates a risk plan that documents these actions.
Exit Criteria	The risk plan is finished.

Brainstorm potential risks

Risks should be as specific as possible. It's true that "The project might be delayed" or "We will go out of business" are risks; however, they are far too vague to do anything about. When a vague risk comes up, the project manager should prod the team into making it more specific. What are the possible sources of the project delay? How have past projects been delayed? For example, if the last project was late because a major stakeholder quit and was replaced by someone who disagreed with his predecessor's vision, the team should write that down as a risk. The assumptions documented in the vision and scope document and identified in a Delphi session are another good source of potential risks. The team should go through them and evaluate each assumption for potential risks as part of the risk brainstorming session.

Estimate the impact of each risk

Once the team has generated a final set of risks, they have enough information to estimate two things: a rough estimate of the probability that the risk will occur, and the potential impact of that risk on the project if it does eventually materialize. The risks must then be prioritized in two ways: in order of probability, and in order of impact. Both the probability and impact are measured using a relative scale by assigning each a number between 1 and 5.

These numbers are arbitrary; they simply are used to compare the probability or impact of one risk with another, and do not carry any specific meaning. The numbers for probability and impact are assigned to each risk; a priority can then be calculated by multiplying these numbers together. It is equally effective to assign a percentage as a probability (i.e., a risk is 80% likely to occur) and a real duration for impact (i.e., it will cost 32 man-hours if the risk occurs). However, many teams have trouble estimating these numbers, and find it easier to just assign an arbitrary value for comparison.

Many people have difficulty prioritizing, but there is a simple technique that makes it much easier. While it's difficult to rank all of the risks in the list at once, it is usually not hard to pick out the one that's most likely to occur. Assign that one a probability of 5. Then select the one that's least likely to occur and assign that one a probability of 1. With those chosen, it's much easier to rank the others relative to them. It might help to find another 5 and another 1, or if those don't exist, find a 4 and a 2. The rest of the probabilities should start to fall in place. Once that's done, the same can be done for the impact.

After the probability and impact of each risk have been estimated, the team can calculate the priority of each risk by multiplying its probability by its impact. This ensures that the highest priority is assigned to those risks that have both a high probability and impact, followed by either high-probability risks with a low impact or low-probability risks with a high impact. This is generally the order in which a good project manager will want to try to deal with them: it allows the most serious risks to rise to the top of the list.

Make a mitigation plan

All of this risk brainstorming and estimation is only useful if it leads to the team taking actions to avoid the most pressing risks. The remainder of the risk planning meeting should be dedicated to identifying these actions. The project manager should start with the highest-priority risk, working with the team to decide on any actions that should be taken. After that, the team should move down the list of risks, until they decide that the priority of each of the remaining risks is low enough that no action would be required.

The team can take any or all of these actions to mitigate a risk:

- *Alter the project plan.* The project schedule can be adjusted to help reduce the risk. Riskier tasks can be moved earlier in the project, or given more time. This will give the team an early warning or a time cushion in case the risks materialize. The project manager can also hold an additional estimation session to break down the riskiest tasks into subtasks. More detailed planning will help reduce the risk.

- *Add additional tasks.* There are certain actions that can be added to the schedule to help avoid risks. For example, if there is a high probability that a critical team member will leave the organization, cross-training tasks can be assigned to other people. This will increase total effort in the project, but it will be worth it if the team member leaves.

- *Plan for risks.* For risks with a high impact that do not need specific tasks or project plan changes, the project manager should have the team spend a few minutes identifying the steps that should be taken in case the risk does occur. These do not need to be added to the project schedule, but they should be written down and added to the risk plan. This way, if the risk does occur, nobody will panic. Problems that have a large impact on the project can be demoralizing to the team and may throw the project into chaos. Simply having preplanned the steps needed to fix the problem is highly reassuring; it keeps the team feeling like they are on track.

Once the mitigation steps are identified, all of these risks and actions should be documented in a risk plan. The easiest way to do that is to create a simple spreadsheet with five columns: Risk (one to three sentences that describe each risk), Probability (the estimated probability from 1 to 5), Impact (the estimated impact from 1 to 5), Priority (Probability × Impact), and Action (the specific actions that will be taken to mitigate the risk, or "None" if the risk is deemed a low enough priority to ignore). Figure 2-1 shows a sample risk plan.

> **NOTE**
>
> A more detailed risk mitigation process is described in *Making Process Improvement Work* by Neil Potter and Mary Sakry (Addison Wesley, 2002).

Project Plan Inspection Checklist

The project plan—including the project schedule—should be reviewed (see Chapter 5) using this inspection checklist:

Statement of work

Does the project plan include a statement of work (SOW)?

Is the SOW complete—does it contain all of the features that will be developed?

Are all work products represented?

If estimates are known, have they been included?

Resources

Does the project plan include a resource list?

Does the resource list contain all resources available to the project?

Risk plan for project	Call center application project			

Assessment team members	Mike, Barbara, Quentin, Jill, Sophie, Dean, Kyle			

Risk	Prob.	Impact	Priority	Actions
Senior management will move call center offshore, which will require an internationalization feature to be built	3	5	15	1. Mike will add a requirements task to the schedule for Quentin to begin investigating internationalization requirements. 2. If the call cener is moved, Mike will call a team meeting to review the schedule and Barbara will inform the rest of senior management of the potential delay.
Jim will be pulled off of this project for Royalty Archive project bug fixes	4	3	12	1. Assign Kyle to work with Jill on the initial programming tasks to make sure he is cross-trained. 2. If Jill is pulled off, she will spend 10% of her time reviewing this project with Kyle.
Reporting feature will be needed	2	4	8	If this happens, Mike will work with Sophie and Kyle to reestimate the programming tasks.
Additional time will be needed to gather requirements from potential users at Boston client	5	1	5	None
Will need to support tie-in to support additional database vendors	1	3	3	None

FIGURE 2-1. Sample risk plan

Are there any resources known to be assigned to other projects at the same time that they are assigned to this one?

Have dates that the resources are unavailable (scheduled downtime for machines, vacations for people, times that facilities cannot be booked, etc.) been taken into account?

Project schedule

Does the project plan include a schedule?

Are there any tasks that are missing or incorrect?

If a WBS was generated by a Delphi session, does the project schedule reflect all of the tasks that were identified by the team?

Does each task have a predecessor?

Is a resource allocated to each task?

If multiple resources have been assigned to a single task, has the task's duration been updated properly to reflect that?

Is there a more efficient way to allocate resources?

Does the project schedule contain periodic reviews?

Risk plan

Does the project plan include a risk plan?

Are there any risks that are not in the plan?

Are there any assumptions (from the vision and scope document or a Delphi session) that represent risks that should be included in the plan?

Is each risk prioritized correctly?

Has the impact of each risk been estimated correctly?

Have the risks been sufficiently mitigated?

Diagnosing Project Planning Problems

If a project is not planned well, it will veer off course fairly quickly. If the project manager does not take the lead in defining the scope immediately, the project will quickly become chaotic. Even if the scope seems to be defined well, the project manager must make sure that all stakeholders really understand and agree to it in order to avoid problems later on in the project. The team must buy into the scope as well, or else they will make decisions that are not in line with the project goals.

Lack of Leadership

It's not uncommon for people to intuitively feel that all they need for a project to be successful is a group of highly talented and motivated people. But even the best people will have trouble starting a project if nobody takes the lead.

One common problem that comes from a lack of leadership is tunnel vision. Each team member knows how to do her specific tasks; however, there's no way to plan for every detail of that task. She will almost certainly encounter decision points. For example, she may see a better way to solve a particular problem that will cost time but lead to a better solution. For some projects, it may be appropriate to pursue this; for others, the delivery schedule is more important than the superior solution.

Without good leadership, the team member might be afraid to make this decision. This usually results in the team member sending emails to peers, managers, stakeholders, and anyone else she can find, requesting confirmation of absolutely every little decision that gets made. People quickly get inundated with notes about project details that they lack the context to even understand.

On the other hand, she may also simply make decisions based on her gut feelings. As the project progresses, not all of her decisions are in line with the needs of the stakeholders. For example, she may choose to pursue the superior technical solution at the expense of the deadline, despite the fact that the stakeholders' needs would have been just as easily satisfied had she chosen the faster solution. As these decisions pile up throughout the course of the project, the scope itself starts to drift away from the organization's needs.

If there is a serious enough lack of leadership, the project may not even get this far. If the scope is never fully defined, then the project may have several false starts. Designers and programmers start building prototypes to demonstrate to stakeholders, only to find that they have to go back and rebuild them because they misunderstood the project needs. Work on the code may begin, only to have programmers moved off of the project for higher priority tasks. People are given conflicting priorities and do not know which one to work on first. The project takes a long time to emerge from the chaos. Even if a product is eventually delivered, it seemed to take much more effort than was necessary, and the team is relieved to be rid of it.

The Mid-Course Correction

A change in the project priorities partway through the project is one of the most frustrating ways that a software project can break down. After the software design and architecture is finalized, the code is under development, the testers have begun their preparation, and the rest of the organization is gearing up to use and support the software, a stakeholder "discovers" that an important feature is not being developed. This, in turn, wreaks havoc on the project schedules, causing the team to miss important deadlines as they frantically try to go back and hammer the new feature in.

This discovery often comes about very late in the project, when a preliminary build of the software is delivered to the stakeholder. Often a team member had already brought the problem to the stakeholder's attention early on in the project. But it was not detected at the time because the stakeholder may not have fully recognized the nature of problem, or he might not have been comfortable bringing the problem up because it would have involved criticizing a design that represented a lot of effort. Either way, the team is now demoralized because it knows it would have been much easier to build the right software in the first place instead of having to change halfway through the project.

Good project planning helps avoid this problem. A vision and scope document describes the features to be developed using straightforward language, and each of the features clearly fulfills a need that the project stakeholders recognize. Stakeholders are not technical people; they might not be fully comfortable reading technical documents, but they are usually very good about talking about their needs and can generally recognize when those needs are taken into account. A project plan developed with the team's buy-in and based on the vision and scope document keeps the project on track and allows everyone to spot problems early on and fix them.

Many design or programming problems can be traced back to an engineer who does not fully understand the needs that are being fulfilled. This is usually not the engineer's fault—perhaps the need itself was never brought up. Having stakeholders review and correct the vision and scope document before the software is designed helps the team recognize those missing needs early on in the project.

The Detached Engineering Team

In many organizations, there is an artificial wall between the people who need the software and the people who build it. The engineering team often sees itself as a separate unit. The priorities of the people in the organization who need the software don't really figure into the way the engineers plan and carry out their work. This seems justified because it will take the team a certain amount of time to do their work, and no amount of bargaining with the business side will change that.

In an organization structured like this, the senior managers and the stakeholders often end up frustrated with the development team. No matter how much pressure they are under, the engineers seem to be going at a slow pace. The engineers, on the other hand, feel like they are already putting in overtime to meet the needs of the other people in the organization, who never seem to be satisfied.

The vision and scope document helps fix this problem by helping the engineers understand the project priorities. It identifies deadlines that are external to the project and that must be treated as constraints. The team can make sure that those deadlines are addressed directly when they are planning their tasks. They can warn senior management early in the project if the deadlines are in danger of not being met, and the stakeholders can be told when their needs are not being met. The stakeholders, in return, will feel like the engineers are taking their needs seriously. All of this can be brought about by a frank discussion of those needs while the vision and scope is developed.

The project plan also fixes this because it represents an agreement between the engineering team, the stakeholders, the users, and the organization's senior management. Because it is based on the engineers' estimates, they know that they are given enough time. The stakeholders, in turn, are given a window into the planning and estimation process, which establishes a level of trust between them and the engineers.

CHAPTER THREE

Estimation

MANY PEOPLE HAVE REFERRED TO ESTIMATION AS A **"BLACK ART."** This makes some intuitive sense: at first glance, it might seem that estimation is a highly subjective process. One person might take a day to do a task that might only require a few hours of another's time. As a result, when several people are asked to estimate how long it might take to perform a task, they will often give widely differing answers. But when the work is actually performed, it takes a real amount of time; any estimate that did not come close to that actual time is inaccurate.

To someone who has never estimated a project in a structured way, estimation seems little more than attempting to predict the future. This view is reinforced when off-the-cuff estimates are inaccurate and projects come in late. But a good formal estimation process, one that allows the project team to reach a consensus on the estimates, can improve the accuracy of those estimates, making it much more likely that projects will come in on time. A project manager can help the team to create successful estimates for any software project by using sound techniques and understanding what makes estimates more accurate.

Elements of a Successful Estimate

A sound estimate starts with a *work breakdown structure* (WBS). A WBS is a list of tasks that, if completed, will produce the final product. The way the work is broken down dictates how it will be done. There are many ways to decompose a project into tasks. The project can be broken down by feature, by project phase (requirements tasks, design tasks, programming tasks, QA tasks, etc.), or by some combination of the two. Ideally, the WBS should reflect the way previous projects have been developed.

A useful rule of thumb is that any project can be broken down into between 10 and 20 tasks. For large projects (for example, a space shuttle), those tasks will be very large ("Test the guidance system"); for small projects (like writing a simple calculator program), the tasks are small ("Build the arithmetic object that adds, multiplies, or divides two numbers"). The team must take care in generating the WBS—if the tasks are incorrect, they can waste time going down a wrong path.

Once the WBS is created, the team must create an estimate of the effort required to perform each task. The most accurate estimates are those that rely on prior experience. Team members should review previous project results and find how long similar tasks in previous projects took to complete. Sources of delays in the past should be taken into account when making current estimates. Postmortem reports (see Chapter 8) are a good source of this information.

No estimate is guaranteed to be accurate. People get sick or leave the organization; teams run into unforeseen technical problems; the needs of the organization change. The unexpected will almost certainly happen. Therefore, the goal of estimation is not to predict the future. Instead, it is to gauge an honest, well-informed opinion of the effort required to do a task from those people in the organization who have the most applicable training and knowledge.

If two people widely disagree on how long a task will take, it's likely that the source of that disagreement is that each person made different assumptions about details of the work product or the strategy for producing it. In other words, any disagreement is generally about what is required to perform the task itself, not about the effort required to complete it. For example, given the same vision and scope document for a tool that sets the computer clock, two different developers might come up with wildly different estimates. But it might turn out that one developer assumed that the implementation would have a simple command-line interface, while the other assumed that there would be a complete user interface that had to integrate tightly with the operating system's control panel. By helping the programmers discuss these assumptions and come to a temporary resolution about their differences, the project manager can help them agree on a single estimate for the task.

A project manager can help the team create more accurate estimates by reducing the uncertainty about the project. The most effective way to do this is to do a thorough job creating a vision and scope document (see Chapter 2)—the more accurate and detailed it is, the more information the team has to work with when generating their estimate. The project manager can also ensure that the team has reached a consensus on the tasks that must be performed. Finally, the project manager can lead the team in a discussion of assumptions.

Assumptions Make Estimates More Accurate

Once the team has agreed upon a WBS, they can begin to discuss each task so they can come up with an estimate. At the outset of the project, the team members do not have all of the information they need in order to produce estimates; nevertheless, they need to come up with numbers. To deal with incomplete information, they must make assumptions about the work to be done. By making assumptions, team members can leave placeholders for information that can be corrected later, in order to make the estimate more accurate.

For the estimates to be most effective, the assumptions must be written down. Important information is discovered during the discussion that the team will need to refer back to during the development process, and if that information is not written down, the team will have to have the discussion all over again. If an assumption turns out to be incorrect, the schedule will need to be adjusted; they will be able to point to the exact cause of the delay by showing that a documented assumption turned out to be incorrect. This will help the project manager explain any resulting schedule delay to others in the organization and avoid that source of delays in the future. The assumptions also provide a way to keep a record of team decisions, share those decisions with others, and find errors in their decisions. (The assumptions should be added to the "Assumptions" section of the vision and scope document—see Chapter 2.)

The team should hold a brainstorming session to try to identify as many assumptions as possible. The bigger the list of assumptions, the lower the overall risk for the project. A project manager may get better results from this session by helping the team see how these assumptions can work to their benefit. Any software engineer who has had a bad experience with an estimate that has turned out to be inaccurate will appreciate the value of assumptions: they serve as a warning to the rest of the organization that the estimate is contingent on the assumptions being true. If even one of these assumptions turns out to be incorrect, the team cannot be "blamed" for the incorrect estimate that resulted.

While identifying assumptions is a skill that improves with experience, there are a set of questions that can help a novice team member figure out what assumptions he or she needs to make in order to properly estimate the software. The project manager (or a moderator in a Wideband Delphi session—see below) can use these questions to help lead the discussion to identify the assumptions:

- Are there project goals that are known to the team but not written in any documentation?

- Are there any concepts, terms, or definitions that need to be clarified?

- Are there standards that must be met but will be expensive to comply with?

- How will the development of this project differ from that of previous projects? Will there be new tasks added that were not performed previously?

- Are there technology and architecture decisions that have already been made?

- What changes are likely to occur elsewhere in the organization that could cause this estimate to be inaccurate?

- Are there any issues that the team is known to disagree on that will affect the project?

The last bullet point is especially important. If one team member believes that the project will go down one path while another team member believes the project will go down a different path, the estimates could vary significantly, depending on which team member is correct. For example, one team member may think that a certain off-the-shelf component should be used because that is cheaper than building it, while another team member may believe that they must build that component themselves because they cannot locate one for sale which suits their particular needs. Instead of reaching an impasse, the team can make an assumption—either assume that they will buy the component, or assume that they will build it—which will enable them to move forward with the estimate. It should be easier to reach an agreement at this point because it is not the final decision. By writing down the assumption, the team keeps a record of the disagreement and leaves open the possibility that this will change in the future. The written assumption will be especially useful later while doing a risk assessment for the project plan because there is a risk that the assumption is incorrect.

In other words, assumptions can help find a compromise to resolve disagreements. If two team members disagree, the team can agree to write down an assumption to temporarily resolve the issue for the purposes of the estimate. It's much easier to get people to agree on one answer temporarily by agreeing to revisit the issue later.

Discussing and writing down the assumptions in a team setting helps the team to identify potential roadblocks. For example, the team may have a genuine disagreement about whether or not to develop a user interface for their clock-setting application. The assumption allows the team to reach a temporary decision, knowing that the final decision is still open. Writing down the assumption allows the team to go back and revise the estimate later if it turns out the assumption is wrong—which means that it is vital that everyone understands that the assumptions are allowed to be incorrect. That way, if the team estimated that they would build a command-line program but later the decision was made to go with a full user interface, everyone will be able to explain why the schedule is delayed.

Another benefit of discussing assumptions is that it brings the team together very early on in the project to make progress on important decisions that will affect development. It's all too common for a developer to make estimates after reading the vision and scope document but before ever talking to anyone about the details of the project. Even if she writes down her assumptions, she has almost certainly missed many others. A moderated discussion of assumptions gives the project team a very effective forum to discuss the unknowns of the project. Identifying unknowns eliminates the source of many inaccuracies in the estimates.

One side effect of writing down the assumptions is that it puts pressure on the senior managers to allow the project to be estimated again if any of the assumptions prove to be incorrect. This is why the project manager should plan on having the vision and scope document updated to include any new assumptions that were identified during the estimation session. This gives the stakeholders and management a chance to review those assumptions and accept or reject them very early on, before they have had a chance to interfere with the development of the software. By having the senior managers review the assumptions, a project manager can reduce a source of future project delays.

Distrust Can Undermine Estimates

Estimates can either be a source of trust or distrust between the project team and their managers. If the team knows that they are given the opportunity to fully justify their estimates, and that they will be allowed to reestimate if the scope of the project changes, that they won't be punished for making an honest mistake in estimation, then each team member will work very hard to produce accurate estimates. In this case, estimation can be an effective tool for team motivation. Estimates are most accurate when everyone on the project team feels that he was actively part of the estimation process. Every team member feels a personal stake in the estimates, and will work very hard to meet any schedule based on those estimates.

Estimation is, by its nature, a politically charged activity in most organizations. When a team is asked to create estimates for work, they are essentially being asked to define their own schedule. Stakeholders need the project completed but usually do not have software engineering experience, so they may not be equipped to understand why a project will take, say, six months instead of three. For this reason, project managers must take care to make the estimation process as open and honest as possible so that the stakeholders can understand what's going on.

It is common for nontechnical people to assume that programmers pad their estimates. They often have a "rule" by which they cut off a third or half of any estimate that they hear, and expect that to be the "real" deadline. They often feel, fairly or not, that the engineering team is "putting one over" on them, mostly because the entire engineering process is, to them, a mystery. This lack of trust causes engineers to automatically pad their estimates, because they know they won't be given enough time otherwise. And even when the situation is not this bad (although it often is), some environment of distrust still exists to a lesser extent in many organizations.

In many of these organizations, there are some kinds of estimates—especially those for quality and requirements tasks—that are particularly likely to not be taken seriously. Senior managers are often willing to take the programmers' estimates at face value, even when those estimates are clearly padded. This is because, to them, programming is opaque: managers and stakeholders don't understand how code is written, so they assume that all programming tasks are difficult. They are more likely to trust programmers' estimates, even when those estimates are highly padded. Requirements analysts, on the other hand, often produce specifications using nothing more than a word processor (and many elicitation sessions—see Chapter 6). A manager or stakeholder is much more likely to trivialize that work and distrust the estimate because he (incorrectly) feels that he has an intuitive grasp on the work being done. Even worse, in some organizations there is a "rule" that testing should always take exactly one-third (or some other fixed ratio) of the programming time, which causes the testing effort to be shortchanged by only allowing exactly that much time for it instead of the actual amount of time testing would require.

Distrust in a software organization can be a serious, endemic problem. It starts with a kernel of distrust between management and the engineering team; the distrust grows until management simply won't accept the team's estimates. For example, a senior manager may decide that the team plans to spend too much time testing the software, even though the team reached consensus and all team members stand behind the estimates. A project manager must be especially careful to explain this and support that consensus when senior managers start to pick apart the team's estimates. If deadlines are handed down that do not allow enough time for the team to complete the work, it can lead to serious morale problems—and the project manager will be blamed for the delay, often by the same people who caused it in the first place.

An important part of running successful software projects is reaching a common understanding between the engineers, managers, and stakeholders. One way to do that is with a consistent set of practices. This allows the engineers' work to be transparent to the rest of the organization. Similarly, the managers' and stakeholders' needs and expectations must be transparent to the engineers. By having key managers attend the estimation session, a project manager can show them that the estimates are made systematically, using an orderly and sensible process, and that they are not just made up on a whim. When the team is having trouble reaching convergence on a task, team members should bring up examples of past results for tasks of similar size and complexity. This transparency helps everyone present (especially the observers) understand why these estimates come out as they do.

Wideband Delphi Estimation

The *Wideband Delphi* estimation method was developed in the 1940s at the Rand Corporation as a forecasting tool. It has since been adapted across many industries to estimate many kinds of tasks, ranging from statistical data collection results to sales and marketing forecasts. It has proven to be a very effective estimation tool, and it lends itself well to software projects.*

The Wideband Delphi estimation process is especially useful to a project manager because it produces several important elements of the project plan. The most important product is the set of estimates upon which the project schedule is built. In addition, the project team creates a work breakdown structure (WBS), which is a critical element of the plan. The team also generates a list of assumptions, which can be added to the vision and scope document.

The discussion among the team during both the kickoff meeting and the estimation session is another important product of the Delphi process. This discussion typically uncovers many important (but previously unrecognized) project priorities, assumptions, and tasks. The team is much more familiar with the work they are about to undertake after they complete the Wideband Delphi process.

Wideband Delphi works because it requires the entire team to correct one another in a way that helps avoid errors and poor estimation. While software estimation is certainly a skill that improves with experience, the most common problem with estimates is simply that the person making the estimate does not fully understand what it is that he is estimating. He may be an experienced software engineer, but if he has not fully explored all of the assumptions behind the estimate, the estimate will be incorrect. Delphi addresses this problem through the discussion of assumptions and the generation of consensus among the estimation team members.

> **NOTE**
>
> The Wideband Delphi process described here depends on a vision and scope document. It is possible to estimate a project without a vision and scope document, instead relying solely on the project team's understanding of the organization's needs. However, if there is no vision and scope document for the project, most project managers will find that writing one will improve the project far more than trying to estimate without it. (Chapter 2 describes how to develop a vision and scope document as part of the software project planning activities.)

---

* The repeatable process for Wideband Delphi was developed in the 1990s by Mary Sakry and Neil Potter of The Process Group. Potter and Sakry offer a software estimation workshop based on their process. Information on their training products can be found at *http://www.processgroup.com*.

The Delphi Process

To use Wideband Delphi, the project manager selects a moderator and an estimation team with three to seven members. The Delphi process consists of two meetings run by the moderator. The first meeting is the kickoff meeting, during which the estimation team creates a WBS and discusses assumptions. After the meeting, each team member creates an effort estimate for each task. The second meeting is the estimation session, in which the team revises the estimates as a group and achieves consensus. After the estimation session, the project manager summarizes the results and reviews them with the team, at which point they are ready to be used as the basis for planning the software project. The script in Table 3-1 describes the Wideband Delphi process.

TABLE 3-1. Wideband Delphi script

Name	Wideband Delphi script
Purpose	A project team generates estimates and a work breakdown structure.
Summary	A repeatable process for estimation. Using it, a project team can generate a consensus on estimates for the completion of the project.
Work Products	*Input* Vision and scope document, or other documentation that defines the scope of the work product being estimated *Output* Work breakdown structure (WBS) Effort estimates for each of the tasks in the WBS
Entry Criteria	The following criteria should be met in order for the Delphi process to be effective: • The vision and scope document (or other documentation that defines the scope of the work product being estimated) has been agreed to by the stakeholders, users, managers, and engineering team. If no vision and scope document is available, there must be enough supporting documentation for the team to understand the work product. • The kickoff meeting and estimation session have been scheduled (each at least two hours). • The project manager and the moderator agree on the goal of the estimation session by identifying the scope of the work to be estimated.
Basic Course of Events	1. *Choosing the team.* The project manager selects the estimation team and a moderator. The team should consist of three to seven project team members. The team should include representatives from every engineering group that will be involved in the development of the work product being estimated. 2. *Kickoff meeting.* The moderator prepares the team and leads a discussion to brainstorm assumptions, generate a WBS, and decide on the units of estimation. 3. *Individual preparation.* After the kickoff meeting, each team member individually generates the initial estimates for each task in the WBS, documenting any changes to the WBS and missing assumptions. 4. *Estimation session.* The moderator leads the team through a series of iterative steps to gain consensus on the estimates. At the start of the iteration, the moderator charts the estimates on the whiteboard so the estimators can see the range of estimates. The team resolves issues and revises estimates without revealing specific numbers. The cycle repeats until either no estimator wants to change his or her estimate, the estimators agree that the range is acceptable, or two hours have elapsed. 5. *Assembling tasks.* The project manager works with the team to collect the estimates from the team members at the end of the meeting and compiles the final task list, estimates, and assumptions. 6. *Reviewing results.* The project manager reviews the final task list with the estimation team.

TABLE 3-1. Wideband Delphi script (continued)

Name	Wideband Delphi script
Alternative Paths	1. During Step 1, if the team determines that there is not enough information known about the project to perform an estimate, the script ends. Before the script can be started again, the project manager must document the missing information by creating or modifying the vision and scope document (see Chapter 2). 2. During either Step 1 or 3, if the team determines that there are outstanding issues that must be resolved before the estimate can be made, they agree upon a plan to resolve the issues and the script ends.
Exit Criteria	The script ends after the team has either generated a set of estimates or has agreed upon a plan to resolve the outstanding issues.

Choosing the team

Picking a qualified team is an important part of generating accurate estimates. Each team member must be willing to make an effort to estimate each task honestly, and should be comfortable working with the rest of the team. Estimation sessions can get heated; a team that already has friction will find that it runs into many disagreements that are difficult to resolve. The free flow of information is essential, and the project manager should choose a group of people who work well together. The estimators should all be knowledgeable enough about the organization's needs and past engineering projects (preferably similar to the one being estimated) to make educated estimates.

The moderator should be familiar with the Delphi process, but should not have a stake in the outcome of the session, if possible. Project managers are sometimes tempted to fill the moderator role, but this should be avoided (if at all possible) because the project manager should ideally be part of the estimation team. This is because the PM needs to take an active role in the discussion of the assumptions. She usually has a perspective on the project priorities that some of the engineers, stakeholders, and users do not see at first.

The role of the moderator is to listen to the discussion, ask open-ended questions, challenge the team to address issues, and ensure that everyone on the team is contributing. The moderator may estimate, but if he does, it is important that he remain unbiased by the team's estimates. A well-chosen team will allow the moderator to sit out on the estimation tasks and remain neutral and open-minded during the discussion.

The project manager should choose the team, and it should include people that she is comfortable working with. The team should include representatives from as many areas of the development team as possible: managers, developers, designers, architects, QA engineers, requirements analysts, technical writers, etc. Most importantly, each of the team members should have a stake in the plan, meaning that his goal is to establish a plan which he can agree to and live with. This allows the Delphi process to serve as an important tool for gaining the engineering team's support for the project plan, giving all involved a feeling of ownership of the estimates on which it is based.

Finally, one or more observers—selected stakeholders, users, and managers—should be encouraged to attend the meeting. The reason that the observers are important is that they often do not understand the engineering process and what goes into building the software. Including observers is an effective way to encourage mutual trust between the team and the nontechnical people in the organization. While the observers do not directly contribute to the numerical estimates, encouraging their involvement in the meetings will increase their feeling of ownership of the final estimates that are generated by the team. When the non-engineers participate in the discussion of assumptions and see how the team arrives at estimates, they walk away with a much greater understanding of how the engineers do their work. What's more, the assumptions are almost always discussed on a level that can generally be understood by most of the nontechnical observers. Since these assumptions usually end up focused on the most problematic areas of development, the observers leave the meetings with a much clearer picture of exactly how the software will be developed.

Kickoff meeting

The goal of the kickoff meeting is to prepare the team for the estimation session. When the kickoff meeting is scheduled, each team member is given the vision and scope document and any other documentation that will help her understand the project she is estimating. The team members should read all of the material before attending the meeting.

In addition, a goal statement for the estimation session should be agreed upon by the project manager and the moderator and distributed to the team before the session. This statement should be no more than a few sentences that describe the scope of the work that is to be estimated ("Generate estimates for programming and testing the first phase of Project X").

The moderator leads the meeting, which consists of the following activities:

- The moderator explains the Wideband Delphi method to any new estimators.

- If any team member has not yet read the vision and scope document and supporting documentation, the moderator reviews it with the team. (If this happens, the meeting should be expected to take an extra half-hour to hour.)

- The moderator reviews the goal of the estimation session with the team, and checks that each team member is sufficiently knowledgeable to contribute.

- The team discusses the product being developed and brainstorms any assumptions.

- The team generates a task list consisting of 10–20 major tasks. These tasks represent the top level of the work breakdown structure—additional detail can be generated later and/or discussed in the assumptions. This high-level task list is the basis for the estimates that are going to be created.

- The team agrees on the units of estimation (days, weeks, pages, etc.).

The team must agree on the goal of the project estimation session before proceeding with the rest of the estimation process. In most cases, the goal is straightforward; however, it is possible that the team members will disagree on it. Disagreement could focus on missing requirements, on which programs or tasks are to be included, on whether or not to estimate user documentation or support requirements, on the size of the user base being supported, or other basic scope issues.

After the assumptions are discussed, the moderator leads a brainstorming session to generate the WBS. The team breaks the project down into between 10 and 20 tasks, representing all of the project activities that must be performed. Once the team is comfortable with the WBS and the assumptions, it will feel much more knowledgeable about the context in which it will be developing the software. This, in turn, will make everyone more comfortable with the team's estimates.

Individual preparation

After the kickoff meeting, the moderator writes down all of the assumptions and tasks that were generated by the team during the kickoff meeting and distributes them to the estimation team. Each team member independently generates a set of *preparation results*, a document which contains an estimate for each of the tasks, any assumptions that the team member made in order to create the estimates, and any additional tasks that should be included in the WBS but that the team missed during the kickoff meeting. (Figure 3-1 shows the format of the individual preparation results.) Each team member builds preparation results by first filling in the tasks, and then estimating the effort for each task. An estimate for each task should be added to the "Tasks to achieve goal" section of the preparation results; the "Time" column should contain the estimate for each task.

Task list		Assumptions
Tasks to achive goal	Time	1. _____
_____	___	2. _____
_____	___	3. _____
_____	___	4. _____
_____	___	5. _____
		6. _____
Calendar waiting time, delays		7. _____
_____	___	8. _____
_____	___	9. _____
_____	___	10. _____
		11. _____
		12. _____
Project overhead tasks		13. _____
_____	___	14. _____
_____	___	15. _____

FIGURE 3-1. Individual preparation results

Each estimate should be made in terms of effort, not calendar time. This means that if the unit of estimation is "days," then the estimate should be for the total number of person-days spent. For example, if a task will require one person to work for 10 days and a second person to work for 6, the estimate should be 16 person-days (or 3.2 person-weeks, assuming a 5-day week). If both people are working at the same time so that their effort overlaps entirely, the calendar time required to do this task is 10 days.

Usually, effort does not overlap perfectly like this; this kind of parallel effort will be factored in later, when the project schedule is created (see Chapter 4). However, one important factor in creating the schedule is taking into account necessary delays in which no work will be done. For example, the team may need to wait for a server to be built or a software licensing agreement to be reached; estimates for any known waiting time can also be added to the preparation results.

Any effort related to project overhead should not be taken into account. This includes things like status meetings, reports, vacation, etc. A separate estimation session can be held for overhead. Any time an estimator identifies a project overhead task, it should be added to the "Project overhead tasks" section of the preparation results. Similarly, estimators may run across potential delays, because certain tasks can't start until after specific dates. These should be added to the "Calendar waiting time" section, and not taken into account while making estimates. (Often, a separate Delphi session will be held specifically to estimate waiting time or overhead tasks. This is the purpose of the checkboxes at the top of the estimation form in Figure 3-2.)

Name	Mike					Date 4/3/2004			Estimation form / / /	
Goal statement To estimate the time to develop prototype for customers A & B									**Units** days	
Category	☑ goal tasks ☑ quality tasks			☐ waiting time ☐ project overhead						
WBS# or priority	**Task name**	**Est.**	**Delta 1**	**Delta 2**	**Delta 3**	**Delta 4**		**Total**	**Assumptions**	
1	Interview customers (A+B)	3	+2	+1					Needs off-site tri	
2	Develop requirements docs	6	+5	-2	+1				Start from scratc	
3	Inspect requirements docs	1	+2	+2	-2				Team of 4 BSAs	
4	Do rework	1	+4							
5	Prototype design	20	-3	4	-2				Includes DB	
6	Test design	5	+3						20% exists now	
	Delta		+3	+5	-3					
	Total	36	49	54	51					

FIGURE 3-2. Filled-in estimation form
(©The Process Group, copied with permission)

While estimating each task, most people realize that they must make additional assumptions in order to estimate tasks. These should be recorded in the "Assumptions" section of the preparation results. They may also discover additional tasks that were not found during the kickoff meeting—these missing tasks should be added to the "Task list" section and estimated along with the rest of the WBS tasks. The final result should be a complete task list, including any additional tasks found, waiting time, and overhead tasks, with an estimate attached to each task. Each team member should bring the results to the estimation session.

Estimation session

The estimation session starts with each estimator filling out an estimation form. Blank estimation forms should be handed out to meeting participants, who fill in the tasks and their initial estimates from their individual preparations. During the estimation session, the team members will use these estimation forms to modify their estimates. After the estimation session, they will serve as a record of each team member's estimates for the individual tasks, which the project manager uses when compiling the results. (Figure 3-2 shows an example of a typical filled-in estimation form.)

Before the team members fill in their forms, the moderator should lead a brief discussion of any additional tasks that were discovered during the individual preparation phase. Each task that the team agrees to add to the WBS should be added to the form; the team will generate estimates for that task later in the meeting. If the team decides that the task should not be included after all, the person who introduced it should make sure that the effort he estimated for that task is taken into account.

At this point, the participants fill out the estimation forms. The estimation form contains one row for each task being estimated. If there are more tasks than rows on the form, more than one form can be used for the session. Each participant starts with a blank form and writes the name of each task on consecutive rows. The estimate for that task should be written into the "Estimate" box next to the task. The estimate boxes are then added up and the total written into the "Total" box at the bottom of the Estimate column.

The moderator then leads the team through the estimation session:

1. The moderator collects all of the estimate forms. The estimates are tabulated on a whiteboard by plotting the totals on a line (see Figure 3-3). The forms are returned to the estimators.

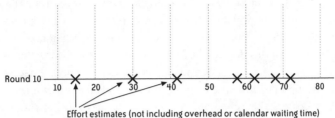

Effort estimates (not including overhead or calendar waiting time)

FIGURE 3-3. Initial estimates

2. Each estimator reads out clarifications and changes to the task list written on the estimation form. Any new or changed tasks, discovered assumptions, or questions are raised. Specific estimate times are *not* discussed.

3. The team resolves any issues or disagreements that are brought up. Since individual estimate times are not discussed, these disagreements are usually about the tasks themselves, and are often resolved by adding assumptions. When an issue is resolved, team members should write clarifications and changes to the task list on their estimation forms. This usually takes about 40 minutes for the first round, and 20 minutes for the following rounds.

4. The estimators all revise their individual estimates by filling in the next "Delta" column on their forms. (Using a delta allows the estimators to write "+4" or "-3" to add 4 or remove 3 from the estimate. They write the new total at the bottom of the sheet.)

This cycle repeats until either all estimators agree that the range is acceptable, the estimators feel they do not need to change their estimates, or two hours have elapsed.

Each round brings the estimates closer to convergence. Figure 3-4 shows what the typical results of an estimation session will look like. It may seem magical to the team—through a straightforward discussion of assumptions and task definition, the team arrives at a consensus that is visible on the whiteboard! This consensus is a result of clarifying these potential ambiguities. Usually the first round brings a long discussion of missed assumptions and changes to the task definition. In the later rounds, the moderator will play an important role in directing the conversation toward where it will be most effective. The moderator should look for the tasks that have the largest spread between the highest and lowest estimates. He should lead a frank discussion of the breakdown or details of that task, as well as places where the team might be over- or underestimating the effort for that task.

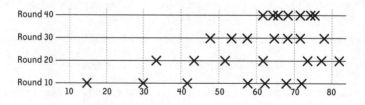

FIGURE 3-4. Converging estimate results

Disagreements often arise, but they are easier to deal with in this setting than later on, when the project is in progress. One effective way to resolve these disagreements is to talk about both sides of the issue, and then agree on an assumption that takes one of those sides. It is easier to make this decision at this stage because the assumption is not permanent; the team can very easily go back and change that assumption, if necessary. But writing down the assumption allows the team to show management that if this assumption turns out to be incorrect, the estimate may no longer be accurate. This way, even though the estimate is not perfect, the team understands why that is the case. If the team has confidence that they did a complete job with the assumptions, they will have more confidence in the value of the estimate.

After the conclusion of the estimation cycle, the moderator leads a discussion on how the session went. The team suggests ways to improve. The moderator notes their feedback, to include it in the final estimation report.

Assemble tasks

After the estimation meeting is finished, the project manager works with the moderator to gather all of the results from the individual preparation and the estimation session. The project manager removes redundancies and resolves remaining estimate differences to generate a final task list, with effort estimates attached to each task. The assumptions are then summarized and added to the list.

The final task list should be in the same format as the individual preparation results (see Figure 3-1). In addition, the project manager should create a spreadsheet that lists the final estimates that each person came up with. The spreadsheet should indicate the best-case and worst-case scenarios, and it should indicate any place that further discussion will be required. Any task with an especially wide discrepancy should be marked for further discussion. Figure 3-5 shows an example of a spreadsheet that summarizes the results. It contains a column for each estimator, as well as columns for the best-case estimate (using the lowest estimates, which assume that everything has gone well), worst-case estimate (using the highest estimates, which assume that the project hit many roadblocks), and average estimate. (When the project manager calculates these numbers, it's often a good idea to remove the highest and lowest estimates in order to eliminate outliers.)

Goal statement	To estimate the time to develop prototype for customers A & B								
Estimators	Mike, Quentin, Jill, Sophie							Units	days
								Shaded items must be discussed	
WBS# or priority	Task name	M.	Q.	J.	S.	Best-case	Worst-case	Avg.- hi & lo	Notes
1	Interview customers (A+B)	6	4	3	3	3	6	3.5	
2	Develop requirements docs	5	10	2	5	2	10	5	Discrepancy between Q. and J.
3	Inspect requirements docs	7	5	6	5	5	7	5.5	
4	Do rework	8	7	9	7	7	9	7.5	
5	Prototype design	28	23	31	25	23	31	26.5	
6	Test design	9	7	6	6	6	9	6.5	
	Total	63	56	57	51	46	72	54.5	

FIGURE 3-5. Summarized results of estimation

The assumptions should also be put into a final form, suitable for inclusion in the "Assumptions" section of the vision and scope document. (If the author of the vision and scope document is not the project manager, then the project manager should turn the assumptions over to the author and help incorporate them into the document.) If the vision and scope document was already inspected and approved, it should be updated and then inspected again prior to being used as the basis for a project plan.

Sometimes there may be a team member who disagrees with the team's assessment estimate for a task, and continues to disagree with it over the course of the project. The project manager must be careful in this situation, especially if the disagreement is over a task that will be assigned to that team member. An important part of the Delphi process is that it generates consensus among the team about the final schedule. That consensus can be much harder to achieve if any of the team members feels like her objections are being ignored. One way for the project manager to make sure that this does not happen is to call an additional meeting to discuss the outlying estimates. During this meeting, the project manager must take the time to listen to everything that the person who differs from the rest of the team has to say. The final decision about the effort still lies with the project manager; however, if there is a genuine disagreement, then the person who disagrees with the rest of the team will at least feel like his objections were heard and evaluated on their merits, rather than just rejected outright.

Review results

Once the results are ready, the project manager calls a final meeting to review the estimation results with the team. The goal of the meeting is to determine whether the results of the session are sufficient for further planning. The team should determine whether the estimates make sense and if the range is acceptable. They should also examine the final task list to verify that it's complete. There may be an area that needs to be refined: for example, a task might need to be broken down into subtasks. In this case, the team may agree to hold another estimation session to break down those tasks into their own subtasks and estimate each of them. This is also a good way to handle any tasks that have a wide discrepancy between the best-case and worst-case scenarios.

Other Estimation Techniques

Wideband Delphi is not the only technique that can be effective in estimating software tasks. Here are a few popular and effective alternatives.

PROBE

Proxy Based Estimating (PROBE), is the estimation method introduced by Watts Humphrey (of the Software Engineering Institute at Carnegie Mellon University) as part of the Personal Software Process (a discipline that helps individual software engineers monitor, test, and improve their own work). PROBE is based on the idea that if an engineer is building a component similar to one he built previously, then it will take about the same effort as it did in the past.

In the PROBE method, individual engineers use a database to keep track of the size and effort of all of the work that they do, developing a history of the effort they have put into their past projects, broken into individual components. Each component in the database is assigned a type ("calculation," "data," "logic," etc.) and a size (from "very small" to "very large"). When a new project must be estimated, it is broken down into tasks that correspond to these types and sizes. A formula based on linear regression is used to calculate the estimate for each task. Additional information on PROBE can be found in *A Discipline for Software Engineering* by Watts Humphrey (Addison Wesley, 1994).

COCOMO II

The Constructive Cost Model (COCOMO) is a software cost and schedule estimating method developed by Barry Boehm in the early 1980s. Boehm developed COCOMO empirically by running a study of 63 software development projects and statistically analyzing their results. COCOMO II was developed in the 1990s as an updated version for modern development life cycles, and it is based on a broader set of data. The COCOMO calculation incorporates 15 cost drivers, variables that must be provided as input for a model that is based on the results of those studied projects. These variables cover software, computer, personnel, and project attributes. The output of the model is a set of size and effort estimates that can be developed into a project schedule. Additional information on COCOMO can be found in *Software Cost Estimation with Cocomo II* by Barry Boehm et al. (Prentice Hall PTR, 2000).

The Planning Game

The Planning Game is the software project planning method from Extreme Programming (XP), a lightweight development methodology developed by Kent Beck in the 1990s at Chrysler. It is a method used to manage the negotiation between the engineering team ("Development") and the stakeholders ("Business"). It gains some emotional distance from the planning process by treating it as a game, where the playing pieces are "user stories" written on index cards and the goal is to assign value to stories and put them into production over time.

Unlike Delphi, PROBE, and COCOMO, the Planning Game does not require a documented description of the scope of the project to be estimated. Rather, it is a full planning process that combines estimation with identifying the scope of the project and the tasks required to complete the software.

Like much of XP, the planning process is highly iterative. The scope is established by having Development and Business work together to interactively write the stories. Then, each story is given an estimate of 1, 2, or 3 weeks. Stories that are larger than that are split up into multiple iterations. (Often, an organization will standardize on a regular story and iteration duration: for example, day-length stories and one- or two-week iterations.) Business is given an opportunity to steer the project between iterations. The estimates themselves are created by the programmers, based on the stories that are created. Finally, commitments are agreed upon. This is repeated until the next iteration of the project is planned.

Additional information on the Planning Game can be found in *Extreme Programming Explained* by Kent Beck (Addison Wesley, 2000).

Diagnosing Estimation Problems

Estimation problems almost always boil down to estimates that are either too high or too low. Padded estimates, where the team intentionally overestimates in order to give themselves extra time, are a chronic source of estimates that are too high. Senior managers giving unrealistic, overly aggressive deadlines are a chronic source of estimates that are too low. In both cases, this can lead to morale problems.

There is a basic tug-of-war going on here. Engineers prefer higher estimates, giving them as much time and as little pressure as possible to do their work. Managers prefer to deliver things more quickly, in order to please stakeholders. The only way for a project manager to avoid this conflict is to work with the team to produce estimates that are as accurate as possible. By adopting a sound estimation process that allows the team and the project manager to reach a consensus on the effort involved in the work, the morale is maintained and the work is much more predictable.

Padded Estimates Generate Distrust

In some organizations, the project team drives the entire estimation process and the project manager simply builds a schedule around their estimates. This can be comfortable for the team, but it does not always work well for the organization, and it can eventually lead to an environment where the managers don't trust the programmers.

There are many reasons why estimates are wrong that have nothing to do with the work being done. Software engineers are often overoptimistic by nature—it's easy to be very positive about a project before doing any of the work, and it's easy to ignore problems that may come up later. It's very tempting to pad estimates, since they lead to longer schedules and less pressure.

The situation is especially bad when someone with no formal training in software engineering and little experience estimating software tasks is asked by her manager to give estimates. She is forced into a difficult situation: if her estimates come up short, she will be penalized at her next review. She could pad the estimates, but that would be dishonest. Her manager will eventually catch on and start cutting down any estimate she provides. Either of these options can lead to unreliable estimates that throw off the entire project planning process. She feels like she's left hanging with little support, and if her manager sees that her estimates are off, he could end up distrusting ones she makes in the future.

A programmer who knows that there will be ramifications—a poor review, a lower raise—if he does not meet his estimates may pad them, often extending his estimates by a factor of two or three. Managers will usually catch onto this, making it clear that they don't trust the programmer's estimates and asking for the tasks to be done early. The programmer, in turn, will only pad the estimates more. This "arms race" usually leads to a complete breakdown of the planning process.

A project manager could avoid the problem of estimates that are chronically padded by having the team reach a consensus on their estimates in an open meeting, where team members are less likely to pad their numbers. Team members who have thoroughly discussed their assumptions about the estimates are much less likely to be overly optimistic—they remain more grounded in the facts of the project, and will not sweep as many details aside. It may be tempting to pad estimates when delivering them by email; it is much harder to pad them when sitting at a table with everyone else on the team, knowing that one's estimates might be challenged and would have to be justified on the spot.

Self-Fulfilling Prophecy

Some project managers respond to an unrealistic deadline by creating "estimates" that are too low but that meet it. Sometimes a team makes up for their project manager's poor estimates through enormous effort and overtime. When this happens, those poor estimates become a self-fulfilling prophecy—instead of being an honest assessment of the work that the team expects to do, the estimate turns into a series of baseless deadlines that the team must meet. The team never agreed to these deadlines, nor did they have any input into them; when this happens, the team will begin to resent their project manager. This is especially common when the top programmer is promoted to project manager, and fails to take into account the fact that he works faster than the rest of the team. (When this happens, the project manager's bond with other programmers will make it more likely for them to agree to the deadline and work much harder.) But any project manager is susceptible to this problem.

Typically, the self-fulfilling prophecy happens when the project manager is the sole source of estimates. He will create a project schedule with aggressive deadlines. Often, he will set the deadline first, and then work backward to fill in the tasks. The effort required to perform each task is not taken into account, nor is the relative expertise of each team member.

If the deadlines are too aggressive but not entirely impossible, the team will work to meet them. This may seem like a good thing to the project manager—he was able to get more work out of the team. But, as the team begins to burn out, they start to realize that they are working toward an unrealistic project schedule. The project does not go smoothly. Instead, it alternates between normal working time and crunch periods, and there is little advance warning before the crunch periods begin.

The first few times that the team meets an unrealistic schedule by working nights and weekends, they are happy to have met the deadline. But each time this happens, the project manager's undeservedly high opinion of his own estimating skills is reinforced. Eventually, the team gets disillusioned and bitter, and the sense of camaraderie that was forged over the many late nights and high-pressure assignments is overwhelmed by anger and frustration.

Had the project manager used a consensus-driven estimation process, the team would have been able to go into the project with a real understanding of what would be asked of them. They would know at the outset that the project would require crunch periods, and would be able to plan their lives around them instead of being blindsided by them. And the project manager would be able to keep the team together, without causing them to feel bitter or exploited.

West Gates | DEPARTURES | East Gates

Time	Number	Train		To	Status	Track		Time	Number	Train		To	Status	Tr
:00P	174	REGIONAL	R	BOSTON	0:05 LATE			1:45P	283	EMPIRE SVC	R	NIAGARA FALLS	ON TIME	
:00P	2159	ACELA EXPRESS		WASHINGTON	0:15 LATE			2:00P	86	REGIONAL	R	BOSTON	0:25 LATE	
:03P	3845	NE CORR SEC EWR		TRENTON		12E		2:00P	486	SHUTTLE	R	SPRINGFIELD	0:25 LATE	
:13P	6631	MID DIRECT SEC		DOVER	ON TIME			2:00P	2121	ACELA EXPRESS		WASHINGTON	ON TIME	
:28P	3847	NE CORR SEC EWR		TRENTON	ON TIME			2:01P	3949	NE CORR	EXP	TRENTON	ON TIME	
:35P	645	KEYSTONE EWR	R	HARRISBURG	ON TIME			2:05P	93	REGIONAL EWR	R	RICHMOND	ON TIME	
:37P	3247	NJCOAST SEC EWR		LONG BRANCH	ON TIME			2:07P	3849	NE CORR SEC EWR		TRENTON	ON TIME	
:39P	6241	MID DIRECT SEC		HACKETTSTOWN	ON TIME			2:13P	6635	MID DIRECT SEC		DOVER	ON TIME	

:54 SEC - STOPS AT SECAUCUS EWR - STOPS AT NEWARK AIRPORT | SEC - STOPS AT SECAUCUS EWR - STOPS AT NEWARK AIRPORT 12

CHAPTER FOUR

Project Schedules

THE PROJECT SCHEDULE IS THE CORE OF THE PROJECT PLAN. It is used by the project manager to commit people to the project and show the organization how the work will be performed. Schedules are used to communicate final deadlines and, in some cases, to determine resource needs. They are also used as a kind of checklist to make sure that every task necessary is performed. If a task is on the schedule, the team is committed to doing it. In other words, the project schedule is the means by which the project manager brings the team and the project under control.

Building the Project Schedule

The *project schedule* is a calendar that links the tasks to be done with the resources that will do them. Before a project schedule can be created, the project manager must have a work breakdown structure (WBS), an effort estimate for each task, and a resource list with availability for each resource. If these are not yet available, it may be possible to create something that looks like a schedule, but it will essentially be a work of fiction. A project manager's time is better spent on working with the team to create a WBS and estimates (using a consensus-driven estimation method like Wideband Delphi—see Chapter 3) than on trying to build a project schedule without them. The reason for this is that a schedule itself is an estimate: each date in the schedule is estimated, and if those dates do not have the buy-in of the people who are going to do the work, the schedule will almost certainly be inaccurate.

There are many project scheduling software products that can do much of the tedious work of calculating the schedule automatically, and plenty of books and tutorials dedicated to teaching people how to use them. However, before a project manager can use these tools, he should understand the concepts behind the WBS, dependencies, resource allocation, critical paths, Gantt charts, and earned value. These are the real keys to planning a successful project.

Allocate Resources to the Tasks

The first step in building the project schedule is to identify the resources required to perform each of the tasks. A resource is any person, item, tool, or service that is needed by the project that is either scarce or has limited availability.

Many project managers use the terms "resource" and "person" interchangeably, but people are only one kind of resource. The project could include computer resources (like shared computer room, mainframe, or server time), locations (training rooms, temporary office space), services (like time from contractors, trainers, or a support team), and special equipment that will be temporarily acquired for the project. Most project schedules only plan for human resources—the other kinds of resources are listed in the resource list, which is part of the project plan (see Chapter 2).

One or more resources must be *allocated* to each task. To do this, the project manager must first assign the task to people who will perform it. For each task, the project manager must identify one or more people on the resource list capable of doing that task and assign it to them. Once a task is assigned, the team member who is performing it is not available for other tasks until the assigned task is completed. While some tasks can be assigned to any team member, most can be performed only by certain people. If those people are not available, the task must wait.

Some tasks may require more than one person to be assigned to them—for example, a programming task may require three programmers. In this case, the *effort* for the task should be divided among those resources. The project manager must keep in mind the difference between effort and *duration*. Duration is the amount of time that elapses between the time the task is started and the time it is completed, measured in hours (or days, weeks, etc.). It does not take into account the number of people performing the task. Effort is measured in *person-hours* (or person-days, person-weeks, etc.), and represents the total number of hours that each person spent working on the task. For example, if 3 people worked on a task together for a total of 2 working days, the duration required to complete the task was 16 hours (at 8 hours per day, with only 5 or 6 of those hours actually devoted to software engineering work). However, since each of the 3 people spent 16 hours on the task, the total effort required was 48 person-hours (keep in mind that some tasks are not divided evenly between resources; the total effort should reflect the actual time worked per resource).

It's possible to allocate one resource to two tasks simultaneously by assigning a percentage of the resource's time to each task. When the task stretches over several days, but the resource is needed only for part of each day or a few days of the task, that resource can be assigned part-time to the task. For example, a resource can be 50% allocated to two tasks, or 30% allocated to one task and 70% to another, etc.

In cases where more than one person is allocated to a task, the project manager must take *overhead* into account. Overhead is any effort that does not go to the core activities of the task but is still required in order for the people to perform it—a sort of "real world" cost of actually doing the work. For example, 2 people performing a task will require more effort than 1 person doing the same task: if the duration of a task is 12 days, it may require 7 days for 2 people to finish it, because they need an additional day to compare and integrate their work. The trade-off is that, while assigning two people to the task requires more effort, the task has a shorter duration.

One useful way to compensate for the extra overhead is to use the range that was generated by the Wideband Delphi estimate (which was for effort, not duration). The project manager can choose an effort estimate from the low end of the range if fewer resources are allocated to the task, whereas an estimate from the higher end can be used for a larger number of resources. The estimation team may have also made assumptions about the number of resources required to perform the task.

It is important to remember that resources are individual people, and no two people will take exactly the same amount of time to perform a task. The project manager should be familiar with the relative expertise of each team member. A senior programmer can often do a job in a fraction of the time that it would take a junior programmer to do the same work. However, the project manager should also pay attention to professional development. Senior team members are scarce; they can't be assigned every task, and some tasks are too difficult to assign to junior people at all. Assigning a junior programmer to work with a senior one will potentially make that junior programmer more valuable on the next project, but can cost more time from both people for training and overhead.

Resource allocation is often the most difficult and time-consuming part of effective project management, because it requires the project manager to know the team. There is no hard-and-fast rule for deciding who is allocated to which task. This is a decision that requires a great deal of attention to the skill sets of the people on the team and to their personal motivation. Some people prefer working on certain kinds of tasks, and are most productive when they are doing those.

Finally, there are two useful and well-known principles to remember when considering how people work on projects. First, Parkinson's Law (named for C. Northcote Parkinson, who first wrote about it in 1958) states, "Work expands so as to fill the time available for its completion." And second, as Fred Brooks pointed out his 1975 book *The Mythical Man-Month*, "Nine women cannot have a baby in one month"—in other words, some tasks can be done only by one person, no matter how critical that task is.

Identify Dependencies

Once resources are allocated, the next step in creating a project schedule is to identify *dependencies* between tasks. A task has a dependency if it involves an activity, resource, or work product that is subsequently required by another task. Dependencies come in many forms: a test plan can't be executed until a build of the software is delivered; code might depend on classes or modules built in earlier stages; a user interface can't be built until the design is reviewed. If Wideband Delphi is used to generate estimates, many of these dependencies will already be represented in the assumptions. It is the project manager's responsibility to work with everyone on the engineering team to identify these dependencies. The project manager should start by taking the WBS and adding dependency information to it: each task in the WBS is given a number, and the number of any task that it is dependent on should be listed next to it as a *predecessor*. Figure 4-1 shows the four ways in which one task can be dependent on another.

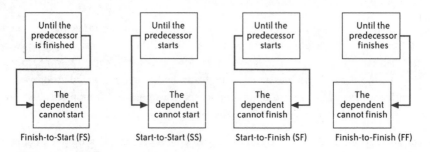

FIGURE 4-1. Four different types of predecessor

There are many reasons why one task may be dependent on another. The most common is the causal relationship: the dependent task relies on a work product generated by the predecessor. For example, the reviewers of a document cannot review it until it is completed, so a review task is dependent on the task that generates the document that will be reviewed. One task may also depend on another because they share the same resource: if there is only one programmer who has the knowledge to perform two different programming tasks, he cannot do them both at the same time; one must be dependent on the other. If there is no specific reason that one of those two programming tasks must be done before the other, then the project manager and programmer have discretion to perform them in either order.

The easiest way to maintain the resource allocations and dependencies is to use a project management software package. Most project management software allows the user to maintain a list of tasks and to associate resource information and predecessor information with each task. (It is possible to do this by hand, but very few project managers create schedules this way. Project management software is almost always used for this purpose.)

Create the Schedule

Once the resources and dependencies are assigned, the software will arrange the tasks to reflect the dependencies. The software also allows the project manager to enter effort and duration information for each task; with this information, it can calculate a final date and build the schedule.

The most common form for the schedule to take is a Gantt chart. This is a type of bar chart developed by Henry Laurence Gantt, an American engineer who was prominent during the first two decades of the 20th century. Over the past century, Gantt charts have been used on major civil engineering projects (including the Hoover Dam and the U.S. interstate highway system), and it is now the standard way to document software project schedules.

Figure 4-2 shows an example of a Gantt chart. Each task is represented by a bar, and the dependencies between tasks are represented by arrows. Each arrow either points to the start or the end of the task, depending on the type of predecessor (see Figure 4-1). The black diamond between tasks D and E is a *milestone*, or a task with no duration. Milestones are used to show important events in the schedule. The black bar above tasks D and E is a summary task, which shows that these tasks are two subtasks of the same parent task. Summary tasks can contain other summary tasks as subtasks. For example, if the team used an extra Wideband Delphi session to decompose a task in the original WBS into subtasks, the original task should be shown as a summary task with the results of the second estimation session as its subtasks.

The Gantt chart in Figure 4-2 demonstrates the following predecessor types:

- Task A is a Finish-to-Start (FS) predecessor of Task B. Task B does not start until Task A is complete. For example, code cannot be reviewed until it is written, so the programming task would be a Finish-to-Start predecessor to the code review task.

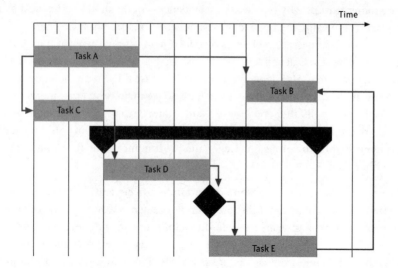

FIGURE 4-2. Gantt chart

- Task A is a Start-to-Start (SS) predecessor of Task C. Both tasks start at the same time. If the start time for Task A were delayed, then the start time for Task C would move forward to match it. For example, a team of software testers might all be expected to start their test executions at the same time. One tester's task would depend on the build being delivered; that task would be a Start-to-Start predecessor for the other testers' tasks.

- Task C is a Finish-to-Start (FS) predecessor of Task D. Task D is a Finish-to-Start (FS) predecessor of a milestone, which in turn is a Finish-to-Start predecessor of Task E.

- Task E is a Finish-to-Finish (FF) predecessor of Task B. Note the delay before Task B starts—it does not start until its planned completion time will match up with Task E. This allows the resources required for Task B to be allocated to another task in the meantime. For example, a test plan can be started as soon as the requirements are complete, but it cannot be completed until after the design is done. So the test plan task would have the requirements task as a Finish-to-Start predecessor and the design task as a Finish-to-Finish predecessor.

Reconcile the Schedule with the Organization's Needs

Once all of the task durations and predecessors have been determined, the project management software can calculate an expected due date for the project. If this date does not fit with the needs of the organization or the project stakeholders, the project manager should first go back to the resource list to see if the tasks can be reallocated more efficiently. One way to do this is to look for large gaps in the schedule; sometimes a small shift or swap in resources can close those gaps.

Another way to deal with a schedule that runs past a non-negotiable due date is to add or rearrange resources (if available). This is one reason it is important to set up different kinds of predecessors. By making a longer task a Finish-to-Start predecessor of a shorter task, for example, a gap in the allocation level for resources might emerge in front of the shorter one. That gap could be moved or filled with another task.

Sometimes there are technical solutions that can help reduce the schedule. It may be possible to return to the assumptions generated during the estimation session. There may be an implementation approach that can be revisited. For example, the team may have assumed that a user interface would be built for a piece of the software, when it could instead be built to run from the command line. Or it might have assumed it would have to build a feature to address a need, when this component could instead be purchased off the shelf.

As a last resort, however, the project can be released in several phases. This requires the project manager to revisit the project's scope, which will have to be adjusted to allow for a phased release: some features will have to be broken into phases, while others may be cut out entirely. This requires that the project manager revise the vision and scope document and go through its review process all over again (see Chapter 2). While this seems severe, it is often the only way to deal with an otherwise unworkable situation in which the organization expects the team to complete a project faster than it is possible for the team to build it.

Add Review Meetings to the Schedule

If a schedule is written down, put in a folder, and never looked at again, the project plan may just as well have never been made. There is no reason to plan a project if that plan is never consulted again, nor corrected when it proves to be incorrect. There is no project plan that perfectly estimates every task; the only way the team members can improve their planning skills is by learning from their mistakes. The way to ensure that this happens is to add regular review meetings to the schedule.

Progress reviews should be held regularly, both to keep track of whether the schedule is accurate and to plan action if the project goes off course. If the team is already holding weekly, biweekly, or monthly status meetings (see below), then these can also function as progress reviews (as long as the specific details of the schedule are discussed at every meeting). To make sure a status meeting functions as an effective schedule review, the project manager must make sure that the agenda at every meeting includes a discussion of whether the project is still on track. The project schedule serves as the agenda for this part of the meeting. The project manager should go through each task that is currently in progress and work with the team to determine the status of the task.

During the review, if the team discovers that a task is going to be late, the project manager must find a way to deal with it in the schedule. In some cases, a late task may cause other tasks to be delayed, though sometimes the delay can be absorbed in the schedule. For this reason, it is important for the stakeholders to be present: if there are major problems, they will know immediately and can help resolve them. The result of this meeting will usually be an adjusted project schedule. However, sometimes delays will cause serious problems that cannot be dealt with in the schedule. If a delay means that an unmovable deadline will be missed, the team will either have to adjust the schedule to put in overtime, or it will have to go back to the vision and scope document and scale back the scope of the project.

Milestone reviews are meetings that the project manager schedules in advance to coincide with project events. The most common way for project managers to handle milestone reviews is to schedule them to occur after the last task in a project phase (such as the end of design or programming). Project schedules are usually broken down into distinct *phases* which correspond to the major software engineering activities: scope, requirements, design, development, and testing. Each of these phases is usually represented on the Gantt chart as a summary task, with a milestone as the final subtask to mark the end of the phase.

Once again, the project manager should make sure that the representatives from the engineering team and stakeholders attend all of those meetings. The difference between a milestone review and a progress one is that the project manager writes up a report after the milestone review. This report should list any schedule delays or changes, any modifications to the scope, and any serious issues that came up since the last milestone review meeting. These reports should be stored with the project plan.

The schedule should always be updated by the project manager. However, the information that is used to update the project schedule should be agreed upon at status meetings. After every status meeting, the schedule should be updated with any changes that were agreed upon in the meeting. If a team member discovers that a problem has occurred between status meetings that could cause a delay, the project manager should be notified immediately. If the project manager feels that the problem is serious enough that it cannot wait until the next scheduled status meeting, an impromptu meeting should be called, and the team should talk about the impact to individual tasks so that the schedule can be kept up to date.

A final milestone should be added to the schedule for a postmortem meeting run by the QA lead (see Chapter 8).

Optimize the Schedule

Many times, the project manager has options in how the schedule is arranged. There is often flexibility in the order in which the tasks may be performed, or to whom they may be assigned. Most schedules end up with several sequences of interrelated tasks: a requirements document may have a string of elicitation, documentation, and verification tasks; software must be designed, coded, and reviewed; test plans must be written, reviewed, executed, repaired, and regressed.

In many schedules, there is some *slack* in these sequences. In a sequence of tasks, slack is the amount of time that any of the tasks can be delayed without causing the due date of the final task in the sequence to be delayed as well. A tight schedule has very little slack; a delay in any task will cause a delay in the due date. For example, a task may depend on a work product, but the person who will perform that task may not be available until three days after the work product is scheduled to be complete; this creates a three-day gap in the schedule. It may be possible to rearrange the tasks in order to reduce that slack—for example, the task that is occupying the resource could be moved to a point later or earlier in the project, or assigned to another resource. These decisions can make an enormous difference in the final due date.

It is important to keep in mind that, while there may appear to be slack in the schedule, it may simply be that all of the resources in the project are allocated to another task; there just happens to be some time between a task and its predecessor. Many project management software packages have a feature that summarizes the allocation of each resource per day in the schedule, which can be used to check for slack periods in which resources are unallocated. This is also helpful for ensuring that no resource is *over-allocated*, or more than 100% allocated to multiple tasks simultaneously. If any resource is over-allocated, it means that there is a dependency between two tasks that was not discovered. When this happens, the schedule is guaranteed to be inaccurate.

Some project managers fall into the trap of using slack in the schedule as a way to mitigate risk. They think that if there is extra space between two tasks, then the second task will have some protection, in case the first task is late. This is usually a mistake. Most project managers who try to do this find that Parkinson's Law kicks in—the work in the first task expands to fill up the slack. Instead of using slack to mitigate risk, the definition of the task should be expanded to include an activity that may mitigate the risk (see Chapter 2 about risk mitigation). This new task will take longer, and the schedule should be updated to reflect that. That said, if there is unavoidable slack in the schedule, it means that the schedule can tolerate some delay without affecting the due date of the project. But it is very important not to rely on this; instead, it's often better to plan other activities (such as training) for the resources with slack time.

One important tool for optimizing the schedule is the *critical path*. The critical path is the sequence of tasks that represents the minimum time required to complete the project. It is the sequence that, if delayed, will delay the schedule. The last task on the critical path is always the last task in the schedule—when the critical path is completed, the project is done. Every project schedule has at least one critical path: most have exactly one, but some may have two or more critical paths that complete simultaneously at the end of the project. There is never slack in the critical path. When the schedule is most optimal, the critical path starts near the beginning of the project and the total effort expended on each day of the project is relatively steady.

It is very important to monitor the critical path closely. If a task that is on the critical path is late, the project will be delayed. On the other hand, some tasks that are not on the critical path can suffer delays without jeopardizing the expected due date for the project. Some project management software packages highlight the critical path on the Gantt chart—this is an especially useful feature that allows the project manager to optimize the chart visually.

Figure 4-3 shows an example of how a critical path would be displayed in a project schedule. The darker tasks represent the critical path; the lighter tasks are off of the critical path. (This figure was created with Microsoft Project 2003.)

In this example, the test preparation tasks are not on the critical path. This means that if there is a delay in building or reviewing the test plans, then the project due date will not change unless that delay is long enough to put those tasks back on the critical path. In this case, that would require nine weeks. (This schedule shows the amount of play in the schedule by depicting slack in the schedule as thin bars to the right of each task. The "1.5wks" label next to the "Execute Test Plan B" task shows that task would have to be delayed by 1.5 weeks to impact the due date.)

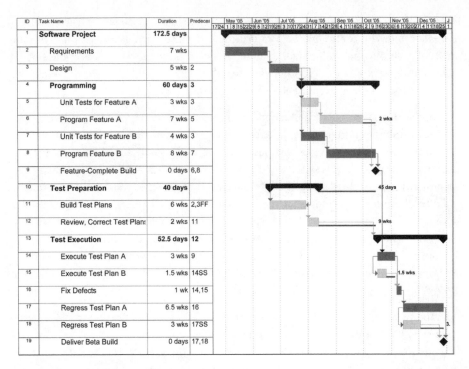

ID	Task Name	Duration	Predeces...
1	**Software Project**	172.5 days	
2	Requirements	7 wks	
3	Design	5 wks	2
4	**Programming**	60 days	3
5	Unit Tests for Feature A	3 wks	3
6	Program Feature A	7 wks	5
7	Unit Tests for Feature B	4 wks	3
8	Program Feature B	8 wks	7
9	Feature-Complete Build	0 days	6,8
10	**Test Preparation**	40 days	
11	Build Test Plans	6 wks	2,3FF
12	Review, Correct Test Plans	2 wks	11
13	**Test Execution**	52.5 days	12
14	Execute Test Plan A	3 wks	9
15	Execute Test Plan B	1.5 wks	14SS
16	Fix Defects	1 wk	14,15
17	Regress Test Plan A	6.5 wks	16
18	Regress Test Plan B	3 wks	17SS
19	Deliver Beta Build	0 days	17,18

FIGURE 4-3. Example of a project schedule showing a critical path

This helps the project manager make decisions about the project. For example, if an extra person becomes available for the project, the project manager can assign him to tasks on the critical path, since assigning him as a resource on a noncritical task won't have any noticeable effect on the due date. It also helps the project manager understand the impact of scope creep or changing requirements, by showing whether those changes will make a difference in the time to deliver.

Don't Abuse Buffers

Many project managers commonly add *buffers* to their schedules. A buffer is a task added to the schedule with no specific purpose except to account for unexpected delays. This practice involves either adding extra tasks or padding existing tasks at strategic points in the schedule where overruns are "expected."

There are times when buffers are useful. For example, on a year-long project, if every programmer has two weeks of vacation and on average takes one week of sick days, then the project is guaranteed to lose three person-weeks of effort over the course of the year. The project manager could sprinkle three person-weeks of buffers at strategic points in the schedule in order to accommodate for this known loss. The use of buffers in this case is appropriate because the size of the loss is known.

However, there are many times when buffers are abused. The idea that overruns are expected means that there is an implicit assumption that the estimate is incorrect. If this is the case, why not increase the estimate to include the buffer? The danger in the buffer is that it lulls people—especially senior managers under time pressure—into feeling that there is lots of extra "play" built into the schedule. They have an expectation that the scope can be changed without any impact to the schedule, because the buffers will absorb the change.

This is especially bad for the team because each person feels that she can ignore "small" errors in her own estimates. For example, a programmer may find that she underestimated her programming task because the technical solution was more difficult than she originally anticipated. If there is a buffer, she may feel comfortable not reporting that mistake because she assumes that it will be absorbed. Unfortunately, if the designer and tester both made similar estimation mistakes and also failed to report them, all three of them are now counting on using the same buffer: there will be a large overrun. Since nobody reported any individual overruns, the project manager will not know about the problem until after the project has already slipped; this will limit his options much more than if he had known about the estimation problems as soon as they were discovered.

The bottom line is that when buffers are added to the schedule, Parkinson's Law will kick in and the work will expand to fill the time allocated to it. Luckily, the project manager already has a tool to help him plan for the unknown or unexpected: he can work with the team to build a risk plan (see Chapter 2). By brainstorming risks and adding mitigation tasks to the project schedule, he can avoid some of the risks. And for the ones that cannot be avoided, there will already be a plan in place to deal with most of them.

Adding a risk plan to a schedule that does not already include risk mitigation tasks requires that the schedule be updated and the project plan reinspected; however, this is not a bad thing. Updating the schedule guarantees that the schedule does not contain any "white lies," and inspecting it effectively communicates the team's true estimate of the work to everyone who will be impacted by it. If the risk plan is thorough, the stakeholders will not be blindsided by the potential problems, because they will see that the team anticipated these possibilities and has a plan to deal with them. This will remove a lot of the pressure usually associated with project overruns.

Track the Performance of the Project

After the schedule is completed and optimized, it is ready for review. The schedule should be inspected by the project team, either on its own or as part of the project plan. (See Chapter 2 for the inspection checklist, which is part of the checklist for the project plan. See Chapter 5 for more on inspections.) It is important that the people on the project team who will do the work all agree that it represents a realistic plan for completing the project.

A copy of the version of the schedule that has been approved should be set aside and used as the *baseline*. A baseline is a fixed schedule that represents the standard that is used to measure the performance of the project. Every time a change to the scope of the project is approved (see Chapter 6 for information on change control), the schedule should be adjusted and a new revision of the baseline should be used instead. Many project management software packages have a feature that allows the project manager to maintain a baseline schedule and track revisions to it.

This means that there are two versions of the schedule. One is a fixed baseline version that is kept as a reference, and the other is an *actual* version of the schedule that is updated to reflect what actually happened over the course of the project. The baseline schedule never changes over the course of the project. Every time a task is delayed or changed, the actual schedule should be updated to reflect that. Each schedule change should be stored as a separate revision, which shows a snapshot of what the schedule looked like at any time in its history.

When the due date for the actual schedule is later than that of the baseline, the project has *slipped*. However, the schedule slip does not tell the whole story. A schedule might slip because the team is waiting for a single person to complete a delayed task. It might also slip because there is a general tendency to underestimate the effort required to perform all tasks. It's important for the project manager to track down the source of each slip in order to help improve the team's estimates in the future, and to work with senior management to determine whether action needs to be taken.

The most common way to understand the nature of the schedule slip is to calculate the *variance*. This is a calculation that dates back to the early 1900s, when it was used by factories to track the difference between their budgeted costs and their actual costs. Variance is now the core of a project management system called *earned value management*, which tracks the project by considering effort "earned" against a budget only after it has actually been performed. For software projects, the variance is a measurement in person-hours (or person-days, person-years, etc.) that shows the difference between the effort planned to date on the baseline and the effort completed on the actual schedule.

The *budgeted cost for work scheduled* (BCWS) is the estimated effort of the actual tasks that appear on the schedule to date. The *actual cost of work performed* (ACWP) is the effort spent on the tasks in the schedule that have actually been completed by the development team members. The data required to calculate this information can be gathered by comparing the effort represented in the baseline schedule (to find the budgeted cost) with the effort in the actual schedule. (Many project management software packages will calculate these numbers automatically.) The variance is the difference between these two numbers (BCWS – ACWP). (BCWS and ACWP are standard acronyms used in most earned value calculations.) If the variance is positive, then the project cost fewer person-hours than were budgeted; if it is negative, then the project overran the budget.

The variance is useful in helping a project manager determine whether a schedule slip is due to an isolated incident or a systematic problem. If there is a large schedule slip but the variance is small (if, for example, it is much smaller than the length of the delay), then the project manager should look for one or two tasks that were delayed. On the other hand, if the variance is large, there may be a problem with the way the team estimated the tasks. The project manager can spend additional time with the team to work on the estimates— for example, extra Wideband Delphi estimation sessions can be performed to decompose the tasks that are more susceptible to delays. This can be used both for future projects and for tasks that have not yet been performed in the current project.

For example, consider a software project where the requirements phase of a project is scheduled to last for six weeks. Over the course of those 6 weeks, 2 software engineers are scheduled to work on the project at 75% allocation, for a total of 360 effort-hours (75% of a 40-hour week is 30 person-hours per week per engineer, multiplied by 6 weeks). At the phase-end review, the project manager finds that the phase actually took eight weeks, and the software engineers put a total of 390 person-hours into the requirements phase. The earned value for this phase is 360 – 390 = -30 person-hours. In other words, the project overran the budget by 30 person-hours. The project manager can even calculate the actual cost (in dollars) of the overrun by multiplying those 30 person-hours by the average cost per hour that the organization pays their software engineers (plus the average overhead cost).

Another way earned value can be used is by generating the *cost performance index* (CPI) for the project. CPI is calculated by dividing BCWS / ACWP and multiplying by 100 to express it as a percentage. A CPI of 100% means that the estimated cost was exactly right and the project came in exactly on budget. If it is under 100%, the work cost less effort than planned; a CPI greater than 100% means that the estimate was not adequate for the work involved. CPI can be used either to compare projects or phases within a project. For example, if the programming tasks took twice as long as estimated but every other type of task in the project took less time than estimated, the total variance for the project might still be low. However, the problem can still be pinpointed by calculating the CPI for each phase of development. If the CPI for the programming phase is well over 100% while the CPI for all other phases is less than 100%, then the project manager should pay extra attention to the estimates for the programming phase in future projects. It is also possible to compare the overall CPI for various projects against one another to see if the CPI goes down over multiple projects. If it does, that shows that the team's estimation skills are improving.

CPI can also be used to find systemic process problems. For example, if, over the course of many projects, the CPI in the coding phase is much lower than the CPI in the other phases, it could mean that there are either problems with the way programming estimates are generated or problems with the execution of the coding tasks. It may also mean that there are uncontrolled changes, which are going unnoticed until the team begins coding. The project manager should take this low CPI as a hint to look more closely at exactly what is causing delays during the programming phase.

In the example given above, the CPI would be (360 / 390) * 100 = 92.3%. This means that the team is only operating at 92.3% efficiency. Since the CPI is below 100%, the team did not perform as efficiently as expected. Since these numbers were just for the requirements phase, the low CPI could simply mean that the team underestimated the requirements tasks. If the average CPI for the requirements phase in the team's other projects is around 90%, then it means the team systematically underestimates requirements tasks. However, if it is much closer to 100%, then there was a specific problem which caused the team to lose effort in this particular project. The project manager can take appropriate action depending on which of these cases is true.

The CPI calculation is useful when comparing projects to one another, as well as phases within projects. The project manager can create a chart of the CPI for each completed phase of the project to determine the accuracy of the estimates. If there are many phases in which the CPI is far from 100%, this information should be taken into account during future estimation sessions. The total CPI of the entire project can be compared to that of other projects, as well, to determine which teams may need estimation training or better management of resources.

The progress of the project should be tracked at the review meetings in terms of slips, variance, and earned value. The simplest way to track the project's progress is by comparing the due date of the actual schedule with the due date of the baseline to anticipate the expected delay in the due date. The variance data and the individual delays that led to the variance should also be recorded, as well as any viable theories or conclusions drawn about why the schedule slipped. This information will be taken into account in the postmortem report (see Chapter 8).

> **NOTE**
> The most popular tool for creating a project schedule is Microsoft Project. There are also free and open source project scheduling tools available for most platforms that feature task lists, resource allocation, predecessors, and Gantt charts. These include:
>
> - Open Workbench (*http://www.openworkbench.org/*)
> - dotProject (*http://www.dotproject.net/*)
> - netOffice (*http://netoffice.sourceforge.net/*)
> - TUTOS (*http://www.tutos.org/*)

Managing Multiple Projects

Many project managers are responsible for multiple projects. If each project is planned well, managing a set of them should not be difficult. When projects don't share dependencies, managing them is straightforward—just manage each project individually, with a separate project schedule for each one.

When projects share dependencies, they are more challenging to manage. There are two ways that one project might depend on another. In the first type, two projects rely on the same resources; in the second type, a work product generated by one project is needed by the other. Getting a handle on these dependencies is the first important step in managing multiple projects.

Understand Dependencies Between Projects

The most common way for projects to be interdependent is through shared resources. One instance of this happening is "pipelined" projects. In many software organizations, software projects go through a set of sequential phases: requirements, design, development, programming, and testing. In each phase, most of the work is done by a small subset of the team, leaving the rest of the team available to work on other projects. To allow the team to work at full capacity, they might be working on several projects at once. Project A is in the requirements phase, while at the same time, project B is in design, project C is in development, and project D is being tested.

The trouble with this system is that no two projects take exactly the same time, and the phases don't always require the same percentage of the total effort. For example, programming is typically 30% to 40% of the total effort of a project. But during that time, a lead tester might be working on a test plan, while programmers might have to stop work for half a day to review the requirements or design documents on another project. When there are more than two or three projects being worked on simultaneously, things can get very chaotic.

Usually, a programmer is fully allocated to a programming task. This means that the programmer is spending all of his time on that task (minus lunch, bathroom breaks, etc.) But in other cases, a resource will be only partially allocated to a task. For example, a conference room may be a scarce resource; it might be reserved only in the morning, but free in the afternoon. Or a designer might work on two projects at once, meeting with stakeholders for one project in the morning while analyzing usability lab data for another in the afternoon.

The project manager's first goal is to make sure that the shared resources are not over-allocated. If one project's schedule has a resource allocated 50% for the entire week, while another has that resource allocated 100% during the same week, that resource has a 150% allocation. Over-allocation problems often do not show up on the schedule.

What's more, if the estimates do not include overhead (going to meetings, reading email, helping customers, talking to senior managers, or other interruptions), then a person can be over-allocated even if the schedule says that she isn't. When taking effort into account on a project schedule, it's important to remember that even though people may be in the office for eight hours each day, they might only be available for project work for five of those hours. Also, the project manager must make sure that changes are controlled properly. If the scope of the project changes but the team is not given a chance to create new estimates, team members will almost certainly end up over-allocated.

Under-allocation is also a danger. If an engineer does not have any scheduled tasks for a week, she can easily get bored. That engineer may not be unhappy about the situation, but if the rest of the team is crunched for time, their morale will be impacted when they see their teammate take off early every day. One way to prevent this is to have low-priority projects where tasks can be assigned to under-allocated team members. However, enough time must be given to allow each person to ramp up on the task and finish enough to feel like the time was not wasted; otherwise, it just feels like busywork.

Modern project management software will often have a "resource pool" feature that allows a project manager to set up a single set of resources available to multiple projects. When a project schedule draws a resource from that pool, the allocation level for that resource is increased accordingly in the pool, so that allocation shows up on all of the other project schedules. Allocation reports can be run to verify that no resource is over- or under-allocated. Alternately, multiple projects can be included on a single schedule. This is slightly harder to maintain, but very easy to understand at a glance.

Another common way for two projects to be interdependent is when one project has a task that has a predecessor in another project. Identifying these predecessors is generally straightforward. Any time a task relies on a piece of software, a document, or another work product that is scheduled to be built in another project, a dependency is created in the schedule. The easiest way to handle this situation is to require that the dependent task does not begin until its predecessor ends. Modern project management software tools have features that help to automate this process by grouping multiple projects together into one master schedule.

The one important pitfall is that each cross-project dependency increases the risk of delay on the dependent project. To mitigate this risk, every predecessor must be reviewed at the project meetings for the dependent project.

Prioritize Projects Realistically

Prioritizing projects is similar to prioritizing tasks—it requires tough decisions, and will almost always make someone unhappy. Priorities are always relative: each project's stakeholder feels that his project is the most important one. And in a way, he's right—it's the most important one to him, but not necessarily to the organization. That doesn't change the fact that if there is a programmer available to work and there are two projects that need to get done, a decision must be made to assign her to one project or the other.

While prioritizing projects seems to require the same actions as prioritizing tasks, it is much more politically charged, and the project manager is under much more pressure to throw away the prioritization entirely and pretend that all of the projects can be done at the same time. This is usually a mistake—unless two projects do not share any resources at all, there will come a time when a resource must be assigned to either one project or the other. If there is no clear priority, this can create confusion and chaos.

Prioritizing projects is about making decisions. Someone has to put his foot down and say that project A is more important than project B. In some organizations, this is the project manager; more often, it is one or more senior managers (often a steering committee) who have the authority to make the decision. One reliable way to figure out who should be making that decision is to follow the money: the person who has the authority to allocate funds to pay engineers and buy computers is generally the person who has the authority to decide which project should be worked on first. Ideally, this responsibility should fall on a single person (often the chair of the steering committee). If no decision-maker can be found, it becomes the project manager's most important responsibility to find that decision-maker.

Once the decision-maker is found, the process of prioritization is straightforward. It is similar to the way risks are prioritized, with the exception that no two projects are allowed to receive the same priority. Without this restriction, the team will end up with only top-priority projects. If the decision-maker has trouble choosing a priority, he can use the same technique used for risk planning. If there are 20 projects to prioritize, he should identify top-priority project and assign it priority 1, then the lowest-priority project and assign it priority 20. Each additional project should then be prioritized in relation to those. (If it is absolutely impossible to decide the relative priority of two projects, he can flip a coin; if the coin's answer seems wrong, he should reverse it. This is a helpful way to "force" him to consider the alternative.)

The final result of the prioritization process is a list of projects that are arranged in order of priority, with a unique priority must be assigned to each project. This list of projects should also indicate which projects are dependent on other ones. This inclusion means that when a team member is identifying the next task to work on, its dependencies can be taken into consideration.

It is often tempting to assign the same priority to two different projects that seem to be equally important to the organization. It is sometimes difficult to make priority decisions; basically, they amount to deciding that one project may be delayed at the expense of another. But if these decisions are not made, that can lead to serious project problems. The most common problem is that the team ends up with several projects that are top priority, and it's not clear which one should be worked on next. This is bad because it's almost always the case that one of those projects really is more important that the others, so there is a good chance the team will work on a less important project. When many projects have a priority of 1 assigned, then the prioritization is essentially useless.

Once priorities are assigned to all projects, it's time to assign resources to the tasks. Each resource should be assigned to the next task on the project with the highest priority that does not yet have work being done. This is not necessarily a hard-and-fast rule: if a task on a lower-priority project must be done in order to make the schedules work out properly and to avoid over-allocation, the schedules should reflect that. And in many cases, there is only one person on the team who has the expertise to perform a specific task. But, wherever possible, the priorities should be honored.

Finally, a periodic priority meeting should be held to reevaluate the project priorities. Some organizations do this weekly, while others do it every two weeks or even monthly. This meeting can be piggybacked on the status meeting, as long as all of the project's decision-makers are there. The important part is that everyone is kept in the loop: the project manager, the lead decision-maker, and the stakeholders for the projects.

Use the Schedule to Manage Commitments

A project schedule represents a commitment by the team to perform a set of tasks. When the project manager adds a task to the schedule and it's agreed upon by the team, the person who is assigned to that task now has a commitment to complete it by the task's due date. Senior managers feel that they can depend on the schedule as an accurate forecast of how the project is going to go—when the schedule slips, it's treated as an exception, and an explanation is required. For this reason, the schedule is a powerful tool for commitment management.

One common complaint among project managers attempting to improve the way their organizations build software is that the changes they make don't take root. Typically, the project manager will call a meeting to announce a new tool or technique—he may ask the team to start performing code reviews, for example—only to find that the team does not actually perform the reviews when building the software. Things that seem like a good idea in a meeting often fail to "stick" in practice.

This is where the schedule is a very valuable tool. By adding tasks to the schedule that represent the actual improvements that need to be made—for example, by scheduling all of the review meetings—the project manager has a much better chance of gaining a real commitment from the team.

If the team does not feel comfortable making a commitment to the new practice, the disagreement will come up during the schedule review. Typically, when a project team member disagrees with implementing a new tool or technique, he does not bring it up during the meeting where it's introduced. Instead, he will simply fail to use it, and build the software as he has on past projects. This is usually justified with an explanation that there isn't enough time, and that implementing the change will make the task late.

By explicitly adding a task to the schedule, the project manager ensures that enough time is built in to account for the change. This cements the change into the project plan, and makes it clear up front that the team is expected to adopt the practice. More importantly, it is a good consensus-building tool because it allows team members to bring up the new practice when they review the project plan. By putting the change out in the open, the project manager encourages real discussion of it, and is given a chance to explain the reason for the practice during the review meetings. If the practice makes it past the review, then the project manager ends up with a real commitment from the team to adopt the new practice.

Diagnosing Scheduling Problems

When a project manager doesn't create a schedule, the organization is given an unrealistic view of how the project will progress. When schedules are not correct, the project manager usually has to resort to drastic measures in order to try to bring the project in line with the organization's expectations, and those measures often don't work. Even when they do, they hurt the morale of the team, and they frequently hurt the quality of the software produced as well.

Working Backward From a Deadline

One of the most common problems that affects a project is that the deadline, which seemed perfectly reasonable when the project started, begins to seem completely unrealistic as the date starts getting closer. This is often caused by a project manager facing a deadline that cannot be changed. Usually, the date comes from marketing or customer relations needs. Instead of being based on estimates of actual effort from the team, expectations are based on agreements between project managers, senior managers, and stakeholders. (For example, a consulting company may take on an overly aggressive deadline in order to satisfy a client seen as important for the company's growth.)

When faced with a non-negotiable deadline for a project, many project managers will work backward from the deadline to determine what work needs to be performed. One misguided way of doing this is to divide the project into phases and assign each phase a certain percent of the schedule. The project manager may decide, for example, that programming should take 60% of the time, testing should take 25%, etc. These numbers don't come from any specific knowledge of the work required; rather, they come from the need to fit that work into a predetermined tomfooleries.

What results is deadline-driven work. If milestones look like they will be missed, key activities like reviews, inspections, and even testing are often abandoned in order to meet unrealistic expectations. The people working on the project are treated unfairly because they are asked to perform an impossible task. They may be told to work overtime or spend weekends in the office to make up for poor planning.

This is also unfair to the stakeholders—especially if they are clients of a business. Many businesses will see certain clients as important and will promise things they can't deliver. A project manager in this situation, who creates an unrealistic schedule to meet those commitments, does not necessarily recognize that the project's deadline is unrealistic. More often, the client is blamed for expecting too much or for being too picky about the deliverable. The project manager may also blame a marketing or sales department for over-promising. But, truthfully, it is the project manager's fault: he agreed to an unrealistic schedule rather than being honest about the likelihood of failure and presenting alternatives like adding resources, reducing scope, proposing a phased release, bringing on consultants, or using different technologies. Had the project manager been up front with the stakeholders from the beginning, they might have avoided this mess.

Misunderstood Predecessors

Sometimes, a deadline that seemed reasonable based on the effort estimates can still go awry, if the project manager has not taken the time to understand how the tasks depend on each other. If a dependency is discovered halfway through the project, it can send the entire team into chaos.

This situation is most common when the team does not sit down to create a work breakdown structure. When a WBS has not been created, it is not uncommon to discover important tasks required to complete the project well after the work has started. By the time the extent of the poor estimate is known, it may be too late to change expectations within the organization.

For example, it may seem like all of the work for a particular project will get done on time. Suddenly, halfway through the project, a programmer discovers that he needs a component that isn't scheduled to be built by another team member for another two weeks. The code that he is building is in turn necessary for another programmer, who will be using it as soon as he is done. Now, instead of being done on time, he will be stuck for the next two weeks; another programmer will be stuck for even longer, waiting for him to complete his work. Unfortunately, the project manager already committed to a deadline. As a result, some team members will have to work overtime to make up for the lost time—while others are left sitting idle.

When predecessors are not discovered until the project is underway, there are usually few opportunities for correction. Critical team members are already working on other tasks, and end dates may have already been agreed upon. What's more, in a tight schedule, predecessor problems often cascade. When one task has to wait, all of the tasks that depend on it will also have to wait, as will the tasks that depend on those, and so forth.

Often, these cascading delays aren't fully recognized by the team until late in the project. Since each person performs each task in the amount of time estimated, the project manager might not realize the problem throughout most of the project. To the project manager, it seems that things are moving along at a steady pace; it is not until the project nears completion that it becomes apparent that the deadline is in jeopardy.

This problem is especially hard on software testers, simply because they are responsible for the tasks at the tail end of the software project. Since the project is in its final phase when the problem is discovered, the testers are responsible for the bulk of the remaining work. This is especially unfair when the root cause of the delay is in an earlier phase of the project: the testers did not create the problem, yet they bear the brunt of the pressure!

CHAPTER FIVE

Reviews

A REVIEW IS ANY ACTIVITY IN WHICH A WORK PRODUCT is distributed to reviewers who examine it and give feedback. Different work products will go through different kinds of reviews: the team may do a very thorough, technical review of a software requirements specification, while the vision and scope document will be passed around via email and have higher-level walkthroughs. (This book was reviewed by a wide range of experts including seasoned project managers, university faculty, and business executives.) This chapter covers several kinds of reviews, each of which may be appropriate for different work products and at various points during the software project.

Reviews are useful not only for finding and eliminating defects, but also for gaining consensus among the project team, securing approval from stakeholders, and aiding in professional development for team members. In all cases, the work product coming out of the review has fewer defects than it had when it was submitted—even though the author thought it was "complete" before the review. Every defect that is found during a review is a defect that someone did not have to spend time tracking down later in the project.

There are many ways that a work product can be reviewed. Each kind of review is appropriate for different audiences or kinds of work product. The purpose of all reviews is to ensure that each reviewer is satisfied that the work product is correct, and that his or her perspective is represented.

The goal of every review is to save the project team time and effort. It's much easier to fix the problems on paper, before they cause software to be built incorrectly. An effective way to make sure defects are caught early is to schedule many reviews over the course of the project to catch the defects before they become deeply embedded in the software. By reviewing each work product before it is approved, a project manager sets those checkpoints and ensures that defects are caught early, before they are repeated in later work products.

Inspections

An *inspection* is one of the most common sorts of review found in software projects. The goal of the inspection is for all of the inspectors to reach consensus on a work product and approve it for use in the project. Commonly inspected work products include software requirements specifications (see Chapter 6) and test plans (see Chapter 8). In an inspection, a work product is selected for review and a team is gathered for an inspection meeting to review the work product. A moderator is chosen to moderate the meeting. Each inspector prepares for the meeting by reading the work product and noting each defect. In an inspection, a defect is any part of the work product that will keep an inspector from approving it. For example, if the team is inspecting a software requirements specification, each defect will be text in the document that an inspector disagrees with. The goal of the inspection is to repair all of the defects so that everyone on the inspection team can approve the work product.

Most project managers have seen their projects get delayed because of scope creep and unnecessary work caused by changes that, had they been caught earlier, would have required much less work to fix. One of the most common complaints from project team members is that they would have built the software differently had they been given a better understanding of what was needed from the beginning. One important root cause of these problems is defects in work products that are not caught until long after those work products have been used as the basis for later project activities.

The most important reason to inspect documents is to prevent defects. If the team starts building software based on a vision and scope document that has a serious defect, eventually the entire project will have to stop and reverse course. This can be very expensive in both effort and morale, because the team will need to backtrack and revise the requirements, design, code, test plans, and other work products that they have already put a lot of effort into implementing. The same goes for defects that were caught in other work products—defects missed in a design specification, for example, will have to be corrected later after they have been coded. The longer a defect goes uncorrected, the more entrenched it is in other work products; the more entrenched it is, the more time and effort it will take to fix.

According to a report by the Software Engineering Institute, it costs more to not do inspections than it does to do them. A national survey of software engineering teams found that in a typical inspection, four to five people spend one to two hours preparing for inspections, followed by one to two hours to hold an inspection meeting. The total effort required for the inspection, therefore, is 10 to 20 person-hours; this effort results in the early detection of an average of 5 to 10 defects. (On the average, these defects, if left in the document, would require either 250 to 500 lines of new code or modification of 1000 to 1500 lines of legacy code to repair if they were eventually caught—which would almost certainly require well over 20 person-hours of programmers' time!) This is a very high return on investment; few tools, techniques, or practices are as effective as inspections for increasing the quality of the software.

Inspections are easy to implement, and have an immediate effect on quality and consensus-building. A small team spending a few hours inspecting a work product will catch errors that could potentially save weeks, or even months, of wasted effort. An effective inspection requires a well-chosen team, a moderator who is able to run the meeting, and an author who is willing to listen to criticism and fix the work product being inspected.

Choose the Inspection Team

The job of the inspection team is to work with the author of the document in order to identify any defects. A *defect* is any problem in the document that will prevent an inspector from approving it. Once a problem is identified, the inspection team must work to come up with a solution that will fix the problem. When the team meets to inspect the document, they will be expected to come up with solutions to the defects that they find. The project manager must select a team that can perform this function. This means that each inspector needs to have enough familiarity with the project and the way the work product will be used to understand its problems and propose changes. (Team members who use the document in their day-to-day work should have no problem with this.)

The project manager must choose a team of 3 to 10 inspectors. Ideally, each inspector should represent a different perspective on the work product. A designer will use a document for different tasks than a programmer will. It is important that each person who will use the document has his views represented in the inspection team. This is critical for catching all of the defects.

During the inspection, the team works to identify any defects in the work product. They are expected to evaluate it from two perspectives. The most important evaluation is from the perspective of their own expertise, where the inspectors identify any issues that will interfere with the development of the project. For this role, they must draw on their engineering skills and experience with past software projects. But inspectors should also evaluate the work product from a common sense perspective. Each inspection team member should think about the ideas in the vision and scope document and consider several questions: does the work product being inspected fulfill the needs laid out in the vision and scope document? Does it really answer the problem posed by earlier work products? Will it be able to serve as a basis for all of the work products that will come later in the product? Good inspection team members will be able to keep these questions in mind.

Select a Moderator

The project manager must choose a moderator to run the inspection meetings. This person must be able to objectively evaluate the work product being inspected and understand any issues that are raised during the inspection. The moderator will also need to be able to control the meeting. If a few inspectors start a discussion to address a defect that might take a lot of time, the moderator will have to be able to stop that discussion and table it as an open issue. It takes some practice to keep control of a meeting.

The project manager should be an inspector, so an independent and unbiased moderator is needed. A good moderator will have sufficient technical background to understand the work product being inspected. It is important for the moderator to be objective, and not to favor one perspective over another during the inspection meeting. In some organizations, the moderator is never a part of the project team, and does not have a stake in the project. However, some people have found it useful to select as moderator a team member who will not be inspecting the document, because the moderator should have an understanding of the issues discussed during the meeting. But in that case, that team member must be willing and able to stay objective by allowing every inspector equal opportunity to bring up defects, and by ensuring that each issue is discussed and either resolved or tagged as an open issue.

The hardest part of the moderator's job is to prepare the inspectors and the author for criticism of the work product. When somebody writes a document, he may be uncomfortable with the idea that it contains errors. It's his work and, in our day-to-day lives, few of us are used to having our work critiqued. But all documents have defects, and authors need to get comfortable with this idea. This is by far the most challenging part of implementing inspections: getting people comfortable with having their work criticized.

To address this, the moderator must help the author understand the benefit of the criticism. It's the moderator's job to make sure that the meeting does not become personal criticism, and that the comments are always constructive. An effective way to do this is to focus the discussion on each defect and come up with a specific resolution. It's the job of the inspection team to do more than just identify the problems; they must also come up with the solutions. The moderator compiles all of the defect resolutions into an *inspection log* (see Figure 5-1 for an example).

# of issues:	16		
Review date:	March 16, 2003		
Attendees	**Read document**	**Time spent preparing**	
Mike (project manager)	Y	Author	
Barbara (VP)	Y	1.0 hours	
Quentin (requirements analyst)	Y	2.0 hours	
Sophie (senior QA engineer)	Y	3.0 hours	
Jill (senior programmer)	Y	0.5 hours	
Issue no.	**Section/page**	**Identified by**	**Issue**
1	Global	Quentin	The term "standard contract" should be replaced with "pro-forma contract."
2	Section 3.1.1 Line 165	Sophie	The contents of the cells in the table are out of order. It looks like some cells were marked down.
3	Section 3.1.2 Line 190	Jill	Specify the look up is by contract number and artist name.
4	Section 3.3b Line 623	Sophie	Tile of the section needs to be changed to "Deletion file (maintenance)." To be consistent with section 3.2.1 #1.

FIGURE 5-1. *Sample inspection log*

At the top of each inspection log is information about the inspection meeting: what work product was being reviewed, when it was held, who was in attendance, whether or not the work product was read by each inspector, how long each inspector spent reviewing the work product, and how many issues (including both defects and open issues) were found. Each work product should have a unique version number, to ensure that the inspection log can be matched up to the proper version of the work product.

The inspection moderator should ask each team member how long he or she spent reviewing the work product and record that number in the log. This stands as a record of how much effort went into the work product, which will help in future estimation, project planning, and impact analysis activities. If any inspector failed to review the work product, the moderator must halt the meeting and reschedule it in order to allow all of the inspectors enough time to review the work product.

The rest of the inspection log contains a list of action items. Each item is marked with the exact location of the defect and the solution proposed by the inspection team. In many cases, the solution is a wording change. The work product contains a specific sentence that is unclear, ambiguous, or incorrect. After a brief (usually under five minutes) discussion, the inspection team identifies wording that will correct the defect. In this case, the moderator writes the new wording in the inspection log, and the author agrees to update the work product accordingly.

In other cases, the solution is too complex to be identified at the inspection meeting. If the discussion lasts too long, the moderator should stop it and add an open issue to the inspection log. This issue must be assigned to the author and, optionally, one or more inspection team members; it is their responsibility to resolve the issue. The log item for this must contain a specific set of actions to be performed ("meet with Marketing to research this missing feature," "rewrite lines 534 through 539 so system will perform data check on report B").

It is important that the inspection log is readily available to all inspectors. After the meeting, it should be distributed to all inspectors, and stored along with previous versions of the document. If the document is checked into a version control system (see Chapter 7), then each inspection log should be checked in along with it. All changes must be made before the work product can be inspected again: open issues must be closed, defects must be repaired, and every issue reported in the log must be addressed.

Inspect the Work Product

During the inspection meeting, a moderator leads the team page by page through a printed copy of the work product. The purpose of the meeting is to identify and fix any defects. The moderator does not actually read each page out loud or give the team time to read the page. The team members read the document prior to the inspection, during their preparation. When the moderator goes through the document page by page, he simply asks the reviewers for their defects on page 1; once those are done, he asks for the defects on page 2 and continues through the rest of the document.

Prior to the inspection meeting, each team member should be given a checklist to help her identify defects. Checklists will be different for different kinds of work products. (In other chapters, checklists will be included for each type of work product that should be inspected.) The script in Table 5-1 describes the process for an inspection meeting.

TABLE 5-1. Inspection meeting script

Name	Inspection meeting script
Purpose	To run a moderated inspection meeting
Summary	In an inspection meeting, a moderator leads a team of reviewers in reviewing a work product and fixing any defects that are found.

Work Products	*Input*
	    Work product being inspected
	Output
	    Inspection log

TABLE 5-1. Inspection meeting script (continued)

Name	Inspection meeting script
Entry Criteria	A moderator must be selected, as well as team of 3 to 10 people. A work product must be selected, and each team member has read it individually and identified all wording that must be changed or clarified before he or she will approve the work product. A unique version number has been assigned to the work product.
Basic Course of Events	1. *Preparation*. The moderator distributes a printed version of the work product (with line numbers) to each inspector, along with a checklist to aid in the review. Each inspector reads the work product and identifies any defects to be brought up at the meeting.
	2. *Overview*. The inspection meeting begins. The moderator verifies that each team member is prepared.
	3. *Page-by-page review*. The moderator runs through the work product page by page. Inspectors indicate where there are defects. Each defect is either resolved or left as an open issue. The moderator adds each defect to the inspection log.
	4. *Rework*. The author repairs the defects identified in the inspection meeting.
	5. *Follow-up*. Inspection team members verify that the defects were repaired.
	6. *Approval*. The inspection team approves the work product.
Alternative Paths	1. During Step 2, if any team member has not read the work product, then the inspection is halted. The meeting is rescheduled and the script returns to step 1.
	2. During Step 4, if an inspection team member discovers additional defects in the work product, then the moderator calls another meeting and the process returns to step 1.
Exit Criteria	The work product has been approved.

Preparation

Each inspector reviews the printed copy of the work product individually, prior to the inspection meeting. Any defects that are found should be marked on the copy so that they can be brought up in the meeting.

In many organizations, the moderator requires that each inspector submit a written list of defects that were found prior to the inspection meeting, and all defects are compiled into a single inspection log and distributed to the entire inspection team. This optional step can reduce the time required for the meeting because instead of going through the entire work product page by page, the moderator only goes through the log, and the author and inspectors have time to prepare in advance to respond to the defects.

Overview

The moderator verifies that each inspection team member has read the printed copy of the work product. If any team member has not prepared, the inspection is aborted and rescheduled for a later date.

Page-by-page review

The moderator turns to the first page of the work product and asks if anyone found any issues on that page. Team members bring up each issue that they found during their preparation. For each issue, the moderator leads a discussion between the team and the author to identify new wording that will resolve the issue. (For work products that are not text or documents, the team describes the change in sufficient detail so that the repair of the defect is unambiguous to the author.) The team should come up with the actual text that will be inserted into the document in order to fix the defect; the moderator should add this fix to the inspection log. If the team cannot come up with a fix on the spot, or if discussion lasts more than about five minutes, the moderator adds it to the inspection log as an open issue and assigns it to the team member who brought it up (and anyone else who is involved), so he can work with the author to resolve it. Once all issues for the page are discussed, the moderator moves to the next page in the work product.

Rework

After the inspection meeting is over, the author makes the changes in the inspection log and works with the inspection team members to resolve all open issues. When the changes are complete, the author turns the updated work product over to the moderator.

Follow-up

The moderator distributes the updated work product to the inspection team. Each team member verifies that he can now approve the work product. If there are any issues that were not fully resolved or additional defects that were not caught, he notifies the moderator, who calls another inspection meeting and starts the inspection process over again. Once the team gets through an inspection without any open issues and can agree on any changes that must be made, the work product can be updated and distributed for approval.

Approval

If any inspector feels that there are still further issues raised by the corrections to the work product, another inspection meeting can be held; however, the project manager and author can also work individually with everyone involved to make sure that the changes are adequate. Once everyone on the team feels that the changes they identified are adequate, they can approve the updated work product without holding another inspection meeting.

The moderator adds a signature page to the work product and distributes a printed version for signature approval. The signed work product is archived.

Manage the Author's Expectations

Many people who have implemented inspections have found that it is very difficult for authors to sit through an inspection meeting without defending their work. Instead of providing clarification that is used to update the work product, they take over the discussion and, by being defensive and loud, get the inspectors to agree not to report defects. This is counterproductive: it leads to situations when the inspection team understands what the author meant, but the work product, which remains unchanged, does not reflect this. It is the moderator's job to keep the discussions on track and prepare the authors for the inspection.

A major challenge of the moderator role is keeping the author from altering the understanding of the document through discussion. The purpose of the discussions is not to teach the inspectors about the project; it is to change the document so that the author and all of the inspectors will approve it. There is a simple rule in document inspection: if there is a misunderstanding about words in the document, they need to be clarified in the document, and not just in the minds of the people who happened to attend the inspection meeting.

Each inspector should keep in mind the fact that if he did not understand something after reading a document, then it is probably the document's fault, not the reader's. If he did not understand it, then it is likely that another reader will also have the same problem (especially considering that most software documents will be used as reference later, by people who are less familiar with the project than the inspectors). For this reason, it is very important that inspectors make it clear when they do not understand something. This is difficult for many inspectors: it's hard for people to admit that they did not understand something that they have read. It is the moderator's job to draw these misunderstandings out of the inspectors during the discussions of each defect.

The author should be prepared to listen to the inspection team discuss defects. It is tempting to get defensive and try to defend each defect. The author must remember that if someone thinks that an issue is worth bringing up in the meeting, there may be some ambiguity there, no matter how clear it seems to the person who wrote the words.

One way to help the author feel less defensive is to take the option (described above, under "Preparation") in which the inspection team members submit their defects to the moderator before the inspection meeting. The moderator compiles all of the defects into a log, which is then sent back to the inspection team. This is helpful because it gives the author advance warning of all of the defects that will be discussed. It also allows the inspection team to prepare solutions to the defects in advance. However, it requires more effort on the part of the moderator, who has to look through all of the defects up front in order to group redundant defects together and make sure that each one is described clearly.

In some organizations, project managers have found it useful to require that the authors not talk in the inspection meetings, to let the document stand on its own. In others, the author is excluded from the meeting entirely, and is simply given the inspection log. Although this sounds drastic and impersonal to some people, some moderators have found this to be a very useful practice, as the team feels that they must put a lot of effort into making the inspection log as self-explanatory as possible. However, while these practices do prevent the author from skewing the results of the inspection, they also cause the author to miss out on important discussions; this is a costly trade-off. As long as the author is able to listen to the moderator's rules, especially when it comes to identifying and addressing defects, he can be a valuable participant in the inspection process.

Help Others in the Organization Accept Inspections

Over the many years that inspections have been practiced in software organizations, project managers have often found that when they attempt to implement inspections, the team pushes back. This opposition occurs because, to some people, it is not intuitively obvious that spending the time inspecting the work products up front will save the team from having to fix the software later. The project manager should prepare for potential resistance by understanding exactly why inspections are important.

Project managers often find that engineers are very unhappy with the idea of inspections. To some, inspections seem unnecessarily "bureaucratic." This is especially unfortunate because inspections are one of the most effective ways to prevent defects and make the most efficient use of the engineers' time. There are few tools or techniques that have such a high potential savings in effort. For each hour spent inspecting documents, the team saves many hours that would otherwise be lost on correcting problems that would have been coded incorrectly—preventing the very tasks that engineers find most frustrating.

Luckily, a small number of objections tend to be raised most of the time, and each of these objections has a straightforward response. In the end, it is usually not hard for a project manager to show most reasonable people that inspections are worth doing.

The most effective way a project manager can sell inspections to the organization is to show the savings in terms of time and money. Each inspection yields defects that would have been much more expensive to fix had they not been found; it should not be hard to give a rough idea of just how much time and money would have been wasted on those defects.

Another way the project manager can sell inspections is by pointing out the knowledge transfer benefits. By instituting inspections and code reviews, engineers other than the author of a work product are cross-trained on it, and can maintain it in the future if the author is busy with another project or has left the organization. Another way a project manager can help people accept inspections and understand their benefit is to run the first inspection meetings using work products created by people who are widely respected in the organization. Once others see the inspections run well and respectfully, they will be much more likely to accept the same practice applied to their own work.

When a project manager starts working toward implementing inspections, there are three objections that come up most often: people feel that inspections take too long, they do not like their work criticized, and they are protective of the final product. Luckily, it is not hard to anticipate these objections and give effective responses. (See Chapter 9 for more advice on making changes in an organization.)

"Inspections take too long."

Some team members seem to be opposed to anything that seems "bureaucratic." To them, inspections are just paper-shuffling meetings that waste their time. They should be writing code (or design specifications, test plans, requirements, etc.), and don't have time to waste just so some manager can check some box somewhere.

To convince someone with this mindset that inspections are necessary, the project manager must show him that every minute spent doing inspections can save many more down the road. Over the years, software engineering researchers have studied thousands of software projects in many different kinds of organizations. They have found again and again that a defect that takes a few minutes to fix in a vision and scope or a use case document will require hours, days, or weeks to fix in code or testing.

The project manager should explain that a typical inspection meeting will take less than two hours. If each person at the meeting finds a single defect, it more than makes up for the time that he spent reading and correcting the document. When looked at from this perspective, doing the inspection saves time.

"I don't like people criticizing my work."

Many people are uncomfortable putting their work up for review. They are unsure of their documents, and they are not used to having people point out their mistakes. It is very important to recognize this, because it often falls on the project manager to help the team members get comfortable with having their work put under a magnifying glass.

When this objection is raised, the project manager can point out that everyone makes mistakes, and that usually those mistakes are not the fault of the author. Frequently, when there is a problem in a document, it is because the author did not have enough information: bringing in the rest of the team can fill in those gaps.

The project manager can also point out that while it may be uncomfortable to have mistakes pointed out during the inspection, it's much more uncomfortable when those mistakes are left in the document. The author of a use case document may feel bad momentarily when defects are pointed out and corrected during an inspection meeting. But if he feels bad then, he will feel terrible if those defects are not caught until after the team spends months designing, programming, and testing the software, only to discover a "bug" that turns out to be a problem in his use case document. Instead of feeling bad when the inspection team points out problems, he should feel relieved that they were caught before they could cause project delays.

Defects should be discussed in terms of what is best for the work product or the project, not as criticisms of the author. It is very important that the moderator be extremely strict during the inspection meetings toward people who make rude personal comments. The moderator should enforce professionalism, and should ensure that every inspection meeting is conducted in a positive manner.

"I built it, and only I can say when it's done."

Some people are very protective of their work, and simply don't want other people to criticize it. In these cases, the author feels that she is the expert, and feels that there's nobody else in the organization who knows more about this subject than she does. Be very careful when confronting her—this is an emotionally charged situation, and it's very easy to turn this person off permanently. It is important for the project manager to be nonconfrontational. The project manager should work to influence this person, not to force her into a situation she doesn't want to participate in.

The best argument in this situation is to show her that the inspection is a tool that is there for her to use. It is like a spellcheck in a word processor: the document is always better after the spellcheck.

Nobody, no matter how good he is at his job, can deliver a perfect document. It is impossible to know exactly what's in the heads of the intended readers. There is no way to include the entire context in a document. There will always be technical or organizational concepts that would take pages and pages to explain, but that everyone is familiar with.

For example, a use case document for accounting software will not explain how double-entry accounting works; it will assume that every reader is familiar with the concept.

When an inspector finds a defect, he is helping the author identify areas that need to be explained. The author assumed that each reader fully understood a concept: it turned out that the reader needed some clarification after all. In this way, the document can be adjusted to the level of its specific readers.

The hesitant author will generally recognize that she has expertise that her readers do not have. Explain that while she can make an educated guess at what context and background needs to be included, she has no way of knowing if it is enough. The inspection process is an efficient technique to help her fix this.

> **NOTE**
> More information on inspections can be found in *Software Inspection* by
> Tom Gilb and Dorothy Graham (Addison Wesley, 1993) and *Peer Reviews
> in Software* by Karl Wiegers (Addison Wesley, 2002). Information on the
> effectiveness of software inspections can be found in the Software Tech-
> nology Roadmap: *http://www.sei.cmu.edu/str/*.

Deskchecks

A *deskcheck* is a simple review in which the author of a work product distributes it to one or more reviewers. In a deskcheck, the author sends a copy of the work product to selected project team members. The team members read it, and then write up defects and comments to send back to the author. Work products that are commonly reviewed using a deskcheck include vision and scope documents (see Chapter 2) and discussion summaries (see Chapter 6).

There are times when a full inspection is neither necessary nor useful. Some work products do not benefit enough to warrant the attention of an entire inspection team because they do not need consensus or approval. In these cases, the author simply needs input from others to prevent defects, but does not require that they approve the document. In these cases, the deskcheck is a useful review practice.

Unlike an inspection, a deskcheck does not produce written logs that can be archived with the document for later reference. There is no follow-up meeting or approval process. It is simply a way for one team member to check another's work. Deskchecks are not formal reviews (where "formal" simply means that it generates a written work product that meets a certain standard and is archived with the rest of the project documentation); there is no standard for the results of the deskcheck. The reviewers simply review the work product and return the results. There is no moderator, and there is not necessarily any consensus generated.

But, despite the lack of formality, the deskcheck is a very important tool for a project team, and there are many times when the project manager will build deskchecks into the organization's software process. If a work product does not need approval by a team but is still a critical part of the software process, the project manager may require a deskcheck in order to ensure that it does not have defects. For example, many QA teams employ automated test scripts, and it is usually necessary to ensure that the finished automated product actually covers the test plan that it was meant to automate. However, it would be unnecessary and very time-consuming to ask programmers, requirements analysts, project managers, and stakeholders to cross-reference each script with a test plan. A deskcheck can be used to verify that the script is correct, and to ensure that more than one QA engineer has taken responsibility for the quality of the script.

Sometimes a checklist is used to ensure that the work product meets the organization's standards. However, unlike an inspection, a deskcheck can be performed without a checklist. The deskcheck usually relies entirely on the reviewer's knowledge of the project and professional standards for the work product.

Figure 5-2 contains an example of comments from a deskcheck that was used by a tester to find defects in an automation script. In this case, the entire review was performed via email: the author mailed the script to the reviewer, and the reviewer read it and emailed the comments back to the author. These comments are much simpler than the inspection log in Figure 5-1. In an inspection, each log entry must either resolve a defect or indicate that it is an open issue that must be resolved. Deskcheck comments can simply point out issues or raise questions without having to supply solutions or promise a resolution. There was no follow-up or approval, and the reviewer had no more contact with this script.

Reviewer's name:	Sophie (senior QA engineer)
Author's name:	Dean (junior QA engineer)
Title:	Contract certification-automated test script #TP-491-A
Review date:	8/12/03
No. of review hours:	2

Location	Comments
Global	Script does not adequately copy databases in when the data changes.
Case 14	The test plan logs in as "Administrator;" this script logs in as "Admin."
Case 52, 53	What exactly is printed? It's not clear, you should be looking for specific data.
Case 61	The test plan tests all of the preferences, but the script only tests the first five.

FIGURE 5-2. Sample deskcheck comments

Deskchecks can be used as predecessors to inspections. In many cases, having an author of a work product pass his work to a peer for an informal review will significantly reduce the amount of effort involved in the inspection. Many defects can be caught by a single person reviewing a document. Approval and consensus is built later on during the inspection meeting; this is simply a way of saving effort. After a deskcheck, many authors will feel much more comfortable sending their document into an inspection—it will often help the author to be more objective and to take the inspection comments less personally.

Finally, a deskcheck can be useful to review a work product that is not meant to be inspected at all. For example, many requirements analysts will generate a discussion summary after a series of interviews and elicitation sessions (see Chapter 6). This is not a work product that is used in later stages of the software process; rather, it is an intermediate document used to generate the software requirements specification. A deskcheck is useful in this case to help interviewees and other requirements analysts identify any information gathered during the interviews that is inaccurate or unclear. No approval is needed, and the requirements analyst is free to ignore any of the comments. The deskcheck simply serves as a checkpoint to ensure that mistakes are caught and addressed as early as possible.

> **NOTE**
> More information on deskchecks can be found in *Peer Reviews in Software* by Karl Wiegers (Addison Wesley, 2002).

Walkthroughs

A *walkthrough* is an informal way of presenting a technical document in a meeting. Unlike other kinds of reviews, the author runs the walkthrough: calling the meeting, inviting the reviewers, soliciting comments, and ensuring that everyone present understands the work product. It typically does not follow a rigid procedure; rather, the author presents the work product to the audience in a manner that makes sense. Many walkthroughs present the document using a slide presentation, where each section of a work product is shown using a set of slides. Work products that are commonly reviewed using a walkthrough include design specifications (see Chapter 7) and use cases (see Chapter 6).

Walkthroughs are used when the author of a work product needs to take into account the perspective of someone who does not have the technical expertise to review the document. For example, a requirements analyst must make sure that the use cases she builds will provide the functionality that the users need, but the user representatives may not have seen use cases before and would be overwhelmed by them. If these users are simply included as part of an inspection team, it is likely that they will read the document and, failing to find many defects, sit silently through the inspection meeting without contributing much. This is not their fault—their training is in the business of the organization, not in reading and understanding software engineering documents. This is where a walkthrough can be a useful technique to ensure that everyone understands the document.

Before the walkthrough, the author should distribute any material that will be presented to each person who will be attending. For example, if the walkthrough is done as a slide presentation, copies of the slides should be emailed to the attendees. If only a portion of that material is going to be covered, that should be indicated as well.

During the walkthrough meeting, the author should solicit feedback from the audience. This is an opportunity to brainstorm new or alternative ideas, and to check that each person understands the document that is being presented. The author should go through parts of the document to make sure that it was presented in as clear a manner as possible.

These guidelines can help an author lead a successful walkthrough meeting:

- Verify that everyone is present who needs to review the work product. This could include users, stakeholders, engineering leads, managers, and other interested people.

- Verify that everyone present understands the purpose of the walkthrough meeting and how the material is going to be presented.

- Describe each section of the material to be covered by the walkthrough.

- Present the material in each section, ensuring that everyone present understands the material being presented.

- Lead a discussion to identify any missing sections or material.

- Document all issues that are raised by walkthrough attendees.

After the meeting, the author should follow up with individual attendees who may have had additional information or insights. The document should then be corrected to reflect any issues that were raised.

> **NOTE**
> Additional information on walkthroughs can be found in *Peer Reviews in Software* by Karl Wiegers (Addison Wesley, 2002)

Code Reviews

A *code review* is a special kind of inspection in which the team examines a sample of code and fixes any defects in it. In a code review, a defect is a block of code that does not properly implement its requirements, that does not function as the programmer intended, or that is not incorrect but could be improved (for example, it could be made more readable or its performance could be improved). In addition to helping teams find and fix bugs, code reviews are useful for both cross-training programmers on the code being reviewed and for helping junior developers learn new programming techniques.

Select the Code Sample

The first task in a code review is to select the sample of code to be inspected. It's impossible to review every line of code, so the programmers need to be selective about which portion of the code gets reviewed. Many teams have found that it takes about two hours to review 400 lines of code (in a high-level language such as Java), although this estimate differs dramatically from team to team and depends on the complexity of the code being reviewed. At that rate, there is no way a team could review all of the code for a software project. Nor would the team want to—in any program, there is a good deal of uninteresting code that looks very similar to the code already developed in previous applications, which has a lower risk of containing as many defects.

The purpose of any inspection is to find and repair defects. Since a relatively small portion of the code will be reviewed, it's important to review the code that is most likely to have defects. This will generally be the most complex, tricky, or involved code.

There are a few useful rules of thumb that are helpful:

- Is there is a portion of the software that only one person has the expertise to maintain? That may be a good candidate for review, for two reasons. First, because the rest of the team will learn how to maintain it; second, it's only ever been looked at by one person, so nobody else has yet had a chance to catch any defects in it.

- Does the software implement a highly abstract or tricky algorithm? The more difficult the algorithm, the more likely it is that a programmer introduced errors in its implementation.

- Is there an object, library, or API that is particularly difficult to work with? Working with a nonintuitive interface causes many programmers to make mistakes.

- Was the code written by someone who is inexperienced or has not written that kind of code before? Does it employ a new programming technique? Is it written in an unfamiliar language? A programmer who is doing something for the first time is most likely to introduce errors.

- Is there an area of the code that will be especially catastrophic if there are defects? A core tax accounting function is more important than the code that renders the splash screen. Select code that must not fail so that more people can look at it—and will be able to maintain it if it does have problems.

It is important to select a sample of code that an inspection team can review in about two hours. The project manager should try to keep the meeting to two hours or less, to avoid "meeting fatigue."

Hold the Review Session

The team selection and preparation in a code review are similar to any other kind of inspection. An inspection team of 3 to 10 people must be selected. Each of these people must be technically capable of reading and understanding the code being reviewed. Before the meeting, the moderator distributes the code sample to each inspector, who does individual preparation exactly as in the inspection.

The main difference between a code review and any other kind of inspection is in the review session. While the code review session is similar to the inspection meeting (see "Page-by-page review" above), there are a few important differences.

In addition to the moderator, there is a code reader who reads the code aloud during the meeting. The code reader can also be one of the inspectors; the only requirement is that the reader must have enough technical expertise to understand the code. The purpose of the reader is simply to keep the team's place during the inspection; the team should have already read the code and identified defects during their preparation. Since code is usually organized in logical units or blocks, it is more useful for a reader to go through those, rather than having the moderator go through the document page by page.

The reader starts at the beginning of the code sample and announces the first block or logical unit. She does not literally read the commands in the code; she simply gives a brief description (about one sentence) of the purpose of that block. If anyone (including the reader) does not understand what the code does or disagrees with the interpretation, the author of the code explains what it is the code is supposed to accomplish. Sometimes the team can suggest a better, more self-explanatory way to accomplish the same thing; often it is simply a matter of explaining the purpose of the code to the person who raised the issue. If any inspectors found a defect in that block of code, the issue is raised and the team either comes up with a fix on the spot or tags it as an open issue for the programmer to fix later. The moderator then updates the inspection log, and the inspection continues until the reader completes the code sample being inspected.

Another important difference between code reviews and document inspections is that the code review is much more focused on detecting defects, and less on fixing them. This is because many defects in documents can be corrected with one or two sentences, or with a change in wording. Defects in the code can be much more involved, and there are often many ways that they could be fixed. The discussion of each defect is longer in a code review than it is during an inspection, and there are usually many open issues at the end of the code review.

In the code review, the moderator needs to be especially careful not to let the meeting turn into a problem-solving session. Programmers love to solve problems. It's easy for them to get caught up in a small detail and turn the meeting into an analysis of a minute problem that covers just a few lines of code. However, long discussions like this will prevent significant amounts of code from being reviewed. That's not to say that these discussions are not valuable—they just don't belong in the code review meeting. If a discussion looks like it will take more than three minutes or so, the moderator should stop the discussion and add it to the inspection log as an open issue. There should be few open issues, however, because most code defects should be straightforward to describe and document once they have been identified.

There are effective ways to modify the code during the review. Many inspectors have found that it is very helpful to refactor the code during the review. By applying refactorings on the spot, the team can make the code much more readable and identify additional defects. (See Chapter 7 for more information on refactoring.)

After the inspection meeting, the code author performs the rework and closes the open issues, and the moderator follows up with each of the inspectors and gains their approval. Instead of getting formal sign-off with physical signatures, it is usually sufficient to indicate the approval in the log comments when the changes are committed to the version control system (see Chapter 7 for more information on version control).

There are several additional benefits for the code review. One is that people learn how their teammates think about the code. A good way to encourage this is to switch off code readers in each review, so every team member gets a chance to be a reader. Reading code aloud and explaining it helps programmers think through problems. Every programmer should be able to explain his ideas well; discussing code during a code review is good practice for that.

Another benefit is that people who know that their code may be inspected tend to write more maintainable software. It's very common for programmers to not include comments or to write very terse, confusing code when they know that they are the only people who will ever read it. But if a programmer knows that someone else will be looking at it, he may put a lot of effort into making it readable. This can have enormous savings in maintenance efforts down the road.

Code Review Checklist

The following attributes should be verified during a code review:

Clarity

Is the code clear and easy to understand?

Did the programmer unnecessarily obfuscate any part of it?

Can the code be refactored to make it clearer?

Maintainability

Will other programmers be able to maintain this code?

Is it well commented and documented properly?

Accuracy

Does the code accomplish what it is meant to do?

If an algorithm is being implemented, is it implemented correctly?

Reliability and Robustness

Is the code fault-tolerant? Is it error-tolerant?

Will it handle abnormal conditions or malformed input?

Does it fail gracefully if it encounters an unexpected condition?

Security

Is the code vulnerable to unauthorized access, malicious use, or modification?

Scalability

Could the code be a bottleneck that prevents the system from growing to accommodate increased load, data, users, or input?

Reusability

Could this code be reused in other applications?

Can it be made more general?

Efficiency

Does the code make efficient use of memory, CPU cycles, bandwidth, or other system resources?

Can it be optimized?

Pair Programming

Pair programming is a technique in which two programmers work simultaneously at a single computer and continuously review each others' work. Although many programmers were introduced to pair programming as a part of Extreme Programming (see Chapter 12), it is a practice that can be valuable in any development environment. Pair programming improves the organization by ensuring that at least two programmers are able to maintain any piece of the software. Pair programming also helps programmers' professional development, because they learn from each other.

Pair programming is like having a continuous code review, without the extra time or effort of holding individual code reviews. It encourages a redundancy among the team members, and everyone is cross-trained on various parts of the code. Junior people can more quickly learn directly from senior people when they are paired together. While it may seem that assigning two people to a single programming task could be inefficient, in fact, productivity often increases. It takes somewhat less time to perform each task, as there are often gaps where one person is "tapped out" and the other can take over. More importantly, the resulting code is of very high quality, so there are far fewer mistakes to go back and fix.

One useful benefit of pair programming is that people tend to write better code when they know that someone else will be reading it. They cut fewer corners, spend more time making the code readable, are more likely to include comments where necessary, and refactor more often.

In pair programming, two programmers sit at one computer to write code. Sometimes they share a single keyboard and mouse, although it is possible to get special hardware or cables that allow each programmer to have his own. Generally, one programmer will take control and write code, while the other watches and advises. But different pairs of people may discover their own dynamic: for example, some pairs will take turns at the keyboard, while others will designate one person as the typist (if one person types significantly faster than the other).

It's straightforward to implement pair programming in any development team—just choose two programmers who are willing to give it a shot, and have them work together at the same computer. However, it's important to remember that, like any programming technique, pair programming is a skill that improves with practice. Some benefits can be realized almost immediately, but there is no substitute for years of experience. But, like any other programming skill, the only way to get experience is to practice.

While efficient pair programming is a skill that requires practice and patience, there are some useful tips that make its initial adoption easier. People will be less resistant to a change if their first experience with a new technique is positive. One way to help guarantee this is to pilot pair programming on a low-risk portion of code. The project manager should choose one where the scope and requirements are well understood going into the project, and where success is easily measured. Both members of the pair assigned to work on it should be people who have done similar projects in the past. These circumstances can provide an opportunity for an easy win, which in turn will increase the programmers' confidence in the technique.

Some teams have found that pair programming works best for them if the pairs are constantly rotated; this helps diffuse the shared knowledge throughout the organization. Any two programmers can potentially make a well-functioning pair, no matter what their relative experience. Some people have found that it helps to choose pairs that include both a senior person and a junior person. This will make it easier for the communication to fit into an existing pattern (mentor and tutor, roles that both people are already used to—although this is not necessarily how all senior-junior pairs will interact). Often, a junior team member will ask a seemingly "naïve" question about the code that turns out to identify a serious problem. This is especially common with problems that the senior member has been living with for so long that she no longer notices them. Sometimes, the extent of a code problem only becomes clear when it is explained to somebody else.

Pair programming is not for everyone. It is difficult to implement pair programming in an organization where the programmers do not share the same 9-to-5 (or 10-to-6) work schedule. Some people do not work well in pairs, and some pairs do not work well together. The project manager should not try to force pair programming on the team; it helps to introduce the change slowly, and where it will meet the least resistance. Some programmers will argue that assigning two people to one task is a waste of time, claiming that two people can get twice as much work done if they work separately. While this may seem true at first glance, the pair will introduce far fewer defects; it may require more man-hours to do the programming, but it will reduce the amount of time spent on bug-fixing and maintenance. However, this may not convince some stubborn programmers. In this case, an effective way to introduce this technique is to begin with the people who are more excited about the idea. Their success can help to convince the stragglers of the value of pair programming.

> **NOTE**
> More information on pair programming can be found in *Extreme Programming Explained* by Kent Beck (Addison Wesley, 1999).

Use Inspections to Manage Commitments

A successful project needs more than just a blanket agreement between team members. It's very easy for someone to "agree" to a document, only to turn around later and decide that he didn't fully understand what he was agreeing to. Instead, the project team needs to reach a true consensus, where each person fully supports the document. The goal of an inspection is to build consensus on the document by gaining a real commitment from everyone who has read it. When a reviewer approves a document, he takes responsibility for its contents, and if the document has defects, he shares some of the blame for missing the mistake.

The best way to reach consensus among the inspection team is for each person to feel like he or she made a real contribution to the document. The inspection meeting accomplishes that by allowing each person to find problems in the document and help the rest of the team find a solution to each problem. This is why it's important for the team to go beyond just pointing out the defects in the document and actually come up with replacement wordings that fix the defects.

By the end of the meeting, nobody remembers that one person suggested this sentence, and another suggested that one; everyone feels a sense of ownership because it was a real group effort. That ownership means that each team member leaves the meeting with a real commitment to the document. This can eliminate many of the conflicts that can cause problems later on in the project.

Inspections are also important for gaining real, meaningful approval for a document. When a document is not correct, that puts the team members in a very difficult situation. Consider a stakeholder who is reading a vision and scope document, and who has a problem with some of the contents. She can't just refuse to approve the document; that would mean that she was personally holding up the project. But if she lets the document move forward as is, that could cause serious problems later in the project. So the stakeholder feels backed into a corner. She can't approve the document as it stands, but she doesn't have the authority to make changes to it. Typically, people who are put in this situation simply avoid reading the document, giving them a sort of "plausible deniability" that lets them avoid blame when the project has problems later.

Inspections are a way out of this situation. The inspection team is given the responsibility of approving the document. To accomplish that, each member is given the authority to withhold approval until any text in the document that prevents them from approving it has either been changed to meet their needs or has been explained to the approver's satisfaction. This allows the project to move forward.

Other kinds of reviews are also useful in managing commitments. Deskchecks are especially important for gathering consensus among people in the organization who do not need to approve specific documents, but whose input is still very important.

Project teams are made up of people who all share a common goal: getting the software project out the door. Stakeholders, users, engineers, and project managers all have this goal in common. This means that each person should be willing to take on responsibility to make sure that every document produced over the course of the software project is correct.

Diagnosing Review Problems

Many organizations rely on their testers (or, in worse cases, their users) to find the bulk of the defects in the software they produce. When the defects are caused by simple coding errors or typos, they are easy to correct. Unfortunately, very few defects are caused by simple coding errors or typos. Most defects are introduced before a single line of code is written. Sometimes a programmer misunderstands the design; at other times, the entire team fails to take a stakeholder's needs into account and fails to build a needed feature into the software. Waiting until after the software is built to discover these problems results in an enormous amount of work to fix defects that should have been caught before a single line of code was written.

Problems Are Found Too Late

There are many problems that can be avoided by having the team adopt vision and scope documents, project plans, software requirements specifications, and other project documents. But what happens when the team doesn't catch an error in one of these documents until the software is built?

One of the most common causes of project failure is that requirements contain a defect that is not caught until much later in the project. Trying to fix that defect after the software is built can be so costly that it can destroy the project entirely. For example, suppose that a team member writes a use case document to describe a critical feature. The document is emailed around to the team, and everyone reads it. However, some of the readers are very busy, so they only skim it and see that it looks about right. Others see problems, but don't want to embarrass the author by bringing them up. A few think that they found very obscure problems and don't want to embarrass the other readers who they think would not have come up with the problem.

Some teams try to find defects by mailing documents around to the team, with no real expectations of what the team is supposed to do with each document. After the author mails the document out, usually nobody responds to the email for a few days. Responses trickle in over the course of the following week. Some of them point out serious flaws, but most of them do little more than point out typos and minor wording changes. In the meantime, the designers start their work to avoid sitting around doing nothing. Eventually the user interface, architecture, and software are built. The product is passed down to the QA team, who start testing the build. They haven't been a part of the development of the software at all, and have only been talking to the users and stakeholders, putting together a test plan to ensure that the software does everything that they expect it to. Within a few days, the QA team discovers a problem: there is a feature that does not work the way the users need it to work.

When this happens, the entire project team is brought together in a meeting, and a split quickly forms. The QA lead and stakeholder insist that the software is broken. The requirements analyst, design lead, and programming lead insist that there is nothing wrong. They finally start going through the documents and find that the software does, indeed, meet all of the requirements laid out in the relevant use case. But the use case is wrong—it does not describe what the users need the software to do. It's clear to everyone present that fixing the problem will be a major endeavor, and that the project will be delayed for a very long time. The team built software that was solid, well-built, and functional—but they built the wrong software.

If the project team had inspected the use cases, this could have been avoided. Everyone with a stake in the project—including QA team members—would be invited to the inspection meetings, and each inspector would have a better idea of what to look for during the inspection process. It costs the same to build the right software as it does to build the wrong software. A few hours of searching for and fixing any problems with the use case document would have saved the team weeks or months of rework.

Big, Useless Meetings

Having a project fail due to a problem in a document that isn't caught until late in the project is traumatic for a team. It's especially bad for the person who wrote the document. Once a team experiences this problem, everyone feels especially motivated to do something about it. In many cases, the solution that seems most obvious to the team and the project manager is to distribute the responsibility for creating the document. The last project was a mess because the team missed something; there's no way that they will let this happen again.

The project manager calls a meeting to get everyone together at the very beginning of the project. He takes no chances, inviting everyone who might possibly have some small input into the project and impressing upon everyone just how important the meeting is. An entire afternoon is blocked out for a standing-room-only session that's supposed to let everybody have a voice in the design of the document. Unfortunately, it ends up having the opposite effect.

Everyone has something to say, and nobody wants to let any stone go unturned. The big meeting seemed like a good idea on paper, but it quickly gets bogged down in details that only one or two people care about. The meeting goes nowhere. Nobody knows what they are supposed to do, and there's no real leadership or direction. Long after meeting fatigue sets in, no progress has been made. Stakeholders are arguing about the minute details of the day-to-day business of the organization, while designers are caught up in potential design problems, programmers can't decide on which tools to use, and, through all of this, nothing is written down. The team adjourns the meeting, having made no progress. After a few tedious marathon meetings, the project team gets sick of waiting and decides to do things the way that they've always been done.

Had the team held an inspection meeting, a deskcheck, or a walkthrough, everyone would have understood his or her role. The reviewers would have been more carefully selected. A single lead author would have had the responsibility of generating the document. Each reviewer would have had a well-defined role, reading the document and bringing up specific defects. Each defect would have been discussed by people with some knowledge to address it, and the responsibility for finding the errors would rest with the people capable of fixing them.

The Indispensable "Hero"

Sometimes a programming team has one "hero" who seems to stand out above everyone else. If a technical problem comes up that nobody can solve, and it looks like the deadline will be blown, the hero will often take the problem home on Friday night, work all weekend, and come in on Monday morning with a solution.

It seems like the hero is good for the team. But there are some serious downsides to his heroics. He's a constant scheduling problem for the project manager, because it seems that no project can be completed without him. He's constantly over-allocated, and there are entire programming teams who cannot move forward because they are waiting for him to finish a project. Meanwhile, he is constantly working 70-hour weeks, and the entire team is afraid that he will burn out or leave the organization.

In some cases, the hero is inadvertently keeping the rest of the team from advancing, either professionally or in the organization. It seems that the hero wrote the core of every code library. Only he knows the details of critical architecture pieces. The hero is tired of people talking about him getting hit by a bus, which seems to come up at least once in every architecture or code planning meeting.

The most difficult problem to deal with in this situation is maintenance. Because of his peculiar over-allocation problem, there is an increasing amount of code that only the hero is able to maintain. This is usually because he was called in to write the most difficult part of the code. Sometimes it is algorithmically difficult, and he's the only one with enough experience to do it. At other times, the coding task relies on a library that he wrote and that only he knows how to use. In either of these cases, if that code needs to be updated, the hero is the only person in the organization who is familiar with it.

Code reviews and pair programming can help alleviate the dependence on the hero. When he writes a piece of especially tricky code, he can hold a code review. If a group of programmers inspects that code, they will be able to maintain his code. In future projects, they'll be able to draw on what they learned in the review session. This will help the entire team's professional development. What's more, the hero is often not much more advanced than everyone around him; he may just know a few tricks that the rest of the team can begin to pick up. Pair programming can be especially helpful if the hero is teamed up with another senior programmer. Sometimes the "hero" status is merely a matter of perception—everyone just "knows" that he's the best programmer around. Pair programming can help everyone on the team realize that they have other people who are just as valuable. For the true hero, sharing his skills with others will help him earn real respect from the team. Team members will be able to continue to learn from his experience, and he will be able to share and teach the team. The team, in turn, will come to see him as a role model and a leader, instead of just a hero who swoops in to fix their problems.

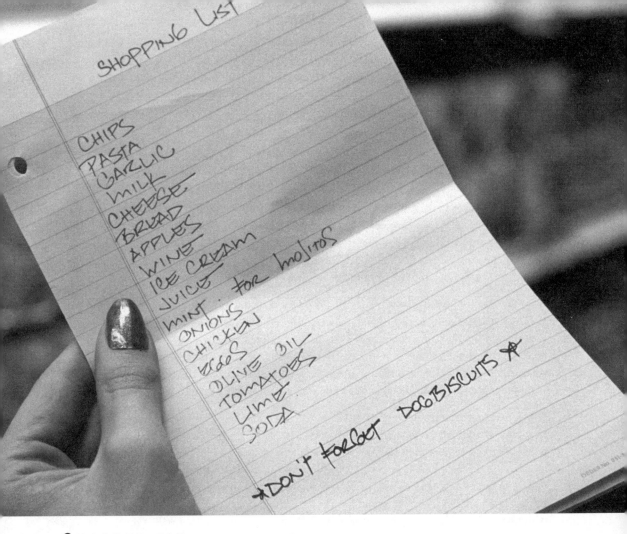

CHAPTER SIX

Software Requirements

IT SEEMS OBVIOUS that we need to know what software is supposed to do before we build it. Nevertheless, many projects are delayed (or fail completely) because development begins before anyone on the project team really understands how the software should behave. The solution to this problem is to take the time to gather and verify the *software require-ments*—documentation that completely describes the behavior that is required of the soft-ware—before the software is designed, built, and tested.

When starting a new project, programmers are often tempted to just dive in, beginning to build the software as soon as they have the general gist of what it is supposed to do. It's not hard to see why people do this: many programmers develop advanced programming skills without ever having to figure out and write down the requirements for even a sim-ple software project. For example, many good programmers hone their craft by building software that they intend to use themselves. In these projects, the programmer does not need to take time to understand the behavior of the software—she intuitively knows what the software is supposed to do from the beginning of the project.

However, most software is built to meet the needs of someone other than the programmer. If those needs are going to be satisfied, the behavior of the software must be planned before the software is built. *Software requirements engineering* is the art and science of developing an accurate and complete definition of the behavior of software that can serve as the basis for software development. Like project management, programming, and testing, software requirements engineering encompasses a set of skills that require training and practice.

Software requirements engineering tasks are usually performed by skilled requirements analysts (who sometimes have the title "Business Systems Analyst"). If a project manager does not have a requirements analyst on his team, he may be able to rely on existing team members to fill this role. There is a good deal of overlap between the skills required for design, programming, and testing, and those required for software requirements engineer-ing. A team member willing to spend time learning new skills (and a team willing to work with him and help him through this task) will often be able to build software require-ments that are sufficient for building and testing. This chapter covers some of the most important practices that a requirements analyst uses.

Requirements Elicitation

Requirements elicitation is the process through which a requirements analyst gathers, under-stands, reviews, and articulates the needs of the software project's stakeholders and users. Elicitation involves fact-finding, validating one's understanding of the information gathered, and communicating open issues for resolution. The objective of this activity is to create a complete list of what the users believe are important requirements. Elicitation activities can include:

- Interviews with the users, stakeholders, and anyone else whose perspective needs to be taken into account during the design, development, and testing of the software

- Observation of the users at work

- Distribution of discussion summaries to verify the data gathered in interviews

When a software system is developed, the first step is to determine what the system will do. This sounds trivial to some people—the vision and scope document tells us what features will be developed, so why not start designing the software once everyone agrees that it's complete? This might seem like a reasonable course of action, but there's a big difference between deciding the features that will go into the software and defining the behavior of each of those features. (If a vision and scope document does not yet exist, developing one will do much more good for the project than jumping directly into the requirements. The requirements engineering activities should wait until after the vision and scope document is ready—see Chapter 2.)

The objective of all elicitation activities is to create a complete list of what the users and stakeholders believe are the important needs that must be filled by the software, the behavior that the software must exhibit, and the constraints to which the software must adhere. A variety of elicitation practices can be used to gain a complete understanding of user needs. Each practice should be considered carefully, to determine which is best suited for a particular project; in addition, several techniques can be used in combination. The goal of using any of the techniques is to gain the commitment of the users so a common view of the system is established.

Conduct Interviews

It's been said that users don't have requirements; they have information. The requirements analyst must figure out how to get that information out of each user, stakeholder, expert, and anyone else who has information that may impact the project. The most straightforward and effective practice for doing this is by conducting interviews.

Interviews with users and stakeholders are the requirements analyst's most important elicitation tool. The goal of the interview is to identify specific needs that the person being interviewed has for the software. This generally requires understanding what the interviewee does on a day-to-day basis that will require her to interact with the software.

The first step in conducting interviews is to identify who the interviewees should be. Start with the list of users and stakeholders listed in the vision and scope document. While they are being interviewed, additional people may be mentioned. The interviewer should determine whether any of those people should be interviewed as well. If the software is being built for a specific industry or area of expertise, the requirements analyst may need to seek out subject matter experts in that area in order to ensure that the software meets the needs of a typical professional familiar with the subject.

When the software is intended to be marketed or sold by the organization, many of the market needs will originate in a sales or marketing department. In this case, it is important that sales and marketing personnel are considered subject matter experts and are interviewed for requirements. If the goal of the project is to enhance or maintain software that is already out in the field, then the interviewees should include actual external users.

The most important rule of the interview is to get the interviewee talking. Software generally doesn't get developed for its own good; a project is usually started because somebody inside an organization needs it. If the requirements analyst is talking to that person, he almost certainly will be happy to talk about it. It is likely that he has been complaining about specific problems and issues for a long time.

There are many leading questions that an interviewer can ask to help uncover important information:

- Why is the software being built? What benefits will the interviewee directly see? What benefits will other people in the organization see?

- What problems need to be addressed with new software? Why do those problems exist? How would you solve them?

- Who will use the software once it is built? Why do they need it? How frequently will they be using the software? Who will support the software?

- In what environment will the software be used? Will it be run within the organization or by its customers? Who will control the hardware?

- Are there any known constraints on the performance, design, or quality of the software?

- What inputs will be used by the software? What outputs will it create? (If examples of these exist, they should be saved for later requirements activities.)

- Are your answers "official," or is there someone else who might be able to answer these questions better? Are there "experts" in the organization who may have additional information?

- How do the users currently do their jobs? How do they expect their jobs to change after the software goes into production? Are there typical problems they currently encounter that they would like to fix?

- Are there any "workarounds" that the users perform, in order to make up for the shortcomings of existing software? Can these workarounds be incorporated into planned features or turned into additional ones? (If the workarounds are not part of the original scope of the project, does that scope need to be expanded to include them?)

- "Is there anything that I missed?"

In the early stage of interviews, any kind of open-ended questions are good for getting the interviewee talking. It is important that the requirements analyst does not interrupt the interviewee. If he has something to say, it could be important. One key to interviewing is to make sure that the predispositions of the interviewer do not interfere with the free exchange of information. Questions should center on the interviewee's problems. The requirements analyst should try to gain an understanding of the real problem without introducing bias into the user's information.

When there are multiple people with similar job functions or expertise, it is often helpful to interview them in groups. When there are too many individual interviews, they will often turn into an endless chain of conflicting statements, making it difficult to reach consensus.

After an initial set of interviews, a requirements analyst should follow up with meetings to verify his or her notes and to gather any new information that the interviewees may have come up with. These meetings may consist of additional interviews, ad-hoc meetings with one or more people, brainstorming sessions, or other kinds of interactions.

NOTE
More information on interviews can be found in *Managing Software Requirements: A Use Case Approach* by Dean Leffingwell and Don Widrig (Addison Wesley, 2003).

Observe Users at Work

Observing a user's workflow in the context of his or her environment allows a requirements analyst to see problems that the user encounters with the current system and to identify ways to enhance and streamline the behavior of the software. Watching users at work provides a more accurate understanding of their activities than simply asking them to communicate the steps involved in performing their tasks. Often there are many details that someone familiar with a task might not think to mention, but that are very important for the requirements analyst to fully understand the task.

Most software is built to help users with a job that they already do. Many software projects have a goal of automating or augmenting existing manual processes, providing new capabilities to existing people in an organization, or replacing and extending legacy software programs. In all of these cases, there are already people in the organization who are doing work that is relevant to the behavior of the software.

Once the requirements analyst has identified people who will use the software and whose day-to-day work is relevant to the behavior of the software, it is useful to observe those people at their jobs.

There are a few guidelines that may be useful:

- Many software projects are started because people who are doing work face tedious or difficult tasks that could be automated. Those people are often happy to open up and talk about the problems that need to be solved.

- Some people may feel self-conscious being observed. It is important that they know that the goal of the requirements analyst is to understand their needs in order to build software to help them. It is also important that they understand that the software is not being built to replace them, but to help make their jobs easier.

- Many organizations have training programs for new employees. If a training program exists for the job being observed, the requirements analyst should attend it. This will often yield more insight into the work, especially if there are training materials that can be used as part of the requirements gathering process.

- If possible, the requirements analyst should try to participate in the work being observed. This is often an effective way to understand the perspective of the users of the software.

Use a Discussion Summary

All of the interaction with the users, stakeholders, and other people who have relevant perspectives will yield a great deal of information. The requirements analyst should capture this information as accurately as possible. Some people find that taking notes on paper (rather than using a computer) allows for better capture of information. However, note-taking software, which captures the interviews in an audio file and links notes to their correct time offset in that file, can also be a useful tool.

Once all of the information has been gathered from the elicitation activities, the requirements analyst should use a *discussion summary* to validate the information. The discussion summary allows all of the notes to be summarized into a single document; that document should be distributed to the main users and stakeholders for a deskcheck (see Chapter 5). This will help catch any potential defects before they make it into the requirements documentation. Table 6-1 contains a template for the discussion summary.

TABLE 6-1. Discussion summary template

1. Project background
a. Purpose of project
b. Scope of project
c. Other background information
2. Perspectives
a. Who will use the system?
b. Who can provide input about the system?
3. Project objectives
a. Known business rules
b. System information and/or diagrams
c. Assumptions and dependencies
d. Design and implementation constraints
4. Risks
5. Known future enhancements
6. References
7. Open, unresolved, or TBD issues

Most, if not all, of the notes gathered by a requirements analyst during the elicitation activities should fit into the discussion summary template. Conversely, the discussion summary template can serve as a guide for a novice requirements analyst in leading interviews and meetings.

The requirements analyst should go through all of her notes when writing the discussion summary. Each note that will be relevant to the behavior of the software should be summarized and added to one of the sections of the discussion summary. The discussion summary will be ready to distribute when it contains all of the information gathered during the elicitation sessions.

This "Project Background" section contains a summary of all the notes that pertain to the background of the project. It contains these subsections:

Purpose of the project
> Every stakeholder and user has a reason that the software should be developed. This section should contain a summary of each of those reasons. The goal is to give the reader an understanding of why these people need the system to be developed.

Scope of the project
> The vision and scope document described the scope of the software to be developed, by listing each feature that would be included. This section should go into greater detail, elaborating on each feature by listing specific behaviors and tasks the software will perform.

Other background information
> This section should contain any additional information that may help a reader understand why the system is needed. (Additionally, most of the notes that don't fit anywhere else in the discussion summary can go into this section.)

The "Perspectives" section is used to identify the people who will help define the behavior of the software. Each person's perspective should be taken into account. Some of these perspectives may conflict with each other; that's okay, as long as they are described accurately. These conflicts will be worked out later, when the behavior is described in the use cases. This section must provide/contain answers to the following key questions:

Who will use the system?
> The people who will be using the software should be divided into categories. Each category of users should have a unique name ("Salesperson") and description ("A member of the North America sales team who will be selling the software in a specific territory."). The names that are given to the categories of users should make sense to people in the organization—most organizations have their own names for different roles or positions, and the requirements analyst should use that terminology wherever possible. The analyst will have many notes that pertain to each of these categories. They should be divided up by category and summarized in this section.

Who can provide input about the system?
> The organization contains many people who can provide some input about the system to be developed. This section should list everyone who was consulted about the system behavior, and summarize any notes that describe the needs of each one.

The "Project objectives" section summarizes the information that was gathered in the elicitation phase, such as the functionality that the software must implement, the work currently being done or planned in the organization that will be affected or augmented by the software, and any constraints that must be taken into account. This section contains:

Known business rules
> This section should contain details of any procedures that are currently being performed or that are needed in the organization and that will affect the software. The section should indicate who is involved or will be affected.

System information and/or diagrams

This section should contain a summary of any notes that describe functionality that must be implemented, existing or planned organizational workflow, specific user interactions, information about the environment in which the software will be used, calculations that must be performed, and any other functionality that must be implemented. This will probably be the longest section in the discussion summary.

Assumptions and dependencies

During elicitation meetings, many assumptions and dependencies will be brought up. They should be summarized in this section. (See Chapter 3 for an explanation of how assumptions affect software development.) Many of these assumptions may already be in the vision and scope document, or in the results of a Wideband Delphi estimation session; it is often sufficient to reference that document, rather than reproduce them in the discussion summary.

Design and implementation constraints

Many times there are constraints that must be placed on the software: known input or output data formats; tools, code libraries, visual controls, programming languages, or APIs that must be used; visual or GUI design standards that must be adhered to; and performance or quality requirements and other known nonfunctional requirements. These should be listed in this section in detail.

The "Risks" section summarizes any risks identified during the elicitation process that are not already included in the vision and scope document or the project plan.

The "Known future enhancements" section lists expected future enhancements. Often, during elicitation, there are feature requests from users or stakeholders that will not be included in the software. Those requests should be described, in order to make sure everyone knows that they are not going to be implemented.

The "References" section should include any internal or external documents needed to understand the software project—for example, any existing system documentation, screen shots, or original system requirements.

The "Open, unresolved, or TBD [to be determined] issues" section is the last part of the discussion summary. There are usually issues that remain unaddressed at the time the discussion summary is distributed for review. Open issues may be under active discussion with users or stakeholders. Some problems may await resolution. And the requirements analyst may not yet have raised some issues. All of these issues should be summarized here.

Once the discussion summary is complete, it should be distributed for a deskcheck (see Chapter 5). Minimally, it should be reviewed by the lead users and stakeholders (who are usually listed in the vision and scope document). But ideally, everyone who contributed to the discussion summary should have a chance to review it and give feedback. The wider the audience, the more likely it is that defects will be caught early. When the reviewers return their comments, the discussion summary does not need to be updated. However, those comments should be archived along with the discussion summary, and should be taken into account in later requirements activities.

Use Cases

Once the initial round of requirements elicitation is done and a discussion summary has been distributed and reviewed, the requirements analyst is ready to begin creating use cases. A *use case* is a description of a specific interaction that a user may have with the software. Use cases are deceptively simple tools for describing the behavior of the software.

A use case contains a textual description of all of the ways that the intended users could work with the software through its interface. Use cases do not describe any internal workings of the software, nor do they explain how that software will be implemented. They simply show the steps that the user follows to use the software to do his work. All of the ways that the users interact with the software can be described in this manner.

A typical use case includes these sections, usually laid out in a table. Table 6-2 shows a template for describing a use case.

TABLE 6-2. Use case template

Name	Use case number and name
Summary	Brief description of the use case
Rationale	Description of the reason that the use case is needed
Users	A list of all of the categories of users that interact with this use case
Preconditions	The state of the software before the use case begins
Basic Course of Events	A numbered list of interactions between the user and one or more users
Alternative Paths	Conditions under which the basic course of events could change
Postconditions	The state of the software after the basic course of events is complete

Name, Summary, Rationale, and Users

Each use case must begin with information that allows the reader to uniquely identify it. Every use case has a descriptive name and a unique identifying number. The number is used as a way to refer to a specific use case in the SRS (see below). In addition to identifying information, each use case has a summary, or a brief description of what the use case does.

The "Rationale" section of the use case contains one or more paragraphs that describe why the use case is needed. This serves as an important quality check to ensure the correctness of the use case. While it is important that the team agrees on the behavior of the software, it is equally important that they also agree on why the software is being created.

Each use case represents a series of interactions between the software and one or more users. The users are divided into categories based on the way they interact with the software; the "Users" section lists the kinds of users that interact with this use case. If all categories of users interact with this particular use case, it should list "any user" in this section.

Preconditions and Postconditions

Any software that is being executed can be thought of as being in a state of operation. When the software is in a certain state, it means that a specific set of operations are available to the user that are not available when the software is in other states. For example, a word processor could have an existing document loaded, a new document displayed, or it could be displaying no document at all. It could be showing a configuration window or a dialog box. These are all different, distinct states that the word processing software can be in. There are certain actions that are only available to the user when the software is in a particular state. For example, the user can enter text into the document if the word processor has an existing document loaded, but not if it is displaying a dialog box.

The *precondition* is the state of the software at the beginning of the use case. This represents the entry criteria for the use case: if the software is not in that state, the use case does not apply. The *postcondition* is the state that the software is left in after the use case is completed. In the use case, each of these states can be described in words ("the word processor is loaded but no document is being edited"), although it is also possible to create a name for each state and refer to it by name.

Basic Course of Events

The *basic course of events* is the core of the use case. Table 6-3 shows a very simple basic course of events for a word processor's search-and-replace feature.

TABLE 6-3. Basic course of events for search-and-replace

Precondition	A document is loaded and being edited.
Basic course of events	1. The user indicates that the software is to perform a search-and-replace in the document.
	2. The software responds by requesting the search term and the replacement text.
	3. The user inputs the search term and replacement text and indicates that all occurrences are to be replaced.
	4. The software replaces all occurrences of the search term with the replacement text.
Postcondition	All occurrences of the search term have been replaced with the replacement text.

The basic course of events consists of a series of steps. The first step will generally be the action that the user takes in order to initiate the use case. The remaining steps are a series of interactions between the user and the software. Each interaction consists of one or more actions that the user takes, followed by a response by the software. In this case, the software is responding to the user entering the search term and replacement text and indicating that the replacement should occur.

This basic course of events does not contain words like "click," "button," "text box or "window." User interface design elements should be left out of use cases to allow the designer as many options as possible. For example, this particular use case could be implemented as a pop-up dialog box that contains text boxes for the search term and replacement text, and a button that says "Replace All." (This is how many word processors, including Microsoft Word, do it). But that's not the only way to satisfy this use case. In the Emacs text editor, for example, the user hits Meta-X and enters "replace-string" on the bottom line of the window, followed by the search term and the replacement term. Either implementation would satisfy this use case.

Sometimes there is functionality that is replicated in many use cases. For example, say the use cases for a program to play music files includes UC-15 (see Table 6-4), a use case that allows a user to explore and edit information in one of his audio files.

TABLE 6-4. Basic course of events for "UC-15: Edit Audio File Information"

Precondition	An audio file is highlighted.
Basic course of events	1. The user indicates that the software is to display information about the audio file.
	2. The software responds by displaying the information fields (track name, artist, length, genre, and year) associated with the audio file.
	3. The user indicates that one of the information fields is to be replaced and specifies a replacement value.
	4. The software updates the audio file with the new value.
Postcondition	Same as precondition state, except the audio file has an updated information field.

If the requirements analyst intends that the user be given the option to select an audio file in many different use cases and edit that file at any time, each of those use cases may have a use case step or an alternative path that reads: "The user indicates that the file is to be edited. Use case UC-15 is executed." In this way, multiple use cases can be extended to include this functionality. The requirements analyst needs to describe it only once, which makes the use cases clearer. This technique has the benefit of giving the designers and programmers hints about where they can reuse code when the software is being developed.

Alternative Paths

Often, a use case has one basic course of events, as well as several alternative courses that are very similar and that share many of the same steps. In these cases, they are documented as different *alternative paths* (rather than in separate use cases), to show that they are closely related. An alternative path provides behavior that is similar to the basic course of events but that differs in one or more key behaviors.

For example, an alternative path for the search-and-replace use case would be to only replace the first occurrence of the search string. Table 6-5 shows the alternative path for this behavior, as well as an alternative path for searching without replacement and another one for aborting the operation:

TABLE 6-5. Alternative paths for search-and-replace

Alternative paths	1. In Step 3, the user indicates that only the first occurrence is to be replaced. In this case, the software finds the first occurrence of the search term in the document being edited and replaces it with the replacement text. The postcondition state is identical, except only the first occurrence is replaced and the replacement text is highlighted.
	2. In Step 3, the user indicates that the software is only to search and not replace, and does not specify replacement text. In this case, the software highlights the first occurrence of the search term and the use case ends.
	3. The user may decide to abort the search-and-replace operation at any time during Steps 1, 2, or 3. In this case, the software returns to the precondition state.

As the requirements analyst defines additional alternative paths, it may become clear that one of them is more likely to be used than the basic course of events. In this case, it may be useful to swap them—make the alternative path into the basic course of events, and add a new alternative path to describe the behavior previously called the basic course of events.

Table 6-6 shows a final use case for a search-and-replace function, which is numbered UC-8 in this example.

TABLE 6-6. Use case for a simple search-and-replace function

Name	UC-8: Search
Summary	All occurrences of a search term are replaced with replacement text.
Rationale	While editing a document, many users find that there is text somewhere in the file being edited that needs to be replaced, but searching for it manually by looking through the entire document is time-consuming and ineffective. The search-and-replace function allows the user to find it automatically and replace it with specified text. Sometimes this term is repeated in many places and needs to be replaced. At other times, only the first occurrence should be replaced. The user may also wish to simply find the location of that text without replacing it.
Users	All users
Preconditions	A document is loaded and being edited.
Basic course of events	1. The user indicates that the software is to perform a search-and-replace in the document. 2. The software responds by requesting the search term and the replacement text. 3. The user inputs the search term and replacement text and indicates that all occurrences are to be replaced. 4. The software replaces all occurrences of the search term with the replacement text.
Alternative paths	1. In Step 3, the user indicates that only the first occurrence is to be replaced. In this case, the software finds the first occurrence of the search term in the document being edited and replaces it with the replacement text. The postcondition state is identical, except only the first occurrence is replaced, and the replacement text is highlighted. 2. In Step 3, the user indicates that the software is only to search and not replace, and does not specify replacement text. In this case, the software highlights the first occurrence of the search term and the use case ends. 3. The user may decide to abort the search-and-replace operation at any time during Steps 1, 2, or 3. In this case, the software returns to the precondition state.
Postconditions	All occurrences of the search term have been replaced with the replacement text.

Develop Use Cases Iteratively

As the use cases are developed, additional information about how the software should behave will become clear. Exploring and writing down the behavior of the software will lead a requirements analyst to understand various aspects of the users' needs in a new light, and additional use cases and functional requirements will start to become clear as well. As this happens, they should be written down with a name, number, and summary—once they are in this form, the analyst can apply the four-step process to complete them.

The first step in developing use cases is identifying the basic ones that will be developed. The list of features in the vision and scope document is a good starting point, as there will usually be at least one use case per feature (usually more than one). This will probably not be the final set of use cases—additional ones will probably be discovered during the development of the use cases.

Many requirements analysts have found that a four-step approach is effective in developing use cases. Table 6-7 contains a script that describes this approach.

TABLE 6-7. Use case development script

Name	Use case development script
Purpose	A four-step approach to use case development
Summary	This approach to developing use cases allows the information to be gathered and documented naturally, in a way that lends itself to an iterative approach of alternating iteration, documentation, and verification of use cases.
Work products	*Output* Use Cases
Entry criteria	A requirements analyst has received feedback from elicitation and is ready to develop use cases.
Basic course of events	1. Identify the basic set of use cases. Assign a name and number to each use case. 2. Add a rationale and summary to each use case. Identify which users will interact with each use case, and add them as well. Create a master list of user categories that identifies all of the information known about each kind of user: titles, roles, physical locations, approximate number of users in the category, organizational policies they must adhere to, and anything else that makes someone part of their category. Where possible, add precondition and postcondition states to the use cases. 3. Define the basic course of events and the alternative paths for each use case. Finish adding the precondition and postcondition states. If additional users and use cases are discovered, add them as well (starting with just a name and number, and then adding the other information as in Step 2). 4. Verify each use case, ensuring that all paths make sense and are correct. Go through each step with user representatives to make sure that they accurately represent the way they expect the users to interact with the software. Look for any steps that are awkward for the user that could be made more efficient. Finish all use cases that were added in Step 3.
Exit criteria	The use cases are complete and no additional information has been uncovered, which may lead to additional use cases being developed. If additional use cases have been discovered, return to Step 1 to fill them in.

A requirements analyst defining a set of use cases for this software would start by creating one use case for each feature. Initially, each of these would have a name and a number. The numbering system does not matter, as long as it is unique. (A number such as "UC-1" is sufficient.) The requirements analyst should create a new use case document with a blank template for each of these use cases, filling in the name and number for each of them and proceeding through each of the four steps to create a complete set of use cases.

> ## NOTE
> An expanded use case format and a great deal of practical information on developing use cases for software projects can be found in *Use Cases: Requirements in Context* by Daryl Kulak, Eamonn Guiney, and Erin Lavkulich (Addison Wesley, 2000).

Software Requirements Specification

A *software requirements specification* (SRS) is a complete description of the behavior of the software to be developed. It includes a set of use cases that describe all of the interactions that the users will have with the software. In addition to use cases, the SRS contains *functional requirements*, which define the internal workings of the software: that is, the calculations, technical details, data manipulation and processing, and other specific functionality that shows how the use cases are to be satisfied. It also contains *nonfunctional requirements*, which impose constraints on the design or implementation (such as performance requirements, quality standards, or design constraints).

The SRS is the most important work product that is produced by the requirements engineering project activities. All later work products—software design and architecture, code, test plans—are based on the SRS.

SRS Template

The SRS contains the use cases, functional requirements, and nonfunctional requirements. It should also contain overall information about the project, in order to orient the team. Table 6-8 shows the SRS template.

TABLE 6-8. Software requirements specification outline

1. Introduction
a. Purpose
b. Scope
c. System overview
d. References
2. Definitions
3. Use cases
4. Functional requirements
5. Nonfunctional requirements

The introduction serves to orient the reader. It describes both the system and the SRS itself:

Purpose

> This section describes the purpose of the document. Typically, this will contain a brief two- or three-sentence description, including the name of the project. For example: "The purpose of this document is to serve as a guide to designers, developers, and testers who are responsible for the engineering of the *(name of project)* project. It should give the engineers all of the information necessary to design, develop, and test the software." This is to ensure that the person reading the document understands what he or she is looking at.

Scope

> This section contains a brief description of the scope of the document. If the SRS is a complete description of the software, then it will state something similar to: "This document contains a complete description of the functionality of the *(name of project)* project. It con-

sists of use cases, functional requirements, and nonfunctional requirements, which, taken together, form a complete description of the software." For complex software, the requirements for the project might be divided into several SRS documents. In this case, the scope should indicate which portion of the project is covered in this document.

System overview

This section contains a description of the system. This is essentially a brief summary of the vision and scope of the project.

References

Any references to other documents (including the vision and scope document) should be included here. These may include other documents in the organization, work products, articles, and anything else that is relevant to understanding the SRS. If there is an organizational intranet, this section often includes URLs of referenced documents.

Definitions

The "Definitions" section contains any definitions needed to understand the SRS. Often, it will contain a glossary, defining terms that the reader may not be familiar with (or that may have a specific meaning here that differs from everyday use). This section may also contain definitions of any data files that are used as input, a list of any databases that may be needed, and any other organizational or workflow-related information that is needed to understand the SRS.

The remaining sections contain a complete description of the behavior of the software. The "Use Cases" section contains each of the use cases. Each use case is represented by a table, which is in the format shown in Table 6-6. The "Functional requirements" section contains the functional requirements, and the "Nonfunctional requirements" section contains the nonfunctional requirements. Each functional and nonfunctional requirement is added to the SRS as a table (using the format shown in Table 6-9).

The SRS should also contain a complete table of contents that includes the name and number of each use case, functional requirement, and nonfunctional requirement.

Functional requirements

Once an initial set of use cases has been created and filled in, the requirements analyst begins documenting the *functional requirements*. Table 6-9 shows the template for a functional requirement.

TABLE 6-9. Functional and nonfunctional requirement template

Name	Name and number of the functional requirement
Summary	Brief description of the requirement
Rationale	Description of the reason that the requirement is needed
Requirements	The behavior that is required of the software
References	Use cases and other functional and nonfunctional requirements that are relevant to understanding this one

The name, summary, and rationale of each functional requirement are used in the same way as those of the use cases. The behavior that is to be implemented should be described in plain English in the "Requirements" section. Most requirements are only relevant to a small number of use cases—these should be listed by name and number in the "References" section. (Some requirements are not associated with use cases.)

The core of the requirement is the description of the required behavior. It is very important to make this clear and readable. This behavior may come from organizational or business rules, or it may be discovered through elicitation sessions with users, stakeholders, and other experts within the organization. Many requirements will be uncovered during the use case development. When this happens, the requirements analyst should create a placeholder requirement with a name and summary, and research the details later, to be filled in when they are better known.

Table 6-10 shows an example of a requirement that might be discovered during the development of the search-and-replace use case in Table 6-6.

TABLE 6-10. Functional requirement example

Name	**FR-4: Case sensitivity in search-and-replace**
Summary	The search-and-replace feature must have case sensitivity in both the search and the replacement.
Rationale	A user will often search for a word that is part of a sentence, title, heading, or other kind of text that is not all lowercase. The search-and-replace function needs to be aware of that, and give the user the option to ignore it.
Requirements	When a user invokes the search-and-replace function, the software must give the option to do a case-sensitive search.
	By default, the search will match any text that has the same letters as the search term, even if the case is different. If the user indicates that the search is to be done with case-sensitivity turned on, then the software will only match text in the document where the case is identical to that of the search term.
	During a search and replace, when the software replaces original text in the document with the replacement text specified by the user, the software retains the case of the original text as follows:
	• If the original text was all uppercase, then the replacement text must be inserted in all uppercase.
	• If the original text was all lowercase, then the replacement text must be inserted in all lowercase.
	• If the original text had the first character uppercase and the rest of the characters lowercase, then the replacement text must reflect this case as well.
	• If the original text was sentence case (where the first letter of each word is uppercase), then the replacement text must be inserted in sentence case.
	• In all other cases, the replacement text should be inserted using the case specified by the user.
References	UC-8: Search

The behavior in the requirement can contain lists, bullets, equations, pictures, references to external documents, and any other material that will help the reader understand what needs to be implemented. The goal of the requirement is to communicate this behavior in as clear and unambiguous a manner as possible.

One pitfall is to get hung up on ambiguity. For example, the example above refers to "the same letters as the search term." This is potentially ambiguous—an overly pedantic reading could interpret it to mean "the same letters as the search term but in any order," and that would technically be correct because the requirement does not specify that the letters should not be out of order. However, it is unlikely that the text will be read that way. In this case, all of the developers will almost certainly understand what the requirements analyst meant when the text was written, and writing the extra explanation into the requirement could make it more confusing.

The requirements analyst has a great deal of discretion about how to break requirements up. For example, the example above could potentially be broken into two separate requirements, with one requirement allowing for a case-sensitive search and another specifying that the replacement text needs to retain the case of the original text when the search is not case-sensitive. A good general rule is that requirements should only be split up when that split offers more clarity. In this case, a split probably would not make the requirement any clearer, so keeping these together makes sense.

Many requirements define behavior that the user can turn on or off (like the user's ability to specify a case-sensitive search in the example). In this case, the requirement should always specify the default behavior (in the example case, the default search is case-insensitive). Requirements often specify behavior that only occurs under certain conditions (like the conditions in which the case is retained). It is also important to specify a fall-through case to show what happens if none of the specified conditions are met ("In all other cases...").

As with the use case, the requirements should not contain any design elements. The requirements analyst should avoid words like window, button, click, checkbox, radio button, form, etc. For example, many search-and-replace features use a checkbox to implement context-sensitive searching. But there is no need to require that the designer use a checkbox—it's possible that an innovative designer might come up with a better way to let the user turn on case-sensitive searching (like with two separate buttons, a radio button, a separate tab, or some other way that isn't immediately obvious). Leaving the design unconstrained allows the designers and programmers more freedom to implement the requirements creatively. The more that the design is constrained in the SRS, the harder it makes their jobs.

Nonfunctional requirements

Users have implicit expectations about how well the software will work. These characteristics include how easy the software is to use, how quickly it executes, how reliable it is, and how well it behaves when unexpected conditions arise. The *nonfunctional requirements* define these aspects about the system. (The nonfunctional requirements are sometimes referred to as "nonbehavioral requirements" or "software quality attributes.")

The nonfunctional requirements should be defined as precisely as possible. Often, this is done by quantifying them. Where possible, the nonfunctional requirements should provide specific measurements that the software must meet. The maximum number of seconds it must take to perform a task, the maximum size of a database on disk, the number of hours per day a system must be available, and the number of concurrent users supported are examples of requirements that the software must implement but do not change its behavior.

There are many kinds of nonfunctional requirements, including:

Availability

A system's availability, or "uptime," is the amount of time that it is operational and available for use. This is specified because some systems are designed with expected downtime for activities like database upgrades and backups.

Efficiency

Specifies how well the software utilizes scarce resources: CPU cycles, disk space, memory, bandwidth, etc.

Flexibility

If the organization intends to increase or extend the functionality of the software after it is deployed, that should be planned from the beginning; it influences choices made during the design, development, testing, and deployment of the system.

Portability

Portability specifies the ease with which the software can be installed on all necessary platforms, and the platforms on which it is expected to run.

Integrity

Integrity requirements define the security attributes of the system, restricting access to features or data to certain users and protecting the privacy of data entered into the software.

Performance

The performance constraints specify the timing characteristics of the software. Certain tasks or features are more time-sensitive than others; the nonfunctional requirements should identify those software functions that have constraints on their performance.

Reliability

Reliability specifies the capability of the software to maintain its performance over time. Unreliable software fails frequently, and certain tasks are more sensitive to failure (for example, because they cannot be restarted, or because they must be run at a certain time).

Reusability

Many systems are developed with the ability to leverage common components across multiple products. Reusability indicates the extent to which software components should be designed in such a way that they can be used in applications other than the ones for which they were initially developed.

Robustness

A robust system is able to handle error conditions gracefully, without failure. This includes a tolerance of invalid data, software defects, and unexpected operating conditions.

Scalability

Software that is scalable has the ability to handle a wide variety of system configuration sizes. The nonfunctional requirements should specify the ways in which the system may be expected to scale up (by increasing hardware capacity, adding machines, etc.).

Usability

Ease-of-use requirements address the factors that constitute the capacity of the software to be understood, learned, and used by its intended users.

The nonfunctional requirements can use the same template as the functional requirements. Table 6-11 shows an example of a nonfunctional requirement:

TABLE 6-11. Nonfunctional requirement example

Name	NF-7: Performance constraints for search-and-replace
Summary	The search-and-replace feature must perform a search quickly.
Rationale	If a search is not fast enough, users will avoid using the software.
Requirements	A case-insensitive search-and-replace performed on a 3MB document with twenty 30-character search terms to be replaced with a different 30-character search term must take under 500ms on a 700MHz Pentium III running Microsoft Windows 2000 at 50% CPU load.
References	UC-8: Search.

Develop the SRS Iteratively

Like use cases, the SRS should be developed in a highly iterative manner. Table 6-12 shows the SRS development script, an iterative process that guides a requirements analyst through the development of a software requirements specification.

TABLE 6-12. SRS development script

Name	Software requirements specification development script
Purpose	To elicit software requirements, document them in a software requirements specification, and verify that it is correct.
Summary	The development of the software requirements specification should be the most iterative part of the entire project. This is the point where the behavior of the software to be developed is at its most malleable—it has only been described in words, and has not yet been realized in design, architecture, code, test plans, or any other work product. The goal of this script is to ensure that as many defects are found as possible, because each defect missed at this stage will be much more costly to detect and fix later on in the project.
Work products	*Output* Software Requirements Specification (SRS)
Entry criteria	A requirements analyst has a vision and scope document for a project and has identified a set of users, stakeholders, and other people who will participate in the elicitation process.
Basic course of events	1. *Elicitation:* The script begins with the elicitation process. The requirements analyst works with users, stakeholders, and other people to elicit their needs and any known requirements. If there are outstanding issues or SRS defects, the analyst resolves them during the elicitation activities.
	2. *Documentation:* The requirements analyst creates or updates the draft of the SRS to reflect the data elicited in Step 1.
	3. *Verification:* A team of reviewers performs a review of the SRS draft. In the first iteration, a small number of reviewers perform a deskcheck of the draft. Later reviews will include more people, and may be inspections instead of deskchecks. Walkthroughs should be conducted for non-technical people who still need to understand the contents of the SRS. The last iteration must be an inspection.
Exit criteria	The script ends after the draft was inspected in Step 3 and no defects were found. If defects were found or there was only a deskcheck performed in Step 3, then the script returns to step 1 for the next iteration.

The goal of the SRS development script is to remove as many defects as possible from the SRS. Many people have trouble figuring out what constitutes a defect. In this case, a defect is any planned software behavior a project team member, user, stakeholder, or decision-maker does not agree with. This means that defects could be caused by any number of problems:

- Somebody does not believe that the planned behavior will satisfy the users' or stakeholders' needs.

- Somebody believes that those needs may be better satisfied with different behavior.

- An inspector does not understand what's written or feels that it is ambiguous or confusing.

- A project team member does not believe that the behavior can be implemented as written.

- Two or more requirements contradict each other—an implementation that satisfies one cannot satisfy the others.

If there is a requirement in the SRS that has one of these problems, it must be identified and fixed so that everyone agrees on everything in the document. There will almost certainly be defects that slip through—no inspection team is perfect—and each of these will cost much more time to fix after it has been designed, coded, and tested than it would have if it had been caught using the SRS development script. The goal is to find as many defects as possible, in order to reduce the amount of time that the team must spend later on in the project undoing the few that slipped past.

One of the most common mistakes in software engineering is to shortchange the SRS. A good project manager knows that the fastest way to finish a project is to take the time up front to get the requirements right. For many managers, however, cutting the requirements short sometimes seems tempting. They are impatient to have the programmers begin working on something concrete that they can use, and do not necessarily see the value of planning the behavior of the software before it is built. But skipping the software requirements activities will always come back to damage the project later. Any defects in the SRS will get magnified in later work products. If a defect is left in the SRS and not caught until testing, that defect will be designed into the software. If the defect is still not caught in the design phase, then code will be built to implement that design, and a test plan will be created and executed that verifies that behavior is accurately reflected in the final build. When that defect is eventually discovered by a user, fixing it will require an enormous amount of effort from the entire project team. This is why it is worth spending time doing extra iterations of reviews at the outset of the project—it's much more efficient to build the software right the first time than it is to go back and fix it later.

The best way to prevent defects is through iteration. This is why the SRS development script calls for repeated reviews of the SRS. It may seem to the project team that they are sitting through redundant deskchecks, walkthroughs, and inspections of a single SRS. It is sometimes tempting to cut this process short and declare that the SRS is "good enough." The project manager needs to resist this urge. When the SRS goes through what some people might perceive as "yet another iteration," it's because somebody found a defect in it that needs to be fixed. If this defect is not fixed now, the effort required to fix it later will dwarf the effort required to do another review of the SRS.

There is a risk that when nontechnical people read the SRS draft, they will fail to understand what is written in it and simply agree to whatever is written down. This often happens in an organization in which software requirements have never been used before. To address this problem, the project manager should work to help everyone understand why it is so important that they take the time to read and understand each SRS draft. This often requires sitting down with each person to make sure he really read and understood the document. Even if that seems time-consuming and patronizing, it's better than losing an enormous portion of the project's effort because the team is busy fixing defects that could have been caught in the first place.

If users and stakeholders are used to playing with intermediate builds and vetoing software features that they don't like, they may object to sitting through a walkthrough meeting rather than waiting until the programmers produce something. However, that's a very costly way to build software. Words on a page are much easier to change than functions and objects in source code. A defect that only takes a few minutes to fix in a draft of an SRS can require days, weeks, or months of the most irritating sort of programming to repair after it's been coded. This is why it's in the project team's best interest to catch the defects as early as possible.

Another problem is that some people may not read repeated drafts; after seeing the first few drafts, they may start to ignore later revisions. One way to reduce the risk of this happening is to keep the initial iterations' review teams very small, and only expand them when the draft is close to completion. People who are not used to reading technical documentation are much more likely to read a single draft than they are to read a half-dozen of them. But in the last iterations, it still may be difficult to get nontechnical people to work their way through a technical document. This is where a walkthrough can be a useful tool to ensure that everyone understands the document. (See Chapter 5 for more information on walkthroughs.)

Requirements Differ from Design

Many people have trouble understanding the difference between scope (which demonstrates the needs of the organization), the requirements (which describe the behavior of the software to be implemented), and design (which shows how the behavior will be implemented). It is hard for them to describe the behavior of a piece of software without talking about windows, forms, buttons, checkboxes, clicking, dragging, etc. The difference between scope, requirements, and design is a very important distinction that the entire project team should be familiar with.

Table 6-13 shows several examples that illustrate the difference between the *user needs* that might appear in a vision and scope document, the *behavior* that might appear in an SRS, and the *design* that might appear in a design specification or code comments. As a general rule, unless the requirements analyst specifically intends to constrain the designers and programmers, design elements should be left out of the SRS.

TABLE 6-13. Examples to illustrate the difference between needs, behavior, and design

Needs	Behavior	Design
The users need to be able to easily search and replace text.	A user indicates that search-and-replace is needed. The software responds by prompting for a search term and replacement text. The user enters the text and indicates that the software is to do a case-sensitive search to replace all occurrences.	A user selects "Search" from the "Edit" menu. The software pops up a window with a text box for a search term, a text box for the replacement text, a checkbox for case-sensitivity (defaulted to unchecked), and a button labeled "Replace All." The user enters the search term and replacement text into the appropriate text boxes, checks the checkbox, and clicks the button to initiate the search.
A user composing email needs to be able to look up contacts in an address book.	A user entering the header information in an email being composed indicates that the current header field should be populated using the address book. The software responds by displaying a list of contacts, including full name and email address. The user specifies one. The software responds by returning to the email and adding the specified name and address to the header field.	The user has the "compose email" window active, selects one of the text boxes that contains the To: or From: header, and clicks the address book button next to the text box. The software responds by popping up a modal dialog that contains the address book entries in a listbox. The user scrolls down to the email address to be added to the field, clicks on the name, and clicks the "Add" button. The software closes the address book window and adds the name to the field that was being edited.
A user needs to search the Internet for web pages that contain certain words.	A user indicates a search term to the search engine. The software responds by displaying a list of pages that match the criteria. The list is limited to 100 results. The user may indicate that the next 100 results are to be displayed, in which case the system displays those results instead.	A user navigates to the home page of the search engine. The software responds by displaying a text box and a button labeled "Search." The user enters the search term into the text box and clicks the button. The software responds by displaying a page with 100 results, with 1 link per result. At the bottom of the page is a link labeled "Next 100 hits." If the user clicks on that link, the search engine displays the next 100 hits, with a link labeled "Next 100 hits" and another labeled "Previous 100 hits."

SRS Inspection Checklist

The SRS development script specifies that its last iteration must include an inspection of the SRS. The following checklist can serve as a guide to SRS inspectors. It is divided into sections that provide criteria for evaluating the SRS document in general, the use cases, and the requirements.

The following checklist items apply to the entire SRS.

Document completeness

Does the document meet all established templates and standards?

Is the document complete?

Is there any information that should be included, but is not?

Is there any information that should be removed?

Are all of the references valid?

Document feasibility

Can the project as specified be accomplished within known cost and schedule constraints?

Document modifiability

Is the document structured so that any changes can be made easily, completely, and consistently?

Document feasibility

Can every element of the SRS be implemented with the available resources and tools?

The following checklist items apply to the use cases.

Use case clarity

Does each use case have a clear flow of events?

Is every action that the system takes performed in response to an action by the user or to a specific event?

Has unnecessary duplication been removed using generalization and/or references?

Is each use case uniquely identified with a name and a number?

Use case completeness

Are all of the steps in each use case necessary?

Are there any steps that are missing?

Are all alternative paths and exceptions accounted for?

Use case level of detail

Does any use case contain details (such as specific calculations, constraints, or other internals that would not directly be observed by the user) that should really be part of the functional requirements instead?

Does any use case unintentionally constrain the design?

Use case testability

Is each use case testable?

The following checklist items apply to the functional and nonfunctional requirements.

Requirement clarity

Is each requirement clear, unambiguous, and readable?

Is each requirement uniquely identified with a name and a number?

Requirement completeness

Is each requirement complete?

Are there requirements that are missing?

Requirement level of detail

Do any requirements unintentionally constrain the design?

Requirement consistency

Are the requirements consistent?

Does any requirement contradict another requirement?

Are all data structures, calculations, and functions named and used consistently?

Requirement functionality

Is every requirement correct?

Are all inputs and outputs clearly specified?

Requirement performance

Are all nonfunctional requirements that constrain performance (speed, resource utilization, etc.) clearly and quantitatively defined?

Requirement testability

Is each requirement testable?

> **NOTE**
>
> More information on SRS development can be found in *Managing Software Requirements: A Use Case Approach* by Dean Leffingwell and Don Widrig (Addison Wesley, 2003) and *Software Requirements* by Karl Wiegers (Addison Wesley, 2003).

Change Control

Throughout the course of most projects, many of the people involved come up with changes to the planned software that could be implemented. Many poorly managed software projects have been driven to failure because the designers, developers, and testers had to repeatedly switch directions because of uncontrolled changes. Changes originate from all over the project: a stakeholder may discover a new need that should be addressed, a senior manager could change his mind about a feature, a programmer could figure out a way to combine behaviors to make the software more efficient, a tester could discover conflicting requirements, etc. Some of these changes will be worth doing, while others should probably be scrapped. But every change will come with a sense of urgency, and the project manager needs a way to sort through them to make sure that only the right changes are made.

Change control is a method for implementing only those changes that are worth pursuing, and for preventing unnecessary or overly costly changes from derailing the project. Change control is essentially an agreement between the project team and the managers that are responsible for decision-making on the project to evaluate the impact of a change before implementing it. Many changes that initially sound like good ideas will get thrown out once the true cost of the change is known. The potential benefit of the change is written down, and the project manager works with the team to estimate the potential impact that the change will have on the project. This gives the organization all of the information necessary to do a real cost-benefit analysis. If the benefit of the change is worth the cost, the project manager updates the plan to reflect the new estimates. Otherwise, the change is thrown out and the team continues with the original plan.

Changes that seem "small" because they are easy to describe in words can have an unexpectedly large impact on the project. Even the most carefully planned and tracked project can be thrown off course by unexpected changes. A project manager can use change control to keep this from happening.

Establish a Change Control Board

The most important part of change control is a *change control board* (CCB). There are certain people in the organization who have the power to change the scope of the project. Usually there is a senior manager or decision-maker who has the authority to make sweeping changes at will; sometimes there are several people in this position. For change control to be effective, these people must be part of the CCB.

In addition, the CCB should contain people from the project team:

- The project manager
- An important stakeholder or user (or someone who understands and advocates the team's perspective)
- Someone who understands the effort involved in making the change (usually, this is a representative from the programming team)
- Someone who understands the engineering decisions that the team makes over the course of the project (a design team member, requirements analyst, or, if neither is available, a programmer who participated in the design of the software)
- Someone who is familiar with the expected functionality of the software and with the behavior being discussed for each individual change (typically a tester)

This last person fulfills a very important role in the change control process. Typically, she is involved in the tracking of changes and defects in the product. When a bug is reported, part of her job is to figure out whether it is a defect (meaning that the software does not behave the way its specification requires it to behave) or a change (meaning that the software behaves as designed, but that this behavior is not what the users or stakeholders need).

Changes will generally be reported through the defect tracking system. (If there is currently no defect tracking system in place, establishing one will have a far greater impact on controlling changes than a change control process will—see Chapter 8). The job of the tester on the CCB is to understand the change: the behavior specified in the requirements, why this behavior is incorrect, and how and why the software should be changed.

Before the project begins, the list of CCB members should be written down and agreed upon, and each CCB member should understand why the change control process is needed and what her role will be in it. The project manager must ensure that everyone buys into the idea of change control and agrees that it is their job to evaluate each change before the software project plan can be altered. The project manager must also reassure them that the programmers and other team members cannot deviate from the plan. This agreement between CCB members is the most important part of the change control process.

Change Control Process

Table 6-14 shows the script for a change control process.

TABLE 6-14. Change control process script

Name	Change control process script
Purpose	To control changes by evaluating their impact before agreeing to implement them
Summary	The change control process ensures that the impact of each change is evaluated before the decision is made to implement that change. A change is proposed by anyone evaluating the software. A *change control board* (CCB), made up of the decision-makers, project manager, stakeholder or user representatives, and selected team members, evaluates the change. The CCB either accepts or rejects the change.
Work products	*Input* Issue report in the defect tracking system that describes the change *Output* Modified issue report that reflects the impact of the change and the decision on whether or not to move forward with it
Entry criteria	A change has been discovered, and an issue report that describes it has been entered into the defect tracking system.
Basic course of events	1. A CCB member (typically a tester) who is familiar with the expected functionality of the software reads and understands the issue report, which describes the requested change. 2. The CCB member familiar with the change meets with the project manager to explain its scope and significance. Together, they identify all project team members who will be impacted by the change, and work with them to evaluate its impact. The project manager updates the issue report to reflect the result of that evaluation. 3. At the next CCB meeting, the project manager presents the scope and significance of the change, along with its expected impact. The CCB discusses the change, and performs a cost-benefit analysis to determine if its benefits are worth the cost. The CCB approves the change. 4. The project manager updates the issue report to indicate that the change has been approved, and then updates the project plan to reflect the change. The team members begin implementing the change.
Alternative paths	1. In Step 1, if the CCB member does not understand the change, it can be returned to the submitter for further explanation. The submitter may choose to either update the issue report to clarify the change (in which case, the script returns to step 1) or drop it entirely (in which case, the change control process ends). 2. In Step 3, if the CCB determines that the benefits of the change are not worth the cost, it can reject it. The change control process ends, and no changes are made to the project. The project manager updates the issue report to reflect the fact that it was rejected.
Exit criteria	The project plan has been updated to reflect the impact of the change, and work to implement the change has begun.

Evaluate Changes in the CCB Meeting

There are points in the course of the project when the CCB may need to meet regularly:

- During the requirements phase, the CCB will need to discuss the scope of the project if it turns out that there are major areas that the vision and scope failed to cover.

- During the design and programming of the software, the team may discover that the requirements need to be changed. For example, programmers may discover requirements in the SRS that seemed reasonable at the time but that turn out to be contradictory or convoluted, which could be changed to simplify the implementation.

- During the testing phase, the testers may discover omissions in the SRS or design that cause defects. For example, an enhancement to a software project may require that a new record type is to be added to one feature, but the requirements and design fail to specify how that record type is handled in another related feature. The programmers never implemented any handling for this new record type in the second feature because the design failed to indicate how that was to be handled.

- The users or stakeholders may discover during a design walkthrough, demo, user acceptance testing, or beta testing that the software does not fulfill their needs.

During the CCB meeting, the project manager explains the change to the rest of the CCB. Once the CCB is brought up to speed, it must determine what project work products will have to be changed. Each change will affect at least one work product that has already been approved—if this were not the case, the CCB would not have to meet because the change could be handled as part of the regular review process.

The CCB must evaluate every change that is requested. This ensures that nothing slips through the cracks, and that a real decision is made for each request. However, this could mean that at some very busy points in the project, the CCB must meet periodically—sometimes weekly or even daily. At each meeting, it may discuss many changes that have been submitted since the previous meeting.

It is important that when the CCB is being organized, the project manager makes sure that each member understands that this sort of time commitment may be necessary. These meetings are an important way for all of the CCB members to stay on top of the issues that come up during development. This knowledge is very valuable later on in the project when it is time to determine whether the software is ready for release (see Chapter 8).

Analyze the Impact of Each Change

It is vital that the project manager understand and manage all of the information produced in the change control process. While all of the project team members' opinions are necessary in evaluating the change, it is the project manager who owns the change, and who makes sure that it is properly understood and evaluated. This is generally a lot of work: the project manager needs to take the time to understand why each change is needed, what needs to be changed, and how much work it will be to make the change. His understanding must be complete enough that he can present this information at the CCB meeting.

The project manager who is responsible for guiding each change through the change control process. This is why it is important that the project manager be the one who updates the issue report to reflect both the effort that was estimated in the evaluation and the final decision of the CCB. And it is the project manager who is responsible for making sure that each CCB member is given enough information to understand the change.

During the change control process, the project manager works with the team to evaluate the impact. One effective way to do this is to use the Wideband Delphi estimation process (see Chapter 3). If this is done, the project manager can append the results of the Delphi meeting to the issue report and present them to the CCB for cost-benefit analysis. But while a full estimation may be necessary for large changes, there are many small changes that do not require the project manager to gather an estimation team and hold a meeting. For example, a change that amounts to a small bug fix may simply require that the project manager talk to the programmer responsible for that code and ask how long it will take to fix it.

There is some overlap here between the responsibility of the project manager and that of the QA team. Some QA engineers may question the need for the project manager to be so involved in updating specific issue reports in the defect tracking system—this is generally a task that is exclusively controlled by QA. This is true both when the issue is a defect and when it is a change; in both cases, the impact must be evaluated, to determine whether the change should be implemented or whether the defect should be fixed.

The reason the project manager is responsible for this is because he serves as a conduit for all of the information relevant to the change. By updating the issue report, he ensures that he has gathered all the information relevant to the change, and that all of the information is in one place. The issue report is still owned by QA, but it makes sense to have the project manager directly update it rather than having to sit down with the QA team each time a change is evaluated. As long as a member of the QA team on the CCB initiates each change, they will still be kept in the loop.

Introduce Software Requirements Carefully

There are plenty of books that tell us that poor requirements are the most common cause of software quality problems. Yet many project managers have had difficulty bootstrapping efforts within their own teams to implement better software requirements practices. Software requirements should make intuitive sense: before a team can build software, they need to know what to build. In practice, however, many project managers have found that it is difficult to convince their teams to adopt good software requirements engineering practices. This is especially true for certain kinds of projects:

- Small projects in which the programmer is confident that he understands all of the requirements already

- Projects in which "everybody" knows what the software is supposed to do

- Projects without a user interface (like batch processes or back-end calculation software)

- Any project considered "technical"— one in which one or more of the stakeholders is a programmer

In all these projects, there is an expectation that a programmer can make all of the decisions about the behavior of the software. It seems intuitive (but incorrect) that since the programmer can already decide on the details of the implementation, he should also have a grasp on what is being implemented. The programmer is often the most confident person in the organization about his own ability to do this, which the rest of the team and the stakeholders always find reassuring.

This is a difficult situation for any project manager. It's never a good idea to try to force the team to accept requirements (or any tool, technique, or practice). But when software requirements are the solution to the team's most pressing problems, it's up to the project manager to convince the team to adopt good requirements practices. Chapter 9 gives many examples of the kinds of problems a project manager may face, and suggests strategies to deal with those problems. With requirements, however, there are a few additional points that may make it easier for a project manager to convince the team to adopt good practices.

Sell the Designers and Programmers First

Software architects, designers, and programmers who are used to working with software requirements tend to find them so important that it's difficult to imagine working without them. But if they have never used requirements before, they instead tend to be resistant to working with them. To the uninitiated, working with requirements may sound restrictive and stifling. In organizations where this is the case, the problem is often compounded by senior managers who do not have as solid a grasp on how their software is developed as they should, and who will be very responsive to any complaints from their technical people. A few negative comments from key programmers can be enough to pull the plug on an entire requirements effort. Even worse, when an organization has not really embraced the idea of software requirements, there is a real danger that the programmers will simply say "yes" to any SRS that comes across their desks, only to ignore or change any requirements that they dislike when they actually build the software.

The key to using software requirements effectively is to help everyone in the organization understand how those requirements will help them build better software. A project manager who is looking to implement requirements should work to bring the designers and developers on board. If a designer feels threatened by the changes, the project manager should show him how the requirements define only the behavior of the software, and not the design. A programmer may object that her creativity is being stifled; maybe she can be shown that the requirements will help prevent the kinds of last-minute changes that cost her weeks of work and made a mess of her code on her last project.

It's not hard to communicate the benefits of change control to the engineering team, because the change control process addresses some of the team's most common complaints. Most software engineers who are working in an organization that does not have good requirements practices are always shooting at moving targets. Changing requirements are a daily fact of life, and even small projects feel like they rapidly spiral out of control because of uncontrolled changes. A project manager can offer to control these changes, so that the team can concentrate on building a good product once rather than rebuilding a poor one over and over again. Once the programmers have been convinced of that, it's not hard to show them how software requirements are clearly a means toward that end.

However, it is important that the project manager does not gloss over the fact that when a designer or programmer is working to a set of requirements, it creates a more restrictive environment than he is used to. This should be out in the open: otherwise, he will feel that the project manager is trying to hide the obvious, which can lead to distrust and reduced morale among the team members. Programmers can be convinced of the benefits as well. It's likely that interviewing users is the programmers' least favorite part of the job, and being handed an SRS that contains everything the users want, so that they do not have to spend time talking to them, is often enough of a trade-off to make up for a small reduction in freedom.

In the end, requirements are good for the designers and programmers, and it should not be too difficult for a project manager to help them understand that. Once the engineering team starts to see requirements engineering as a way for them to increase their quality, reduce their rework, and make their projects go much more smoothly, it is much easier to get the management of the organization on board.

Speak the Managers' Language

Building software without requirements is similar to building a house without blueprints. It's possible to start hammering nails into wood, and the builders will probably come up with some sort of structure that will stand on its own and provide shelter. But if those builders start hammering nails before the blueprints are done, it's almost impossible that they will end up building a house that matches the blueprints. But this doesn't stop managers from trying to get the programming team to start building the software before the requirements are complete.

Many managers do not understand why requirements engineering is important. All they see is people sitting around and writing a bunch of documents instead of writing code. It's not immediately obvious to them why the team is "wasting" so much time on this. The code has to be written, and they don't see why the programmers have to wait until they get these documents to begin writing it. It seems to them that the programmers can at least get started on writing *something*. For a lot of managers, it's very frustrating when programmers are not writing code—every day they see the team writing requirements is one more day that the programmers didn't get started building the software. When the designers and programmers are not sold on the idea of requirements engineering, there is little chance that anyone else in the organization will accept it.

Many managers don't speak the language of software engineering. When this is the case, any attempt to sell them on software requirements by giving a technical explanation about software behavior and quality attributes will cause their eyes to glaze over. Some managers are good at convincing engineers that they understand technical issues that are really beyond them; a project manager might walk away from this conversation thinking that no other person had agreed that the team should implement requirements engineering on a project. But this is probably the manager's reaction to any technical change suggested by a team member, and he will withdraw his "support" (or claim that he never understood it in the first place and never really agreed) at the first sign of friction between engineers.

The way to sell the managers on requirements engineering is to speak their language. Most senior managers who are in charge of making project decisions are most concerned with getting the product out the door faster, and with getting fewer calls from users who have found that the software does not do what they need it to do. The project manager who is trying to put the software requirements tools in place should show the manager how they can fix these very serious problems that have plagued past projects. The goal is not to drive a wedge between the programmers and the stakeholders and users. Rather, requirements help everyone reach the same goal.

A common complaint among stakeholders and users is that programmers have not taken the time to listen to them before starting in on building the software. If this goes unchecked in an organization for too long, people can start to see the programmers as cocky. A project manager working on selling the idea of requirements can look for examples of this in the organization. There are probably instances in the past when a programmer has assured a stakeholder or user that he understands exactly what she needs, only to go ahead and build something that only does half of what the stakeholder wanted, plus a bunch of stuff that doesn't make any sense at all. There may be a piece of software out in the organization that has a bunch of confusing buttons or menu options; it's possible that the intended users don't even know what they do. There may have been a rollout in the past where the users had to alter the way they did their work in order to accommodate the software. These are all advertisements for adding software requirements engineering activities to the next project, and the project manager can use them as examples of the kinds of problems that software requirements can fix.

Selling the idea of requirements to senior managers and decision-makers usually takes a lot of effort. The project manager will have to repeat herself many times. In many organizations, the managers do not really understand how the software gets built—they leave those "technical details" to the engineers. Luckily, software requirements engineering activities lend themselves to explanations in simple, layman's language.

It should make intuitive sense to a senior manager that the programmers are not mind-readers. It's likely that they have neither the time nor the inclination to sit down and interview everyone who may have something to add to the project. And the experts do not have time to make themselves available to the programmers for the entire length of the project. The solution is clearly to have someone sit down and talk to the people who need the software built. That person should be a software engineer capable of eliciting software requirements and building a feasible software requirements specification. Most managers should understand this on a "gut" level.

Diagnosing Software Requirements Problems

Project teams that have problems specifying the software requirements often find that their projects suffer from a few typical problems. Strangely, many programmers and project managers do not realize that they are problems at all. There is a common and mistaken belief that they are just characteristics of how software is typically developed. But when software teams adopt good requirements engineering practices, they find that these problems are greatly reduced, and that their projects go much more smoothly.

Iteration Abuse

Iteration, or the repetition of a particular task or activity with the goal of improving its main work product, is a practice employed by many programmers. There are several popular development methodologies (Extreme Programming and Rational Unified Process, for example—see Chapter 12) that rely on iterative development. These methodologies use iteration effectively, by planning and executing a series of small steps that build on previous iterations to produce a series of intermediate builds; each successive build adds new functionality to a previous build. Each build is intended to be production quality, and is fully tested. Changes are controlled by having each new iteration concentrate on adding new functionality, rather than making many changes to existing behavior.

However, many software teams abuse iteration. They do not use successive iterations to add new functionality to a build that is already production quality. Instead, the iterations are meant to be a sort of guessing game. The first iteration is presented to users and stakeholders, who are expected to tell the programmers what's wrong with it. The programmers then go back, fix those things, and deliver a second build, which the users and stakeholders again correct. This is expected to continue until the software does everything that the users and stakeholders need it to do.

This sort of iteration makes intuitive sense to everyone involved. The programmers like it because they can dive right into the project and do what they do best: program. And it feels right to the users and stakeholders as well, because it's much less work for them than sitting down and really thinking about what they need out of the software. All they have to do is play with the demo versions and give their opinions.

Unfortunately, this is all too good to be true. The first iteration is easy to deliver—expectations are low, and people are excited to get their hands on a build so quickly and to give their input. The next iterations seem to be doing their job, and the software does look like it's starting to get better. But as the software gets more complex, each iteration takes longer and longer to do. There seem to be more bugs in each new build. The programmers find that they have to take more time to rip out things that they put in earlier. The code starts to degenerate into an unmaintainable mess because the programmers keep patching and repatching code that they should have built differently in the first place. The iterations finally end, but not with fully working software. Rather, the users and stakeholders get increasingly fed up with long delays and with buggy software that doesn't do what they need. They eventually settle on a build that is close enough to something that fulfills their needs; they can concoct workarounds for any remaining problems that keep them from getting their work done.

This sort of "iterative" development falls apart because software is difficult to change. After an object or function is written, it is generally used elsewhere in the code. The objects or functions that reference it, in turn, are called from other objects or functions, and so on.

Any changes made to one function can ripple through the rest of the software, causing many unforeseen problems. Even a minor change in the basic behavior of the software usually requires that the programmers make extensive alterations to its design. As the changes pile up, they become increasingly awkward because the programmer needs to patch existing code without breaking it. Each additional design change requires another layer of patching, and most of those patches require some compromise between implementing new behavior and not breaking existing behavior. This is a messy and difficult way to code, and tends to introduce many defects and delays after a few iterations.

Had someone written down a description of the behavior of the software before the programmers started building it, many of these iterations could have been avoided. It's much easier to change the behavior of the software on paper than it is to change the code. By adopting a highly iterative software requirements engineering process, the project team can identify most of the changes before a single line of code is written. They may still have to make changes to the software, but those changes will be much smaller and therefore much less risky.

Scope Creep

Many software projects have been driven to failure by poorly controlled changes. Typically, one of the project team members, users, stakeholders, or decision-makers sees a change that he thinks ought to be implemented. The change seems "small," so programmers begin altering the software to include it. But the change turns out to be difficult to implement, and the entire project is thrown off track. This problem is usually referred to as *scope creep*, because the scope of the project slowly drifts over the course of many incremental changes.

Scope creep is so common that many project managers don't realize that it's a problem at all. They feel that refusing any change request would be considered "inflexible" by others in the organization, and that any project manager or team member who refuses to make a change is not being a team player. But in a team that does not control changes, progress on the project starts to slow as the changes pile up. At every status meeting, the team reports that they are 90% done—but it seems that they have been 90% done for the last 3 months, and they don't seem to be making any headway on that last 10%. Terms like "quagmire" and "death march" get tossed around. The project plan is a joke, a product of wishful thinking that was abandoned months ago. When projects finally do deliver, it feels less like the team successfully met their goal than they finally crawled out from under a suffocating mess.

In a project like that, the programmers usually understand the problem. They can point to portions of the code that had to be rewritten several times in order to accommodate changes. The team members know that had they been asked to do the correct project the first time, they could have built it much more quickly and easily, but that it took many changes to finally arrive at the product they have now. And nobody even wants to think about maintenance—the code is a mess, because it had to be patched and hacked so many times.

To many people, this is all just a fact of life: it's the reality of how software is developed. They feel that changes happen, and that there's really nothing that can be done about them. But it doesn't have to be that way. As with iteration abuse, if more of these changes can be identified on paper during requirements elicitation and reviews, by the time the programming team starts building the software they are much closer to the goal and will have to deal with far fewer changes.

However, there will still be requests for changes, and those changes should be controlled using a change control process. One reason changes are easy to sneak through is because it's often easy to describe a difficult change using simple language. It's human nature to be accommodating, so the programmers are willing to incorporate that change because it seems like it would be easy to implement. The change control process requires that a description of the change be written down, and that engineering team members take the time to estimate how much effort the change would require. This forces the project's decision-makers to decide if the change is worth the effort. If it is, the schedule is updated. But many changes that seem "simple" turn out to be much more involved than the person asking for them realizes, and many changes turn out not to be worth the extra effort. If the changes are starting to make it harder to develop the software, this will cause each additional change to have a greater impact, which in turn will make it less likely to be approved. Even if the changes are all approved, the team does not have to fight against an unrealistic deadline to get them done—instead, the project plan is updated, and it remains realistic.

CHAPTER SEVEN

Design and Programming

THERE'S A FAMOUS QUOTE ATTRIBUTED TO **KENT BECK,** a widely respected software engineer who's responsible for many advances in the field: "I'm not a great programmer; I'm just a good programmer with great habits." This chapter is about introducing some of those great habits. A good programmer who adopts these habits will build better software.

Programmers spend their time designing and building software, and all of their project work revolves around the source code. But many programming teams find that they lose control of their own code. Sometimes they lose track of the changes that they make; new additions might occasionally disappear, and old bugs routinely pop up. They might lose control of the design of the code, finding that no matter how much care they put into designing the software well, they still end up with messy code that's difficult to maintain. Some programmers have never known any other way, and don't realize that these problems can be eased. A project manager can improve the code by helping the team adopt good programming practices.

While many development problems originate outside of the programming team, there are some basic changes that the programmers can make that will improve the quality of the code they produce. Most teams, even ones with skilled and talented programmers, are vulnerable to the same design and programming problems. These problems can be addressed with a few basic tools and techniques—which can often be put in place entirely within the programming team, without involving anyone else in the organization.

A programming team that adopts the tools and techniques in this chapter will avoid many common project pitfalls. This chapter only covers their most fundamental use—there are many advanced operations that can be done with all of them that are not covered here. With these practices in place, the team will find that they have a much firmer grasp on their own source code. If these tools are not yet in place, working with the programmers to implement them should be high on the project manager's priority list.

Much of this chapter is an introduction to refactoring and unit testing. Many experienced programmers will recognize that refactoring and unit testing are important skills that require practice, reading, and training. We tried to write this book in such a way that someone could read each chapter and immediately use the tools and techniques on a project. Unlike the other practices, however, we don't expect the reader to be able to fully develop unit tests or refactor code after reading this chapter, any more than we would expect to be able to give a thorough presentation of object-oriented programming in one section of a chapter. Instead, our goal is to give the reader an introduction to the theory and practice of both refactoring and unit testing, illustrated with simple examples of each.

> **NOTE**
>
> We encourage anyone interested in developing unit testing and refac-
> toring skills to read these excellent books:
>
> - *Pragmatic Unit Testing in Java with JUnit* or *Pragmatic Unit
>   Testing in C# with NUnit* by Andy Hunt and Dave Thomas
>   (The Pragmatic Programmers, 2004).
> - *Refactoring: Improving the Design of Existing Code* by Martin
>   Fowler (Addison Wesley, 1999), and Martin Fowler's
>   web site *http://www.refactoring.com.*

Review the Design

In many project teams, the programmers begin coding as soon as they have a software requirements specification that everyone agrees on. Typically, the first programming tasks usually involve building a user interface that supports each use case, and creating an object model that implements each of the functional requirements.

The designers and programmers have several options:

- The programmers can simply start building the code and create the objects and user interface elements.

- Designers can build a user interface prototype to demonstrate to the users, stakeholders, and the rest of the team. Any code used to develop the prototype is typically thrown away once the design has been finalized.

- Pictures, flow charts, data flow diagrams, database design diagrams, and other visual tools can be used to determine aspects of the design and architecture.

- An object model can be developed on paper, either using code, simple class diagrams, or Unified Modeling Language (UML) diagrams.

- A written design specification is written, which includes some or all of these tools.

In order to ensure that the software is designed well, the project manager works with the team during the creation of the work breakdown structure and estimates (see Chapter 3) to determine which of these options is appropriate for the project. The design tasks should be estimated and included in the project schedule; this requires that the team agree on a single design approach from the outset of the project.

The design tasks should always include reviews, even when there is no written design specification. If the programmers dive immediately into the user interface design, they should hold a walkthrough with the users. This may involve taking screenshots of the UI and turning them into a slide presentation, or it may mean that the programmers give a thorough demonstration of the user interface.

Any written documentation should be reviewed and, if possible, inspected. However, it is important that the reviews and inspections reach the correct audience. Many users who have important input for the user interface may be uninterested or confused by object models and UML diagrams. If all of these elements are bundled into a single design specification, it is important that the scope of each review is clear—it's reasonable to have individual people review only the part of the design specification that they are interested in.

Version Control with Subversion

The purpose of a *version control system* is to bring a project's source code under control.* The main element of the version control system is the *repository*, a database or directory that contains each of the files that make up the system. Bringing a group of files under control means that someone can pick a point at any time in the history of the project and see exactly what those files looked like at the time. It is always possible to find the latest version of any file by retrieving it from the repository. Changing a file will not unexpectedly overwrite any previous changes to that file; any change can be rolled back, so no work will accidentally be overwritten. Modern version control systems can identify exactly what changed between two different versions of a file, and allow the team to roll back those changes—even if they were made a long time ago, and the affected files have had many modifications since then.

This is very important for source code. When source code files are stored in a shared folder, for example, it is easy for changes to be lost when more than one programmer is working on the software. Even a single programmer, working on source code that resides in a folder on his computer, can run into problems. He might make a large change, only to realize that he needs to roll it back. Or he may find that he's got several copies of the code on his hard drive and laptop, and that each of them contains a different set of changes that all need to be integrated.

Subversion is a free and open source version control system. It is available from *http://subversion.tigris.org* for many operating systems and platforms, including Linux, BSD, Solaris, BeOS, OS/2, Mac OS X, and Windows. Subversion provides many advanced features for bringing source code under control, but it takes only a few basic commands for a programming team to use a simple version control repository effectively.

The examples below are based on Version 1.2, the latest version available at the time of this writing. The remainder of this chapter assumes that this version (or later) is installed on the programmer's machine. The Subversion installation procedure does not install a graphical user interface—all functions are accessed through command-line programs. There are graphical utilities and web interfaces that work with Subversion, including TortoiseSVN (*http://tortoisesvn.tigris.org*), ViewCVS (*http://viewcvs.sourceforge.net*), and SmartSVN (*http://www.smartcvs.com/smartsvn*).

---

* Some people use the term "configuration management" in place of "version control." We've selected the narrower term because in some software engineering organizations, "configuration management" includes not only version control (identifying baselines and controlling changes to work products), but also tracking change requests, establishing configuration management records, and performing configuration audits.

This is the only section in this book in which a specific software package is recommended. However, Subversion is not the only option for version control. Other popular version control systems include:

- CVS (*http://www.nongnu.org/cvs*)

- RCS (*http://www.gnu.org/software/rcs*)

- Arch (*http://www.gnu.org/software/gnu-arch/*)

- Aegis (*http://aegis.sourceforge.net/*)

- Perforce (*http://www.perforce.com/*)

- Visual SourceSafe (*http://msdn.microsoft.com/vstudio/previous/ssafe/*)

Multiple People Can Work on One File

Programming teams that do not use a modern version control system usually have a rule that only one person at a time can work on any given file. Sometimes this rule is enforced by using an antiquated version control system, which allows only one person to check out a file. Some teams use a master folder to store all of the source code, and individual programmers must rename files that they are using or move them temporarily to a "checkout" folder.

There are version control systems that essentially function as an automated checkout folder. A system like this requires that a programmer check out a file from the repository before modifying it, and keeps track of the checkout status of each file in the repository. The system prevents anyone from modifying any file until it is checked back in. This is known as the "lock-modify-unlock" model, and it is very intuitive to many programmers. However, it is a very restrictive way to manage code, and can cause delays and problems for the team.

One worst-case scenario that some teams encounter is a schedule delay caused by having many programming tasks that must occur on a single piece of code, when that code can be updated by only a single person at a time. For example, programmers might run into trouble when they must add behavior to a complex window in the software that contains many tabs and controls, all of which reside in a single file. If they are only using a folder to store the code, only one person can work on the file at a time. Even if the modifications themselves are relatively straightforward, this process could take a lot of time, and may even require a senior developer to be pulled in to perform the work as quickly as possible (which could lead to extra delays because he can't be assigned to any other task until this one is done.)

When a team has to work with large files that contain a lot of code that is not under control, or that is checked into a lock-modify-unlock version control system, it runs into "unavoidable" delays because only one person can edit each file at a time. Adopting a modern version control system like Subversion is one effective way to fix this problem. Subversion allows multiple people to work on a single file at the same time, using an alternative model called "copy-modify-merge." In this model, a file can be checked out any number of times. When a programmer wants to update the repository with his changes, he retrieves all changes that have occurred to the checked out files and reconciles any of them that conflict with changes he made before updating the repository. (See below for details about how copy-modify-merge works.)

Many programmers who have never worked with a copy-modify-merge version control system will find it counterintuitive. The idea that multiple people can use their own working copies to work on a snapshot of the code may seem like an invitation to disaster. It seems intuitive to him that programmers will step on one another's toes all the time, constantly overwriting changes and eventually creating an unmanageable mess.

In practice, the opposite is true: it turns out that it is usually easy to merge changes, and that very few changes conflict. Code is almost always built in such a way that the functionality is highly encapsulated in functions. And even within individual functions, there are small, independent blocks of code. Even if two neighboring blocks are altered at the same time, it is rare for a conflict to be introduced.

Copy-modify-merge is very efficient. Teams lose much more time from schedule bottlenecks caused by waiting for files that are checked out than they do from trying to figure out how to merge the changes. Giving multiple people the ability to merge changes into a shared repository is an important way to eliminate those bottlenecks. Version control systems based on the copy-modify-merge model have been used for years on many projects. This is especially true for large teams or teams in which the members are distributed over a large geographical area—their work would grind to a halt waiting for people to check code back in.

Understanding Subversion

The Subversion repository contains a set of files laid out in a tree structure (similar to the file systems in most operating systems), with folders that contain files and other folders, as well as links or shortcuts between files. The main difference is that the Subversion file system tracks every change that is made to each file stored in it. There are multiple versions of each file saved in the repository. The files in the repository are stored on disk in a database, and can only be accessed using the Subversion software.

A Subversion repository has a revision number. This revision number gets incremented every time a change is made to the repository—this way, no revision number is used more than once. The standard convention for writing revision numbers is a lowercase "r" followed by the number of the revision; all output from Subversion will adhere to this convention.

The Subversion repository keeps track of every change that is made to every file stored in it. Even if a file is modified by adding or removing lines, or if that file is removed entirely, all previous revisions still can be accessed by date or number. Subversion can also generate a list of differences between any two revisions of a file.

For example, consider a repository that contains Revision 23 of the file *cookies.txt* in Table 7-1, which was checked in on March 4.

TABLE 7-1. cookies.txt r23 as it looked on March 4

```
2 1/4 cups flour    1 tsp baking soda    1/2 tsp salt
1 cup butter        3/4 cup sugar        3/4 cup brown sugar
1 tsp vanilla       2 eggs               2 cups chocolate chips

Mix butter and sugars. Beat until creamy. Add vanilla. Beat in
eggs, one at a time. Mix in rest of ingredients. Drop by
spoonfuls on cookie sheets. Bake at 350 degrees.
```

Subversion uses global revision numbers, which means that the revision number applies to the entire tree in the repository. Any time that a change is made to any file in the repository, the global revision number of the repository is incremented. Table 7-1 shows a file as it looked on March 4, when the repository was at Revision 23. Some people may refer to this as "Revision 23 of *cookies.txt*," but what they really mean is "*cookies.txt* as it appeared in Revision 23 of the repository." If someone updates a different file in the repository on March 5, the repository's revision number will increment to 24. When that happens, there is now an r24 of *cookies.txt*—it just happens to be identical to r23.

Now, let's say that time has passed since the file was checked in. It's May 13, and other people have added several other files to this repository, so the repository is now at r46. If someone (let's call her Alice) decides to check out *cookies.txt* and add the line that calls for chopped nuts, when she commits her change the repository increments to r47, and this revision, r47, will contain the new version of *cookies.txt* in Table 7-2.

TABLE 7-2. cookies.txt r47 committed by Alice on May 13 (with chopped nuts added)

```
2 1/4 cups flour    1 tsp baking soda    1/2 tsp salt
1 cup butter        3/4 cup sugar        3/4 cup brown sugar
1 tsp vanilla       2 eggs               2 cups chocolate chips
1 cup chopped nuts

Mix butter and sugars. Beat until creamy. Add vanilla. Beat in eggs, one
at a time. Mix in rest of ingredients. Drop by spoonfuls on cookie
sheets. Bake at 350 degrees.
```

The next time someone checks the tree that contains *cookies.txt* out of the repository, they will get r47 of the file. However, they can specifically ask for a previous version in one of several ways:

- Specifically ask for r23 of *cookies.txt*.

- Ask for any revision of *cookies.txt* between, say, 21 and 43. For example, requesting r36 will retrieve the revision associated with r36 of the repository—and since the file has not changed since r23, this is the revision that will be retrieved.

- Request a copy of *cookies.txt* as it looked on April 6.

Any of these requests will yield the version of the recipe without the nuts in Table 7-1. Even if the file is later deleted from the Subversion repository, previous revisions are still available and can be retrieved by revision number or date. (This means that the file is never permanently deleted from the repository. When a file is "deleted," the repository simply no longer lists it in the current revision. If a user checks out an old revision from before the file was removed, the version of the file associated with that revision is still available.)

Check Out Code into a Working Copy

Before a Subversion repository can be accessed, it must be checked out. Checking out a repository simply means retrieving a snapshot of the repository and copying it to the user's local machine. The repository is not altered in any way when files are checked out. The local copy of the repository is called a *working copy*. This is the core of the copy-modify-merge model: any changes that the user needs to make are done in the working copy, which must be brought up to date before it can be checked back in.*

Everybody gets their own working copy; one person can have any number of working copies. When files are checked out from a repository, the Subversion client creates a new working copy for those files. Usually a programmer will check out only one copy of a given directory or tree at a time, but there are occasions when a programmer will have several working copies that contain different snapshots of different parts of the repository. (Only directories or trees can be checked out—Subversion does not allow a programmer to check out a single file in a directory.)

There can be many working copies of the same code, even on the same machine. Each working copy keeps track of both who checked out the files and when they were checked out. The user can retrieve the differences between the working copy and the revision that he had originally checked out at any time, even if the user's machine does not currently have access to the server from which the working copy was checked out.

Additionally, a programmer can check out all of a repository, or just part of it. The checkout can include a single folder or an entire branch including all subfolders. (It can also include the entire repository, but in Subversion this is almost never done, because it can cause an enormous amount of data to be retrieved.) When the files are checked out, the latest revision of each file is copied to the working copy. When the programmer looks in the working copy, she sees all of the files and folders that she checked out, plus another hidden folder called *.svn*. This folder contains all of the data that Subversion uses to check for differences and to keep track of the state of the working copy.

The programmer edits the files in the working copy, and, when she is satisfied that the files in the working copy are ready, she can *commit* them back to the repository. It is only during the commit that the repository is updated to look like the working copy. The commit is the step that the programmer takes to finalize the changes and integrate them back into the source code stored in the repository. When someone commits changes to the repository, Subversion updates only those files that have changed since the working copy was checked out. Once changes have been committed, they will be accessible to anyone looking at the repository.

---

* Some people refer to this as the *sandbox* model—each person gets to play in his own sandbox, and only has to clean up later when it's time to merge the code back. They will often refer to Subversion's working copy as a sandbox.

Subversion performs an *atomic commit*, which means that either all of the changes go into the repository completely, or none of them make it at all. This way, the programmer does not need to worry about only half of the changes making it into the repository. (Some older version control systems suffered from that problem.)

Since multiple people can each check out their own working copies, they can all work on the same file simultaneously. There is no limit to the number of times a file can be checked out at once; any part of the repository can be checked out into multiple working copies on multiple machines at the same time. If several people have files checked out of a repository, it is likely that there are earlier versions of some files in some of their working copies, and later versions in other ones.

If the repository has not changed since the working copy was checked out, then the user can simply commit the change, and Subversion will update the repository. However, if the repository has changed, Subversion will not allow the user to commit the changes just yet—it will tell the user that the working copy is out-of-date. At this point, it is up to the user to bring the working copy up-to-date by telling Subversion to update the working copy. Subversion will then retrieve any changes that have been committed to the repository since the working copy was checked out.

Often, most of the changes that have been committed to the repository since the working copy was checked out are *mergeable*, meaning that none of the lines that changed in the repository have changed in the working copy. When this happens, Subversion will update all of the files in the working copy to reflect all of the changes that have been committed to the repository.

However, if a *conflict* occurs, it is up to the user to resolve it. A conflict occurs when two people (let's call the second person Bob) introduce different changes to the same line in the same file in their separate working copies. A conflict occurs when Alice and Bob both need to make different changes to the same lines in the same file. They both check out the file and make changes to it, and Alice commits it back to the repository first. But when Bob attempts to commit the change to the repository, Subversion discovers that there is a conflict. That conflict must be resolved in Bob's working copy before it can be committed to the repository.

To illustrate this idea, consider what would happen to the previous example (*cookies.txt* r47 in Table 7-2) if Alice committed her changes under different circumstances. Suppose she checked out r23 (see Table 7-1), but Bob checked in r38 (shown in Table 7-3) before she could commit her changes.

TABLE 7-3. *cookies.txt r38 committed by Bob on April 26 (with M&Ms added)*

```
2 1/4 cups flour      1 tsp baking soda      1/2 tsp salt
1 cup butter          3/4 cup sugar          3/4 cup brown sugar
1 tsp vanilla         2 eggs                 2 cups chocolate chips
1 cup chopped M&Ms

Mix butter and sugars. Beat until creamy. Add vanilla. Beat in eggs, one at a time.
Mix in rest of ingredients. Drop by spoonfuls on cookie sheets. Bake at 350
degrees.
```

This version contains a change: Bob added chopped M&Ms to the recipe. This change occurred on April 26, a few weeks before Alice checked in r47. So when it was committed, Subversion did not complain; at the time, there were no conflicts. It simply allowed the change and was able to update the repository without requiring any input from the user.

When May 13 rolls around and Alice tries to commit r47 in Table 7-2, Subversion discovers that the working copy is out of date (because the revision number of the repository is greater than it was when the working copy was checked out). She updates the working copy to incorporate any changes. When she does this, Subversion detects the conflict in line 4: the version in her working copy contains chopped nuts, while the version in the repository contains M&Ms. Alice will then be required to decide which version of that line should be kept; once she makes that decision, the file can be committed to the repository. (See below for more details about how she specifies this.)

This is how the working copy allows two people to check out the same file, and even alter the same lines in that file. They did not have to coordinate with each other, and the first person was never even aware that a conflict occurred. It's up to each person to resolve the individual conflicts that arise. What's more, a full audit trail is available, so if it turns out that someone made the wrong choice, then that choice can be undone later and it will be possible to figure out who made the mistake.

Access the Subversion Repository Using a URL

A Subversion repository exists on a computer as a folder. It's easy to recognize a Subversion repository: it usually contains subfolders named *conf, dav, db, hooks,* and *locks.* These folders contain different important elements of the repository: for example, the *conf* folder contains configuration files, the *db* folder contains a database that stores all of the files and revision history, and the *hooks* folder contains scripts that can be triggered automatically when Subversion performs certain actions.

There are two commands that are installed with Subversion that programmers will typically use to access and maintain the repository. The repository administration tool svnadmin performs actions directly on a repository. It can create a new repository, verify its contents, make a copy of an entire repository, dump the repository to a portable format, recover from a database error, and perform other administrative tasks. svnadmin always works on a local directory—when a user executes it, the repository is always passed as a path to a local folder, in whatever format the operating system expects.

The command-line client tool svn is the main interface that most programmers use to check out and update files in the repository. The svn command-line client can access a repository using any of several different methods: accessing the folder directly on the hard drive or a shared drive, connecting to the svnserve server, using svnserve server over SSH, or using Apache to serve the repository via HTTP or HTTPS.

The svn client uses a URL instead of a simple path, in order to differentiate between the different kinds of access methods. This way, the programmer using it does not need to change the way she works in order to accommodate different kinds of access methods. Table 7-4 shows the schema for each access method.

TABLE 7-4. Repository access URLs

(reprinted with permission from Version Control with Subversion*)*

Schema	Access method
file:///	Direct repository access (on local disk) Example: file:///usr/svn/repos/
http://	Access via WebDAV protocol to Subversion-aware Apache server
https://	Same as http://, but with SSL encryption
svn://	Access via custom protocol to an svnserve server
svn+ssh://	Same as svn://, but through an SSH tunnel

For the most part, Subversion's URLs use the standard syntax, allowing server names and port numbers to be specified as part of the URL. One difference is that the file:/// access method can be used only for accessing a local repository—if a server name is given, it should always be file://localhost/. It should always be followed by the full path of the repository:

```
file:///usr/local/svn/repos
```

If the repository contains folders, those folders can be appended to the repository. (These are the virtual folders contained within the repository, not the physical folder that contains the repository database.) For example, to access */recipes/cookies.txt* in the repository */usr/local/svn/repos*, the client must be passed the following URL:

```
file:///usr/local/svn/repos/recipes/cookies.txt
```

The file:/// URL scheme on Windows platforms uses the unofficially "standard" syntax for specifying a drive letter by using either X: or X|. Note that a URL uses ordinary slashes, even though the native (non-URL) form of a path on Windows uses backslashes. It is important to use quotes so that Windows does not interpret the vertical bar character as a pipe:

```
C:\>svn checkout file:///C:/Documents and Settings/Ed/Desktop/repo
C:\>svn checkout "file:///D|/svn/repository/path/to/file"
```

Most of the Subversion examples in this chapter will use UNIX-style command syntax and pathnames.

Create a Repository

The Subversion installation procedure does not create a repository—that must be done using the svnadmin command.

Use svnadmin create to create an empty repository:

```
svnadmin create REPOSITORY_PATH
```

The svnadmin command requires that the repository path be specified in the operating system's native format. On a UNIX system, the following commands will create a repository in the */usr/local/svn/repos/* directory:

```
$ mkdir /usr/local/svn
$ svnadmin create /usr/local/svn/repos
```

On a Windows system, svnadmin uses a Windows-style path to create the repository. The following commands will create a repository in the *c:\svn\repos* directory. Note that this is a raw path, and not a file:/// URL:

```
C:\>mkdir c:\svn

C:\>svnadmin create c:\svn\repos
```

A shared folder on a network is all it takes to set up a repository that multiple programmers can use. A single programmer can do the same on her own machine to store her own work in a local repository.

Once the empty repository is created, an initial set of files can be added to it using the svn import command, which allows files to be added to a repository without checking it out:

```
svn import [PATH] URL
```

There are several ways that the directories in a repository can be structured. One easy way to do it is to have a root-level folder for each project. Each project folder contains three subfolders: *trunk, tags,* and *branches.* The working version of the source code is stored in the *trunk* folder. (The other two folders are reserved for more advanced version control activities, which are beyond the scope of this book.)

For example, to import a project called *hello-world* that contains two files, *hello-world.c* and *hello-world.h,* they should be put into a folder:

```
$ mkdir tempimport
$ mkdir tempimport/hello-world
$ mkdir tempimport/hello-world/trunk
$ mkdir tempimport/hello-world/tags
$ mkdir tempimport/hello-world/branches
```

[copy hello-world.c and hello-world.h into the import/hello-world/trunk directory]

```
$ svn import tempimport/ file:///usr/local/svn/repos/ -m "Initial import"
Adding         tempimport/hello-world
Adding         tempimport/hello-world/trunk
Adding         tempimport/hello-world/trunk/hello-world.c
Adding         tempimport/hello-world/trunk/hello-world.h
Adding         tempimport/hello-world/branches
Adding         tempimport/hello-world/tags

Committed revision 1.
```

Note that a log message reading "Initial import" was passed to svn using the -m flag. If this is omitted, Subversion will launch the default editor to edit the log message. The environment variable SVN_EDITOR can be used to change the default editor. (Many Windows users prefer to set this variable to notepad.)

The Subversion repository is now ready for use. Additional files can be added either by using the svnadmin import command or by checking out a branch of the repository and using the svn add command.

Share the Repository

A Subversion repository can be accessed by programmers using any of the access methods listed in Table 7-4. The simplest way to do this is to use a shared folder and the `file:///` URL schema. However, this is not secure and may be problematic to share on an intranet or over the Internet.

Running a server is very straightforward using the svnserve program. Many people think that the word "server" is synonymous with "administrative headache." In fact, setting up and running a Subversion server is simple, and can be done on any machine where a repository is installed. The following command will run a read-only server:

```
$ svnserve -d -r /usr/local/svn/repos/
```

It works equally well on a Windows platform:

```
C:\>svnserve -d -r c:\svn\repository\
```

If this is running on a machine called mybox.example.com, the repository can be accessed using the URL svn://mybox.example.com. (Note: At the time of this writing, svnserve does not work with Windows 95/98/ME.)

By default, the server is read-only, which means that it only allows users to retrieve files, not to commit changes. However, it does not take much work to turn on password authentication. First a password file must be created in the *conf* folder in the Subversion repository. In this example, the file *passwords.txt* contains the following lines:

```
[users]
andrew = mypassword
jenny = anotherpw
```

Then the following lines must be added to the end of svnserve.conf in the same folder:

```
[general]
anon-access = read
auth-access = write
password-db = passwords.txt
```

Now when the svnserve command listed above is executed, it will run a server that supports authentication. The username and password can be passed to svn on the command-line with the --username and --password flags. When the repository is checked out, the working copy remembers the authentication information, so the username and password only need to be supplied when files are checked out.

```
$ svn checkout svn://servername/trunk --username andrew --password mypassword
A  trunk/hello-world.c
A  trunk/hello-world.h
Checked out revision 1.
```

Note that in this example, since no destination folder name is given, it checks out the working copy into a folder named *trunk*, which corresponds to the path given in the URL.

A third way to share files is using svnserve tunneled over SSH. All that is required here is that Subversion be installed on a computer that is running an SSH server. A programmer just needs to pass the correct URL schema to svn. Subversion establishes an SSH connection and executes svnserve on the server to connect to the specified repository. Note that this example uses the abbreviation co on the command line:

```
$ svn co svn+ssh://user@server/usr/local/svn/repos/hello-world/trunk/ hello-world
Password: *****
A  hello-world/hello-world.c
A  hello-world/hello-world.h
Checked out revision 1.
```

The http:// and https:// URL schemas require that an Apache server be set up to work with Subversion using WebDAV and mod_svn. (Configuring an Apache server to support access to a Subversion repository is beyond the scope of this book.)

The Subversion Basic Work Cycle

The authors of *Version Control with Subversion* (O'Reilly) recommend a basic work cycle that programmers use on a day-to-day basis to do their work. This work cycle is described in the script in Table 7-5.

TABLE 7-5. Subversion basic work cycle script

Name	Subversion basic work cycle
Purpose	Programmers use this work cycle for their day-to-day programming tasks.
Summary	Subversion has numerous features and options, bells, and whistles, but most programmers use only the most important ones in the course of a day's work.
Work Products	*Input* Source code in a Subversion repository *Output* A new revision of the source code has been added to the repository.
Entry Criteria	The programmer needs to modify code in the repository.
Basic Course of Events	1. Update the working copy of the code using svn update. 2. Make changes to the code by altering the files in the working copy and using svn add, svn delete, svn move, and svn copy. 3. Examine all changes that were made using svn status and svn diff. 4. Use svn update to incorporate any changes that were made to the repository since the working copy was checked out. Resolve changes made by other people since the working copy was checked out by using svn resolved. 5. Commit the changes by using svn commit.
Alternative Paths	1. In Step 1, if there is no working copy yet, a new copy is checked out by using svn checkout. 2. In Step 3, changes can be undone by using svn revert. This does not alter the repository, only the working copy. 3. The programmer can discard all changes in the working copy by simply never committing them to the repository and deleting the working copy.
Exit Criteria	The repository is updated with the modified code.

Update the working copy of the code

When a programmer needs to modify the code for a project, the first thing to do is to bring his working copy up to date so that it reflects all the changes that are in the latest revision. If he does not yet have a working copy, he can check one out of the repository with the svn checkout command.

The programmer supplies the URL to the repository and, optionally, a path to check it out into. If no path is specified, Subversion makes a new subdirectory in the current directory and checks it out there. The following action will check out the "trunk" branch from the example above:

```
$ svn checkout svn://servername/hello-world/trunk hello-world --username andrew
A  hello-world/trunk
A  hello-world/trunk/hello-world.c
A  hello-world/trunk/hello-world.h
A  hello-world/branches
A  hello-world/tags
Checked out revision 1.
```

Since the username andrew was given during the checkout, the working copy will remember that username. Before any changes are committed to the repository, it will ask the user for a password. To avoid this, the --password flag can be used to specify the password. (It is important for the URL to contain the *trunk* folder—otherwise, Subversion will grab a copy of every branch and tag in the repository, which could be an enormous amount of data.) The third parameter passed to the svn command is the checkout folder—in this case, the user specified *hello-world* in order to check out the contents of the trunk into a folder called *hello-world*. Without this parameter, Subversion would instead check out the working copy into a folder called *trunk*.

The svn update command brings the working copy up-to-date. If someone has committed the file hello-world.c since it was checked out and that file has not been altered in the working copy, the following command will update it in the working copy:

```
$ svn update hello-world
U  hello-world/trunk/hello-world.c
Updated to revision 2.
```

The svn update command can also be called from anywhere inside the working copy. In that case, the path should be omitted from the command line:

```
$ cd hello-world/trunk
$ svn update
U  hello-world.c
Updated to revision 2.
```

The letter next to hello-world.c is a code to indicate what action Subversion performed for that file:

- A for a file that was added to the working copy
- U for a file that was updated in the working copy

- D for a file that was deleted

- R for a file that was replaced (meaning that the file was deleted and a new one with the same name was added—which will be considered a new file with a distinct revision history)

- G for a file that was changed and those changes were successfully merged into the working copy

- C for a file that could not be merged because of conflicting changes

Make changes to the code

Once the working copy is up to date with the latest revision, the programmer can make changes. Generally, these changes will be done using whatever editor or IDE the programming team has always used. Subversion does not require that the working copy is up to date in order for the user to make changes. The repository will generally change while the user is making changes; the programmer will merge these changes into the working copy before committing it back to the repository.

Sometimes files need to be added. For example, the programmer might add a file called *Makefile* to the *hello-world* project. Subversion won't recognize the file if it is simply added, so the programmer must also let Subversion know that the file is there:

```
$ cd hello-world/trunk
$ svn add Makefile
A          Makefile
```

This tells Subversion that the file Makefile has been added to the working copy. The programmer must commit the working copy in order to add the file to the repository. The delete, copy, and move commands all work in a similar manner (see Table 7-6).

TABLE 7-6. Commands to make changes to the working copy
(reprinted with permission from Version Control with Subversion*)*

svn add foo
Schedule file, directory, or symbolic link *foo* to be added to the repository. When you next commit, *foo* will become a child of its parent directory. Note that if *foo* is a directory, everything underneath *foo* will be scheduled for addition. If you only want to add *foo* itself, pass the --non-recursive (-N) switch.
svn delete foo
Schedule file, directory, or symbolic link *foo* to be deleted from the repository. If *foo* is a file or link, it is immediately deleted from your working copy. If *foo* is a directory, it is not deleted, but Subversion schedules it for deletion. When you commit your changes, *foo* will be removed from your working copy and the repository.
svn copy foo bar
Create a new item bar as a duplicate of *foo*. *bar* is automatically scheduled for addition. When bar is added to the repository on the next commit, its copy history is recorded (as having originally come from *foo*). svn copy does not create intermediate directories.
svn move foo bar
This command is exactly the same as running svn copy foo bar; svn delete foo. That is, bar is scheduled for addition as a copy of *foo*, and *foo* is scheduled for removal. svn move does not create intermediate directories.

Examine all changes

When the programmer is ready to commit all of his changes to the repository, he should use the svn status command to ensure that his working copy contains only the changes he intends.

```
$ svn status hello-world/
M      hello-world/trunk/hello-world.c
A      hello-world/trunk/Makefile
```

The svn status command generates a list of all of the files in the working copy that have changed since it was checked out. It does not connect to the repository to do this. Instead, it uses the reference copy of the checked-out revision that was stored as part of the working copy.

Each file listed by svn status has a one-letter code next to it. Table 7-7 contains a list of codes that svn status will return. (If the programmer passes a specific path to svn status, it only returns the status of that file.)

TABLE 7-7. Output codes for svn status command
(reprinted with permission from Version Control with Subversion)

A item
: The file, directory, or symbolic link *item* has been scheduled for addition into the repository.

C item
: The file *item* is in a state of conflict. That is, changes received from the server during an update overlap with local changes that you have in your working copy. You must resolve this conflict before committing your changes to the repository.

D item
: The file, directory, or symbolic link *item* has been scheduled for deletion from the repository.

M item
: The contents of the file *item* have been modified.

X item
: The directory item is unversioned, but is related to a Subversion externals definition.

? item
: The file, directory, or symbolic link *item* is not under version control. You can silence the question marks by either passing the --quiet (-q) switch to svn status

! item
: The file, directory, or symbolic link *item* is under version control but is missing or somehow incomplete. The item can be missing if it's removed using a non-Subversion command. In the case of a directory, it can be incomplete if you happened to interrupt a checkout or update. A quick svn update will refetch the file or directory from the repository, or svn revert file will restore a missing file.

~ item
: The file, directory, or symbolic link *item* is in the repository as one kind of object, but what's actually in your working copy is some other kind. For example, Subversion might have a file in the repository, but you removed the file and created a directory in its place, without using the svn delete or svn add command.

I item
: The file, directory, or symbolic link *item* is not under version control, and Subversion is configured to ignore it during svn add, svn import, and svn status operations. Note that this symbol only shows up if you pass the --no-ignore option to svn status—otherwise the file would be ignored and not listed at all!

In addition to svn status, the programmer can use svn diff to see the specific changes that have been made to each file. The svn diff command can take a file parameter to generate a list of differences for that file; if no file is given, then it generates a list of differences for every file that was changed. The differences are displayed using the unified diff format.

The svn revert command can be used to roll back changes. If the programmer issues that command and gives it the filename of a file in the working copy, then that file is overwritten with a "pristine" copy that is identical to one in the revision that was checked out of the repository.

Merge any changes made since the working copy was checked out

Before the changes can be checked in, the user should update the working copy. This causes any changes made to the repository since the working copy was checked out to be changed in the working copy as well. The programmer does this by using the svn update command.

Most of the time, the svn update will automatically merge any changes that were made. But occasionally a programmer will have a change in his working copy that overlaps with another change that was made to the repository since he checked out.

In the example above, Alice wanted to update *cookies.txt* and checked out r23 of the recipe (which contained neither nuts nor M&Ms—see Table 7-1). She planned on adding nuts to the recipe but, before she could commit that change to the repository, Bob added M&Ms and committed r38 (see Table 7-2). When Alice attempted to commit her new revision (see Table 7-3), Subversion gave her the following message:

```
$ svn commit -m "Added nuts"
Sending        cookies.txt
svn: Commit failed (details follow):
svn: Out of date: 'cookies.txt' in transaction '46-1'
```

This told Alice that she needed to update her working copy in order to integrate any changes by issuing the svn update command:

```
$ svn update
C cookies.txt
Updated to revision 46.
```

When Subversion detects a conflict, it updates the file and marks the conflict using a string of greater-than and less-than signs. Table 7-8 shows the conflicts marked in *cookies.txt* after the update.

TABLE 7-8. Subversion found conflicts in cookies.txt

```
2 1/4 cups flour      1 tsp baking soda    1/2 tsp salt
1 cup butter          3/4 cup sugar        3/4 cup brown sugar
1 tsp vanilla         2 eggs               2 cups chocolate chips
<<<<<<< .mine
1 cup chopped nuts
=======
1 cup chopped M&Ms
>>>>>>> .38

Mix butter and sugars. Beat until creamy. Add vanilla. Beat in
eggs, one at a time. Mix in rest of ingredients. Drop by
spoonfuls on cookie sheets. Bake at 350 degrees.
```

The text between <<<<<<< .mine and ======= indicates the changes that were found in the working copy. The text between ======= and >>>>>>> .r38 indicates the conflicting changes that were found in r38 (see Table 7-3). It is up to the user to choose one or the other of these changes. The user can also come up with a way to use both of them—for example, indicating that the chopped M&Ms are optional.

Once the user has resolved the changes, the svn resolved command is used to indicate that the conflict has been resolved:

```
$ svn resolved cookies.txt
Resolved conflicted state of 'cookies.txt'
```

Now Alice can commit the changes to the repository.

Commit the changes

Once the working copy has been updated and all of the conflicts have been resolved, it is time to commit the changes by using svn commit. In the example above, Alice would issue the following command:

```
$ svn commit -m "Updated the recipe to add nuts"
Sending        cookies.txt
Transmitting file data .
Committed revision 47.
```

> **NOTE**
>
> Additional information on version control and working with Subversion (including branches, tags, and setting up Apache to work with Subversion) can be found in *Version Control with Subversion* by Ben Collins-Sussman, Brian W. Fitzpatrick, and C. Michael Pilato (O'Reilly, 2004). It can be downloaded free of charge or browsed online at *http://svnbook.red-bean.com/*.

Refactoring

To *refactor* a program is to improve the design of that program without altering its behavior.* There are many different kinds of improvements—called *refactorings*—that can be performed.

Every programmer knows that there are many ways to write code to implement one specific behavior. There are many choices that do not affect the behavior of the software but that can have an enormous impact on how easy the code is to read and understand. The programmers choose variable names, decide whether certain blocks of code should be pulled out into separate functions, choose among various different but syntactically equivalent statements, and make many other choices that can have a significant impact on how easy the software is to maintain.

---

* Some people have a much narrower definition of the term *refactoring* than we use in this chapter. They use it to refer only to the specific activity of making source code smaller by taking specific code paths and turning them into runtime data or structures.

Many programmers think of coding as a purely constructive task, for which the only reason to add, remove, or change the source code is to alter the behavior of the software. Refactoring introduces a new concept: adding, removing, or changing the source code for the sole purpose of making it easier to maintain. There are many different *refactorings*, or techniques, through which programmers can alter their code to make it easier to understand.

Refactoring is a new way of thinking about software design. Traditionally, software is designed first and then built. This is especially true of object-oriented programming, where the programmers might be handed a complex object model to implement. But most programmers who have worked on a reasonably complex project have run across instances when they discover ways that an object could have been designed better. They could not have predicted most of these improvements because they only became apparent during the construction of the code. Refactoring provides them with a way to incorporate those improvements in a structured, repeatable manner.

Because each refactoring is a change to the design, it may impact the design review process. If the software design has already been reviewed by project team members, then any changes that arise from refactoring activities should be communicated to the people who reviewed it. This does not necessarily mean that design specification must be reinspected after each refactoring; since refactoring changes the design without altering the functionality, it is usually sufficient to distribute just the changes to the design and have the team members approve those changes. In general, people do not object very often to refactoring, but they appreciate being given the opportunity to discuss it and suggest alternatives.

Each refactoring has a set of steps—similar to the scripts we use to describe the tools in this book—which makes it much less likely for the programmer to introduce defects. It also has two design patterns that show what the code looks like before and after the refactoring. There are dozens of refactorings, each with its own particular pattern and steps. The example below demonstrates four of these refactorings: *Extract Method, Replace Magic Number with Symbolic Constant, Decompose Conditional*, and *Introduce Explaining Variable*. A comprehensive catalog of refactorings can be found at *http://www.refactoring.com/catalog*.

Refactoring Example

In this example, a programming team in an investment bank is reviewing a block of code for a feature that calculates fees and bonuses for brokers who sell a certain kind of investment account to their corporate clients. The programmer who wrote the code uses refactoring to clarify problems that were identified during the code review.

The inspection team performed a code review on this block of Java code, which included the class Account and a function calculateFee from a different class:

```
1 class Account {
2     float principal;
3     float rate;
4     int daysActive;
5     int accountType;
6
7     public static final int  STANDARD = 0;
8     public static final int  BUDGET = 1;
```

```
9      public static final int  PREMIUM = 2;
10     public static final int  PREMIUM_PLUS = 3;
11 }
12
13 float calculateFee(Account accounts[]) {
14     float totalFee = 0;
15     Account account;
16     for (int i = 0; i < accounts.length; i++) {
17         account = accounts[i];
18         if ( account.accountType == Account.PREMIUM ||
19             account.accountType == Account.PREMIUM_PLUS ) {
20             totalFee += .0125 * ( account.principal
21                         * Math.exp( account.rate * (account.daysActive/365.25) )
22                         - account.principal );
23         }
24     }
25     return totalFee;
26 }
```

At first, the code seemed reasonably well designed. But as the inspection team discussed it, a few problems emerged. One of the inspectors was not clear about the purpose of the calculation that was being performed on lines 20 to 22. The programmer explained that this was a compound interest calculation to figure out how much interest was earned on the account, and suggested that they use the *Extract Method* refactoring to clarify it. They performed the refactoring right there during the code review. Since this calculation only used data that was available in the Account class, they moved it into that class, adding a new method called interestEarned (in lines 12 to 15 below):

```
1 class Account {
2      float principal;
3      float rate;
4      int daysActive;
5      int accountType;
6
7      public static final int  STANDARD = 0;
8      public static final int  BUDGET = 1;
9      public static final int  PREMIUM = 2;
10     public static final int  PREMIUM_PLUS = 3;
11
12     float interestEarned( ) {
13         return ( principal * (float) Math.exp( rate * (daysActive / 365.25 ) ) )
14                 - principal;
15     }
16 }
17
18 float calculateFee(Account accounts[]) {
19     float totalFee = 0;
20     Account account;
21     for (int i = 0; i < accounts.length; i++) {
22         account = accounts[i];
23         if ( account.accountType == Account.PREMIUM ||
24             account.accountType == Account.PREMIUM_PLUS )
25             totalFee += .0125 * account.interestEarned( );
26     }
27     return totalFee;
28 }
```

An inspector then asked what the number .0125 in line 25 was, and if it could ever change in the future. It turned out that each broker earned a commission fee that was equal to 1. 25% of the interest earned on the account. They used the *Replace Magic Number with Symbolic Constant* refactoring, replacing it with the constant BROKER_FEE_PERCENT and defining that constant later in line 31 (and adding a leading zero to help people read the code quickly):

```
1  class Account {
2      float principal;
3      float rate;
4      int daysActive;
5      int accountType;
6
7      public static final int  STANDARD = 0;
8      public static final int  BUDGET = 1;
9      public static final int  PREMIUM = 2;
10     public static final int  PREMIUM_PLUS = 3;
11
12     float interestEarned( ) {
13         return ( principal * (float) Math.exp( rate * (daysActive / 365.25 ) ) )
14                 - principal;
15     }
16 }
17
18 float calculateFee(Account accounts[]) {
19     float totalFee = 0;
20     Account account;
21     for (int i = 0; i < accounts.length; i++) {
22         account = accounts[i];
23         if ( account.accountType == Account.PREMIUM ||
24              account.accountType == Account.PREMIUM_PLUS ) {
25             totalFee += BROKER_FEE_PERCENT * account.interestEarned( );
26         }
27     }
28     return totalFee;
29 }
30
31 static final double BROKER_FEE_PERCENT = 0.0125;
```

The next issue that was raised in the code review was confusion about why the accountType variable was being checked in lines 23 and 24. There were several account types, and it wasn't clear why the account was being checked for just these two types. The programmer explained that the brokers only earn a fee for premium accounts, which could either be of the type PREMIUM or PREMIUM_PLUS.

By using the *Decompose Conditional* refactoring, they were able to clarify the purpose of this code. Adding the isPremium function to the Account class (lines 17 to 22) made it more obvious that this was a check to verify whether the account was a premium account:

```
1  class Account {
2      float principal;
3      float rate;
4      int daysActive;
5      int accountType;
6
```

```
7      public static final int  STANDARD = 0;
8      public static final int  BUDGET = 1;
9      public static final int  PREMIUM = 2;
10     public static final int  PREMIUM_PLUS = 3;
11
12     float interestEarned( ) {
13         return ( principal * (float) Math.exp( rate * (daysActive / 365.25 ) ) )
14                  - principal;
15     }
16
17     public boolean isPremium( ) {
18         if (accountType == Account.PREMIUM || accountType == Account.PREMIUM_PLUS)
19             return true;
20         else
21             return false;
22     }
23 }
24
25 float calculateFee(Account accounts[]) {
26     float totalFee = 0;
27     Account account;
28     for (int i = 0; i < accounts.length; i++) {
29         account = accounts[i];
30         if ( account.isPremium( ) )
31             totalFee += BROKER_FEE_PERCENT * account.interestEarned( );
32     }
33     return totalFee;
34 }
35
36 static final double BROKER_FEE_PERCENT = 0.0125;
```

The last problem found during the inspection involved the interestEarned( ) method that they had extracted. It was a confusing calculation, with several intermediate steps crammed into a single line. When that behavior was buried inside the larger function, the problem wasn't as glaring, but now that it had its own discrete function, they could get a clearer look at it.

The first problem was that it wasn't exactly clear why there was a division by 365.25 in line 13. The programmer explained that in the Account class, daysActive represented the number of days that the account was active, but the rate was an annual interest rate, so they had to divide daysActive by 365.25 to convert it to years. Another programmer asked why principal was being subtracted at the end of the interest calculation. The explanation was that this was done because the fee calculation was based only on the interest earned, regardless of the principal that initially was put into the account.

The refactoring *Introduce Explaining Variable* was used to introduce two intermediate variables, years on line 13 and compoundInterest on line 14, to clarify the code:

```
1 class Account {
2      float principal;
3      float rate;
4      int daysActive;
5      int accountType;
6
```

```
7    public static final int  STANDARD = 0;
8    public static final int  BUDGET = 1;
9    public static final int  PREMIUM = 2;
10   public static final int  PREMIUM_PLUS = 3;
11
12   float interestEarned( ) {
13       float years = daysActive / (float) 365.25;
14       float compoundInterest = principal * (float) Math.exp( rate * years );
15       return ( compoundInterest - principal );
16   }
17
18   public boolean isPremium( ) {
19       if (accountType == Account.PREMIUM || accountType == Account.PREMIUM_PLUS)
20           return true;
21       else
22           return false;
23   }
24 }
25
26 float calculateFee(Account accounts[]) {
27     float totalFee = 0;
28     Account account;
29     for (int i = 0; i < accounts.length; i++) {
30         account = accounts[i];
31         if ( account.isPremium( ) ) {
32             totalFee += BROKER_FEE_PERCENT * account.interestEarned( );
33         }
34     }
35     return totalFee;
36 }
37
38 static final double BROKER_FEE_PERCENT = 0.0125;
```

After these four refactorings, the inspection team agreed that the new version of this code was much easier to understand, even though it was almost 50% longer.

The code after refactoring must behave in exactly the same way it did beforehand. In general, every refactoring should be combined with an automated test to verify that the behavior of the software has not changed, because it is very easy to inject defects during refactoring. A framework of automated unit tests can ensure that the code behavior remains intact. Luckily, the team already had a set of unit tests. They had to add tests to verify the new Account.isPremium method, but the new code passed all of the other unit tests and the new version of the code was checked in (along with the new tests).

Refactoring Pays for Itself

Many people are initially uncomfortable with the idea of having programmers do tasks that don't change the behavior of the code. But, like time spent on project planning and software requirements engineering, the time spent refactoring is more than recouped over the course of the project. In fact, refactoring can help a team recover code that was previously written off as an unmaintainable mess, and can also help to keep new code from ever getting to that state.

Refactoring makes intuitive sense, when one considers the main reasons that code becomes difficult to maintain. As a project moves forward and changes, code that was written for one purpose is often extended and altered. A block of code may look pristine when it's first built, but it can evolve over time into a mess. New functionality or bug fixes can turn clear, sensible code into a mess of enormously long and complex loops, blocks, cases, and patches. Some people call this spaghetti code (a name that should make intuitive sense to anyone who has had to maintain a mess like that), but it is really just code whose design turned out not to be all that well suited to its purpose.

The goal of refactoring is to make the software easier for a human to understand, without changing what it does. Most modern programming languages are very expressive, meaning that any one behavior can be coded in many different ways. When a programmer builds the code, he makes many choices, some of which make the code much easier or harder to understand. Each refactoring is aimed at correcting a common pattern that makes the code harder to read. Code that is easier to understand is easier to maintain, and code that is harder to understand is harder to maintain.

In practice, maintenance tasks on spaghetti code are extraordinarily difficult and time-consuming. Refactoring that code can make each of these maintenance tasks much easier. Well-designed code is much easier to work on than poorly designed code, and refactoring improves the design of the software while it is being built. Any programmer who has to maintain spaghetti code should make extensive use of refactoring. It usually takes about as much time to refactor a block of spaghetti code as it does to simply try to trace through it. In fact, many programmers have found that it's much faster to use refactoring to permanently detangle messy code than it is to try to just fix the one problem that popped up at the time

In addition to saving time on programming, refactoring can also help a programmer find bugs more quickly. Poorly designed code tends to have more defects, and tracking these defects down is an unpleasant task. If the code is easier to read and follow, it is easier to find those bugs. And since much of the duplicated code has been eliminated, most bugs only have to be fixed once. Of course, the clearer the code is, the less likely it is that defects get injected in the first place.

There is no hard-and-fast rule about when to refactor. Many programmers find that it's effective to alternate between adding new behavior and refactoring the new code that was just added. Any time a reasonably large chunk of new code has been added, the programmer should take the time to go through it and find any possible refactorings. The same goes for bug fixes—often, a bug is easier to fix after the code that it's in has been refactored.

NOTE
Additional information on refactoring can be found in *Refactoring: Improving the Design of Existing Code* by Martin Fowler (Addison Wesley, 1999) and on his web site at *http://www.refactoring.com.*

Unit Testing

Before a build is delivered, the person or program building the software should execute *unit tests* to verify that each unit functions properly. All code is made up of a set of objects, functions, modules, or other non-trivial *units*. Each unit is built to perform a certain function. The purpose of unit testing is to create a set of tests for each unit to verify that it performs its function correctly. Each unit test should be automated: it should perform a test without any input or intervention, and should result in a pass (meaning that the test generated the expected results), failure (the results of the test differed from what were expected), or error (meaning the code reached an error condition before the test could pass or fail). Many people require that unit tests have no dependencies on external systems (networks, databases, shared folders, etc.).

Automated unit testing is a stepping stone to *test-driven development*. Test-driven development is a programming technique in which a programmer writes the unit tests before he writes the unit that they verify. By writing the tests first, the programmer ensures that he fully understands the requirements. It also guarantees that the tests will be in place, so that they aren't left until after all of the other programming activities are completed (and then possibly dropped, due to schedule pressure).

The main activity in unit testing is creating *test cases* that verify the software. A test case is a piece of code that verifies one particular behavior of the software. Each test should be able to run without any user input; its only output is whether it passed, failed, or halted due to an error. The test cases for a software project are generally grouped together into *suites*, where there may be a number of suites that verify the entire software. It's often useful to design the suites so that each one verifies specific units or features; this makes the test cases easier to maintain.

The most common (and effective) way for programmers to do unit testing is to use a *framework*, a piece of software that automatically runs the tests and reports the results. A framework typically allows a programmer to write a set of test cases for each unit. Most frameworks provide an automated system for executing a suite of unit tests and reporting the results. This allows a full battery of unit tests to be executed automatically at any time, with little or no effort. Unit testing frameworks are available for most modern programming languages.

The framework usually provides some sort of object model, API, or other language interface that provides test cases with functionality for reporting whether the test passed or failed. Most frameworks allow the programmer to indicate which tests are associated with various units, and to group the test cases into suites. Table 7-9 shows some of the test frameworks available for various languages. (This list is by no means exhaustive—there are many other frameworks available for these and other languages.)

TABLE 7-9. Test frameworks available for languages

Language	Framework name (URL)
Java	JUnit (*http://www.junit.org*)
Visual Studio .NET	NUnit (*http://www.nunit.org*)
C	CUnit (*http://cunit.sourceforge.net*)
C++	CppUnit (*http://cppunit.sourceforge.net*)
SmallTalk	SUnit (*http://sunit.sourceforge.net*)
Perl	Test (*http://search.cpan.org/~sburke/Test*)
Python	PyUnit (*http://pyunit.sourceforge.net*)
Borland Delphi	DUnit (*http://dunit.sourceforge.net*)

Test All of the Code, Test All of the Possibilities

The name "unit test" comes from the fact that each individual unit of code is tested separately. In object-oriented languages like Java, C#, and SmallTalk, the units are objects. In imperative languages like C, the units will correspond to functions or modules; in functional languages like Lisp and SML, the units will generally be functions. (Some languages, like Visual Basic and Perl, can be either imperative or object-oriented.)

It takes multiple tests to verify a single unit. The framework will have a way to build suites of test cases and indicate that they correspond to a specific unit.

A good test verifies many aspects of the software, including (but not limited to) these attributes:

- The unit correctly performs its intended functions.
- The unit functions properly at its boundary conditions (like null or zero values).
- The unit is robust (it handles unexpected values and error conditions gracefully).

Unit tests must be able to run within a developer's test environment. Real-time or production resources like databases, data feeds, input files, and user input are not necessarily available to the test. To get around this limitation, a programmer can use a *mock object*—an object that simulates a resource that is unavailable at the time of the test. (It is beyond the scope of this book to describe how to implement mock objects.)

JUnit

JUnit is the unit testing framework for Java. It was created by Erich Gamma and Kent Beck, based on Beck's work with SmallTalk. JUnit has been very influential in the world of unit testing; many unit test frameworks are ported from, or based on, JUnit. The test case examples below are JUnit test cases, which are part of an automated suite of unit tests for the FeeCalculation( ) function above. The unit tests allowed the programmers doing a code review of this function to successfully refactor it without injecting defects. After each refactoring, they executed the unit tests. If any of them failed, the programmers tracked down the problem and fixed it.

The tests use a few additional commands defined by JUnit to tell the framework whether the unit test passes or fails:

assertEquals([String message], expected, actual [, tolerance])
: Causes the unit test to fail if expected is not equal to actual. If tolerance is specified, the equality for floating point numbers is calculated to that tolerance.

assertSame([String message], expected, actual)
: Causes the unit test to fail if expected does not refer to the same object as actual.

assertTrue([String message], boolean condition)
: Causes the unit test to fail if the Boolean condition evaluates to false.

assertFalse([String message], boolean condition)
: Causes the unit test to fail if the Boolean condition evaluates to true.

assertNull([String message], java.lang.Object object)
: Causes the unit test to fail if object is not null.

assertNotNull([String message], java.lang.Object object)
: Causes the unit test to fail if object is null.

fail([String message])
: Causes the unit test to fail immediately.

Each assertion can optionally be given a message. In that case, if the test fails, the message is displayed in the test report generated by the framework. In JUnit, a test that completes without failing is considered to have passed.

Every test in JUnit must be able to be run independently of every other test, and the tests should be able to be run in any order. The individual tests are grouped together into a test case. Each test is a method in a test case object, which inherits from *junit.framework. TestCase*. (The above assert commands are inherited from this class.) Each test case can optionally have a setUp( ) function, which sets up any objects or values required for the tests, and a tearDown( ) function, which restores the environment to its condition before the test was run.

Unit Testing Example

The examples in this section are the individual test methods from a test case object called testFeeCalculation. There are many tests that would exercise the fee calculation function shown in the Refactoring section above. This example shows six of them. All of them require an instance of the *FeeCalculation* class, which is set up using this setUp( ) function:

```
public FeeCalculation feeCalculation;
public void setUp( ) {
    feeCalculation = new FeeCalculation( );
}
```

The first test simply verifies that the function has performed its calculation and has generated the right result by comparing the output to a known value, which was calculated by hand using a calculator:

```
public void testTypicalResults( ) {
    Account accounts[] = new Account[3];

    accounts[0] = new Account( );
    accounts[0].principal = 35;
    accounts[0].rate = (float) .04;
    accounts[0].daysActive = 365;
    accounts[0].accountType = Account.PREMIUM;

    accounts[1] = new Account( );
    accounts[1].principal = 100;
    accounts[1].rate = (float) .035;
    accounts[1].daysActive = 100;
    accounts[1].accountType = Account.BUDGET;

    accounts[2] = new Account( );
    accounts[2].principal = 50;
    accounts[2].rate = (float) .04;
    accounts[2].daysActive = 600;
    accounts[2].accountType = Account.PREMIUM_PLUS;

    float result = feeCalculation.calculateFee(accounts);
    assertEquals(result, (float) 0.060289, (float) 0.00001);
}
```

This test passes. The call to feeCalculation( ) with those three accounts returns a value of 0.060289383, which matches the value passed to assertEquals( ) within the specified tolerance of .000001. The assertion does not cause a failure, and the test case completes.

It's important to test unexpected input. The programmer may not have expected feeCalculation( ) to receive a set of accounts that contained no premium accounts. So the second test checks for a set of non-premium accounts:

```
public void testNonPremiumAccounts( ) {
    Account accounts[] = new Account[2];

    accounts[0] = new Account( );
    accounts[0].principal = 12;
    accounts[0].rate = (float) .025;
    accounts[0].daysActive = 100;
    accounts[0].accountType = Account.BUDGET;

    accounts[1] = new Account( );
    accounts[1].principal = 50;
    accounts[1].rate = (float) .0265;
    accounts[1].daysActive = 150;
    accounts[1].accountType = Account.STANDARD;

    float result = feeCalculation.calculateFee(accounts);
    assertEquals(result, 0, 0.0001);
}
```

The expected result for this test is 0, and it passes.

It's not enough to just test for expected results. A good unit test suite will include tests for *boundary conditions*, or inputs at the edge of the range of acceptable values. There are many kinds of boundary conditions, including:

- Zero values, null values, or other kinds of empty or missing values
- Very large or very small numbers that don't conform to expectations (like a rate of 10000%, or an account that has been active for a million years)
- Arrays and lists that contain duplicates or are sorted in unexpected ways
- Events that happen out of order, like accessing a database before it's opened
- Badly formatted data (like an invalid XML file)

A few tests will verify that these boundary conditions are handled as expected. This unit test verifies that calculateFee( ) can handle an account with a zero interest rate:

```
public void testZeroRate( ) {
    Account accounts[] = new Account[1];

    accounts[0] = new Account( );
    accounts[0].principal = 1000;
    accounts[0].rate = (float) 0;
    accounts[0].daysActive = 100;
    accounts[0].accountType = Account.PREMIUM;

    float result = feeCalculation.calculateFee(accounts);
    assertEquals(result, 0, 0.00001);
}
```

This test passes in an account with a negative principal (a calculator was used to come up with the expected result by hand):

```
public void testNegativePrincipal( ) {
    Account accounts[] = new Account[1];

    accounts[0] = new Account( );
    accounts[0].principal = -10000;
    accounts[0].rate = (float) 0.263;
    accounts[0].daysActive = 100;
    accounts[0].accountType = Account.PREMIUM;

    float result = feeCalculation.calculateFee(accounts);
    assertEquals(result, -9.33265, 0.0001);
}
```

In this case, the programmer expects the correct mathematical result to be returned, even though it may not make business sense in this context. Another programmer maintaining the code can see this expectation simply by reading through this unit test.

The next test verifies that the software can handle a duplicate reference. feeCalculation( ) takes an array of objects. Even if one of those objects is a duplicate reference of another one in the array, the result should still match the one calculated by hand:

```
public void testDuplicateReference( ) {
    Account accounts[] = new Account[3];

    accounts[0] = new Account( );
    accounts[0].principal = 35;
    accounts[0].rate = (float) .04;
    accounts[0].daysActive = 365;
    accounts[0].accountType = Account.PREMIUM;

    accounts[1] = accounts[0];

    accounts[2] = new Account( );
    accounts[2].principal = 50;
    accounts[2].rate = (float) .04;
    accounts[2].daysActive = 600;
    accounts[2].accountType = Account.PREMIUM_PLUS;

    float result = feeCalculation.calculateFee(accounts);
    assertEquals(result, 0.0781316, 0.000001);
}
```

It's also possible to create tests that are expected to fail. The programmer expects calculateFee( ) to choke on one particular boundary condition—being passed null instead of an array:

```
public void testNullInput( ) {
    Account accounts[] = null;
    float result = feeCalculation.calculateFee(accounts);
    assertTrue(true);
}
```

The assertion assertTrue(true) will never fail. It's included for the benefit of any program-mer reading this unit test. It shows that the test is expected to get to this line. Unfortu-nately, calculateFee throws a *NullPointerException* error.

In this case, that's exactly the behavior that the programmer expects. The unit test can be altered to show that it expects the call to calculateFee( ) to fail:

```
public void testNullInput( ) {
    Account accounts[] = null;
    try {
        float result = feeCalculation.calculateFee(accounts);
        fail( );
    } catch (NullPointerException e) {
        assertTrue(true);
    }
}
```

The fail( ) assertion is placed after calculateFee( ) to verify that it throws an exception and never executes the next statement. The assertTrue(true) assertion is then used to show that the call is expected to throw a specific error, and the test expects to catch it.

These test methods by no means represent an exhaustive test case for the FeeCalculation class. But even this limited set of tests is enough, for instance, to ensure that a refactoring has not broken the behavior of the class. It would not take a programmer much longer to come up with a more exhaustive test case for this example.

Test-Driven Development

Test-driven development means that the unit tests are created before the code is built. Before a programmer begins to build a new object, she must first create the test case that verifies that object. By the time the test case is finished, she has defined all of the expected inputs, outputs, boundary cases, and error conditions for the object, and she has a test case that verifies that it works. As she builds each part of the object, she can run its unit tests to verify the code that has just been built. Many defects found by testers or users have to do with unexpected inputs or error conditions; since the programmer has already planned out all of the ways that the object might fail, she will catch many more of these the first time she builds the software.

Test-driven development also helps programmers understand the requirements better. It's possible—and often tempting—to begin coding with only a partial understanding of what it is that the code is supposed to do. It is not uncommon for a programmer to "go off half-cocked" and begin coding before really taking the time to understand the behavior of the code. This is understandable; it's more fun to write code than it is to sit and pore through requirements documents. It's even more tempting when there are no requirements documents. If the programmer has to build the software simply based on notes from some conversations and a vague understanding of the scope, it's much more fun to just jump in and start coding! Taking the time to write the unit tests really firms up the requirements in the programmer's mind, and often helps her to see exactly where she is missing information.

There are several important benefits of test-driven development. The most obvious one is that it guarantees that unit tests are always written. When a team is under pressure to release, it's very tempting to release the code that seems to work. And when the unit tests are the last thing that the team has to do, a senior manager facing a deadline will often decide to release the build as is. Without the unit tests, the code will have more defects. These defects will have to be fixed later, often after the programmers have moved on to other projects and this code is no longer fresh in their minds.

Another important benefit of test-driven development is that the unit tests have a very positive influence on the design of the code and the object model. Many design problems stem from the fact that when an object is built, the programmer makes a decision about the interface that later turns out to make that interface difficult to use. By the time she writes code that uses that interface, the object is already written, and it may be difficult to rewrite it to accommodate the way it really needs to be used. The unit test forces her to start by writing code that uses the object; many poor interface decisions immediately become apparent, before the code for the object is written.

A complete suite of unit tests also makes it much easier to refactor the software. The unit test suite can be run after each refactoring, helping the programmers to immediately identify any defects that they might have accidentally injected. Running unit tests after each refactoring removes most of the risk and ensures that the refactoring really does not alter the behavior of the software.

Unit testing is an efficient way to build better software. Test-driven development often yields code that has fewer defects than standard development, and many programmers who do test-driven development find that they are able to produce that code more quickly than they had in the past.

Everyone Is Responsible for Quality

In some organizations, there seems to be a growing tension between the programmers and testers. The testers will find an increasing number of defects, which they feel should have been caught before the build was delivered to them. The programmers, on the other hand, start to feel that they aren't responsible for testing of any kind—not even unit tests—because they feel the testers should catch every possible problem. Project managers who start to sense this tension often feel powerless to do anything about it. In situations like this, automated unit tests can help.

Many programmers are confused about exactly what it is that software testers do. All they know is that they deliver a build to the QA team. The QA people run the program and find bugs, which the programmers fix. It is often hard for them to figure out where unit testing ends and functional testing begins. A good project manager will keep an eye out for this confusion, and help to clarify it by making sure that the programmers understand what kinds of testing are expected of them.

There are different kinds of testing that serve different purposes. The purpose of unit tests is to verify that the software works exactly as the programmer intended. Software testers, on the other hand, are responsible for verifying that the software meets its requirements (in the SRS) and the needs of the users and stakeholders (in the Vision and Scope Document). Many defects arise when a programmer delivers software that worked as he intended, but did not meet the needs of the users. It's the software tester's job to catch these problems (see Chapter 8). This is why both the programmers and testers must test the software—they are looking for different problems. If this distinction is clear to the programmers, they should understand why unit testing is their responsibility.

By adopting unit tests and test-driven development, the programmers can develop a very clear picture of exactly what their testing responsibilities are. Before the programmers deliver their code to QA, the code should pass every unit test. This does not necessarily mean that the software does what it's supposed to do, but it does mean that it works well enough that a tester can determine whether it does its intended job.

It should make intuitive sense that, since the QA team runs the software as if they were users, they do not have access to the individual units (objects, functions, classes, database queries, modules, etc.) that the programmers create. If these units are broken, it is often possible for those defects to be masked, either in the user interface or elsewhere in the software. Even if those units seem to function properly, there may be defects that will only be found when those units are used together in complex ways. This is what QA engineers do—they simulate complex actions that could be performed by the users in order to find these defects. From this perspective, it is not hard for a programmer to see that only the programmers can test those units, and that those units must be working before the testers can do their jobs. Implementing automated unit tests can ensure that those units work, letting the QA team concentrate on more complex behavior. By helping the programmers understand the line between unit testing and functional testing, and take on the responsibility for unit testing, the project manager can help reduce the tension on the project.

Unit Testing Saves Programming Time and Effort

Some project managers find that programmers are resistant to unit tests. Sometimes the programmers resent the assumption that their code isn't perfect, even when there is a history of defects that had to be fixed on previous projects. Other times, they assume that the QA team's job is simply to find the programmers' bugs. But mostly, they don't like spending time writing and running unit tests that won't be delivered in the build. It feels like a waste of time, without adding much value. But in fact, the opposite is true. Most programmers who adopt unit tests find that it actually reduces the total time it takes to build software. It may take time to write the tests up front, but it costs more time to go back later and fix all of the bugs that the unit tests would have caught.

One way that unit tests help the programmers deliver better code is by improving the object interfaces or function definitions that the programmers use. Many experienced programmers will recognize the feeling of regret that comes when they start using an object that they built to encapsulate some functionality, only to realize later that they should have designed the interface differently. Sometimes there is functionality that the object needs to provide that the programmer didn't think of; at other times, it may be that the methods are awkward to work with, and could have been laid out better. But the code for the object is already built, and it's too late to fix it. She will just have to work around the awkwardness, even though building the object right from the beginning would have saved her some time and effort. Or she may be frustrated enough to go back and rebuild the object entirely, which costs even more time. This is a common trap that plagues object-oriented design—there's no way to know how easy it is to use an object until code is built that uses it, but there's no way to build that code until the object is done.

In practice, test-driven development is an effective way to avoid that trap. The programmer can build a series of simple unit tests before the object is built. If the object is needed, she can build a mock object to simulate it. By the time she is ready to define the interface, she has worked out many of the details and has discovered and avoided the potential problems with the interface before the object is built.

Programmers also find that effort is unnecessarily wasted in situations when one person has to use an object that was designed by someone else. Often a programmer finds that the object's interface is not clear. There could be ambiguous function names or variables, or it could be unclear how to use objects that are returned by certain functions.

This is another case when unit tests can be very useful. When a programmer consults documentation for an object or an API manual, the first thing she usually looks for is an example of the functionality that she is trying to implement. The unit tests serve the same purpose. When an object comes bundled with a series of unit tests, the programmer can consult them to see how the object was intended to be used. Not only do they provide her with a substantial amount of example code, but they also show her all of the behavior that the object is meant to exhibit, including the errors that it is expected to handle.

> **NOTE**
> Additional information, tutorials, and examples of unit testing can be found in *Pragmatic Unit Testing* by Andrew Hunt and David Thomas (The Pragmatic Bookshelf, 2003).

Use Automation

There are many tasks over the course of a software project that can be automated. Unit tests are a good example of automation—before programmers started using automated unit tests, they had to manually verify each function and user interface element before delivering a build. By automating unit tests, the programmers were able to make them much less time-consuming tasks and, as a result, many more programmers take the time to build unit tests.

But unit tests are not the only manual programming task that can be automated. Automation can ensure that the software is built the same way each time, that the team sees every change made to the software, and that the software is tested and reviewed in the same way every day so that no defects slip through or are introduced through human error.

When projects become complex and require many steps to build, it's easy for programmers to forget a step. A programmer may build a version of the software that is missing a library, or is compiled with incorrect options. What's more, some programming teams have discovered that, as their build process becomes more and more complex, they have to dedicate more of a senior team member's time to generating new builds on a regular basis, which can cause delays in the project. Eventually, it becomes difficult for the team to even generate a reproducible build. When the build is delivered to users, there are often defects that can be traced back to missing libraries, or to required files that should have been included.

There are many automated build tools that address all of the problems caused by an unpredictable and difficult-to-reproduce build process. Popular ones include:

- Make (which ships with most Unix-like operating systems and some IDEs)
- GNU Make (*http://www.gnu.org/software/make*)
- Apache Ant (*http://ant.apache.org*)
- Jam (*http://www.perforce.com/jam/jam.html*)

Each of these tools automates a set of steps required to build the project. There are ways to ensure that dependencies are honored, so that a piece of code is only built after the tool first builds every library that it depends on. With an automated build tool, a programmer can cut a new build at any time and without extra input or interaction. The team can be sure that the software is built the same way each time and includes all of the necessary files and dependencies.

One of the most important ways a software project can be automated is with a development monitoring system. Two of the most popular ones are CruiseControl (*http://cruisecontrol.sourceforge.net*) and TinderBox (*http://www.mozilla.org/projects/tinderbox*), both of which are free and open source. These tools allow a project team to construct a set of tasks to be run automatically on a schedule. These tasks include:

- Retrieving the latest build from the version control system, building it, copying it to a folder, and reporting any build warnings or errors
- Running automated unit tests, generating a test report, and reporting critical failures
- Running automated code review tools and reporting any warnings or rule violations
- Listing any changes that have been committed and by whom, including links to code listings for the changes
- Emailing results as text or visual reports (or sent via SMS text messages or some other communications system)

These tasks can be configured to run on any chosen schedule. Many teams will schedule daily builds. Some will require builds on an hourly basis (or another schedule), while others will only require automated builds to kick off when changes are checked in. The important aspect of this is that the team can depend on these tasks being run the same way each time. They are kept aware of every change made to the code, and they are always aware of the health of the current build. If code is checked in that causes the build to break or important unit tests to fail, the team will know about it immediately and will be able to fix the problem early on, before any other changes are made.

It is especially useful to combine the reports from a development monitoring system with code reviews. This is an especially common practice on successful open source projects, where every change or patch applied to the code is emailed to the developers and reviewed before it is incorporated into a production release.

Be Careful with Existing Projects

An overeager project manager can easily sour a programming team on these tools, if the team doesn't see the benefits. While it's easy for a team to migrate an existing project to a new version control system, it is much harder to begin to build unit tests for an existing codebase. (It's also much more risky, since the old repository can be kept around so that the code can be moved right back if the new version control system does not work out.)

Migrating from files stored in a folder to Subversion is trivial—just build the repository, import the files, and rename the old folder. Migrating from an antiquated source control system to Subversion is a little more involved, but it's still relatively straightforward. The simplest way to do it is to import a copy of the latest revision. This will not make previous changes available in Subversion; however, an Internet search will usually turn up scripts that will automatically import repositories from the most popular version systems into Subversion. Either way, as long as the old repository is kept around in case of disaster, migrating to Subversion can be done at any time, and it can bring immediate benefits to both new and legacy projects.

Refactoring can also bring immediate benefits, but programmers should be careful about how it is applied. It is generally safest to introduce refactoring in code reviews and bug fixes. This will ensure that the benefits of refactoring are applied to where they will do the most good: complex, difficult-to-maintain, or bug-ridden code. Refactoring can also be implemented in new development tasks without much difficulty, as long as the programmers doing the refactoring feel comfortable with the task. However, it is usually a mistake to just pick a block of code at random and try to refactor it. While the refactoring will probably work just fine, the benefits will not be noticed by the programming team, and they will start to question its usefulness.

Many people are uncomfortable introducing refactoring unless there are already unit tests in place. Unit tests are often considered a necessary prerequisite for refactoring, because they ensure that the refactoring does not change the behavior of the code. However, while having unit tests in place is the ideal situation, it is still possible to gain many of the benefits of refactoring without unit tests, as long as the refactored code is thoroughly reviewed in order to find any defects that may have been introduced. This is another reason code reviews and refactoring should be combined.

Unit testing should probably be avoided on large legacy code, and kept to new development. While it is possible to develop unit tests for older code, and those tests will probably catch defects, the process of building them will be very time consuming. This is because it's necessary to fully understand the behavior of a block of code before writing its unit tests, and regaining that understanding usually requires a large ramp-up period for the programmer to familiarize herself with code that has not been touched recently. This ramp-up will probably require a lot of reverse engineering, and may require the programmer to dig around to recover requirements that are unclear from the code and were never written down. Most programmers forced to go through this exercise will be turned off to unit testing entirely. When unit testing is being introduced to an organization, it should generally be confined to new code until the programmers are comfortable using test-driven development in their daily tasks.

Diagnosing Design and Programming Problems

There are several typical design and programming problems that can be avoided by using the design and programming tools and techniques in this chapter. To illustrate these problems, the three following scenarios show how a programming team can grow increasingly frustrated over the course of their software projects as a result of losing control over their source code.

Haunted by Ghosts of Old Problems

Many programming teams use a shared folder to store source code. Even though they are generally diligent about making backups, and everyone is careful about maintaining the integrity of the code, mistakes sometimes slip through. Despite their best efforts, the team finds that new code seems to disappear with some regularity, while defects that were fixed months ago mysteriously resurface.

At first, the problems happened because one programmer would overwrite another's changes. One programmer would copy the code to his hard drive to work on it. While he was working on his copy of the code, a second programmer would copy it to her drive. The first programmer would copy his changes back to the shared folder. But when the second programmer copied her changes back, it would overwrite the changes made by the first programmer. This caused problems that were difficult to track down; the first programmer did not realize that his code was no longer in the folder (and neither did anyone else).

This problem seemed to get steadily worse as the code base grew. After the team had to redo a week's worth of work because an entire feature was overwritten, they were motivated to search for better solutions. The first solution they tried was creating a "checkout" folder underneath the source code folder. When a programmer needed to work on a file, he first moved it to the checkout folder, and then copied it to his local hard drive. Nobody would work on the file until it was "checked in" by copying it back to the shared folder and removing the old version from the checkout folder. But this still caused problems— occasionally someone would accidentally copy an old version of a previously checked-out file into the shared folder. Nobody would know that it happened until a client complained about the reappearance of an old bug that had been fixed months earlier. The checkout folder "solution" was not good enough.

The team eventually put in place version control software, which put the entire source code into a repository. They chose one that was made by the same vendor as their other programming tools, because it was included and installed automatically. The software forced programmers to check out the code before they could alter it and update it back in the repository, and it locked any checked-out files so that they could not be altered until they were checked back in by the person who checked them out. This was definitely better than a shared folder, but it still caused problems. People would constantly complain of leaving code checked out on their office machines, only to find that they couldn't edit important files when working from home. Occasionally, someone would go on vacation with an entire project checked out, and nobody could figure out which files she intended to check back in. And, worst of all, there were some files that everyone needed to alter all the time. Since only one person could check them out at a time, the programmers were constantly waiting for each other to finish their tasks. The integrity of their code seemed safer, but it came at the cost of schedule delays.

Had this team gone with a version control system like Subversion, they could have prevented all of these problems. With Subversion, a programmer can update any file at any time, no matter how many people are working on the project. By being forced to resolve conflicts in the latest version of the code before committing any changes, he can prevent old code from leaking into a new build. By running the unit tests afterward, he can ensure that the build he is checking in works properly and that no defects have been accidentally introduced.

Broken Builds

Most programmers on the team know that they need to unit test their code. And when it comes time to do it, they try to be as thorough as possible. Before a programmer delivers a build to QA, he goes through each feature and clicks every button and UI widget to ensure that they seem to work. The programmers always make sure to take at least a few hours— sometimes an entire day—after the software is built, making sure that it works.

But all of that effort does not seem to matter. No matter how hard the team tries, the lead programmer always seems to get into the same argument with the lead tester in the status meeting after the first build of a project is delivered. The lead tester reports that the tests had to be halted because some basic functionality is missing or broken. The programmer explains that the entire team took a lot of their time to unit test the build, and that everything looked like it worked. The QA lead explains that this clearly wasn't enough, because the software is too broken to be tested. The programmer gets exasperated—isn't it the job of the QA team to figure that out and tell them what to fix? In the meantime, the testers have to sit around and wait for the new build, and their entire schedule is blown. There never seems to be a solution, just a lot of work to try to get the build good enough for the testers.

A software tester will often find defects that slipped past the programmers, because her test strategy causes her to take actions in the software that require many different units in the code to work together. Had the programmer built a unit test suite that thoroughly tested each of these units, he would have caught many of those problems before they ever reached the QA team. More importantly, if the programming team adopts a test-driven development strategy, each programmer will be clear on exactly where his responsibility lies in verifying the quality of the software. The team will know that they test each unit, letting the testers concentrate on verifying that the requirements have been met.

Spaghetti Code

Maintaining old code is the least desirable programming job in many organizations. Code that was patched by a dozen different developers over the years seems to be held together with the software equivalent of duct tape and paper clips. With each successive version of the software, certain aging functions just seem to get longer and more convoluted. Trying to track down bugs is a tedious and frustrating task, and even the simplest modifications can be daunting.

In an environment where aging code has turned into a twisted mess of complex and tangled execution paths, loops, blocks, and patches, the team is usually at a loss. Everyone recognizes that it's a problem, but the only solution that anyone ever suggests is rewriting some, or even all, of the code. Sometimes a rewrite is justified by upgrading to a newer version of a language, programming tool, IDE, database, or operating system—but the team knows that the only reason the idea has merit is because the old codebase has essentially become unmaintainable.

The programming team can make maintenance of such difficult code much easier by introducing refactoring. Any time a programmer encounters a twisted, tangled block of code, she could take the time to refactor it into a much more manageable block before attempting to do any work on it. Not only would refactoring make each individual maintenance task easier, but eventually a large portion of the code could be detangled so that it is approachable and much more easily maintained. Unit tests can be used to ensure that the behavior of the software does not change during the refactoring steps.

CHAPTER EIGHT

Software Testing

THE QUALITY OF THE SOFTWARE IS THE RESPONSIBILITY OF THE ENTIRE TEAM. Throughout the entire software project, the team does many things to find and prevent defects. Once the software has been built, it's time to look back and make sure that it meets the requirements. The goal of software testing is to make sure that the product does what the users and stakeholders need it to do. Software testers review the final product to make sure that the initial requirements have been met.

In software testing, *quality* is defined as "conformance to requirements." Every use case, functional requirement, and other software requirement defines a specific behavior that the software must exhibit. When the software does not behave the way that the requirements say it must behave, that is a *defect*. This means that your software testers are responsible for figuring out whether the software that was produced by the team behaves in the way that the requirements it was built from say that it should.

Every engineering discipline defines quality in exactly this way. When an auto manufacturer provides a specification to a subcontractor to create a part for a car, that specification contains tolerances for various measurements for that part. When the subcontractor ships a box of those parts back to the manufacturer to be built into the car, any part that does not meet the requirements in the specification is considered defective. And it's exactly the same with software—any feature that does not meet the requirements in the specification has a defect.

This means that if an organization does not have good requirements engineering practices (see Chapter 6), then it will be very hard to deliver software that fills the users' needs, because the product team does not really know what those needs are. It's not a coincidence that many problems that seem to originate with the software testers are really requirements problems that simply have not been caught yet.

This chapter gives an overview of what testers do in a software organization, and clears up some misconceptions about what they do not do. By putting in place good software testing practices based on solid software requirements specifications, a project manager can help assure the quality of the software.

Test Plans and Test Cases

The goal of test planning is to establish the list of tasks that, if performed, will identify all of the requirements that have not been met in the software. The main work product is the *test plan*. There are many standards that can be used for developing test plans. Table 8-1 shows the outline of a typical test plan. (This outline was adapted from IEEE 829, the most common standard for software test plans.)

TABLE 8-1. *Test plan outline*

Purpose
> A description of the purpose of the application under test.

Features to be tested
> A list of the features in the software that will be tested. It is a catalog of all of the test cases (including a test case number and title) that will be conducted, as well as all of the base states.

Features not to be tested
> A list of any areas of the software that will be excluded from the test, as well as any test cases that were written but will not be run.

Approach
> A description of the strategies that will be used to perform the test.

Suspension criteria and resumption requirements
> Suspension criteria are the conditions that, if satisfied, require that the test be halted. Resumption requirements are the conditions that are required in order to restart a suspended test.

Environmental Needs
> A complete description of the test environment or environments. This should include a description of hardware, networking, databases, software, operating systems, and any other attribute of the environment that could affect the test.

Schedule
> An estimated schedule for performing the test. This should include milestones with specific dates.

Acceptance criteria
> Any objective quality standards that the software must meet, in order to be considered ready for release. This may include things like stakeholder sign-off and consensus, requirements that the software must have been tested under certain environments, minimum defect counts at various priority and severity levels, minimum test coverage numbers, etc.

Roles and responsibilities
> A list of the specific roles that will be required for people in the organization, in order to carry out the test. This list can indicate specific people who will be testing the software and what they are responsible for.

The test plan represents the overall approach to the test. In many ways, the test plan serves as a summary of the test activities that will be performed. It shows how the tests will be organized, and outlines all of the testers' needs that must be met in order to properly carry out the test. The test plan is especially valuable because it is not a difficult document to review, so the members of the engineering team and senior managers can inspect it.

The bulk of the test planning effort is focused on creating the *test cases*. A test case is a description of a specific interaction that a tester will have, in order to test a single behavior of the software. Test cases are very similar to use cases, in that they are step-by-step narratives that define a specific interaction between the user and the software. However, unlike use cases, they contain references to specific features of the user interface. The test case contains actual data that must be entered into the software and the expected result that the software must generate. A typical test case includes these sections, usually laid out in a table:

- A unique *name* and *number*

- A *requirement* that this test case is exercising

- *Preconditions* that describe the state of the software before the test case (which is often a previous test case that must always be run before the current test case)

- *Steps* that describe the specific steps that make up the interaction

- *Expected results* that describe the expected state of the software after the test case is executed

Table 8-2 shows an example of a test case that would exercise one specific behavior in requirement FR-4 from the discussion of functional requirements in Chapter 6. This requirement specified how a search-and-replace function must deal with case sensitivity. One part of that requirement said, "If the original text was all lowercase, then the replacement text must be inserted in all lowercase."

TABLE 8-2. Example of a test case

Name	TC-47: Verify that lowercase data entry results in lowercase insert
Requirement	FR-4 (Case sensitivity in search-and-replace), bullet 2
Preconditions	The test document TESTDOC.DOC is loaded (base state BS-12).
Steps	1. Click on the "Search and Replace" button. 2. Click in the "Search Term" field. 3. Enter *This is the Search Term.* 4. Click in the "Replacement Text" field. 5. Enter *This IS THE Replacement TeRM.* 6. Verify that the "Case Sensitivity" checkbox is unchecked. 7. Click the OK button.
Expected results	1. The search-and-replace window is dismissed. 2. Verify that in line 38 of the document, the text *this is the search term* has been replaced by *this is the replacement term.* 3. Return to base state BS-12.

Note that this test case includes interactions with design elements like text fields, buttons, and windows. This is one of the main differences between a use case and a test case. A use case specifically does not talk about design elements, in order to avoid constraining the designers. Test cases must be very specific about how they plan on doing their interaction because the design has been decided upon, and the part of the purpose of the test case is to exercise that design. This means that the test case cannot be completed until the design of the software is finished.

A project manager should be aware of the characteristics of a good test case. A test case describes in complete detail everything that the tester must do. It contains the names of the buttons that the tester must click on, the menu items that should be selected, the exact data that must be typed in, etc. All of the expected behavior of the software (such as windows dismissed or error messages displayed) must be described. The goal of that is to make each test case repeatable, so that no two people will test the software differently.

Table 8-3 shows an example of a test case that is widely open to interpretation. It may seem specific at first glance, but there are some serious problems with it:

• The test case does not specify exactly how the search-and-replace function is accessed. If there are several ways to bring up this function, and a defect is found that is specific to only one of them, it may be difficult to repeat precisely.

• The test case is not data-specific. Every tester could enter a different search term and replacement term. If a defect only occurs for certain terms, it will be difficult to reproduce.

- The test case does not specify how the data is entered into the field. It is possible that a problem might come up when the user uses the tab key to navigate between fields, but cannot be reproduced by clicking on them.

TABLE 8-3. This poorly designed test case does not describe the interaction precisely enough

Steps	1. Bring up search-and-replace.
	2. Enter a lowercase word from the document in the search term field.
	3. Enter a mixed-case word in the replacement field.
	4. Verify that case sensitivity is not turned on and execute the search.
Expected results	1. Verify that the lowercase word has been replaced with the mixed-case term in lowercase.

In short, this test case is not repeatable. It may seem intuitive to make the test case more general, in order to capture a wider range of functionality. However, the test case itself will be run only once during each test iteration. Instead of trying to make the test case more general, multiple test cases should be added to the test plan, in order to verify each specific type of test. For example, there should be separate test cases for clicking in the text field and tabbing between them. If the tester wants to verify that the find-and-replace function works with long strings as well as short ones, or for numbers and symbols as well as alphabetical characters, all of those things should be separate test cases. (The test case name should be used to differentiate between these tests.)

Another important characteristic is that each test case describes one—and only one—test. The reason for this is that the test case should isolate the specific behavior that is being tested, to ensure that any defect that is found is a problem with that feature only. One of the complexities of software is that there are usually an infinite number of possible feature combinations, and the only way to make sure that those combinations are not interacting improperly is to isolate each specific behavior. That makes it much easier to determine the root cause of any defect found.

For example, Table 8-4 contains the "Expected Results" section of a poorly designed test case that exercises all of the bullet points in requirement FR-4. If a defect were found in bullet point number 4, it would be difficult to determine whether the defect arose because those specific actions were done in sequence, or if it were simply an isolated defect.

TABLE 8-4. This poorly designed test case has more than one interaction

Expected Results	1. The search and replace window is dismissed.
	2. Verify that in line 36 of the document, the text *THIS IS THE SEARCH TERM* has been replaced by *THIS IS THE REPLACEMENT TERM*.
	3. Verify that in line 38 of the document, the text *this is the search term* has been replaced by *this is the replacement term*.
	4. Verify that in line 43 of the document, the text *This is the search term* has been replaced by *This is the replacement term*.
	5. Verify that in line 44 of the document, the text *This Is the Search Term* has been replaced by *This Is the Replacement Term*.
	6. Verify that in line 44 of the document, the text *thIS is the SEarCh Term* has been replaced by *This IS THE Replacement TeRM*.

Test cases are usually strung together in one long interaction with the software. This means that the results in Table 8-4 should really be verified using five different test cases, one per bullet point in requirement FR-4. For example, since test case TC-47 verifies the second bullet point in FR-4, TC-48 could verify the third bullet point and have in its precondition that TC-47 has been run. The precondition for TC-47, in turn, would require that TC-46 be run.

To ensure that the test cases all start out with the same document open, each test case depends on a *base state*, or a condition of the software that can be reproduced at any time. A base state is an anchor point that is easy to navigate to. Test case TC-47 contains two references to a base state labeled BS-12. The first reference is in the Precondition section: the test case requires that the software be in its base state. The second reference is at the end of the Expected Results section: the tester must return the software to the base state after the test case, in order to reset it for the next one. This ensures that whether the test passes or fails, it will not have any side effects on any tests that are executed after it. Table 8-5 shows the definition of this base state. It is in the same form as a test case (note that since it is not exercising a particular requirement, the "Requirement" section contains the text "N/A").

TABLE 8-5. Base state BS-12

Name	BS-12: Load test document TESTDOC.DOC
Requirement	N/A
Preconditions	No user is logged in and no applications are running.
Steps	1. Log in as user "joetester" with password "test1234".
	2. Launch the application.
	3. Select the File/Open menu item.
	4. Enter "/usr/home/joetester/TESTDOC.DOC".
	5. Click OK.
Expected Results	1. Verify that the Open Window dialog box has been dismissed.
	2. Verify that the file TESTDOC.DOC is loaded.
	3. Verify that the file TESTDOC.DOC is given focus.
	4. Verify that the file TESTDOC.DOC is active.

It is not necessary for every test case to start out in a base state. In fact, it is often useful to string a set of test cases together so that the precondition of each one depends on the previous test case passing. However, when there are strings of test cases that go for a long time without returning to a base state, there is a risk that areas of the application will go untested in the event of a failure. If a test case fails, the results of the following test cases simply cannot be trusted until the software is returned to a base state.

Once all of the test cases and base states are defined, they should be combined into a single *test case document*. This document is usually far longer than any other document produced over the course of the software project. It contains a separate table for each test case and base state. Each of the test cases and base states should be cross-referenced with the "Features to be Tested" section of the test plan. This section should contain the complete Name field of each test case and base state. Typically, the test cases and base states appear in the test case document in the same order that they appear in the test plan.

The test case document should have an outline that follows the software requirements specification: it should contain one section for each use case and requirement, and in that section, there should be a set of test cases that fully test that requirement. This makes the test cases much easier to inspect, because a reviewer can look at a single section and judge whether the test cases in that section fully exercise the requirement that they are supposed to be testing.

Once the test cases are complete, they should be inspected by the engineering team (see Chapter 5). The test plan and test cases should be collaborative documents; if the team does not give input into them, then it is likely that the software will fail to implement certain behavior that the users expect. This inspection will generally have a narrower audience than the test plan because the document is much longer and more technical. Minimally, it should be reviewed by another software tester, the requirements engineer who built the requirements that are being tested, and the programmer who implemented them.

Inspection Checklist

The following checklist items apply to the test plan.

Completeness

Does the document meet all established templates and standards?

Is the document complete?

Are there any requirements that are not tested?

Are there any features that are planned for testing but should be excluded?

Feasibility

Can the testing as planned be accomplished within the known cost and schedule constraints?

Can every test described in the test plan be reasonably conducted?

Environment

Is the description of the environment complete?

Is the test plan traceable to any nonfunctional requirements that define the operating environment?

Performance

Does the test plan account for the expected load for concurrent users, large databases, or other performance requirements?

Can the performance tests be traced back to requirements in the specification?

Acceptance Criteria

Do the acceptance criteria match the standards of the organization?

The following checklist items apply to the test cases:

Clarity

Does each test case have a clear flow of events?

Does each test case test only one specific interaction?

Does each test case describe the interaction using specific user interface and data elements?

Is each test case repeatable by someone uninitiated on the project?

Completeness

Is every requirement in the SRS verified fully with individual test cases?

Are all of the steps in each test case necessary?

Are there any steps that are missing?

Are all alternative paths and exceptions accounted for?

Accuracy

For every action, is there an expected result?

For every behavior in the requirement, is there a verification of the actual behavior?

Is the test case data specific—if data must be entered or modified, is that data provided?

Traceability

Is each test case uniquely identified with a name and a number?

Can each test case be traced back to a specific requirement?

Test Execution

The software testers begin executing the test plan after the programmers deliver a build that they feel is feature complete. This is referred to as the *alpha build*. The alpha should be of high quality—the programmers should feel that it is ready for release, and as good as they can get it. This build should have been code reviewed (see Chapter 5) and should have passed unit tests (see Chapter 7); it should have already been minimally functionally tested by the development team, as well.

There are typically several iterations of test execution. The first iteration focuses on new functionality that has been added since the last round of testing. (If this is the first time this software product has been tested, then every test case is executed.) If no defects are uncovered that are considered high enough priority to fix (see below about defect triage), then the testers move on to perform a regression test.

A *regression test* is a test designed to make sure that a change to one area of the software has not caused any other part of the software that had previously passed its tests to stop working. Regression testing usually involves executing all test cases that have previously been executed. In other words, it's not enough to verify that the software has been altered: it's also necessary to ensure that the change did not break any other part of the software that previously worked.

It is rare for no defects to be uncovered in the first test iteration. Usually, some test cases fail and defects must be reported. Once the iteration is complete, the defects are triaged (see below) and the programmers begin repairing the software. When a new build is delivered, the next iteration of testing begins.

After each iteration, the testers create a *test report*. This is a document (usually a spreadsheet or word processor document) that simply contains a list of all test cases that failed or were not executed. The purpose of the report is to give the project team a good idea of how much of the application was exercised in the test.

For each test case that failed, a tester creates a *defect report*. These reports are used to determine the general health of the product, in order to allow the project team and stakeholders to understand its maturity and readiness for release (see below about defect tracking).

Testing is complete when either no defects are found or (more likely) all of the defects that have been found satisfy the acceptance criteria in the test plan. These criteria will typically include several rules: that all test cases have been executed, that the project stakeholders have reviewed all of the defects and personally determined that the software can be released with those known defects, and that there is consensus among the engineering team that the product is ready for release. Table 8-6 shows an example of typical acceptance criteria from a test plan.

TABLE 8-6. Acceptance criteria from a test plan

1. Successful completion of all tasks as documented in the test schedule.
2. Quantity of medium- and low-level defects must be at an acceptable level as determined by the software testing project team lead.
3. User interfaces for all features are functionally complete.
4. Installation documentation and scripts are complete and tested.
5. Development code reviews are complete and all issues addressed. All high-priority issues have been resolved.
6. All outstanding issues pertinent to this release are resolved and closed.
7. All current code must be under source control, must build cleanly, the build process must be automated, and the software components must be labeled with correct version numbers in the version control system.
8. All high-priority defects are corrected and fully tested prior to release.
9. All defects that have not been fixed before release have been reviewed by project stakeholders to confirm that they are acceptable.
10. The end user experience is at an agreed acceptable level.
11. Operational procedures have been written for installation, set up, error recovery, and escalation.
12. There must be no adverse effects on already deployed systems.

The list of acceptance criteria can also include any specific performance requirements ("server must support 80 users," "product must perform under high load for 72 hours without failure," etc.), as well as any security requirements specific to the software.

The majority of the acceptance criteria in the example focus on the consensus of the people involved in the software project. It is important that everyone agrees that any defects that the software ships with will not affect the users.

Note that these criteria assume that there will be defects that will not be fixed. The goal of test execution is not to remove every defect from the software; rather, it is to make the people in the organization aware of the individual issues encountered during testing. This way, everyone is aware of the risks (if any) involved in releasing the software, so an informed decision can be made about whether or not to fix the defects and retest the software.

Defect Tracking and Triage

All defects that are found by the testers must be replicated, repaired, and verified. This means that many people must be able to see and reproduce the behavior that causes each defect. To do this, a defect report must be created for every defect found that includes:

- A name and a unique number.
- A priority (determined by the tester, but that may be modified later in defect triage).
- A description of the defect. The description must include the steps required to replicate the defect, the actual behavior observed when the steps were followed, and the expected results of the steps.

When a tester discovers a defect, it should be entered into a *defect tracking system*, a database used for storing information about defects and routing them through a workflow of evaluation and repair. There are many defect tracking systems available, including commercial systems and ones that are free and open source. Many of the metrics used to measure the health of the product are gathered from the defect tracking system (see below). It is also useful when planning regression tests: testers use it to keep track of defects that were repaired, in order to verify that they were fixed before getting into the rest of the functional tests.

Once a defect is entered, the defect tracking system routes it between testers, developers, the project manager, and other people, following a workflow designed to ensure that the defect is verified and repaired. The specific workflow used to enter, evaluate, and repair defects can vary from organization to organization. Minimally, the defect workflow should track the interaction between the testers who find the defect and the programmers who fix it, and it should ensure that every defect can be properly prioritized and reviewed by all of the stakeholders to determine whether or not it should be repaired. This process of review and prioritization is referred to as *triage*. This somewhat dramatic name comes from the triage of patients in an emergency room: the patients with the most severe injuries must get medical attention first. It is the same way with software defects, where the most severe defects are given the highest priority.

Triage should be done by project stakeholders, or at least one person who is trusted by the stakeholders to make those decisions for them. It is important to be sure that the person or people who are responsible for the quality of the application are given control over the defect triage process so that the high-priority bugs get fixed. In some organizations, one senior-level manager reviews and makes decisions on contentious bugs. In others, individual team members are empowered to make release decisions on their own. One manager in a room may decide all of the priorities on the defects, or the team may meet and review each defect to determine which ones need to be fixed and which do not. However, it is generally not the sole responsibility of the tester to make such decisions. One of the most effective ways to determine release-readiness is to have the entire project team reach a consensus on which defects are important to fix and which can be released in the product.

While it is one of the most straightforward concepts in quality assurance, triage is also one of the most important and time-consuming. Every single defect must be reviewed and prioritized. This can mean daily meetings for project stakeholders, and it is often difficult to delegate this responsibility because only the stakeholders really know whether a defect will prevent the users from doing their jobs.

In other words, there is an important division of responsibility. The testers are only responsible for reporting what they see when they use the software. They are not in a position where they can judge whether the defects they find will impact the organization. That's not their focus, and they do not have the expertise to make those judgements. Only a person who has a real stake in the software can use that information to judge its health. A software crash that is caused using certain steps or data may seem very important to a tester; someone with a lot of knowledge of the way the users will use the software might see an obvious workaround that will make perfect sense to them, or see that the users would not encounter that crash at all. That does not mean the software should be released if it crashes, but it does affect the priority of that bug being fixed.

Test Environment and Performance Testing

It is important for the project manager to get involved in setting standards for verifying that software has sufficient performance. It may seem like this is a detail that can be left up to the testers, but it can't. In fact, it's absolutely necessary that the project manager work with the team to try to forecast how the product will be used.

Performance requirements really should be in place as early as the scope definition phase. When the project manager is writing (or helping to write) the vision and scope document for the product, she should ask questions about the environment in which the product will be deployed:

- How many users will be using the software?
- How many of those users will be using it concurrently?
- Does the software need to be available 24 hours a day, 7 days a week?
- Are there peak usage times?
- How much data will be stored in the database?
- What physical hardware will the software be running on?
- What version of the operating system will be used?
- Is security a concern?
- Will the software need to run under multiple environments (OS, hardware, etc.)?
- Will the software need to be updated or maintained after it is rolled out?

All of these things will affect how the software is tested. Even though all of the details are not known when the vision and scope document is written, all of these issues should at least be raised, and any known information should be recorded. That way, the requirements analysts will make sure to discover the answers to these questions and include them in the software requirements specification as nonfunctional requirements (see Chapter 6). The testers, in turn, will take those nonfunctional requirements and use them to build a test environment and plan a set of performance tests.

Most performance testing requires automated tools. Sometimes these tools can be bought off the shelf; at other times, they must be developed separately by the programmers. Performance requirements should be known as early as possible in order to properly plan for them. It is a very common mistake for an organization to demand performance requirements, yet fail to budget for licensing fees for performance testing tools (which can be expensive), a hardware environment that mirrors the production environment (which costs as much as the production environment itself), and, most importantly, the time for the testers to set up this environment. This is another reason the project manager must be highly involved in planning for the performance testing—it can be a very costly operation, but it is one that must be fought for if the software is to perform adequately.

Even when the software under test does not have to meet demanding performance requirements, it can be challenging to plan for, budget, and set up an adequate test environment. If the users will use multiple hardware or operating system platforms, each of those must be replicated in the test environment. If web-based software has a specific network configuration (routers, load balancers, separate network segments, firewalls, DMZ, security, etc.), then the test environment must have all of the same equipment. If not, the testers will never be able to replicate the real-world conditions under which the software might break.

It is very common to shortchange the test environment by using virtual machines, by using one machine for both the database and the web server, by getting rid of load balancers, or by introducing other differences between the test environment and the production environment. That amounts to a waste of time when it comes to performance testing. Maybe the team will find some memory leaks and bugs, but much of the time, performance problems are in configuration, not in code. This is often overlooked, and it can lead to large problems and user dissatisfaction when the software is rolled out.

It is important that the test environment be completely separate from production. This is especially true of software that has already been released to the clients (especially web-based software, or software that depends on a central database located in the same office as the programmers and testers, or that relies on their network). It is surprisingly easy to take down a production system during testing if the test environment is not completely separate. For example, it may seem "safe" to save money by sharing only a firewall, load balancer, or router. Yet there are serious kinds of bugs that may occur only in the test version, which will make it effectively impossible for production requests to reach the software. If this happens, the software testers will be blamed for the production downtime—even if it was caused by a bug introduced by the programmers!

The primary reason people typically shortchange their test environments, or do not perform adequate performance tests, is money. It is expensive to perform these tests, and often difficult to convince senior managers that they need to double their hardware budget. The project manager must fight for adequate resources for performance tests, and plan this hardware need from the very beginning (rather than tack it on at the end). The truth is that if it is too expensive to set up an adequate test environment, then the organization simply cannot afford to produce this software and should seek another solution.

Smoke Tests

A *smoke test* is a subset of the test cases that is typically representative of the overall test plan. For example, if there is a product with a dozen test plans (each of which has hundreds of test cases), then a smoke test for that product might just contain a few dozen test cases (with just one or two test cases from each test plan). The goal of a smoke test is to verify the breadth of the software functionality without going into depth on any one feature or requirement. (The name "smoke test" originally came from the world of electrical engineering. The first time a new circuit under development is attached to a power source, an especially glaring error may cause certain parts to start to smoke; at that point, there is no reason to continue to test the circuit.)

Smoke tests can be useful in many scenarios. For example, after a product has been tested, released, and deployed into production, a configuration management team member may manually run through a smoke test each time a new installation of the software is put in place at a client, in order to ensure that it is properly deployed. Another good use is to allow programmers to judge the health of a build before they give it to the software testers for testing: once a product has passed all of its unit tests, it may make sense to install the build and manually run the smoke tests, in order to ensure that it is ready for testing.

Unfortunately, smoke tests are often abused by senior managers or stakeholders who are impatient for the software to be complete. Typically, they will learn of a reduced battery of tests that takes very little time to run, but will fail to understand how these tests differ from the complete regression tests that are normally run. Suddenly, there is a new option that doesn't take very long. The project manager will start seeing requests to cut down the testing tasks by substituting the smoke tests for actual tests.

What's worse, the deployment scenario, in which a new deployment is verified with a smoke test, will be abused. The idea behind the deployment scenario is that no changes have been made—the smoke test is simply to help verify that the act of deployment has not accidentally broken the environment. (It's not uncommon for a complex deployment environment to have slight configuration or network differences that can break the software—or for someone to leave a network cable hanging!) The smoke test is there for the people responsible for deploying the software to be sure that the installation was successful. If, however, changes are made to the environment or (even worse) the code in production, the smoke test will almost certainly fail to uncover the problems that have been introduced.

Many people are skeptical when project managers warn them of potential problems with deploying untested or poorly tested code. It's important to remember some of the most historic and costly defects that were caused by a "tiny" change in the code. In 1990, an engineer in AT&T rolled out a very small change to a switch that had one defect in one line of code (a misspelled "break" statement in C). The long-distance network failed for over 9 hours, causing over 65 million calls to fail to go through and costing AT&T an enormous amount of money. There are plenty of other very costly examples: the NASA Mars orbiter crash due to one team using metric units and another using English units, eBay's outage in 1999 due to a poor database upgrade, the Pentium processor bug that had a few numbers off in a floating point lookup table… all of these problems were "tiny" changes or defects that cost an enormous amount of money. In the end, nobody cared how small the source of the problem was: a disastrous problem was still disastrous, even if it was easy to solve.

This does not mean that the entire test battery needs to be run every single time a deployment is made or a change is made. What it means is that an informed decision must be made, and risks assessed, before the test battery is cut down for any reason. For example, test procedures that target specific areas of functionality could be reduced when changes are limited, and when the risk of those changes is low. There is no one-size-fits-all test that will result in proper coverage for your applications. Any time a limited change is made to the software, it should be carefully considered, in order to make sure that the appropriate tests are executed.

Test Automation

There are software packages available that allow a tester to automate test cases. Typically, this software uses either a record-and-playback system where mouse movements and keystrokes are recorded and played back into a user interface, a programming or scripting languages that accesses the user interface using a class model, or a combination of the two. Automation can be a powerful tool in reducing the amount of time that it takes to run the tests.

However, setting up and maintaining test automation adds an enormous amount of overhead. Now, instead of simply writing a test case, that test case must be programmed or recorded, tested, and debugged. A database or directory of test scripts must be maintained, and since there can be hundreds or thousands of test cases for even a small project, there will be hundreds or thousands of scripts to keep track of. What's more, since the scripts hook into the user interface of the software, there must be some plan in place to keep the scripts working in case the user interface changes.

There have been some advances recently (at the time of this writing) that help cut down on test automation maintenance tasks. These advances include canned functions to automate multiple tasks at once, generalization of scripts so that the tester refers to general business processes instead of specific user interface interactions, and the use of databases of test scripts that can be maintained automatically. But even with these advances, it is still highly time-consuming to automate and maintain tests—it often means that test planning takes several times as long as it would without automation.

It is a common misconception that automation will free the test team of most of their work. This simply is not true. Automation requires more effort than manual testing; the trade-off is that the test scripts can be reused, so that a series of automated tests run much more quickly than a manual test.

One good reason to adopt automation is that the test battery will never shrink. As the product matures, the test battery will get bigger and bigger because the software will do more and more. This means that manual testing will require more and more effort as time goes on, and will take longer each time the functionality increases. Automation, on the other hand, requires a constant amount of overhead, and can help keep the test effort under control because the automated tests do not require much effort to run. They do, however, require a lot of effort to interpret once they have run. Instead of a tester manually executing a test case, finding a defect, and recording that defect immediately, the tester must first look at a report document to find the reported failures and then track each failure down in the application, research it, and enter it as a defect.

Another misconception is that test scripts will somehow eliminate the need for test cases. This is absolutely untrue. Automation actually requires more planning than manual testing. Each test script must first be developed as a written test case. Writing a script without a test case is like writing software without requirements—if the tester simply goes in and starts recording, there is no way to define the expected result of the test. It's not enough to just record a script; the test case itself must be written, and then the recording made to automate the test that has been planned. If this is not done, there is no way to verify that the tests really do cover all of the requirements. And if there is no written test case, there is no way to interpret the results if the script fails, because there is no record of what it is that the script was supposed to do!

There are also many logistic difficulties in automation that must be overcome, especially if there is a team of testers who will maintain and run the tests. The scripts must be stored somewhere, and people need to be able to collaborate without overwriting each others' work (which may require that the automation script files be stored in a version control system like Subversion—see Chapter 7). It may be difficult to estimate how long it will take to actually run and interpret the scripts. And another trade-off is hardware: adding more and more powerful test machines can cut down on the amount of time required to test the software, but, since they do not cut down on how long it takes to interpret the results and enter defects, there may be some diminishing returns in that area.

All in all, automation is often a net gain for the project, especially if the project will be tested many times and maintained over a long period of time. However, there is absolutely no benefit in automating a product that will not face repeated regression tests over the course of multiple releases. If there will be just one release, the cost of automation will not be recouped. It is very important for a project manager to understand the pros and cons of automation, and to guide the organization toward its wise use.

Postmortem Reports

After the project is done, there is a lot of important information out in the organization that can help a project manager run future projects better. There is a brief period after the software is released to the users when everyone is done with the tasks, but when they still have a lot of strong opinions and remember specific details about how the project went. If this information is documented in a way that can be used to help in the future, it will be a valuable resource for the organization.

A *postmortem report* is an overall account of the team's experience in building the software, and of the experience of the users and stakeholders in working with the team. The report should contain an honest assessment of how the team members, users, and stakeholders perceived the end product and assessed the decisions made throughout the project. The purpose of the postmortem report is to highlight the team's successes and identify any problems that should be fixed in future releases.

Often, a project manager will gather the project team together with anyone who had anything to do with the software project into a large meeting so they can talk about the project. This is rarely effective—it just turns into a big, useless meeting (see Chapter 5). In the same way that people are uncomfortable criticizing each others' work or taking that criticism for individual work products, they can be equally uncomfortable doing it for the entire project. This is especially true when it comes to taking criticism about the project from people outside of the team.

A much more effective way to gather this information is to rely on the quality assurance team members, who have expertise gathering and objectively reporting both positive and negative information about the project. In the same way that they assess the health of a single build and write a report that describes it, they can assess the health of the entire project and write a postmortem report that describes the results of that assessment. The project manager can then gather the team, users, and stakeholders together to review the results.

One effective way to gather information for the postmortem report is to use a survey. It is important that this survey covers every phase of software development, so that nobody is left out or singled out. The survey should be constructed so that participants can respond anonymously. Respondents should be asked for both a numeric rating and for their thoughts and comments. Table 8-7 shows some typical questions that might appear on a postmortem survey.

TABLE 8-7. Sample postmortem survey questions

The "Accounting Rules Automation" feature is complete.						
(strongly agree)	5	4	3	2	1	(strongly disagree)

Do you have additional comments about this?

The "Accounting Rules Automation" feature is useful.

(strongly agree)   5   4   3   2   1   (strongly disagree)

Do you have additional comments about this?

The Vision and Scope document said that the software was intended to address the business need that our client team was missing critical assessment numbers. How well did the software project fill this need?

(very well)   5   4   3   2   1   (poorly)

Do you have additional comments about this?

The survey should gather a wide range of information about how well the team performed their function, features of the software that was built, the effectiveness of specific work products and activities, and how well the team met the objectives of the project and of each phase of development. Survey questions typically cover:

- Were the tasks divided well among the team?
- Were the right people assigned to each task?
- Were the reviews effective?
- Was each work product useful in the later phases of the project?
- Did the software meet the needs described in the vision and scope document?
- Did the stakeholders and users have enough input into the software?
- Were there too many changes?
- How complete is each feature?
- How useful is each feature?
- Have the users received the software?
- How is the user experience with the software?
- Are there usability or performance issues?
- Are there problems installing or configuring the software?
- Were the initial deadlines set for the project reasonable?
- How well was the overall project planned?
- Were there risks that could have been foreseen but were not planned for?

- Was the software produced in a timely manner?

- Was the software of sufficient quality?

- Do you have any suggestions for how we can improve for our next project?

Once the survey results are collected, they should be summarized and presented in the postmortem report. The report should focus on the overall results rather than individual responses. Figure 8-1 shows a typical summary section that would appear at the top of a postmortem report. In this example, the questions in the survey were grouped into six categories, and the results were divided into positive, neutral, or negative ratings.

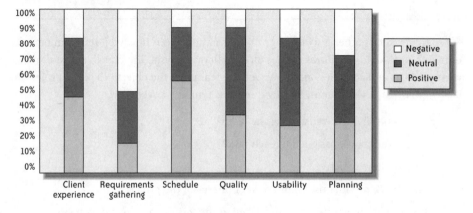

Post-Mortem Survey Results
Now that we've released the software to 83% of the client base, it's a good time to take stock of the things that we did right when releasing the software, and to point out places where we can improve. To help us determine our areas for improvement, we sent a survey to everybody involved with the release: the Software Engineering team, Sales, Client Support, Level 1 Technical Support, the Implementation Team and selected other people who played a part in the release. Of 66 possible respondents, we received 34 responses.

FIGURE 8-1. Sample summary section from a postmortem report

Each of the remaining sections in the report shows details about the response for each individual question, followed by final sections that offer recommendations and specific actions to take. (The actual postmortem survey should be attached to the report as an appendix.) Each section should summarize the results of one question in the survey and present any comments given (without any identifying factors). It is important to preserve the respondents' anonymity so that they can feel comfortable giving their uncensored opinions. If several respondents had similar or related comments, those comments should be combined into one single statement that summarizes all of them. Not every comment will be constructive; the QA engineer preparing the report should use judgement to decide which comments are relevant. Table 8-8 shows an example of a section of the report that summarizes one question.

Beta
Was the beta test effective in heading off problems before clients found them?
Score: 2.28 out of 5 (12 Negative [1 to 2], 13 Neutral [3], 9 Positive [4 to 5])

All of the comments we got about the beta were negative, and only 26% (9 of 34) of the survey respondents felt that the beta exceeded their expectations. The general perception was that many obvious defects were not caught in the beta. Suggestions for improvement included lengthening the beta, expanding it to more client sites, and ensuring that the software was used as if it were in production.

Individual comments:

- I feel like Versions 2.0 and 2.1 could have been in the beta field longer so that we might have discovered the accounting bugs before many of the clients did.
- We need to have a more in-depth beta test in the future. Had the duration of the beta been longer, we would have caught more problems and headed them off before they became critical situations at the client site.
- I think that a lot of problems that were encountered were found after the beta, during the actual start of the release. Shortly thereafter, things were ironed out.
- Overall, the release has gone well. I just feel that we missed something in the beta test, particularly the performance issues we are experiencing in our Denver and Chicago branches. In the future, we can expand the beta to more sites.

Once the postmortem report has been compiled, the project manager should call a meeting to review it. The attendees should include project team members, stakeholders, users, and any other people who were asked to respond to the survey. The meeting should be a walkthrough (see Chapter 5) of the report. The project manager should write down suggestions or comments that are brought up during the meeting.

The final section of the report is an action list, which should be added after the postmortem meeting. Throughout the review, there will be many recommendations suggested by stakeholders, team members, and other people. The project manager should work with everyone at the meeting to identify specific actions that can be taken to make sure those recommendations are implemented. If possible, he should gain a real commitment to those actions, if the right people are there; if not, he should commit to following up on each of them, in order to make sure that the next project is performed better. By writing down the list of specific actions to take and including the commitments that people make during the meeting, the project manager can ensure that those changes are incorporated into future projects.

Using Software Testing Effectively

Software testing is often the most difficult area of software development for a project manager to put in place because, unlike other disciplines of software engineering, many people have a negative attitude toward it. Some people think that good programmers simply don't write bugs, so if they hire good programmers, then they don't need testers. Others only see software testing as something that holds back development. However, there are many organizations where software testing is used as an effective tool for reducing project schedules and increasing user satisfaction. If a project manager works to combat the negative attitudes about testing, he can achieve these results on his own projects.

Commonly, people (mistakenly) think about software testing in one of two ways. Sometimes they expect testers to be "all-powerful." They should be able to catch every single bug in the software so that there will never be a user error or complaint, ever. To someone with this mindset, any complaint that comes from a user is seen as a failure of the software testers. On the other hand, people sometimes consider software testers to be little more than bean counters, whose job is to simply look for typos and for "insignificant" errors that the programmers might have missed in their "exhaustive" testing. Paradoxically, some people can even hold both of these misconceptions simultaneously. In other words, the expectations put on software testers are not only impossible to meet, but often contradictory.

When people have one of these common misunderstandings about what it is that software testers do, it generally leads to an even bigger misunderstanding of what quality is. They do not think about quality as how far a product has deviated from its specifications. Instead, they think about it as some sort of theoretical limit that would be really great to achieve, but could never actually be accomplished in practice.

Much of this confusion about quality and software testing comes from the fact that software testers do not add to the software; they "just" run it and report any problems. The actual mechanics of testing seem almost stagnant to somebody who does not really understand its purpose. They feel that the software is built, yet there are these testers who are running the same tests over and over on the same piece of software, keeping the organization from releasing it. It falls to the project manager to defend the software quality by keeping the test activities from being shortchanged.

Understand What Testers Do

Testers are not a special breed of person. Software testing is a skill; it is a discipline of software engineering, just like programming, design, requirements analysis, and project management. Yet many people think that someone needs to be a certain kind of person in order to be a successful tester. They feel that being an effective software tester is purely a matter of disposition, rather than an acquired skill. It is very common for good testers to constantly hear their peers say things like, "I can't understand how you could do what you do" and "I could never do that to people."

Even highly respected thinkers in software engineering tout the virtues of having your software tested by people who don't know anything about software engineering at all. It has even been suggested that software testing involves no skill and could be done by temps, college students, smart teenagers, and retirees. The thinking goes that anyone who is qualified to be a good tester would not want to be one because the job is somehow so horrible that anyone who would be really good at it would opt for programming instead.This is ridiculous. Yet it is by far the most common opinion on software testing in the industry.

To understand what testers do, it's important to debunk certain popular myths. The first myth is that anyone off the street can test software. This is no truer than it would be of any other software engineering discipline. Testing requires training, skill, experience, and an understanding of the requirements and design of the application under test. A software requirements specification would be essentially unreadable to, say, a college student or temp with no software engineering background. How would such a person then be able to design a test strategy to verify it?

Many people mistakenly believe that software testing is a stepping-stone to programming. This is complete nonsense. The skills are completely different, and a good programmer will not learn any more about programming by testing software than a tester would by programming. They are different jobs with different skills. Nobody suggests that a programmer should first be a requirements analyst or project manager before beginning to program. But for some reason, many people suggest exactly this about those who work in quality assurance. All of those jobs have different skill sets, and all are necessary in order for a team to develop software. A good project manager will help her organization see that no one of those jobs is more important than any other.

Another myth is that testers have to be "nasty." The thinking behind this is that testers must enjoy criticizing other people about minute details. (This is also often what people mean when they say that testers should be "detail-oriented." Shouldn't everyone involved in software development be equally detail-oriented? Details can make or break the project.) In truth, testers do not need to be nasty; rather, they should be scientifically-minded. Each test case is really an experiment: if the user interacts in this way, does the software produce the desired results? The testers really want the software to pass, and would prefer to be able to move on to the next test rather than to have to enter a defect.

The most common myth is that testers want to keep the organization from releasing software, and want to criticize the programmers who built it. It is common to talk about a "battle" between programming and QA, in which there is a lot of tension and competition between the two groups in the organization. This myth is highly counterproductive, because it drives a wedge between software engineers working toward the same goal. A good tester simply wants the truth about the software to be known, so that responsible and accurate decisions can be made about its health. Testers do not want to keep the software from being released; they just want the stakeholders and managers to make an informed decision about releasing it.

In other words, testers don't want to be mean to the programmers; they want to help them make the code better, so that everyone can be proud of the product. There is no mystery to what motivates a good software tester. Testers want to do a good job and take pride in a well-engineered product, just like all other software engineers. It's their job to catch defects; if they miss defects, they look like lousy testers. They aren't hired to abuse programmers; they're hired to "abuse" software—by people who have the software's best interests in mind. Software testers certainly do not want to make specific comments about individual programmers. In fact, when they are testing, they rarely even know who wrote the code that broke. All a tester wants to do is report that taking certain action with the software does not yield the results she expected. It's up to management to decide how to handle that.

By and large, these myths are not true. However, there are some people who were attracted to software testing specifically because of these myths and, as a result, turn them into self-fulfilling prophecies. There's a tiny minority of people in the software testing world who really do enjoy being nasty to programmers. Often, these people do not have much skill in software testing. However, these people represent the exception and not the rule. Treating all software testers based on this stereotype is always counterproductive.

Divide Quality Tasks Efficiently

When looked at from a high level, it seems that testing tasks can be easily divided between testers and programmers. The programmers are responsible for making sure that the software does what they intended it to do; the testers are responsible for making sure that the software does what the users and stakeholders intended it to do. However, when testing is actually under way, there are often grey areas of responsibility that emerge between programming and QA that can be a source of contention that inside the team. It is up to the project manager to make sure that tasks are distributed according to what is efficient, and by how people define their jobs.

Many people mistakenly believe that software testers can test "everything" in an application. When a defect is found after the software is released, they expectantly look to the QA team to figure out why they did not catch it. Sometimes it is true that QA should have caught a defect. If there is a requirement written into the specification or design that is planned, but the software does not properly implement the requirement or design, the testers should have caught it. If there are test cases that were supposed to execute the behavior and were marked as "passed," then it is reasonable to assume that a tester made a mistake. But it is unreasonable to think that every client complaint, every crash, or every "bug" should be caught by QA. Not only is it unreasonable, it is simply impossible to do this. The job of a software tester is to verify that the software met its requirements. If there is a core behavior that users will expect and that stakeholders need, the only way for the tester to know this is for a requirements analyst or designer (or a project manager, if necessary!) to write down exactly how the software should behave. It is unreasonable to expect the tester to come up with that independently.

Quality is everyone's responsibility. Some programmers look at QA as a sort of "quality dumping ground" where all quality tasks can be relegated. Study after study, book after book, and, most importantly, practical experience show that this approach fails every time. Software testers just can't tack quality onto a product at the end of the project. Quality must be planned in from the beginning, and every project team member needs to do his or her part to make sure that the defects are caught.

Consider the example of a defect that is found in a test that is very complicated—for example, it may occur in only one environment with a specific set of data. In some organizations, rules put in place by management require that the software testers spend days researching what might be causing this problem: reconstructing scenarios, attempting to reproduce it in different environments, trying to recreate corrupted data...all of which are highly time-consuming. This is a very inefficient use of engineering time, if it's the case that a programmer could have just loaded the software into a debugger in the same environment that the tester originally found it in, recreated the problem using the same test data, and fixed it on the spot.

Another example of a grey area is a critical crash in the software that makes an important feature of the software essentially impossible to use, and that is immediately apparent on installation. For example, the crash may occur as soon as the feature is launched. This is a common argument between programmers and testers: the tester immediately rejects the build, but the programmer may insist that it was perfectly reasonable to send such a broken build to QA. What the programmer may not realize is that the tester may have spent several hours setting up the test environment (imaging machines, redoing the network, installing database software, etc.), only to abort the test within five minutes. And, because the install has been done already, the entire environment will have to be done again. This is clearly an inefficient use of time. The programmer could have taken a few minutes to compile the build and launch the software—he would have found the problem immediately. This is why it is important that there are quality-related activities like unit tests and smoke tests in place that are always performed by the programmer (and passed) before the build is turned over to the testers.

Decisions about who is responsible for quality tasks should not be made based on an argument about who is responsible for what. It should not be about what programmers or testers feel should or should not be in their job descriptions. Instead, the decision should be made based on what is most efficient. If a task will take two hours for a programmer but three days for a tester, then clearly that task should be assigned to the programmer. This is why the project manager needs to have a solid understanding of what it is that the testers do, and of what's involved in setting up the test environment. That way, if there is an argument about whether or not a programmer should take on a certain quality task, the project manager can demonstrate why it is much more efficient for the programmer to do so—or choose to assign the task to the tester, if that's what makes sense. The most important part of this is for the project manager to make optimal decisions that have the smallest impact on the schedule.

Manage Time Pressure

The most common complaint about testing that project managers hear from senior managers is that the testers are wasting time, when a build could be released today. It is often very frustrating for a senior manager to hold a CD or see a web site that looks complete, only to be told that he has to wait for the testers to finish their jobs. The features seem to work, the software seems to do what it needs to do, and everything looks correct. Can't the software be rolled out now?

It is possible that even the very first build that gets created could be ready to be shipped before a single test is executed. In fact, this is what the QA team is hoping for! If the team did an excellent job of defect prevention through requirements gathering, unit testing, inspections, and reviews, then it is possible that not a single defect will be found that is serious enough to prevent the software from shipping. But it is very unlikely for this to be the case; few (if any) experienced testers have seen this. It is much more likely that the tests will uncover a defect that the senior managers decide must be fixed before the software is shipped. This is why testing tasks are necessary, and why the project manager must fight for time to finish testing the software.

Testing tasks cannot be cut any more than programming tasks can. Yet, when the project is late, senior managers and project stakeholders will often put a great deal of pressure on the project manager to do exactly that. Sometimes they will insist that regression tests be replaced with smoke tests (or cut entirely); other times, they will cut out environments, performance tests, or other activities that are critical to ensuring the software functions. It is the project manager's responsibility to resist this and assure the quality of the software.

One way that software quality is often compromised through time pressure is by putting pressure on testers to make overly aggressive estimates, and then to work overtime to meet those estimates. This happens in testing more than it happens anywhere else in a software organization, simply by virtue of the fact that testing activities are the last ones performed on the project, and the fact that few people really understand what it is that testers do. The key to avoiding this is for a project manager to use a repeatable estimation process (see Chapter 3), to resist the urge to cut quality tasks from the schedule, and to constantly stand up for the fact that the time that was estimated is what will actually be needed to test the software.

For example, if it's known that one iteration of regression tests takes three weeks, and the stakeholders choose during triage to repair defects and cut a new build, then it must be made clear to them that they are making the decision to spend three more weeks testing the software. There are two options at that point: either release the software as is, or bite the bullet and take the three weeks. One effective way to explain this is to point out that had the last iteration of regression testing not been done, the team would not even know about the defects that they want to fix, so not testing is a big risk.

Another common misguided request is that testers cut out any test cases that are not seen as representative of typical user behavior. For example, in the test case example in Table 8-2, the five bullet points in the requirement being tested require at least five different test cases. A manager putting pressure on the tester may insist that only one of the tests for that requirement be executed. Yet that manager would never go to the programmer and suggest that they only implement one of the five bullets. (This is especially likely with negative cases and boundary cases.) The bottom line is that if a feature is important enough to build, then it's important enough to make sure that it works properly.

The project manager must fight for the estimated time frame. If the estimates are overly aggressive and the testers need to work overtime to meet their own goal, that's fine. The testers should not have agreed to the inaccurate estimates. However, it's important not to routinely undercut the tester. It's very common for a manager under pressure to require, for example, that the testers come in on weekends to meet a deadline, or to arbitrarily cut down the amount of time that it takes to run a regression test. This is unfair. It's no different than telling a programmer who needs three weeks to build a feature that she only has two. Something will give and, in either of these cases, it will lead to problems with the software.

Gather Metrics

Metrics are statistics gathered over the course of the software project in order to identify accomplishments and areas for improvement. With a good metrics program, it's possible to compare projects to one another, regardless of size or scope. The ability to make these comparisons will help a project manager make consistent judgements and set standards for project teams across multiple projects.

It is not difficult to gather most simple metrics. The information needed to calculate them is available in the defect tracking system and the project schedule. (In Chapter 4, valuable earned value metrics were gathered and discussed.) In addition to earned value, there are several other metrics that can be useful to a project manager. The project manager should work with the senior management of the organization to determine what is worth measuring.

All metrics should be taken on an organization-wide level. It is important that the numbers that are gathered are used for improving the organization, and not for rewarding or penalizing individual software engineers. It is tempting, for example, to make part of an annual bonus dependent on the team reducing certain defect measurements. In practice, that is an effective way to make sure that defects do not get reported or tracked properly. Here is a list of metrics commonly used in software projects:

- The *Defects per Project Phase* metric provides a general comparison of defects found in each project phase. This metric requires the person entering the defect in the defect-tracking database to enter the phase at which the defect was found. It also requires that defects from document reviews be included, and that those defects be prioritized in the same manner as all other defects. (For example, defects found during an SRS inspection would be classified as found during the requirements phase.) This metric is usually shown as a bar graph, with the project phases on the X-axis, the number of defects on the Y-axis, and the data points being the number of defects found per phase (one sub-bar per priority).

- The *Mean Defect Discovery Rate* metric weighs the number of defects found by the effort on a day-by-day basis over the course of the project. This is a standard and useful tool to determine whether a specific project is going according to a projected defect discovery rate (based on previous projects and industry averages). This rate should slow down as the project progresses, so that far more defects are found at the beginning of software testing than at the end. If this metric remains constant or, even worse, is increasing over the course of several test iterations, it could mean that there are serious scope or requirements problems, or that the programmers did not fully understand what it is the software was supposed to do.

- The *Defect Resolution Rate* tracks the time taken to resolve defects, from the time that they are entered until the time that they are closed. It is calculated by dividing the number of non-closed problems by the average time to close. This can be used to predict release dates by extrapolating from the current open defects.

- *Defect Age* is used to measure how effective the review and inspection process is. A defect that was introduced in the scope or requirements phase but not discovered until testing is far more costly to fix than it would have been had the inspection caught it early—so the lower the mean defect age, the better. To capture the defect age metric, the root cause, or the project phase in which each defect was introduced, must be determined during triage and entered into the defect tracking database. (This is referred to as root cause analysis.) An age can then be assigned to each defect based on which phase it was discovered in and which phase it was introduced. By comparing the average defect age for the entire project with the average age for defects introduced in a specific phase, the project manager can identify which inspections and reviews are most effective and introduce better inspection practices to target the costliest defects.

- The *Percentage of Engineering Effort* metric compares how software effort (in man-hours) and actual calendar time break down into project phases. These two measurements will be useful in determining where additional training, staff, or process improvement is needed. This metric measures the average number of man-hours spent in each project phase. Some phases consume a lot of calendar time, but do not require many man-hours. A project manager can use this measurement to gauge whether the effort is being used efficiently over the course of the project schedule.

- *Defect Density* measures the number of defects per KLOC (thousand lines of code). This is one of the most common metrics used in software engineering. It is often used to determine whether the software is ready for release. A test plan may have a maximum defect density listed in the acceptance criteria, which requires that the software not contain any critical or high-priority defects, and contain less than a specific number of low-priority defects per KLOC.

> **NOTE**
>
> More information on software testing can be found in *Testing Computer Software* by Cem Kaner, Jack Falk, and Hung Quoc Nguyen (Wiley, 1999).
>
> More information on software metrics can be found in *Software Metrics: Establishing a Company-wide Program* by Robert Grady and Deborah Caswell (Prentice Hall, 1987).

Diagnosing Software Testing Problems

There is an old programming saying: "There's no such thing as bug-free software." Many people simply accept that there are quality problems, and that no piece of software is perfect. This is true—but it is also irrelevant. The goal of testing is to make sure that the software does what the users need it to do, not to make sure that it is perfect. (After all, does anyone really know what a "perfect software project" is?) With that in mind, there are real, specific problems that plague many software projects that can be solved by software testing.

Requirements Haven't Been Implemented

When a software team delivers a product that's missing features, the users tend to notice. It seems like this should never happen—aren't there many reviews and checkpoints along the way that ought to prevent it? In fact, the only time when the original requirements are ever checked against the final software is during software testing. And if there is a problem with testing, the most serious symptom is unimplemented requirements.

There are many reasons why requirements do not get implemented. Sometimes a designer or programmer does not understand what's written in the specification, or has a different understanding than what was intended. But sometimes it's simply an oversight. Good review, requirements, and programming practices will help reduce this—instead of missing features, there might only be a few requirements that have rules that are not fully implemented. But it is rare for the programmers to deliver software that completely meets every single requirement.

Missing requirements are especially insidious because they're difficult to spot. It's not hard to tell that something is there that shouldn't be; it's much harder to recognize when something important is not there at all. Often, a programmer will be completely taken by surprise when a user comes back to her and asks where a certain feature is in the software.

It's especially likely that the missing requirements are difficult to spot because even the programmer missed them when looking over his own work. Programmers tend to be careful and meticulous people; they would have caught the obvious ones.

What's more, the programmers do not necessarily see which requirements are more important to the users and stakeholders—they all have to be built, and it's up to the users and stakeholders, not the programmers, to prioritize what is developed. So by the time the software is built and delivered to the users, the requirements that are missing are difficult to spot, but are still just as important to the people who asked for them. It is not uncommon for a programmer to be surprised that a user even noticed that a business rule in a requirement was not implemented: the programmer didn't know that it was important, even though the user saw it as absolutely critical. When this happens, the programmer is both embarrassed and upset that all of his good work is ignored because some tiny rule was missing; the user, on the other hand, considers the software unusable, and has trouble even evaluating the rest of the work that's been done.

Obvious Bugs Slip Through

In many software organizations, there is a general feeling that the software testers are not very good at their jobs. Things that were written down and reviewed don't get tested. Applications are released with huge, glaring bugs, even though the testers passed the build and said it was fine to release. There are several common reasons this happens.

Sometimes bugs slip through because of ill-trained software testers. Organizations that are just setting up a software engineering group for the first time often don't have a software testing group at all, and don't realize that software testing—like programming, requirements engineering, or design—is its own engineering discipline, requiring both training and experience. In an organization like this, it is not uncommon to draft technical support staff, junior programmers, end users, outside temps, and sales people as "testers." They see their job as simply "banging on the software" and providing comments as to whether or not they like it. If the programmers have not done sufficient unit testing (see Chapter 7), it is likely that these people will find places where the software breaks or crashes. However, it's a crapshoot: while they may find valid, great defects, it's likely that many more will slip through unnoticed.

The problem is that it's not enough to understand the business of the organization. To test the software, a tester needs to be more than an educated user; she needs to understand the requirements and be able to verify that they have been implemented. When the testers do not have a good understanding of the software requirements, they will miss defects. There are many reasons testers may have this problem. If there are not good requirements engineering practices in place at the organization, the testing strategy will certainly go awry. This happens when there are uncontrolled changes to requirements, when requirements and design documents are constantly changing, or with software development that is not based on specifications at all (for example, when stakeholders have approached programmers directly).

Programmer "gold plating" is especially problematic for testing. Most programmers are highly creative, and sometimes they have a tendency to add behavior to the software that was not requested. It is difficult for testers—especially ones who are not working from requirements documents—to figure out what behavior in the software is needed by the users, and what is extraneous. However, all of the software must work, and since the gold-plating features may never have been written down (or even discussed), the tester has difficulty figuring out what the software is even expected to do.

In some organizations, the testers are completely out of the loop in the software project until the product is complete. The programmers will simply cut a build and "throw it over the wall" to the testers; the testers are somehow supposed to intuit whether or not the software works, despite the fact that they were not involved in the requirements, design, or programming of the software, and have no prior experience with it. The testers are not told what the software is supposed to do; they are just supposed to make the software "perfect."

But most commonly, defects slip through because of schedule pressure. The most effective, careful, and well-planned testing effort will fail if it is cut short in order to release the software early. Many project managers have trouble resisting the urge to cut testing and release the current build early. They see a build of the software that seems to run. Since the software testing activities are always at the tail end of the software project, they are the ones that will be compressed or cut when the project runs late and the project manager decides to release the software untested.

"But It Worked For Us!"

When a product is not tested in all environments in which it will be used, the tests will be thrown off. The tests will yield defects, but it's much more likely that users will find glaring problems when they begin to use the software in their own environment. This is frustrating because the tests that were run would have found these problems, had they been conducted in an environment that resembled actual operating conditions.

Sometimes the tests depend on data that does not really represent what the users would input into the software. For example, a tester may verify that a calculation is performed adequately by providing a few examples of test data and comparing the results calculated by the software against results calculated by hand. If this test passes, it may simply mean that the tester chose data with the same characteristics that the programmer used to write the software in the first place. It may well be that when the software goes out to be used, the users will provide all sorts of oddball data that may have unexpected and possibly even disastrous results. In other words, it's easy to verify that an addition function calculates "2 + 2" properly; but it's also important to make sure it does the right thing when the user tries to calculate "2 + Apple."

It's common for a system to work fine with test data—even with what seems to be a lot of test data—yet grind to a halt when put in production. Systems that work fine with a small dataset or few concurrent users can die in real-world usage. It can be very frustrating and embarrassing for the engineering team when the product that they were highly confident in breaks very publicly, because the testers did not verify that it could handle real-world load. And when this happens, it's highly visible because, unless those heavy load conditions are verified in advance, they only happen once the users have gained enough confidence in the system to fully migrate to it and adopt it in their day-to-day work.

Some of the trickiest problems come about when there are differences—whether subtle or large—between the environment in which the product is being tested and the environment that it will be used in. Operating systems change often: security patches are released, and various components are upgraded or have different versions in the field. There may be changes in the software with which the product must integrate. There are differences in hardware setups. Any of these things can yield defects. It's up to the software tester to understand the environment the software will be deployed in and the kinds of problems that could arise. If she does not do this, entire features of the software could be unusable when it is released, because tests that worked fine on the tester's computer suddenly break when the software is out in the field.

PART TWO

Using Project Management Effectively

CHAPTER NINE

Understanding Change

IT MAY SEEM LIKE THE TOOLS AND TECHNIQUES IN THE FIRST PART OF THIS BOOK are enough to help you build better software. You've diagnosed problems that affect your organization, you have tools that will help you fix those problems, and you have plenty of tips and examples to help you put them in place. Isn't that enough?

Unfortunately, it's not. Building better software is also about changing the way things are done in your organization, and change makes many people very uncomfortable. Project managers around the world have tried to implement straightforward improvements to the way they build software, only to find that they can't convince the other people in their organizations to agree to discuss those changes, much less to actually alter the way their projects are carried out.

It's very frustrating to see a problem, feel like you have the solution, and not be able to do anything about it. Luckily, there are some straightforward techniques that make it easier to get an organization to change how the software is built. By understanding the most common ways that people respond to change and learning how to convince or reassure the ones who are resistant to change, it is possible to overcome these obstacles and successfully make the changes that your organization needs.

Why Change Fails

A project manager who is trying to get an organization to build better software must make changes to the way the work is performed. This is easier said than done. Most project managers are not in a position in which they can simply demand that everyone in the organization abandon their old ways and adopt new tools and techniques. But even in an organization where it's possible to simply issue a memo requiring everyone to change the way they do their jobs, people will usually be uncomfortable changing so quickly.

The planning and the execution of the change are very important, and there are aspects of any change under the project manager's control that can cause it to fail. Not all obstacles are political: if you introduce a poor practice or tool, or you implement a tool poorly, it will not go well. When your projects suffer from poor planning, insufficient training, or simple bad timing, your attempt to change your own project may fail.

But there are problems that are bigger than just your project. Sometimes the biggest obstacles to your projects come from outside of what a project manager typically controls. Sometimes there are people impacted by your change who will resist it. If you feel that the change is necessary despite the resistance, you will need to handle it politically.

Most technical people have an aversion to politics. They feel that the only way for one person to influence another is to first lay out all of the facts; the only logical conclusion should be obvious. Unfortunately, when you are working with other people, it may take more than just facts to win them over. Most people who will be persuaded solely by facts will already agree with you. When you encounter resistance to your ideas, it may be from someone whose objection may seem irrational to you. This is especially true when you are trying to make a change that influences someone outside of your project in your organization (like a stakeholder or senior manager) who can prevent your change and who does not necessarily need your project to be successful. To be successful, you will need to understand this person's motivation and persuade him to come around to your point of view. That's politics, and it may be necessary in order for your project to be successful.

Many project managers—especially ones who have a technical background—tend to ignore the fact that their organizations are made up of people who need to be convinced of the importance of a change before they will adopt it. Some of these people will have an emotional or even irrational response to any attempt at change; it could take a sea change in the organization before they agree to it.

Irrational attitudes about software development usually boil down to two basic beliefs. First, people believe that most or all software projects are delivered late and delivered with many bugs, and that this is just a fact of life. Second, they believe that their organization is unique, and that the problems they are experiencing are particular to their organization and have never been seen before in any other organization.

(This second belief may seem odd, considering the many thousands of software organizations around the world that have all used similar tools and techniques to fix very similar problems and make real, lasting improvements. It's possible that the belief in uniqueness comes from the fact that the software being built truly is unique, in that it has never been built before; it's not a leap to assume—incorrectly—that the software project and all of its problems are therefore also unique to that particular organization.)

Many times, resistance is not irrational at all. Anyone who has been through a change previously—possibly a passing management fad—that didn't fix the problem (or failed outright) may be resistant to another change. It may seem unfair, but if people in your organization have previously gone through poorly planned changes, it will be harder for you to make changes of your own.

When you are introducing new tools, techniques, or practices in your organization, you may encounter resistance for a number of reasons. By exploring the feelings, fears, and justifications for resisting change that project managers commonly encounter, these reactions can be unraveled and understood.

Change Is Uncomfortable

Most people in your organization are trying to do a good job. They want their peers and supervisors to see that they are good at performing the tasks assigned to them. When someone has developed a level of comfort and familiarity with his job, the last thing he wants is to have someone come along and make him adopt an entirely new way of doing things.

People can also be afraid of change. Most people prefer to feel like they know what they are doing. They want their jobs to be stable and the tasks assigned to them to remain within their capabilities, and, most of all, they want everyone around them to recognize that they are competent and doing a good job. A new tool or technique may seem like a good idea to you. But if someone in your organization who is affected by your change doesn't understand how it would benefit her, then she will only see and respond to the potential problems that it might create. In other words, it's not enough to show that the benefits of a change outweigh its costs on an organizational level; if people do not see how a new tool or technique personally benefits them, they may see it as a burden with no benefits and will be resistant to adopting it.

Resistance to change is not necessarily a bad thing. For example, when a project's scope or requirements are repeatedly changed, delays and defects usually result. In Chapter 6, a change control process was introduced to make sure that changes are only made after their costs and benefits have been fully explored. If it is important for projects' changes to be controlled, it is even more important that an organizational change is made only after its costs and benefits are well understood. It would be difficult to work in an organization that welcomes any change from anyone, without considering the impact of that change.

It makes sense to be prudent in evaluating the nature of changes made to the way you build software. Too drastic a change can cost you your project. Everybody on the team needs to understand why new practices are put in place, and each person should feel like he understands how his role fits into the big picture. If the way the team builds software is constantly being "improved," it can become too difficult for each person to keep track of his day-to-day tasks, and people can lose their sense of purpose. This can lead to prioritization problems, quality problems, and almost certain delays.

Yet despite the fact that changes can be hard to introduce, you will want to introduce new tools, techniques, and practices. But even when you are fully prepared to show that the benefits outweigh the costs, people in your organization may still resist those changes.

This can lead to a very frustrating situation. You may make a great case for a change: there is a real problem and you have the evidence to support it; many people, both inside and outside your organization, see the problem. The senior managers and the project team all agree that there is a problem. But when you start suggesting changes that address this problem, everyone gets uncomfortable. As each person starts to think about how he would have to change how he does his own job, some will simply start to resist any change. They may resist it because it would require learning a new way of doing things, because it would require them to do more work, or just because it is different.

And even when you convince others of the need for a change, it can sometimes be difficult to prove to the people in your organization that adopting a particular tool or technique will really solve the problem. Often, people will question whether they should go through all of the pain of changing, without knowing for certain that the change will result in a real solution. It can be very difficult in this situation to convince them otherwise.

We Already Build Software Well

Denial is a common response to change. You may have identified a glaring problem, but people around you fail to even recognize it (or simply refuse to acknowledge it). Many professional software engineers and managers have never experienced a project that did not have enormous delays and serious problems; it's often assumed that this is just part of how software is built. After all, they usually delivered something—most projects were eventually completed, and the software they built is now being used. Sure, some projects seem to always be eternally 90% done (with 90% left to go), but most of them seem to get *something* onto the users' desktops (although many patches and bug fixes needed to be rolled out afterward). Isn't that good enough?

The truth is that software development does not have to be painful. It is possible for schedules to come in on time, for teams to work normal hours, and for project managers to feel like they are actually in control of their projects.

The denial mindset should seem familiar to anyone who has tried to implement inspections, only to meet with enormous resistance from the project team. Just as people are not used to seeing their documents criticized and corrected, they are not used to, or comfortable with, their projects being branded "failures." Part of your job as a project manager is to help people in your organization learn from their mistakes. This means that they first need to learn to acknowledge those mistakes.

Sometimes project managers find that people want to know how projects in other organizations have turned out. When people in your organization ask for this, what they are really looking for is the bar that they are being measured against. They don't necessarily want to know what techniques are out there in order to help them build better software; they are just looking for corroboration that they are doing enough already, and don't need to make any changes. But the truth is, projects usually go wrong because of specific problems. Many research groups (including the Software Engineering Institute and the Standish Group) have found that when organizations implement process improvements (like the tools and techniques in this book), those problems often get fixed, leading to software development that costs less and results in better software. Many organizations around the world have verified this in practice.

Also, people in your organization may be willing to acknowledge that there is a problem, only to go back into denial when past performance is discussed. Getting people to talk about their problems is a start, but it's not enough. The same people who complain about project delays and scope creep will often suddenly reverse their opinion when talking about past projects. Most professional people need to see themselves as successful—it's part of each person's identity. For many people, talking about the need for improvement means digging up old, painful projects and examining problems that they would just as soon leave buried. It's easier to look back at a troubled project and see only the successes, forgetting the delays, arguments, difficulties, dead ends, and failures along the way.

In an organization where people are in denial about their problems, it is common for people to shoot down changes by saying that "we've never done it that way before." That's obviously true—it's different, so clearly it hasn't been done that way before; the objection sounds like nonsense. The reason this excuse makes sense to the people who say it is because any change amounts to an implicit criticism of the status quo. If a change is needed, then it means we've been doing things wrong; therefore, any change is bad. Making changes to the status quo seems too risky because the organization has always developed software this way.

Another important reason that changes may seem uncomfortable is that the people in the organization may not fully understand how the software is built. Many senior managers have a great deal of experience with the problems that the software solves: for example, the CEO of a company that builds financial or accounting software knows a lot about finance or accounting. But, frequently, the details of what is involved in building the software are a mystery to them. When senior managers are disconnected from the design and development of the software, they begin to see it almost as a "magic formula." They are clearly making money selling software, so they must have made the right decisions. Now some project manager is coming along and telling them to make changes to this formula, which they don't understand. A senior manager does not like feeling ignorant of his own organization, and he does not like being told that the organization that he built needs to be fixed.

Ironically, in many organizations where people claim that they already build software well, there is no standardized way of building software. Sometimes there are requirements written before the programming begins; other times, there aren't. Sometimes there is a project schedule, but often, there's just a single deadline. In one project, the software may be tested; in the next, it's dumped on the users. Since no two projects are ever done the same way, it's always true that the team has "never done it that way before"—and this excuse is still used to shoot down anyone trying to come up with a way to build better software.

"Not Invented Here" Syndrome

"Not Invented Here" syndrome (NIH syndrome) is a name given to a common type of organizational culture where people intentionally avoid research or innovations that were not developed within the organization. When faced with a problem, the people in the organization will typically reject a solution that is known to have worked elsewhere in the industry, solely on the grounds that it did not originate from inside the organization. They opt instead to build their own solution, often at far greater cost.

This may seem ridiculous or silly to people who have not directly experienced it, but NIH syndrome is a serious problem. Some teams will waste many hours defining procedures, creating tools, and building their own solutions to problems that have already been solved elsewhere, rather than adopting or adapting an existing solution that can be purchased off the shelf or learned from a book, training course, or outside expert. One motivator behind NIH syndrome is that people are often rewarded for building new software when they would not be rewarded for buying something that does the same work. For example, a programmer who would get a lot of recognition for spending months building a component might not get any recognition for buying an equivalent one, even though it would cost a tiny fraction to buy rather than build.

If you think about it, you may recognize at least a small example of this behavior in your own organization. For example, many programmers will "reinvent the wheel," building functions or components that could be purchased or downloaded. If your organization commonly develops proprietary technology instead of using an alternative that's available from a third party, it may suffer from at least a mild case of NIH syndrome.

A project manager attempting to change an organization with a bad case of NIH syndrome faces unique challenges. In most organizations, once people recognize that there is a problem, it's often sufficiently convincing to show them that people in other organizations solved the same problem with a solution that already exists. But people in an organization that has NIH syndrome will reject the idea that anyone else in any other organization could possibly have had the same problems. There is simply a pervasive idea that "we're different," which leads to immediate resistance to any ideas that come from outside.

There is an especially virulent strain of NIH syndrome that is commonly found in small entrepreneurial companies. It goes beyond simply believing "we're different"; instead, the people at afflicted organizations believe "we're better." They consider larger companies to be inflexible and laden with bureaucracy. They feel that their small size is an advantage. People in companies like this will often refer to things like their "flat organizational structure" (which, oddly, still features four or five layers of hierarchy, similar to most medium-sized companies), and will talk about how they can respond much more quickly to clients' needs than their larger competitors. Such a mindset often leads to outright rejection of any change based on a tool or technique that works for large companies. Anything that a large company does is dismissed as "too bureaucratic" (see below), and would "clearly" slow down a small, nimble company. In truth, however, every single tool and technique in this book has successfully been used on small projects employing as few as two people. When it comes to NIH syndrome, size really doesn't matter.

It's "Too Theoretical"

When an idea does not make intuitive sense, many people will dismiss it as a result of "academic research," which could not possibly apply to the world they live in. For example, to someone without a project management or software engineering background, it may not be immediately obvious that reviews reduce defects, or that it's important to write a specification before building software. To him, these procedures are time-consuming, with no obvious benefit. They sound good in a book, but would never work in the organization. In other words, they are "too theoretical."

Some managers—especially ones who consider themselves "hands-on" and who value technical knowledge above management skill—will say that many of the tools and techniques in this book are "too theoretical," and therefore somehow do not apply to their particular organizations. This attitude is common among managers who worked their way up from programming or other IT positions and who have only served as a manager in one organization. It is also common among people who have never experienced a successful project that was on time, on budget, and with few delivered defects.

Declaring a particular tool or technique "too theoretical" may seem like an odd response. These practices arose from software engineering practices that were developed, implemented, and refined over the course of countless projects in thousands of organizations. Most people would consider any solution that is well accepted and has been implemented across the industry to be anything but theoretical. But for many managers, a technique described in a book is of less value than one that was learned or discovered in the field. If someone has never seen a project that went smoothly, it seems natural to assume that all projects suffer delays, scope creep, and other problems that stem from poor planning and engineering; they consider any proposed "cure" for these problems to most likely be nothing but an academic theory that would never work in the real world.

It is especially common to hear the "too theoretical" excuse from the manager or leader of a small team facing growing pains. This typically occurs when programmers are added to a very small team. The team slowly gets less and less productive, and adding more programmers does not seem to help. Many of the problems described in Part I start to occur, and the manager gets frustrated. Unfortunately, this is a very difficult (yet common) position for a new manager to find himself in. Typically, he finds himself trying to doing everything the same way it's always been done, but his projects continue to break down. It seems like every trick he's tried has backfired. He's called big meetings that turned out to be worse than useless. He's yelled at his team, other managers, even the CEO. It seems that everyone knows that something is wrong, yet nothing will fix the problem.

Still, this manager will often reject tools and techniques like the ones in Part I as "too theoretical" because he has not personally experienced them. When there were only two or three people on the team, the projects apparently went just fine. It seems intuitive to him that adding a few more people should not make much of a difference in managing the project. To this person it's not intuitively obvious, for example, that writing a vision and scope document or creating a project schedule will help his projects run more smoothly. Anything that he has not tried, and especially anything that does not directly affect the code, must be "too theoretical."

The problems that are diagnosed in the first part of this book really do affect very small teams; they are just not nearly as difficult to overcome when only two or three people are affected. It is not hard for one person to keep track of changes, communications, and project status for a very small team. However, as the team grows, these problems compound. The team starts to lose track of changes to the scope, requirements, and code. The project schedules get more complex and less accurate. Stakeholders and users start to feel that the project is getting out of control.

A manager in this situation will be very cautious about adopting any change. He knows that just making changes at random makes the problem worse. He's probably read management books and tried applying the information in them, only to find that didn't work; he's come to distrust this sort of advice. By demanding changes that are not "theoretical," he's really saying that the team must be careful not to implement any more changes unless they are already proven—preferably on one of his own projects. Unfortunately, that creates a chicken-and-egg situation: how can the team take a particular technique from theory to practice, when every technique is too theoretical to be implemented?

It Just Adds More Bureaucracy

An especially damaging attitude in some organizations holds that programming is the only important activity in a software project. Project management tools and techniques are seen as distractions that drain energy and effort away from the programmers' "real job" of writing code. Any project activity that takes place before the programmers begin writing code simply amounts to "spinning our wheels," and the goal of all early project activities should be to get the programmers doing the "real work" as quickly as possible.

A manager in this sort of organization will typically think that if she just adds more programming hours, a project that seems to be failing will get back on track. Since programming is the main activity in the project, all project problems amount to programming problems. In fact, there are project managers who believe that all they need for a successful project is a team of top-notch programmers. They wonder, "Why do we need to quadruple our documentation by creating schedules and project plans and change control procedures?" After all, it's been shown time and time again that a great programmer is 10 times as productive as a mediocre one. Isn't it enough to pay top dollar getting the very best programmers and setting them loose on the problem? Why all the extra "bureaucracy"?

In reality, programming is usually less than 40% of the effort on a successful project. Most project problems are caused by the team not understanding what it is that the software should do. Estimation problems happen when the team members don't explore all of the assumptions that they are making and, as a result, don't have a handle on what information is known and what is unknown. Project planning goes wrong when the scope creeps, or when there are problems that could have been foreseen. When bugs are found in the software, often it's not because the software is broken; the software is usually working exactly as the programmer intended it to work, it's just not doing what the users need it to do.

The solutions to these problems do not involve programming. But, to some people, any action that the team takes that does not directly relate to programming is "bureaucratic." Planning the project, writing down requirements, and holding inspection meetings is seen as just pushing paper around. There may be a project schedule, but this is just used as a tool to help the rest of the organization understand what it is the programmers are doing—in other words, the schedule is created by asking the programmers their opinion, and the project manager's job mostly boils down to simply reporting that opinion to the rest of the organization. (Even worse, of course, is the project manager who simply makes up the schedule out of thin air, or bases it solely on the boss's expectations.)

When the project manager's role is reduced like this, there is usually an implicit assumption that a schedule is just a guess, and an expectation that it will almost certainly slip. At least the project managers and other software engineers believe that it's implicitly assumed. Unfortunately, this is a dirty little secret among the engineering team. The rest of the organization takes these estimates and schedules at face value. They believe that the team made a real commitment, and they make important decisions based on what they believe is a real date. This leads to a general feeling of distrust between the software engineering group and the rest of the organization. It all starts with the project manager's mistaken attitude that it's just not possible to estimate a project accurately, and that you just can't predict what's going to happen when the team starts building the software. (See Chapter 3 for more information on how to estimate a project accurately.)

In an organization where this attitude is prevalent, it is common to see a much higher value placed on anything that has to do with programming, with a lower value placed on all other areas of software engineering. If the programming team requests new computers, often senior managers will not hesitate to spend thousands of dollars on them. Yet the project manager may be refused permission to spend a few extra hours talking to stakeholders and users in order to write a vision and scope document, even though it would save an enormous amount of project time (and only cost the equivalent of a few hundred dollars of people's time). When this happens, it's usually because it is easy to justify any activity or expense that is done to benefit programming, while all other expenses are regarded suspiciously.

You Can't Give Me More Work!

Most of the changes that a project manager makes will increase the workload of other people. Software engineers, managers, and stakeholders who were not directly involved in building software will suddenly find themselves expected to attend status and review meetings, participate in planning and estimation activities, work with someone creating a vision and scope document or eliciting requirements, or perform other tasks that were never expected of them before. If you are making these changes, then you are the person piling additional work onto someone's already overflowing plate. Not surprisingly, there are people who will not be happy with this arrangement.

People are often unhappy to be asked to attend meetings, especially in organizations where most meetings lack direction, focus, or even an agenda. In organizations like this, the meetings tend to meander. Often they boil down to a discussion between two people about a topic that has nothing to do with anyone else at the meeting. Sometimes, meetings are called simply to give a captive audience to a senior manager. If you are in an organization where everyone hates going to meetings, when someone suddenly finds out that she has to attend your weekly status meeting, she might be unhappy—and provoked into doing something about it.

A common response from a recipient of this new workload is surprise and shock. It's very uncommon for people to have tasks assigned to them by people to whom they do not report, yet here's some project manager doing exactly that. Often, when someone is surprised by extra work, he feels especially motivated to take action to remove it from his plate. He will complain to his boss and to his boss's boss, and he may even try to go over your head to get your entire project shut down. When a project manager tries to put new tools or techniques in place, it is frustrating to encounter resistance from the very people who will benefit from the practices simply because they seem like extra work. (It is especially frustrating when team members agree in principle that those practices will reduce the total effort required to build the project, yet do not agree to adopt them!) Even if you win the battle and get your senior managers to agree to force him to do the extra work, you could still lose the war: now a participant in your project cannot be relied upon, and could cause damage to your project by stonewalling and causing delays. He could even sour your organization to any future improvements if the senior managers hear only his complaints and do not see immediate results.

It's Too Risky

The celebrated economist John Maynard Keynes once wrote, "Worldly wisdom teaches that it is better for the reputation to fail conventionally than to succeed unconventionally." Legendary investor Warren Buffett put it this way: "Lemmings as a class may be derided but never does an individual lemming get criticized." In other words, any manager who backs a change puts his reputation on the line; if that manager does nothing, he will not be criticized for maintaining the status quo.

When you make a change in an organization, you aren't just altering the activities that the team performs. You're also affecting how people relate to each other in the organization. A change that goes wrong can ruin someone's reputation (and, if it's serious and public enough, their career).

Nobody gets blamed if things stay the same. If a project fails, but many other projects failed in the same way, the failure is usually seen as inevitable and the people in charge of the project are not held accountable for the failure. And even the most flawed deliverable can be painted as a success, even if the software that is finally produced barely does what it's supposed to and requires many patches and bug fixes. (In fact, for many software professionals, this is a fact of life—every project they have ever worked on turned out that way!)

Many people equate questioning what has always been done with insulting the organization as a whole. They consider it to be something a team player would never do. To someone with this attitude, the fact that you are pointing out problems and suggesting changes sets you apart from the accepted culture. They feel that since you are making wide-ranging criticisms of the organization, you do not buy into its culture and are simply being counterproductive. Paradoxically, to these people, it is considered more productive to make bad decisions and let projects fail than to question the way things are done.

This means that when people complain that making changes is risky, they are not incorrect. However, a manager shooting down a proposed change as "too risky" may be sensing risk to his own reputation, rather than to the project.

When looked at from a pure cost-benefit perspective, most of the tools and techniques in this book have a very limited risk to the project. Usually, it only takes a few hours to run a Wideband Delphi session, set up a version control system, write a vision and scope document or hold an inspection meeting. Even if these tools and techniques fail to produce any results at all, the total cost to the project is minimal. Yet these same tools are routinely shot down as "too risky," and in a sense they are—but not with respect to the project.

When people talk about these tools and techniques being risky, often they are not trying to say that the tools will somehow damage the project; rather, the risk is that if the project still runs into problems, the manager who implemented the new tools can be held responsible for those problems. In other words, there's an implied rule in most organizations: "you break it, you bought it." If you make a change to an existing process, you're now responsible for any failures that result, even if those failures are only tangentially related to the changes you made.

People are justifiably reluctant to go against the conventional wisdom in their organization. No matter how misguided, the popular opinion is very powerful and difficult to change. People who are willing to point out a series of singular, unrelated mistakes may be unwilling to admit that there is a more general problem with their organization—especially if admitting the problem calls into question their knowledge of software development. People do not like to feel like they don't have all the answers. And if you point this out in your effort to change your organization for the better, you might inadvertently cause people to feel that you are publicizing their mistakes and calling them out as incompetent.

Incidentally, this is one reason many people are turned off by the idea of process improvement. They have only seen attempts at change partway through a project that has gone awry. Managers start making out-of-context changes in desperation, usually based on something they have read but don't fully understand. Even worse, the changes are frequently used as a means of forcing a stakeholder or client into compliance with an already delayed schedule. This is not so much a way to save the project as it is a way for some manager to protect his reputation. Not all improvements will help in every situation.

For example, one of the most common places where changes should not be introduced—but often are—is when a project is starting to fail and the stakeholder is starting to get angry. This mistake is especially common in consulting companies that gave unrealistically low estimates for their projects and now find themselves in trouble. They see a client who rightly points out that the software has many defects, and that it does not fulfill his needs. A common (and unfortunate) response from the project manager is to try to change the organization, instead of admitting that the client was given an unrealistic plan and working to better fill the client's needs. A change control process is implemented to clamp down on any new feature requests, and a hard-and-fast schedule is put in place that forces the client to accept the work that the team has already done, whether or not it fulfills the client's needs. This results in a frustrated client and increased friction between the client and the project team.

Forcing a stakeholder to accept poor software is a terrible reason to make changes to the software process. Organizations are right to resist changes that are made for any reason other than building better software more quickly. If there are client or stakeholder relations problems, they need to be dealt with directly, instead of trying to solve those problems by changing the way the group builds software.

How to Make Change Succeed

Progress comes not just from making changes, but from making smart changes. However, it is often difficult to tell the difference—and no organization should be entirely comfortable with change. It's often difficult to tell the difference between a real, substantive change for the better and a management fad that will cost time and effort, but yield little or no reward. Using the techniques in this section can help you demonstrate to the people in your organization that the practices you want to implement are appropriate, and help you to get your proposed changes accepted by the project team and the organization's managers.

However, while these techniques are useful and proven, they are not cure-alls. It's possible to run across organizational problems or roadblocks that are beyond your ability to fix (for example, there may not be enough money to hire a test team). The Achilles' heel of the approach to improving organizations that's described in the first part of this book is that there are people who will resist change for irrational and emotional reasons, and, if they have more power than you in your organization, you simply may not be able to make the changes that your projects need.

You can't stop people from being averse to change, and you can't always stop them from shooting down your ideas. Even if your ideas make perfect sense, you may still be unable to implement them simply because there is someone above you in your organization who feels uncomfortable with your proposed changes. However, if you are creative, forgiving, and flexible, the most daunting organizational problems can be addressed and sometimes even overcome.

One important element for successful change is understanding how the people in your organization think about and react to changes. Good planning, along with some understanding of the psychology of the people affected, will help convince people to accept them. By understanding the ways people think about and react to change, and by applying certain techniques that may make them more comfortable with the changes, you can improve your chances at successfully changing your organization.

Prepare Your Organization

Before you can begin to implement changes, you need to deal with the attitudes that will cause people to reject those changes. It's up to you to figure out your organization's culture. Try to feel out the sorts of arguments that you will run into, in order to get a feel for your audience. Then you can tailor your pitch for change—and it really is a sales pitch in many ways—to your organization.

There are several possible strategies that you might use to "sell" your change to the people in your organization, depending on the environment in which you are working. Here are a few that have been effective in the past. There's no single solution to any of the problems in the previous section, though—you will have to use your own judgement to figure out an approach that will work with the people in your organization. With luck, you can start to combat the poisonous attitudes in your organization that would stand in the way. Of course, even after all of this, there's no absolute guarantee that you will actually be able to change your organization—but at least now you have a better shot.

"We've always done it like this"

Organizations uncomfortable with any kind of change are the hardest to deal with. In this situation, it often makes sense to make it appear as though the change you are making isn't a change at all. Pitch the effort as preserving the status quo: "We've always built software like this; now we're just writing down the best practice so we apply it consistently."

This is especially helpful in growing organizations, where you can talk about a need to write down how things are done already, in order to help new people adjust to the environment. It's important to remember that people have a need for consistency—when your actions are aligned with past projects, it's much easier to persuade others in your organization.

This strategy can also be pitched as a training program. All organizations must train people, so it's possible to pitch your improvement effort as a way to bring them up to speed by writing down how things are done.

Keep in mind that this approach is not completely honest—you're trying to pretend that a change is the same as the status quo, and may be taking advantage of the fact that few people in your organization have sufficient understanding of how software is developed in their own organization to see the difference. But this approach can often buy you enough time to get people used to some of the changes that you want to make.

Be positive about the work that's already being done

When people are in denial about the need for change, it is often because they need to see themselves as successful and do not want to admit that their past projects have been less-than-perfect. Use this feeling to help you implement your change by praising the work that's been done in the past, and positioning the change as a way to build on those past successes. Keep your tone positive when talking to people about the need for change.

Find examples in past projects of things that went well that support your changes. For example, you may have had a positive meeting at the outset of a project generally viewed as a success in which the team dealt with scope issues. This can be the kernel of justification for an effort to build a vision and scope document for a future project.

If anyone in your organization has ever discussed the sorts of things that you are proposing, you'll be in better shape. You can use these people to help you make your case by showing them that you are building on their ideas. This can help you build consensus among the project team and in the organization.

Take credit for the changes

It usually helps to show that the changes you are proposing have worked in other organizations. But if your organization suffers from NIH syndrome, this approach could be damaging. It's counterintuitive, but it may make sense for you to act like you thought of the changes yourself.

Don't talk about the changes as a process improvement effort that standardizes the way you build software. Instead, step away from the big picture and concentrate on solving individual problems. Justify the changes as if they are solely in response to specific problems in your organization, and not as tools that are standard across the industry.

Some people are understandably uncomfortable taking credit for the ideas of others. But while you may not have come up with the idea of a vision and scope document or a project plan yourself, you did have the idea of applying it to a specific project in your organization.

This may seem manipulative (although that's not necessarily a bad thing). But it doesn't have to be. A project manager can help the whole team take credit for changes as a way to motivate them and help them move forward. This is especially useful when combined with being positive about the work that's already been done. A project manager might say something like, "Folks, we've done a great job with these first five work items. I'm very proud of what you've done. But I'm convinced these next three are different in nature from those five and we need to approach them differently than we have in the past. Here's how...." It doesn't matter that the proposed change is a tool or technique from a book; it can still be pitched as a change that builds on the work the team has already done.

Make the changes seem straightforward

When someone feels that a tool or technique is "too theoretical," what he is really saying is that he's never heard of it before, doesn't fully understand it, and can't immediately imagine an actual situation in which it would work. He typically talks about the "real world," and he may feel like you don't necessarily live in that world, if you're proposing a change that has not been directly borne out by his experience.

Be careful in this situation. Consider someone who has been in the industry for a long time, but has not come into contact with these ideas before. It's likely that he has seen countless projects fail, and has come to grips with—and possibly built his career around—the idea that a lot of projects simply go wrong. By telling him that there is a straightforward way to fix this problem, you are challenging a fundamental assumption in his career. He will rightfully take that personally, and you must take his feelings into account.

If this person is senior to you in your organization, this also becomes an issue of credibility. If you put yourself in the position where you are questioning the experience of someone senior to you, he will want to know where your credibility comes from. It's a mistake to say that your credibility comes from doing research; a better approach is to look for corroboration from within your organization and your projects to prove that your ideas are valid. The best way to handle this situation is to build consensus among your peers. It's much easier to have this conversation with a senior manager when your credibility is already validated by the people around you, and when it's clear that the organization's culture is ready for the change.

Another way to approach this situation is to pitch the changes you want to implement as technical tools, rather than as core software engineering concepts. Most people who have been in the field for a long time are used to routinely applying new technical tools that have never been tested in the organization. This is also a good way to gain consensus among the programming team for your ideas.

Build support from the team

If you can bring the programming team on board, you have a much better chance of convincing the rest of the organization to follow. In most organizations, people who do not have technical skills often defer to the programmers any time there is a disagreement. If the programming manager in your organization is on board with the improvements, he can pitch an improvement as a technical change instead of a more general, far-reaching process change. Once the programmers start demanding changes, they usually get their way.

There are a lot of project problems that the team is very aware of. When the scope creeps, the programmers have to tear down code they previously built and replace it with code that is patched together and not built as well as they would like. The programmers would much rather fix a bug before a client sees it. Poorly defined requirements lead to changes and frustration. All of these problems are exactly the ones that you are trying to fix.

Show the team that you are working to help them. For example, using Wideband Delphi estimation and building a project schedule may seem needlessly "bureaucratic" to them—until you show them how it will help them avoid working overtime later on in the project. By showing that there are clear benefits to what you are doing or suggesting, you can avoid some of the knee-jerk reactions from your team against your changes, and instead get them on board.

Show that the changes will save time and effort

When someone talks about a change adding too much bureaucracy, what she usually means is that it takes time and effort that she is not used to spending. This is where an explicit justification is necessary. That justification is not about showing them charts, graphs, or numbers; rather, your goal should be to show how you are working to reduce the overall effort required for the team to build the software.

People do not want to come to meetings unless those meetings are proven to work. You need to convince them that for every hour they spend in a meeting, they are shaving off at least an hour at the end of the project. It's not hard to make an intuitive case for this, as long as you tailor it to each individual person that you are talking to. Explain the impact of the problems on each person's work, and show how the tool will reduce that impact.

For example, if a technical support manager is balking at attending inspection meetings, point out that you are trying to get more defects out of the software so she'll have to deal with fewer support calls about them. Programmers are often concerned with scope creep because it requires tedious and unnecessary rework; show them how a vision and scope document or use cases will help to reduce the time spent on rework.

Work around stragglers

There are some people who simply cannot be convinced that a change is worthwhile. They resent being given any extra work. They may even be against the entire project for entirely selfish reasons. For example, it's not unheard of for a programmer who is highly skilled with a particular platform or technology to sabotage efforts to migrate the software to an entirely different platform, simply to protect his expertise. Some stragglers don't even look like stragglers—they may be "heroes" who are used to waiting until there is an emergency before jumping in and saving the day. But whatever the reason, if someone is firmly against your changes, you are not going to be able to bring them on board—at least not by yourself and not now.

Before working around a straggler, see if you can bring him around. One good way to do this is to have a respected team member talk to a straggler so that, instead of ignoring or working around him, you're putting him in a situation in which he can learn to be more productive. Unfortunately, not all people will be convinced, even by those they respect.

The way to handle stragglers who refuse to adopt your changes is to work around them. Build consensus among everyone else on your level in the organization. Don't worry too much about people who oppose you for reasons that can't be dealt with: if your changes eventually become part of the organizational culture, they will either come on board or leave on their own.

Again, the idea of consistency is very important in this situation. If someone takes a public stand on an issue, she feels an enormous psychological need to remain consistent with that opinion. This means that if you push someone who is initially opposed to your ideas, she will feel pressured to fight harder and harder against you: the more she argues against the change, the less she feels like she is "allowed" to change her mind without losing face. On the other hand, if you leave her alone initially, you give her an environment where it could be much easier for her to come around later.

You can also use consistency in a positive way. It is very important that you have gained a real (and written, if possible!) commitment from the people around you before you try to pitch your change upward. Not only will this help you show senior management that you have real support, but it will also help people to stay committed, because they feel the need to remain consistent with their past decisions.

It is important not to go to senior management too early. If you do, you are essentially going over the heads of everyone around you who has not already committed to your change. This is counterintuitive: you have a solid case for change, and you know that you can convince your boss to make it, so why not just go there first?

The problem is that the ideas you are pitching are very powerful and often very convincing. It is often possible to implement wide-reaching changes that affect many people in your organization without actually involving them at all, simply by going over their heads. The minute that one of those people sees additional work that you have managed to get assigned to him without first asking him, he will turn against the change. Had you given him a chance to come on board first, he probably would have seen the benefits and supported you; now he's working against you, simply because you backed him into a corner.

This isn't about the personal aspects of them supporting or not supporting you. If the changes that you are making are good ones that will increase productivity, then people will probably jump on your bandwagon once they recognize the value of the changes. Everybody wants to be part of a winning team, and the key is to make it easy for them to join your team. If people have an adverse reaction to what you are saying, let it go—they'll come around later.

Once you have a *real* consensus, you can go to senior management. It will be clear to them that the entire culture is asking for this. One of the most important principles of organizational change is that changes do not stay in place without support from senior management.

Stick to the facts

People respond well to someone who speaks directly to them and who does not have any hidden agendas. Be clear about your motives; make sure that you talk about the costs as well as the benefits of any change that you suggest. You must make an effort to understand your audience: being a straight-talker to a sales manager is much different than being one to a programmer, so you need to really think about who you are presenting these ideas to before you do it. Learn their perspectives and frame your arguments in ways that are interesting to them. Another important part of being a straight-talker is having a solid grasp on the ideas behind the changes that you are making. If you really understand them, then you can put the ideas into terms that anyone else can understand.

"It's too risky" can be the best possible objection that you can hear. It means that the people you are talking to are listening, thinking about implementing the change, and coming up with ways that it could go wrong. They are really thinking about what it would take to do what you are suggesting. This means that they can be convinced with facts, not just persuaded with emotions and politics.

In a situation like that, you can get approval to start a pilot project, and show the benefits of changes on that pilot. You can present research that shows that the changes you want to make are accepted industry standards. You could get approval to study the problems that exist in the organization, and plan an improvement project to come up with an answer to those problems. You can figure out how much the projects cost in terms of time and effort, and show how your changes will reduce those numbers. And, most importantly, you can show how it's even riskier to keep things the way they are. That's a productive conversation any way you look at it, because you'll come out of it with a list of problems that you need to address with your improvement effort.

(Unfortunately, "It's too risky" can also be the worst possible objection that you can hear. It could mean the person you are talking to has shut you out, and is no longer listening. When this happens, you can't make any more progress from this angle.)

Plan for Change

Once you have made some headway in overcoming resistance, the most important way to ensure the success of your change in your organization is to plan for the change. Planning for a change is similar to planning for a software project, in that the scope must be defined and tasks need to be assigned to people who will carry them out. By treating a change to your organization like its own project, you can use the same planning tools as you would for a software project.

There is a fundamental difference between a project to change an organization and a project to build software: the bulk of the effort in a software project is devoted to building work products, while the effort in changing an organization is focused on training (or retraining) the people who will then turn around and build the software differently. But in both cases, the scope should be written down and agreed to, and the resources assigned and trained.

Create a vision and scope document

The way to make a successful change is to ensure that the problem you are solving is the most important one that the organization faces. Before people in your organization will accept a change, they must be convinced that the change is necessary. To an eager project manager who wants to implement new tools and techniques, this can be a frustrating situation. But it's actually a good thing—if people are too willing to accept changes to the way they do their work, then any changes you make will quickly be replaced with the next popular idea to come along.

In Chapter 2, the vision and scope document was introduced as an important planning tool that helps ensure that each of the project's features addresses a specific user or stakeholder need. Each person's needs are written down, and each of the planned features is tied back to one of those needs. The document is then reviewed by everyone who will be affected by the project, to ensure that all of their needs and concerns are met.

A vision and scope document can also be used to plan a change to the organization. Table 9-1 shows a typical outline for a vision and scope document.

TABLE 9-1. Vision and scope document outline for a change project

1. Problem Statement
a. Project background
b. Stakeholders
c. People affected
d. Risks
e. Assumptions
2. Vision of the Solution
a. Vision statement
b. List of changes
c. Changes that will not be implemented

This document is developed in exactly the same way as described in Chapter 2. The stakeholders are identified, their needs elicited, and the scope of the change is defined.

There are just a few differences between this outline and the one for a software project:

- Instead of a "Users" section, there is a "People affected" section. This section describes the specific people in the organization who will have to change the way they do their jobs. This is the first important reality check for a project manager attempting to make changes. It is very easy to think about changes in abstract terms, forgetting that real people will have to change the way they work. It's even easier to gloss over the fact that people will be affected when you're selling the change. This section helps everyone be clear on who is affected from the very beginning. Listing the affected people in the document also ensures that they are included when it is reviewed, which allows them to have a say in how they do their jobs.

- Instead of listing features that will or won't be implemented, this vision and scope document lists changes that will be implemented. Each of the changes in the "List of changes" section should include a full explanation of exactly what changes will be made. For example, if use cases are to be implemented, include the use case template that will be used and a description of any elicitation tasks and other tasks that will be performed in order to create them, as well as any additional resources that will be needed.

- There is no "Scope of phased release" section. If the changes need to take place in a certain order, that should be incorporated into the description of each individual change.

Writing a vision and scope document before making the actual changes allows the project manager to gather evidence that those changes will address real problems in the organization. It is important to point out specific instances that other people will agree are problems. A successful vision and scope document will show everyone in the organization that there is a real, troubling problem. If you only include real evidence in the document, an objective reader will see that there is a serious problem—and by proposing a change that will fix it, you can throw them a rope by offering a real solution.

Inspect the vision and scope document

Once the document is written, it should be reviewed by all stakeholders and everyone in the organization who will be affected (see Chapter 5). This will accomplish several things. It will make sure that the changes you are proposing really solve the problems that they are supposed to solve, because they will be documented as needs in the "People affected" section. But more importantly, it will ensure that the change is communicated to everyone who needs to see it—and by incorporating their feedback, you will help gather consensus among them.

This is a check both for you and the other people who this affects. It is important for them to see that your changes will help them. But it is also important for you to choose the changes that will do the most good in the organization. It is much easier to propose an unnecessary change in a meeting than it is to do it in writing. By writing down the rationale for all of the changes, you can make sure that people see that there are real problems to be solved, and that you are proposing solutions to those problems.

The reason it is important to write down the rationale for each change is that it is tempting to try to "fix" a problem that doesn't really exist, simply because the change is easy to implement. Many people decide to make a change or implement a certain practice, and then "find" problems to justify it. (In much the same way, if you lose your keys in the dark, it's easier to search for them under a streetlight because it's easier to see.) By identifying the rationale for each change, you can find the real problems that need to be fixed. This helps you prioritize your changes, in order to address those problems that hurt the most.

The audience for the review should be as large as possible, to ensure that everyone who is affected by the change sees that it is coming. The review will give them ample opportunity to give their input. People are less likely to react irrationally to a change if they are given a chance to give input when it is proposed. Most importantly, since everyone who is in a position to object can be included in the review, you can get those objections out in the open early. That way, you can address their objections early on. Many people object to changes simply because they were blindsided; by asking for their input before the change is implemented, you can avoid that problem. Once the vision and scope document is approved, it is much less likely that there will be surprises later on.

Schedule the changes

Once the team has approved the scope of the changes that will be made, it is time to implement those changes. By updating the project schedule to include those changes, you can make it more likely that they will actually be carried out on the project.

Building changes into the project schedule is an effective way to "seal them in" to guarantee that they actually happen. Many changes unravel because while everyone agrees that they are a good idea, they never actually make it into practice. By adding tasks to the project schedule that reflect the change, you ensure that time and resources are dedicated to implementing it. You also help the team members see that the change is coming, and give them time to plan for it.

It's also important to allocate time for training. You may understand the details of the new tools and techniques, but many of the people on the project do not have that advantage. Make sure to include meetings to introduce the team members to the new practices. If additional training sessions are necessary, schedule them as well. Plan to give the other people in your organization the time they need to learn how to use the new tools and techniques. This may mean adding time to tasks that will be done differently than in the past, due to the changes. (Allow time for a learning curve—people will not be as efficient at using the new tools and techniques initially as you hope they will become after some practice.)

For example, if you are implementing code reviews, you should add training and review meetings to the schedule. You should also extend the programming tasks, in order to allow the programmers time to make changes found during the review. When the schedule acknowledges that additional time should be spent on these tasks, the programmers are much more likely to actually perform the code review tasks.

> ### NOTE
> A more detailed process for scoping and planning an improvement project is described in *Making Process Improvement Work* by Neil Potter and Mary Sakry (Addison Wesley, 2002).

Push for Consensus

It's difficult to change an organization alone. It is much easier to make a change if you have the support of others in your organization. Identifying potential allies is an important step in changing an organization. The most effective way to change an organization is to build consensus within your project team, among your peers, and up through the management chain.

People will be more positive about your change when they see that other people are already on board with it. If you can recruit early supporters, it will be easier to bring other people around to your way of thought. The best way to convince someone to make that investment is to show that there is already a consensus among the software experts in the organization.

The first step in generating consensus is to find people who also recognize the problem that you are trying to solve. This should not be hard—if your organization's problem is serious enough to warrant a change, there will probably be other people around who have noticed this problem as well. Put aside for now the fact that people may not believe you have a real solution; it's sufficient to start with a basic agreement that there is a problem.

Many people feel that change should either be "top-down" (meaning that the changes originate from management) or "bottom-up" (meaning that they originate from the team). However, while it is absolutely critical that you have the support of your organization's senior management before implementing a change (unless it is for a change that affects only your project), there is no need to make this decision while still generating consensus. If you can convince a senior manager that there is a real problem and that you have a solution, that person will be a very valuable ally. But it's also important to convince people who are on your level in the organization. To many senior managers, the most convincing argument is that several people who report to him agree on something. This is why it is especially useful to get multiple people on different levels of the organization to agree that your changes will improve the way software is built.

Once you have found people who recognize that there is a problem, you can work to show them that you have a solution. An effective way to convince people to join your effort is to show them that you are not just suggesting change because you don't like the way things are done: you are also helping them with problems that they wish would be solved. Most people are never really asked if they are having trouble. Take the time to listen to each person's complaints. If you can show someone that her problems are not her fault but, rather, could be attributed to something external (like a lack of planning or change control), she will be much more open to your solutions.

It's not enough just to find people on the team who are willing to talk about their problems. There are many people who just love to complain about work. It's easy enough to get people like this to talk about what's wrong, and even to acknowledge that there are endemic problems. But once it comes time to make real changes, someone who has not really bought into your solution may disappear from your effort at the first sign of resistance. Also, beware of people who come around too easily—it may be that they are simply easily swayed, and will abandon your effort for the next big idea that comes along.

Gathering allies is also a good reality check for your change effort. If you cannot convince even a small number of people that there is a real problem to be solved, and that your proposed change will solve it, then that is a good indicator that you will run into serious problems when attempting to sell your changes to the rest of the organization.

Give yourself a lot of time to do this. Organizations do not change overnight, and consensus is not generated with a single meeting. It is important not to steamroll anyone. If someone has an objection, make sure that he feels that you are taking that objection seriously. It is easy to get frustrated with disagreement; try to find ways to help the people who disagree with you, rather than simply ignoring or going around them. If someone disagrees with you, it may be that he sees that there is a more important problem that you should be concentrating on instead. Show each person that you are trying to keep his best interests in mind. Try to learn what his biggest problems are and work to solve them.

Use a Pilot Project to Build a Track Record

The best way to build credibility in your organization is to show a real track record of past success. Running a pilot project is an effective way to build a track record.

A pilot project is simply a project that you have selected on which you will test specific changes before rolling them out to the rest of the organization. Before running a pilot project, make sure that the changes that you want to implement are limited in scope. Making more than a small number of changes at a time is usually difficult to manage.

Choose pilot projects carefully. You will want to select ones that will have a visible effect but carry little risk. Some tools and techniques are easier to implement than others—choose the "low-hanging fruit" by selecting the changes that you feel are most likely to succeed.

The best pilot projects are ones that are likely to succeed. A good candidate project might involve problems similar to ones that the team has solved in the past. It should use technology the team is already familiar with. Avoid projects that have a higher risk of failure, such as ones that implement new technology or involve new, unproven team members. Even if a pilot project fails for a reason that has nothing to do with the change being piloted, there is a chance that your change will be blamed for its failure.

During the pilot project, keep careful records of any project problems or issues. Keep senior management in the loop for any serious problems—if it looks like the change is causing the team to miss a goal, it is better that the news come from you, and that it come as early as possible. It is helpful to adopt a scientific attitude toward the project: treat it as an experiment (preferably one with a high likelihood of success), and be as objective as possible about the outcome.

If your pilot project is successful, you now have a valuable publicity tool for your change. It is no longer "theoretical," because it was successful in the organization. And it's much less likely to be seen as "risky," because the change has shown to be successful on a project.

However, it is important to keep in mind that a pilot project is not necessarily a cure for an organization that resists change. The very characteristics that make a project a good candidate for a pilot can also cause it to be vulnerable to criticism. By selecting a project that is smaller in scale and less important than most other projects in the organization, you invite criticism that the tools and techniques you are piloting might work in a small and low-pressure environment, but would fall apart under more difficult conditions. They may claim that the new tools and techniques would never work for more difficult projects in which users, stakeholders, and clients are putting pressure on the programmers, when there are deadlines, and where the projects are much bigger. And they are not necessarily wrong—you have not stress-tested your changes. Just because a change is successful in the least risky environment possible doesn't mean that it will be successful in the rest of the organization. That's not to say that the pilot project is not an important tool; it simply has its limits.

NOTE
More information on piloting changes can be found in *The Art of Project Management* by Scott Berkun (O'Reilly, 2005).

Measure Your Progress

Measuring your improvements is a critical part of changing the way your organization builds software. Measurements provide a way to track progress, as well as a way to communicate this progress to senior management and the rest of the organization.

There are two important ways that most project managers want to improve their projects. They want their projects to cost less, and they want fewer defects in the final product. Showing improvement in both cost and quality provides powerful evidence that the changes you have made are working.

Measuring cost

The most common criticism that project managers receive when trying to improve the way they build software is that the new procedures and changes cost too much. Therefore, an astute project manager will gather the actual number of hours that the changes cost. This information should be gathered during a pilot project and any other time changes are implemented.

Every activity that you have inserted into the development process in order to build better software should be measured in terms of time and effort. You can track this information in a spreadsheet (see Figure 9-1).

Week	Activity	Hours	People	Effort (person-hours)	Participants
4-APR	SRS inspection	2	4	11	Mike, Sophie, Jill, Quentin, Dean
4-APR	Change control	3	5	14.5	Barbara, Anthony, Mike, Jill, Quentin
11-APR	Unit test development	5	1	5	Jill
18-APR	Code review	3	2	5.75	Jill, Kyle
18-APR	Unit test development	3	1	3	Jill
18-APR	Test plan review	2	5	14.5	Mike, Sophie, Dean, Jill, Kyle

FIGURE 9-1. Spreadsheet to measure the cost of improvements

Each activity performed over the course of this project is measured in terms of the total calendar time that elapsed while the activity was performed ("Hours"), the number of people involved ("People"), and the total number of person-hours (see Chapter 4) that were expended in both preparing for and performing the activity ("Effort"). In addition, the week, activity name, and participants are listed. This is not a difficult spreadsheet to maintain—in the example above, the project manager only had to add one to three lines per week to the spreadsheet—but it is very useful for showing that the benefits of the changes were worth their costs.

This information is easy to gather, and it will be valuable when it comes time to judge whether the benefits of the improvements were worth the cost. You can put the cost of the improvement in context by using the project schedule (see Chapter 4—and if you do not have a project schedule yet, it is more valuable to build and maintain one than it is to gather this data!). From the schedule, you can find the calendar time elapsed over the course of the project, and the amount of effort performed over the course of the entire software project.

One goal is to show that the effort required for the improvements is relatively small. By adding up the effort in the spreadsheet and dividing by the total effort in the schedule, you can calculate the percentage of the effort that your improvements cost. Many of the tools and techniques—especially ones that are typically labeled "bureaucratic," such as inspections, code reviews, and developing a vision and scope document—require a very small percentage of the project's effort. And it is often not hard to point to specific results (like problems that were avoided by developing the vision and scope document, or defects that were found during an inspection or code review) that, had the tasks not been performed, would have clearly cost more time than they saved.

Another goal is to show that even though the improvements took time and effort, they did not add calendar time to the schedule (since the final due date was not delayed). This is not hard to do, if your organization has done another project of similar size or complexity in the past and you know how long that project took to build. If the tools and techniques were effective, that project should have taken more calendar time than your project. Subtract the total number of hours required to build the current project from the total number of hours required to build the similar project. If this result is much greater than the number of hours spent on the improvements, it shows that the improvements saved more time than they cost. (The earned value metrics in Chapter 4 are also helpful when comparing two projects.

In addition to comparing projects, you can also compare tasks within a project. You can compare the hours or effort required for a specific task with the benefits of that task. For example, if another project in your organization took 3 months (13 calendar weeks, or 520 hours) developing a feature that eventually had to be scrapped because it did not meet the needs of the users, you can show that far fewer than 520 hours would have been needed to develop and inspect a vision and scope document that could have prevented the wasted effort.

Measuring quality

One straightforward way to measure the quality of the software is to measure the total time and effort required to test the software. This metric covers all of the effort expended, from the time that the programmers deliver an alpha build that they consider complete to the time that the test activities yield results that the senior managers agree are acceptable for release (see Chapter 8 about the release readiness process). This measurement should include not only the testing activities, but also any work programmers do to fix defects that are found. If the testing team finds requirements or scope defects, this number should also take into account time and effort spent on activities performed by the project manager, requirements analysts, stakeholders, users, and anyone else involved in fixing that defect.

Any tools and techniques that you put in place in order to improve the way software is built should reduce the time and effort required to test the software. To use this measurement, use the schedule to figure out both the calendar time and the effort required to test the software as a percentage of the total calendar time or effort required for the entire project. You can then compare these numbers to other projects of similar complexity. If these numbers decrease over the course of several projects, your improvements are working. In many cases, the change will also lead to fewer delivered defects (but it can take a while to observe that effect).

It is important to select projects for comparison that match the current one in complexity. This means that the comparison projects should use similar technology, require similar expertise from the team, and preferably use many of the same team members. This works especially well when comparing maintenance releases of a single software project.

Bring In an Expert

Sometimes the best way to make sure that your changes are implemented effectively is to bring in an expert. There are many consultants who will assist in improvement efforts and train your organization to implement the tools introduced in this book. Sometimes, corroborating your improvement initiatives with an expert's opinions is just what people in your organization need, to feel reassured that the ideas have merit.

Experts and consultants are especially helpful in training people in a wide range of specific techniques, including estimation, inspections, code reviews, unit testing, and project planning practices. They can also be pivotal in helping to establish metrics, testing, or requirements efforts. What's more, there are many pitfalls that inexperienced project managers and organizations can fall into: experts can identify these pitfalls and help you avoid them. In this way, bringing in a consultant or expert can more than pay for itself.

Perhaps most importantly, experts' training sessions are morale boosters—there is little that can get a team more excited about a new technique than training them all at the same time on it. Everyone feels like they have a common understanding, and the culture changes to accept that idea much more quickly than it would have, had it only been introduced by someone internally.

Don't be afraid to go outside of your own organization to get training. Some project managers are tempted to develop their own training programs, but they often underestimate the effort involved. Doing it right is extremely time consuming, and it's likely that you won't do nearly as good a job as someone who has used and refined his training many times. In addition, you'd be reinventing the wheel—just like programmers with NIH syndrome do with regard to new practices.

When an improvement effort seems to lose some steam, an effective way to get it back on track and renew the organizational commitment is to engage in group training about process improvement techniques, and raise general awareness about your efforts. Hearing from an outside authority figure that you are on the right track can be enough to gain support from those who might not have agreed with you in the past.

When you bring an outside expert into your organization, the fact that this person is paid to give advice will cause many people to treat this person as an authority figure. People naturally defer to an authority. In many organizations, bringing in an expert will cause people to change their minds, even if that person is saying the same thing you already said. Even if you are in an organization with NIH syndrome, bringing in an outside expert or a consultant can help bring people around. By hiring an expert, the organization already has committed to listening to the person. The expert's advice can immediately become "how things are done here," because money has been authorized and spent on the expert. Once money has been spent to obtain an expert opinion, people are much more likely to take suggestions for change seriously.

NOTE

More ideas on organizational change can be found in *Peopleware: Productive Projects and Teams* by Tom DeMarco and Timothy Lister (Dorset House, 1999). Information on the psychology of influence, attitudes, and persuasion can be found in *Influence: Science and Practice* by Robert Cialdini (Allyn and Bacon, 2001).

CHAPTER TEN

Management and Leadership

MANY MANAGEMENT BOOKS sell themselves as lists of "best practices" that, if followed, will yield projects that are planned and executed smoothly and without any problems. Most people who try to follow those practices find that it is much harder to do in practice than the books led them to believe. Projects are not always predictable. The organization's needs may change; people may quit or be transferred into or out of the team; or the goals of the project or the climate in which the organization does its business may change. A project manager usually cannot control any of these things.

The tools and techniques in this book will help solve the most common problems that plague software projects. But there are many other ways that a project can go wrong, and it is impossible to prepare in advance for all of them. It is up to you, the project manager, to be smart. You should use these tools when you can. But you will undoubtedly come across issues or problems that these practices simply do not address, and it is your job to think your way through the solution. If you keep in mind some sound engineering principles and fundamental ideas about management, you stand a better chance of leading your projects through these problems and, in the end, delivering better software.

It is also part of your job as a manager and a leader to adequately explain the decisions that you are making, and to keep the team's interest in line with the organization's interests—and vice versa. You must do this by working with senior management to understand their goals and needs, and helping them understand that the changes you are making will help them achieve those goals. You must also work with each team member to understand her goals and needs, and help her understand the job that she must perform. If you do this, you will ensure that the software is mutually beneficial for both the organization and the individuals building it.

In a sense, part of the job of the project manager is to serve as an information conduit. You help information flow from the team up to senior management in the form of project status and analysis information. It is your job to understand all of the work being done, so that it can be summarized to the people who make the decisions about the future of the project; they need this information to make informed and intelligent decisions. This requires that the project manager put a lot of effort into understanding what it is the team is doing and why they are doing it. The project manager cannot simply ask for estimates, fit those estimates in a schedule, and quiz the team on the percentage they've completed. He must understand what actions each team member is taking to complete the task, and what possible complications they are running into. The project manager is the only person looking at how the tasks interrelate; he is the only one with the perspective to see the problems and, ideally, fix them.

Take Responsibility

The world is full of frustrated project managers. Frustrations come in many forms. Some project managers are assigned projects, but have to fight for the people to do those projects. Others have inadequate office space, computers, or networks. Many project managers are constantly clashing with other managers because of "dashed-line" organization structures where their teams do not report directly to them. Some find that their project team members are routinely pulled off of their projects without warning, or that their projects are reprioritized and thrown into disarray.

There is a common root cause of most, or all, of these problems. The cause is that the project manager is told that she has responsibility for her projects, but, though she is held accountable for their success, she is not given sufficient authority to do her job.

Managers routinely throw around the word "responsibility," often in the context of a subordinate "not taking responsibility" for a task. To many of them, "take responsibility for this task" is synonymous with "go away and don't bother me until the task is complete." This is an unfortunate attitude, and it is a root cause of failed projects and depleted morale in organizations around the world. A good project manager must have a more sophisticated understanding of responsibility in order to avoid these problems.

A person has *responsibility* for a task only if he is given sufficient authority to perform the task and is held accountable for the results. When you assign a task to your project team, you must ensure that each team member has sufficient authority to perform the task, as well as an understanding of his or her accountability. For the project to be most effective, the team members should understand these concepts as well.

Ensure That You Have Authority to Do the Project

A person has *authority* to perform a task only if he is has adequate control over the resources necessary to complete the task. Giving a project manager authority to carry out a project means giving him control over the resources (people, office space, hardware, software, etc.) required to complete it. Since resources cost money, sufficient budget for the project must be allocated within the organization.

This does not mean that the project manager must have direct control over these resources. For example, the team members do not necessarily need to report to him. However, if they do not report to him, he must have the full cooperation of the direct manager of each resource assigned to the project, so that he can assign tasks to the team members directly without having to obtain permission for each task. If there is a single person on the project whose involvement is not guaranteed from the outset, the project manager cannot say with certainty that he has all of the resources that he needs to complete the project. In this case, he does not have sufficient authority to do his job.

In the same way, the project manager does not need to have a corporate credit card to buy the necessary hardware or software. But he does need to have a guarantee from the person who has the budgetary authority that he will be allowed to obtain these resources. Without this guarantee, his authority will still be incomplete.

You Are Accountable for the Project's Success

A person is *accountable* for a task if failure to adequately perform that task carries professional consequences. These professional consequences can take one or more of four possible forms:

- His reputation is damaged among his peers and in the organization.
- His manager gives him a poor performance review.
- His compensation is reduced.
- His responsibilities are changed (or taken away altogether, if he is fired).

When someone is held accountable for a task, he must have some understanding of the professional consequences if he fails. If there are no consequences, or those consequences are not particularly damaging, then there is little incentive to complete the task.

That does not mean that someone who does not have incentive to complete a task will do a poor job. She may still perform it well, usually out of a sense of duty, loyalty, or personal responsibility. But if failure does not carry consequences, she is not really accountable. She is doing the task as a favor, and any success is coincidental.

Grant Authority and Accountability to Team Members

When you are responsible for a software project, you are accountable for its success. However, you are not the only person accountable—you must distribute that accountability fairly among the project team. The way to do that is to make sure each team member is responsible for her task by ensuring that she has sufficient authority to carry it out and understands how she will be held accountable for its completion.

The best way to ensure that each team member has sufficient authority is to discuss it directly at team meetings. When you discuss the status of a project, verify that each person has everything necessary to perform her assigned tasks.

The most common way that authority is removed is when a team member is pulled off of the task. If you have been given a person's time for your project, you must be able to depend on that to last for the course of the project. Many people will not tell you that they have additional demands on their time unless you ask them directly.

Never assign a task to a person who does not have the authority to perform it. All engineers must have control over their time. Requirements analysts must be allowed to call meetings with stakeholders. User interface designers must be allowed to make UI design decisions without having to clear them with a string of senior managers. Programmers must be allowed to use the tools and techniques that they need. Testers must be allowed to request requirements specifications, technical specifications, and preliminary builds, and must feel free to report defects without being blamed.

If the project is late or runs into problems, you must give every project team member your guarantee that you will work hard to identify the root cause of the problem. For example, many delays that are introduced due to poor planning or scope creep are not recognized until late in the project, during the testing activities. The testers may have done their jobs and met all of their estimates, but, since they are in charge of the active task at the time that the project delay is discovered, they are held accountable for problems that they had no authority to prevent. It is your job to prevent this from happening by holding the people responsible for the delay accountable. You must share in the consequences because you failed to recognize the problem until too late. And you must take steps to prevent it in future projects, by implementing additional tools and techniques.

Defend Your Project Against Challenges to Your Authority

If resources are pulled off of your project, your authority is being challenged. You only have authority to do a task if you can command the resources necessary to complete it, and, when people are pulled off of your project, those resources are no longer available to you. However, the accountability is still in place. If you want to avoid being held accountable for the project's failure, you must recognize the challenge to your authority and defend your project against it. This is difficult, and often requires patience and negotiation.

For example, it is very common for programmers to be interrupted "for just an hour or two." If a senior manager or executive needs help with something small—say, he's having trouble using a program that he knows the programmer wrote a few months ago—he will often approach the programmer directly, without your knowledge. This puts the programmer in a difficult position, because she does not feel like she can tell this senior person that she is too busy to help. She will want to be helpful, and may simply take on the extra work without mentioning it to you.

If something like this happens, it is your job to address the situation. Though it seems innocuous, this is an indirect (though probably unintended) challenge to your authority, because a resource has been pulled off of your project. It is also a challenge to the programmer's authority, because she no longer has enough time to do her task. This is a difficult situation to fix. You might approach the senior manager directly and explain that this will cause a delay in the project, and that both you and your programmer will be held accountable for her delay. If the senior manager balks, you might ask him to share the accountability by writing an email to the project's stakeholders explaining why the project will be delayed, so that you won't get blamed.

You may have to be creative in how you solve this problem, because this can be a politically charged situation. Approach it with a cool head. Do not accuse people of trying to interfere with your project. Remember that the person you are talking to is just trying to do his job, and he probably did not realize that he was putting your project at risk. Try to talk about how this affects you and your project team, and be very specific about the consequences. Give examples of how a delay in the programmer's task will ripple down the project and cause additional delays. Most importantly, make sure that you have your facts straight before you meet with the other manager, and make sure that your own manager knows everything you are about to say, and approves.

If your manager does not back you up in defending your authority, your hands are tied. You will either have to renegotiate the schedule or accept the consequences. This is hard for many people to deal with. The best way to prepare is to make sure that you have plenty of documentation, so that when you are called upon to explain the delay, you can show what caused it and, if necessary, that your manager knew about it and did not let you fix the situation.

Do Everything Out in the Open

It is a very frustrating situation for a project manager when he makes a decision or takes an action, and then finds that a colleague or senior manager disagrees with him for seemingly no reason at all. Many times, these disagreements arise from a lack of communication. If everyone in your organization has constant access to everything that you and your team produce, the mystery behind why you make your decisions goes away. People may still disagree with you, but at least they will be disagreeing with your ideas and not simply because they felt like they were kept out of the loop.

It's not possible to tell everyone everything all of the time. But if it is known to the organization that a project manager is sharing his project information, and all of his colleagues know where they can find that information, they are much less likely to feel like information is being hidden from them.

Whether you are interacting with your team or with your organization's management, it is important that everything that you do is *transparent*. This means that when you create a document, hold a meeting of interest to others, or make an important project decision, you should share all of the information produced and used with everyone involved.

Publish Your Work Products

All work products should be kept in a public repository. This could be a shared folder or directory, a version control system, a Wiki or other sort of web interface, a knowledge base, or some other system for information storage. This ensures transparency for both team members and the organization's management.

When each person on the team knows that the work she is doing can be read and used by all other team members, she will feel much more accountable for her work than if she were doing the same thing in private. In general, people tend to create more readable documents, build more maintainable designs, and write more readable code if they know it will be shared with others.

Managers also benefit from transparency of work products. For example, if a product ships and a client encounters a defect, a client support manager can consult the test plan for the part of the product in which the defect was found. He might want to see the defects reported in the defect tracking system, or check the specification for the feature to verify that it is indeed a defect and not a misunderstood feature. Publishing the work products allows everyone in the organization to use them as reference materials.

Your senior managers will especially benefit from transparency. If it is your responsibility to specifically summarize and report every aspect of every product, it is highly likely that you will, on occasion, leave out an important item. However, if your boss is used to looking at the project documents himself, there is no chance that you will leave him in the dark. This will help build trust between you, and will also help discover any impending problems.

Another problem that is avoided through work product transparency is information hoarding. Sometimes an insecure person feels that he needs to keep certain aspects of his day-to-day work secret from the rest of his organization—even his manager. This helps him feel more important to the organization, since any time anyone needs access to that information, they must go through him. In some cases, it even (unfairly) provides job security: if he's the only person who has maintained that particular work product, it is much harder to fire him if he's doing a poor job. That secrecy also makes it difficult to judge how poor a job he's doing.

Make Decisions Based on Known Guidelines

If you do things the same way every time, the people who work with you will come to understand the reasoning behind your decisions. They will feel much more comfortable with you than if you make decisions in a less predictable manner. One way to help others understand your perspective, and avoid surprising them, is to publish the standards by which you manage.

There are several ways that guidelines can help make your decisions more predictable:

- Use published *standards documents* to help others understand the way certain roles must be filled. For example, a standard for interacting with a version control system might require that each programmer verify that the code builds without compilation errors before it is checked in. Programming standards may include naming conventions for variables or files. A testing standard might specify that a test plan must be executed by somebody other than the person who wrote it. Acceptance criteria and release readiness criteria are useful standards to help the organization make unbiased and objective decisions about when to release the software into test or to the general public. In addition, inspection checklists are also a kind of standards document.

- Documents should be based on *templates* when possible. This ensures that all of the information that is needed in the document is included, and that important omissions are noted by the person writing the document. For example, a template might require that a vision and scope document always have a section for future releases. For projects that are only expected to have a single release, this section will contain "N/A" or a placeholder. This will prevent the reader from wondering whether the author meant that there would be a single release, or whether it was an oversight.

- *Process documents* ensure that each project is done using a repeatable process. That ensures that the same activities for the current project are done in the same order as previous projects. This helps each person on the project understand how their work fits into the big picture, and reassures them that they are doing the right tasks. Process documents also give them the ability to compare the team's performance from project to project, to determine whether the organization is improving over time. The scripts used throughout this book are examples of process documents.

- Use *performance plans* to set expectations for individual team members. Each person in the organization should have her performance measured against a written standard, and she should be given an active role in helping to define that standard. This helps her gauge how she is performing and provides a positive environment for her manager to help fix performance problems and reward good work.

Manage the Organization

An important part of the project manager's job is managing upward in the organization. The way that you interact with your organization's senior management can make or break your projects. When you make changes for the better, you are changing their organization, and, whether or not you are successful, your boss will want to be involved.

Senior Managers See Software Projects as a Cost Burden

Many project managers face an uphill battle when interacting with their organizations' senior management. They find that senior managers have an increasingly antagonistic view of their software projects. The senior managers only see the cost of the development, and often fail to see how the software projects help the organization. These problems are compounded when projects come in late, or do not fill the needs of the stakeholders.

In the mid 1990s, Mary Lacity and Rudy Hirscheim published a study of 14 Fortune 500 companies in which they interviewed over 60 senior managers about their attitudes toward IT projects. They found that the overwhelming majority of them thought of their IT departments as a "cost burden" that steadily increases their costs without adding to the profitability of the company. This attitude is pervasive not just in large companies, but in organizations of all types and sizes.

Unfortunately, most project managers cannot just sit down with their organization's senior managers and explain the value of their projects. They must show over time that there is a real reason that each project is developed, and that each project's benefits justify the cost of development.

Many of the project management practices in Part I are aimed at communicating this. The vision and scope document is the project manager's first opportunity to ensure that each project is developed based on real and specific needs, and that the features of the software are aimed at fulfilling those needs. The vision and scope document and the project plan communicate the real costs and benefits of development to senior managers in terms that they understand. And a change control process ensures that the managers are kept apprised of all changes to the project, and that those changes are worth their costs.

A project is successful if its costs are justified by its benefits. Establishing a track record of successful projects is the most effective way for a project manager to reverse dangerous attitudes in senior management.

Show Senior Managers the Impact of Their Decisions

The first step in working with senior managers is to know what a best-case scenario looks like. In good organizations, decisions are based on objective standards and metrics that were developed in advance to determine the health of the application. The goals of the project are decided from the outset, and a successful project will have met those goals. Project decisions—approval of schedules, deadlines, budgets, and resources—are made by a single person or a group of people who make those decisions based on objective evidence.

Unfortunately, in small- to mid-sized companies, this is not usually the case. Decisions are frequently made based on gut feelings instead of objective analysis. The people in charge of project decisions are not necessarily experienced in working with software projects—in many cases, this may be the first time they have encountered software projects. Even in software companies, a small or young company may be run by a manager or management team with industry, business, or organizational experience—but without much experience managing software projects. While gut decisions can be successful, they will often lead to serious project problems.

It's true that project decisions based on gut instincts are often correct. If that were not the case, people would never get into the habit of making gut decisions in the first place. But the fact is, most small businesses are run entirely on gut instincts. And if you have a small product with a small and well-understood user base, those gut decisions make intuitive sense to anyone who understands both the product and the clients. That usually includes the upper management of such a company. As a result, many small businesses have successfully built and sold software products using mostly gut instincts to govern their decisions.

One typical example of project management by gut instinct is release readiness. The typical reasoning sounds like this: "We've tested the product longer than we did for the last release, and we have not encountered any major problems. So let's release it!" In contrast, a release readiness process that was based on objective facts would require that a certain percentage of the code base is covered by the tests, and that the number of defects that are discovered falls below a certain threshold (based on the size of the application). For example, the product might only be considered releasable if at least 70% of the code has been executed under test, if no critical defects are found, and if there are fewer than 3 medium-priority and 10 low-priority defects per 10,000 lines of code. Keep in mind that the exact same testing activities could be performed in both cases; it's just that in the second case, everyone has already agreed that if these objective and measurable criteria are not met, more testing is needed.

In a small company, the senior managers are happy if they are making more money this year than last year. Most of the time, they don't try to figure out why that happened. They know that what they are doing is working, and there's no need to question it. This attitude is very common, and you must recognize its relevance to your projects.

Some senior managers feel that they have navigated more difficult problems than whether or not to put the code under source control or add another round of testing. These things seem like details to them, and they don't feel that they need to read a book to figure them out. To someone with this attitude, the very fact that you are concerned about these "details" makes you seem like an alarmist—you are up in arms about something that they consider very minor. Or, even worse, they feel that they have done a fine job of building a software organization, and are insulted that you think that you can make it better by introducing changes.

If an organization is in the software business, the people running that organization need to understand the details of making software. Making those decisions is uncomfortable for a senior manager with little software experience: it is hard to make sound decisions about building software when one has only a simple, high-level view of software design, programming, and testing.

One common senior-management response to this problem is to attempt to delegate—probably to you, since you have read a book about it and seem to know what you are talking about. Unfortunately, this is a shallow commitment that can cause its own problems. If your boss does not understand the goals of the improvements you want to make or the reasons behind them, he will not make consistent decisions. The actions that you take in implementing new practices on your project will impact other people: they will create additional work for some of them, and many will perceive that you are taking away some of their power, flexibility, or freedom. And, in some poorly run software organizations, there may be people assigned to software tasks who are not very good at those tasks; they might prefer not to have their work measured or analyzed. If they see you as an interloper, they will complain to your boss. If he does not understand why you are doing what you are doing, all he will see is conflict—conflict that you created with the changes that you made. Since he did not take the time to understand the benefits of your actions, he will simply blame you for making changes and causing conflict. Your improvement effort will grind to a halt.

The solution—and it is not an easy one—is that upper management must be better educated about the details of your project. The person who has the authority to tell you (and everyone else on your level) to undertake a project should understand the purpose behind every step in the software process. This means more than just understanding that software needs to be designed, developed, and tested. He needs to know why the software is being developed that way.

It means that if, for example, you are trying to implement inspections, then the senior manager must understand what an inspection is, what is being inspected, what kinds of defects it will find, why those defects are there, who needs to attend the inspection meetings, and what will happen if the inspection is skipped—and he needs to understand this before the inspections are implemented. He must be sold on the idea. If he does not agree that this is the most efficient and effective way to develop software, he will fold the first time someone decides that inspections are "bureaucratic," unnecessary, or somehow getting in her way. It is only with some genuine understanding of the changes you want to make that he will be able to make a real commitment to them.

The process of educating your organization's senior management must go both ways. You need to put time and effort into understanding the goals and needs of the organization and its senior managers. The easiest way to do this is to call a meeting with them. The purpose of this meeting is to write down their goals and needs. These should be written in their language (e.g., improving profits, increasing the customer base, reducing support calls, etc.). Be sure to meet with them periodically in order to keep this list up-to-date. You should be able to use it to show how your improvements will help them meet these goals.

Don't Confuse Flexibility with Always Saying Yes

There are many situations when a project manager disagrees with the people around her. Sometimes a project is going off track or experiencing problems. Other times, people disagree with her approach to a project. It is important to be flexible in these situations. But sometimes it is hard to figure out just what it means to be flexible. Flexibility might mean making sure that everyone understands that the project is in a difficult situation, and agrees on the course that it will take. But it might also mean listening to the dissenting opinions and making changes to the way the project is being managed. Flexibility should never mean having to cave in to unreasonable requests.

Don't agree to an unrealistic schedule

When somebody asks you to do something, it is natural to want to satisfy them—especially if that person is above you in your organization. Many project managers operate in a climate of constant pressure from above, and they want to alleviate that pressure by being positive and agreeable.

Some senior managers think that all dates are negotiable, and that teams can always be pressured into releasing software earlier—even if the team's projected date is based on realistic estimates and solid project planning. Sometimes upper managers will just challenge the team's opinion because they believe that anything can be done sooner if the team works harder. Unfortunately, just increasing the pressure on the team is a poor motivator. It makes people feel as though their opinions have been second-guessed, that their expertise is not valued, and that their work is not respected. Nevertheless, it's a common situation.

For example, consider a project in which the senior manager in charge has set a deadline, but it is clear to the project manager that this deadline is too aggressive and the team will never meet it. If she simply goes to the manager and tells him that the project is headed for failure, he will probably just think that she is not being a "team player". He will probably put a great deal of pressure on her to just accept his deadline and work the team harder, possibly forcing them to put in overtime in order to meet the goal. He would consider that being "flexible." But in reality, that's a recipe for team demotivation, and probably disaster. The senior manager's "solution" does not solve the problems that are keeping the project from delivering at that time. In fact, simply agreeing to the deadline is actually being inflexible, in that it ignores the reality of the situation and fails to present alternatives that might actually help the team meet the deadline (or, at least, satisfy the organization's needs that motivated the decision to impose the deadline).

Creating transparency and gathering consensus are the most effective ways to address this. When a project slips, the project manager needs to diagnose where the planning went wrong or what risk was not previously considered. Hopefully, she has done enough planning (see Chapter 2) that she has real evidence that the project will not meet the deadline. In this case, true flexibility would involve presenting the senior manager with options, such as doing a phased release, scaling back the features to be developed, or adding resources.

Change your approach when necessary

Sometimes a project manager is faced with a project that is coming in early. The schedule was the result of a difficult negotiation, and moving the date earlier means giving up the hard-won project time. It seems counterintuitive to move the deadline up and give up the extra padding. But there are cases when this is necessary.

One of the most common situations that results in decreasing the schedule is when a programmer discovers a shortcut. For example, a project may have gone through a solid estimation process, and a project plan was created when one of the assumptions for the estimates was that a certain component would have to be built from the ground up. For example, if a programmer discovers that this component can be replaced with one purchased off the shelf, this reduces the effort required to build the software.

Many project managers would happily sweep this under the rug and keep that extra schedule time as a buffer against future schedule slips. This feels like "flexibility" to the project manager, because it keeps her options open in the future.

The temptation to keep the buffer in the schedule must be resisted. Just as the overly aggressive deadline had to be resisted with transparency and honesty, the project plan must be kept honest in this case as well. The reason this is the truly flexible option is that the extra effort can then be reused by the organization, either to extend the current project or to apply it to a future one. Keeping that effort on the current project schedule denies it to the organization and limits its ability to develop other projects.

Don't confuse "easy to describe" with "easy to implement"

Many changes are very easy to describe in words. Yet most programmers can tell horror stories about being asked for a "tiny change" that turned out to require an enormous amount of effort. A manager asking for an easy-to-describe change will often assume that any project manager who balks at immediately implementing the change is being inflexible.

It is a common myth that having a software process—that is, deciding on how you are going to build the software before you actually build it—is inflexible. The feeling is that requiring that the software be planned and designed before it is built will prevent programmers from just jumping in and making any small changes that are needed by the organization. This is one of the most common complaints that project managers hear when trying to implement a reasonable planning process.

In fact, it is the planning process itself that provides the most opportunity for flexibility. It's very difficult to figure out which changes are easily contained, and which ones will have much larger consequences. Sometimes a change that seems tiny will require a large coding effort, while a change that seems large from a user perspective is actually relatively minor to implement but could have a lot of testing implications. The only way to get an accurate picture is by engaging the team and having them estimate the impact of the change—preferably using a change control process (see Chapter 6). Controlling the changes will give the organization the most flexibility.

Manage Your Team

Many project managers—especially those who have been promoted from technical positions—feel like their primary job function is to understand the job each team member is doing. Often the best programmer, designer, or tester will be promoted into a management position. And in many cases, this is a very good choice, because it's important for a manager to understand the work being done by the team. Sometimes the project manager is also the direct manager of each team member, and in this case, he is especially vulnerable to certain management pitfalls.

Understanding the work that the team is doing is very important; however, the primary task of a manager is to have the right people do the correct work and, ultimately, to get the tasks done in the most efficient and least problematic way. The first instinct of a manager who got to where he is by being a good programmer will be to be the best programmer on the team. That's not what the team needs—they need someone to make decisions, provide guidance, and prioritize their tasks. If all he does is "get his hands dirty" by solving programming problems for his team, they will not only sense a lack of direction from their manager, but may also feel demotivated because their work is not valued.

In contrast, some managers understand that their job is to delegate. But while delegation is an important part of management, it must be done with a good understanding of the work being delegated. The manager may not be the best engineer in the group, or even be able to perform all of the engineering tasks he assigns. He should, however, understand the goals and limitations of each task, and be able to offer real guidance if team members get stuck or need help. That's much harder than delegating: while he's trusted a team member to accomplish the task, he must still understand enough about it to be useful if that team member encounters a problem.

Good managers usually feel a little guilty about being managers. They know that their people are good, and they want them to succeed. But this necessarily involves riding their coattails. As a manager, you might feel that in some ways you are not making a direct contribution by producing work products. This is a good feeling: embrace it. Recognize that your role is to "grease the wheels" by providing an environment in which work gets done. And the best way to provide that environment is to show the team that you trust them to do the work. Show the team that you are there for them when they need you. When you make decisions about the project, make sure that you are always fair, just, consistent, and predictable. That way, when people disagree with you, they can at least understand why you made that decision and will remain motivated and loyal to the project.

Avoid Common Management Pitfalls

Poor managers are distinguished by their poor habits. They tend not to question their own authority, and they frequently don't have much faith in the people who work for them. They distance themselves from their projects, and tend to see their jobs as simple, intuitive, easy, and straightforward. A manager who acts this way projects hubris and arrogance; some people find that reassuring, but most engineers find it condescending. The best way to improve as an engineering project manager is to avoid these pitfalls.

The best way to avoid these pitfalls is to question each decision that you make:

- Is the decision based on facts, or are you automatically jumping to a decision based solely on intuition and gut instincts?
- Are you unfairly questioning your team's honesty, integrity, or skill?
- Are you making a decision that is politically motivated? Are you simply siding with the person you like better?
- Are you oversimplifying a task or avoiding its internal details out of laziness?

By understanding the root cause of many common pitfalls, a project manager can keep his team motivated and avoid bad decisions that lead to serious project problems. It requires constant vigilance to avoid those problems.

Don't manage from your gut

There is a common belief among many managers that decisions should make intuitive sense. This is generally true. However, the converse—that all ideas that make intuitive sense are good decisions—is definitely not true. Software projects are complex. They involve many people serving in different roles, sometimes with multiple roles per person. They involve numerous tasks and subtasks, where each task may be assigned to several people. As a manager, you can't expect to intuit all of that complexity. Just because you, as the project manager, have the authority to make decisions about the project, that doesn't mean that it's your job to overrule people all the time. It's your job to understand the issues that face the team, and to help the team deal with those issues.

Think about it rationally: if a team member disagrees with a decision that you have made, and comes up with a well-researched and logical explanation for her disagreement, is it fair to dismiss her opinion simply because it does not immediately make intuitive sense to you? There are many things in the world (especially in complex engineered products) that simply are not intuitive to most people.

For example, it seems intuitive that doubling the staff on a project should allow them to complete it in half the time. However, in the real world, projects are much more complex: there is overhead in the extra communication, certain tasks on a critical path cannot be split, it takes time for new team members to ramp up, etc. But that doesn't stop many project managers from trying over and over again to throw additional team members at a late project, only to find that it becomes an even later project.*

Unfortunately, software project managers have to make decisions based on complicated information all the time. To make good decisions, you have to understand software engineering concepts and technological concepts that are not intuitive, and remain open to the idea that there have been recent innovations or changes in software engineering and technology that may contradict your current beliefs. This job is about being informed, not about feeling your way through problems.

A project manager must make many individual decisions: who to assign tasks to, how long they should be expected to take, whether to implement certain features or requirements, the dependency between tasks and software behavior, and many other design, development, and testing decisions. There is no way that even the best project manager can be on top of every detail in an average-sized software project. But these decisions still must be made. So how can you make them without simply relying on your intuition, but also without being overwhelmed by the details?

Luckily, your project team is staffed by competent software engineers who are capable of building the software. (If your team is not competent, you have bigger problems!) This means that you have at your disposal people who can help you make those decisions. You should enlist their help and work to understand the perspectives of all of the people involved in the project. When you make a decision, you must understand which team members it affects and take their perspectives into account. If you don't know those perspectives yet, ask the team members their opinions. Most people will be more than happy to help you decide the direction of their tasks, and you will almost certainly get better results because they participated in the decision-making process.

If you try to learn all of the details for every decision that must be made, you will find that your projects will quickly get bogged down, with everyone waiting for you to decide on at least one issue. But if you work with your team to make well-informed decisions, you can share that load…and everybody wins. That's why you have a team: so people can collaborate.

Don't second-guess estimates

Many managers fall into a common trap when considering their team members' estimates: they automatically cut those estimates, no matter how reasonable or well researched they are. There are generally three reasons this is done.

---

* Fred Brooks pointed this out in his 1975 book *The Mythical Man-Month*. He referred to it as Brooks' Law: "Adding manpower to a late software project makes it later."

One reason is that the organization already committed to an earlier date for the software, and changing that expectation is difficult or impossible for the manager. This means that the project was not planned properly. The solution is to apply the project planning and estimation tools and techniques to bring the project under control. If the estimate does not meet the needs of the organization, the manager has several options: the scope of the project can be scaled back; the software can be released in phases; the deadline can be renegotiated; resources can be added; or some combination of all of these can be done. The team will generally respect the decision, as long as it was clearly based on honest estimates and planning rather than an artificial date.

The second reason that an estimate may be second-guessed is that this second-guessing is a misguided attempt to motivate the team. For some reason—and nobody is really sure why some people believe this—there are managers who think that telling somebody that they can do a task in less time than they estimated will cause them to "step up to the plate." Somehow, knowing that their manager believes that they can do it is supposed to increase their productivity. Unfortunately, this sort of second-guessing becomes a self-fulfilling prophecy. As the team realizes that their estimates will always be cut, they will start padding those estimates. This can create an environment of distrust between the team and their manager.

The third reason managers will second-guess their teams' estimates is to force them to work overtime. By enforcing an overly aggressive deadline, some managers find that they can squeeze five, ten, or more extra hours per week out of all of their team members. This is especially dishonest, and it almost always breeds resentment. If the team is expected to work overtime—and in some cases, this is a valid and realistic expectation—that should be taken into account when the effort estimates are turned into a project schedule. This way, the team is not blindsided by the extra work and can plan their lives around it. (Sometimes managers forget that people have lives outside the organization!)

In all of these cases, the key to understanding how the team members react to second-guessing is to recognize that they believe their manager is sending them a clear message: he does not trust their estimates. The solution to this is to establish trust by making decisions in a transparent manner. (A good way to do this is to use a repeatable estimation process like Wideband Delphi—see Chapter 3.)

This does not mean that the project manager does not need to understand estimates. It is important for a project manager to not only understand the reasons why the team estimated a certain effort for a task, but to question the estimate if it looks inaccurate, unrealistic, or seems to be based on incorrect assumptions. As long as the questions are reasonable and can be answered with facts, the team will generally respect them and work to answer them. If it turns out that the estimate is, in fact, unrealistic, the team will be glad that the project manager pointed out a potential problem with it!

Don't expect consensus all of the time

Over the course of almost any project, there will be disagreements between team members. Some project managers make the mistake of expecting the team members to settle all of these disagreements, reaching a consensus on their own. The project manager treats all disagreements as if they were merely petty or politically motivated, rather than based on a genuine difference in opinion over some important issue that affects the project.

When two team members have a genuine disagreement, it is the manager's job to make a decision. That decision is going to leave at least one of the team members—and possibly both—unhappy. It is important to share the reasoning behind the decision with everyone, and to stand behind the decision. If it turns out to be wrong, it's the project manager's fault, not the fault of the person who originally proposed the solution or of the person who didn't fight hard enough for the alternative.

To make a good decision, the manager must understand both perspectives. It's not enough to just tell the two people to go decide among themselves: if they could do that, they would not have brought the disagreement up with their manager in the first place. Sometimes a compromise can be reached, but most team members are capable of recognizing when a compromise is available, and implementing it themselves.

If you treat each conflict as if it were a trivial or petty argument and tell your team members that it's their own responsibility to solve it, you are essentially asking one of them to acquiesce on something that he clearly thinks is important. That is unfair and divisive, and it makes both team members feel as if you do not care about their concerns or the project itself.

That's not to say that there are no problems that cannot be left to the team. Sometimes a problem really is petty ("Bill stole my stapler!") and the team members really should at least try to work it out between them before involving their manager. But even these problems can escalate, and if that happens, a concrete decision ("Buy another stapler") is the only way to make the problem go away. It's important for a project manager to learn to differentiate between trivial problems ("Someone keeps taking the last donut") and more serious ones ("Tom won't let go of his ridiculous database design").

Regardless of the magnitude of the problem, if two people on your team care enough about a problem to come to you with it, you should take it seriously. If you dismiss it and tell them that it's their problem to solve among themselves, you are making it clear to them that even though you are their manager, you do not care about the team members' problems (and, by extension, the project itself).

Avoid micromanagement

When a manager is overly involved in each task to the point that she personally takes over the work of each person on her team, she is *micromanaging*. From her point of view, there are a lot of benefits to micromanaging her team:

- It endears her to the people at or above her level, because it seems like she always knows everything there is to know about what's going on with her team.

- She knows that no mistakes will ever make it out of her team.

- She does not have to trust the people who work for her to do a good job. Instead, she can review everything they produce to ensure that each work product meets her standards—and she will redo anything that does not meet those standards.

- It makes her feel very important, because nothing gets done without her.

- It allows her to feel superior to everyone who works for her.

- She gets to steal her team's thunder, taking credit for all of their accomplishments while blaming them for any failures.

Her micromanagement has a devastating impact on the people who work for her. They feel that they have no responsibility whatsoever for what they do. They are not trusted. If they produce poor work, she will fix it, usually without explaining what they did wrong and often without even telling them. They feel like they do not have any impact, positive or negative, on the final product. And they're right.

Many people will put up with this situation for a long time. They can continue to collect a paycheck. The job that they do is not particularly stressful, because any work that does not meet the organization's standards will be redone for them. They are not trusted to set priorities, make decisions, or do any aspect of their jobs. This is very inefficient for the organization, and very demotivating for the team members. While they will tolerate the situation, the team members are neither challenged nor fulfilled. Meanwhile, their manager is drowning under all of the work. Nobody is happy with this situation.

There are a few easy rules that will help you avoid micromanagement:

Don't expect to review everything

Many people think that to be an effective manager, you have to have read, reviewed, and redone all of the work of the people who work for you. A good manager will spot-check the team's output, but reviewing (and possibly redoing) every piece of work that the team creates is a terrible use of a manager's time. Delegation requires trust; if you do not trust your team to do their jobs, then you should fire them and replace them with people who you do trust (or don't replace them, so the organization does not have to pay their salaries).

Don't fall into the "hands-on manager" trap

There is a general perception in the technology world that management is not an actual job. It's often believed that competent engineers manage themselves, while their incompetent "pointy-haired" bosses just get in the way. This is simply untrue. Competent engineers can be trusted to produce good requirements, designs, test plans, and code; their focus is not on prioritizing or managing teams of people. They can't do your job for you, so don't try to do theirs for them.

Many managers assume that because they are responsible for the work that their team produces, they should be able to do all of it. That's just not true—the individual team members have time to build up their expertise in developing the software, while you only have time to manage the project. Instead of trying to fill in as a technical team member, work on building up your project management skills.

Use transparency to your advantage

Some people fall into the trap of thinking that the job of project manager consists of constantly bugging each team member for status reports. Team members have trouble with this. They are surprised and unhappy that their project manager doesn't know enough about the project to glean even the most basic status; they also feel that they are not responsible for reporting their status upward. The project manager always goes to the team members, so they don't ever feel the need to report problems unless directly asked.

If all project plans and work products are kept as a matter of public record, the team members don't need to deal with a project manager constantly bugging them for status reports. If the project has transparency, each team member is responsible for his own status communication.

If your team is falling behind, don't just ask them for their status—this will encourage them to give you excuses. Instead, gather the status yourself using the documents that you have made public, and ask them about specific problems. Transparency only works if you make it clear that there are consequences for poor performance, and that poor performance is evident from public documents. Given this, people will see what's required of them in order to do a good job.

Don't be afraid to let your team make mistakes

People learn from their mistakes, and it's important that they be given the opportunity to make them and take responsibility for them. If they are going to grow professionally, it is going to be through their own experiences and through trial and error. Without this, team members will never see that their success takes effort to achieve. If a micromanager simply corrects all of their mistakes and redoes their work, they have no incentive to learn or improve.

It's okay for your team to make mistakes, as long as you're on top of it. The way to stay on top of mistakes is through the peer review tools. This allows team members to share information and help each other to grow to a standard that is in line with what the project needs and what the organization requires.

Make your mistakes public

If you make mistakes, you need to communicate them to everyone around you. It's okay to make the wrong call. Good managers recognize when they have made mistakes and correct them. The best managers publicize those mistakes so that everyone can learn from them, and so no one is blindsided by them.

When a team member makes mistakes, the project manager should share in the responsibility. Many project managers don't realize that they are culpable for the mistakes made by their team members. The reason the manager is culpable is because he assigned the task to the team member, allocated the resources to do it, set the priorities for the project, and set and communicated the deadlines—all of which were contributing factors.

For example, if somebody makes a bad decision because she failed to understand the project priorities, the project manager shares the responsibility for the error. That doesn't mean the project manager is solely to blame—if there were 20 people in the meeting where that priority was communicated, and 19 of those people understood it, the one person who ended up making the mistake should have spoken up at the time. But it still means that the project manager was not entirely clear, and failed to communicate the project priorities to everyone on the team. So when that mistake gets made, it's still partially the project manager's fault.

Just as it is okay for team members to make mistakes as long as they learn from them and corrective action is taken, it is okay for project managers to make mistakes as well. That's not to say that there are no consequences for mistakes—a serious mistake can lead to delays, which could lead to reprimands and even failed projects. As a project manager, if you find that one of your team members has made a mistake, it's your job to figure out what role you played in that mistake. And when you communicate that mistake up to senior management, you should highlight your role in it and try to shield the individual team members as much as possible.

This is very difficult to do. It's human nature to blame others. But by taking the blame yourself, you protect the team and keep them motivated, and help prepare them to recover from the mistake. If you stick your neck out for the team, they will know it, and they'll be much more loyal to you. On the other hand, if you let the blame roll downhill, the team will resent you and begin to work against you.

Some project managers don't think this is fair. They feel that if someone makes a mistake, it's that person's responsibility to take the blame for it. But the project manager is in a position of authority, and just as other people are accountable for their individual responsibilities, the project manager is accountable for everything he is responsible for. And he's responsible for the entire project.

Avoid lists

Some managers do little more than hand their team members lists of tasks or action items. When a team member is handed a list of tasks, but has no understanding of the rationale behind each action, he does what he can to complete the task. But without a real understanding of the needs that drive the project and the rationale behind each task, he will often make basic mistakes that would be obvious if he were given the proper context. There will always be decisions that a manager cannot predict and put on a list; without context, a team member has little chance of making those decisions correctly.

It's easy for a team to feel comfortable working from a list. It means that they are not responsible for anything other than this list of tasks. They don't have to think about overall project goals or the bigger picture. Most importantly, they don't have to make decisions. Accomplishing everything on a list of tasks is gratifying—a team member can go home at night knowing his job is 100% complete. But someone who feels responsible for the project, and not just his own tasks, knows his job is not really complete until the software is delivered and accepted. Sadly, once a team member understands the big picture, he feels like he's never done.

Your job as a manager is to get everybody on the team to see the big picture. The vision and scope document is a valuable tool for this, as are the rationale sections of the use cases and requirements. These tools allow the team members to more fully understand the context that surrounds the work that they are doing.

Software project teams are made up of smart people. It's far better to leverage their minds than to treat them like robots. Many people like to throw around the term "grunt programmer," as if there were a lot of programming tasks that were little more than cutting and pasting program recipes. But even the lowest impact programming tasks involve decision-making on the part of the programmer.

Accept Criticism

There are two ways that managers encounter criticism from a team member. One way is when the team member disagrees with the way a manager wants work done. The other is when the manager disagrees with how the team member is doing the work. Dealing with criticism is a potentially demotivating situation, but it's also a potentially encouraging one if handled well.

Sometimes the team members solve a problem differently than you would. As a manager it is important to recognize the work that has gone into these solutions, even if they contradict your preconceived ideas about that work. Being able to accept the team member's criticism of your solution means that you are making decisions in the project's and organization's best interests, and motivates your team to keep thinking their way through such problems in the future.

Everybody solves problems differently, and it's a fact of life in software engineering that most problems have many correct solutions. When you ask a team member to solve a problem, it's likely that she will come up with a correct solution that is different than the way you would solve the problem. If a member of your team offers a solution that is technically correct, but you don't accept it because you would do the work in a different (but equally valid, or even slightly more efficient) way, the team member will feel crushed.

A good manager's default action should be to accept, not reject, ideas. You must take it very seriously when you reject somebody's work, and when you do, you should always explain and defend your decision. There are many good reasons to reject a team member's solution. Sometimes it's incorrect, and sometimes it's not well thought out. But people will become very attached to such solutions, even when they are dead-on wrong. In those cases, you must be willing to stick to your guns. When you do, it must be for the right reasons, and you must take the time to explain your reasoning.

Criticism goes both ways. Sometimes a manager will want the team to do their work one way, and some team members will disagree. In fact, sometimes the entire team will disagree with a decision and come to the manager en masse. In this case, it is very tempting to just roll over and give in; it is equally tempting to refuse to even consider their opinions. Neither of these options is good, because no real discussion takes place in either case. Instead, a good manager will come up with a real justification for why he wants the work done that way, and will expect the team to do the same. If there is a real, verifiable reason for going with one alternative, everyone should be able to see it. And most importantly, the manager should show that he considered the argument, even if he essentially rejects it.

Ultimately, you won't be able to make everyone happy. It's always better if everyone can agree, but there are many times when there is a genuine difference of opinion. In this case, the manager is within his rights to pull rank. However, if he just rejects an argument outright or ignores a valid argument just to get his way, he is abusing his power, and his team will resent him and try to figure out ways to work around him. They will also avoid coming to him in the future, opting to apologize later rather than ask permission now.

Another way to help team members accept your decisions is to have written guidelines that they can follow. If you can point to a published document that guides the way that your team does their work, your team members will recognize that and respond to your consistency. It's much easier to work with a manager who is consistent and predictable than with one who may randomly reject ideas with no real justification. The tools in this book are examples of the kinds of guidelines that a team can adopt. For example, a manager may have a written guideline that says that every programmer should follow the Subversion basic work cycle (see Chapter 7). Then, even if a programmer feels that it's not her responsibility to merge changes that occurred since a file was checked out, the manager can refer back to the guideline and show that he is being consistent in his decision to have her merge her changes.

Understand What Motivates Your Team Members

Talk to your team about their goals. If an employee's goals are incompatible with his company's goals, he should not be working for that company. However, each person's goals go beyond simply finishing the current project: people want to move ahead in their careers, and part of your job as project manager is to help them achieve their professional development goals. The organization gains when employees improve, because a more experienced employee will deliver superior work. A team with people who have more experience can take on more complex projects and come up with more creative solutions.

People work for money. For some reason, many bosses feel uncomfortable with this—they pretend that people work out of loyalty, love of the job, or blind devotion to the organization's goals. This leads to an unfortunately pervasive attitude where managers act like their employees are lucky to have jobs. Compensation also comes in many forms: in addition to money, some organizations will give flexible hours, training, books, stock options, free lunches, senior titles, access to new technology, or other perks in place of money. But in all of these cases, people need to feel that they are being fairly compensated for the effort that they are putting in.

Another motivator is loyalty. Many people naturally develop some loyalty to the organizations where they work—it is human nature. This is why teams of people who are poorly managed and undercompensated will still work 80-hour weeks on projects that are clearly doomed to failure. Unfortunately, it's very easy to redirect loyalty, especially through dishonesty. In some cases, a poor manager can keep secrets from the team and lie to them about organizational decisions, in order to redirect the team's loyalty from the organization to him. In other cases, senior management themselves can, through lying, incompetence, and obvious lack of appreciation, lose the team's loyalty.

Don't Be Thrown by Dishonesty

People lie. They will say that they have completed things that they haven't, or that they understand things that they don't. They will make commitments, and then claim they never made them. Having a dishonest person working on a project is possibly the most difficult situation a project manager can face.

There are some things a project manager can do to discourage dishonesty. By keeping all work out in the open and admitting your own mistakes, you can create an environment where people are more honest. But this only goes so far—sometimes people lie, and you'll have to deal with it.

The best-case scenario is one in which you have evidence that directly contradicts the lie. If you find that somebody is lying, you need to present him with that evidence. The purpose is not to make him feel bad; rather, it is to help him understand that it's wrong, and that he shouldn't do it again. Don't get caught up trying to understand why someone is being dishonest—it could be a misunderstanding, it could be malicious, or it could be something else entirely. Sometimes the person doesn't even realize that he's lying. The key is to have enough information available so that you can set the situation right and keep it from threatening the project.

Unfortunately, in some cases, there is no evidence to counter the lie. When this occurs, there may be nothing that you can do about the situation. If you think that someone is lying and you don't have evidence, you can set about collecting that evidence. Usually a lie is about a commitment that was made: the person may have agreed to do a certain task in a certain way, and is now claiming that she never made that commitment. Information about the commitment may be in an email, a project document, or a task definition in the project plan. But if the commitment was less formal (such as a verbal agreement), there may simply be no record of it.

If there is not enough evidence, you may have to let the lie pass and live with the consequences. This is a very frustrating situation. In this case, your job is to improve the way you manage your commitments and those of your team, in order to prevent problems like this from happening in the future. You can collect better information, change your expectations, help people feel more comfortable letting you know if there are problems, and, in extreme situations, avoid working with people who have trouble being honest.

> **NOTE**
>
> More information on commitment management can be found in *Managing the Software Process* by Watts Humphrey (Addison Wesley, 1989).

Address Performance Problems Early

It is difficult to effectively manage teams without defining their goals up front. The best way to do that is to involve each person in the definition of his or her own goals. Each of these goals should be specific, measurable, should pertain to their work, and should be attainable.

One effective way to do this is to work with each team member to develop a *performance plan*, which is simply a list of goals that the manager and team member agree to.

People need to feel that they understand what is expected of them. The purpose of the performance plan is to set standards that are fair and attainable, and that are developed with the involvement of the team member (when possible). Your team members will feel more comfortable with their jobs if they feel they are being asked to meet reasonable goals and perform within their abilities. On the other hand, when someone does not know what is expected of him, you may feel he is doing a poor job when, in reality, he simply does not know what you expect of him. (You may not know, either—which is another reason a performance plan is useful!)

The manager should measure each team member's progress in meeting the goals listed in the performance plan. If the organization's operating environment changes, the manager should work with the team members to change those goals.

In many organizations, team members do not report directly to project managers; rather, they report to people who manage development or QA groups in the organization. However, a project team member whose goals are poorly defined or in conflict with the objectives of the project can threaten the project's success. When the success of the project is threatened, it is the project manager's responsibility to remove the threat. This may require that the project manager help the direct manager establish a performance plan.

You may find that your project team members' professional goals, set by their direct managers, conflict with the objectives of your project. For example, a programmer on your team may feel that meeting the deadlines for delivering code is more important than carrying out code reviews and unit testing, which he sees as optional, "extraneous" activities. By failing to do code reviews and build unit tests, he meets his personal deadlines, but he causes the project to be late because it spends more time in testing. If the programmer reports to a development manager, for example, it is your job to bring this up with that manager. One way that you can suggest that he fix the problem is by building a performance plan that includes goals that are quality related.

It is important to correct performance problems as early as possible. Many project managers make the mistake of waiting until the end of a project to try to address performance issues. If a team member is not doing his job properly, the project manager may not have the authority to fire or discipline the team member. But he can have that team member removed from his project, if he is unable to correct that person's behavior by either dealing directly with the team member or going to the direct manager. By addressing the problem as early as possible, the project manager limits the risk to the project.

CHAPTER ELEVEN

Managing an Outsourced Project

MANAGING PROJECTS IS HARD. Scope creeps, changes go uncontrolled, defects are introduced, schedules are delayed…and that's all in your own organization, where your software engineering team is right down the hall. Imagine how difficult it is to get even these results when your team is in another organization in an entirely different building—and possibly in a city halfway around the world! When you hire a company outside your organization to build your software, you open up yourself, your project, and your organization to exactly these problems.

Unfortunately, that straightforward reasoning seems to be lost on many people. The fact is that outsourcing is risky, and many people find that their projects go awry. Gartner, a respected research and consulting group, recently (at the time of this writing) published a report that predicted that half of IT outsourcing projects in the next 2 years will fail, and that 60 percent of organizations that outsource customer-facing processes will find that hidden costs and customer problems have wiped out any cost savings. This implies that leading an outsourced project requires a different set of skills than most project managers are familiar with. If you are used to working with an in-house team, you personally will need to change your approach to project management if you want to get your outsourced project done right.

There are a lot of overly optimistic books, articles, and papers written about outsourcing. Mary Lacity and Rudy Hirscheim propose reasons for this phenomenon in their book *Beyond the Information Systems Outsourcing Bandwagon*. They point out that much of the outsourcing literature is written during the "honeymoon" period, after the contract is written but before any project milestones are met (or blown). Many only report projected savings, not actual savings. And most of all, they point out that only the successes tend to be documented, because few organizations want to publicize their mistakes.

The truth is that the project manager for an outsourced project faces all of the challenges she would face on a project developed within the organization, plus a slew of additional difficulties. However, if she is able to navigate these issues, she can lead a successful project.

Prevent Major Sources of Project Failure

By getting involved in your software projects and not leaving all of the decisions up to the vendor, you can prevent many of the most common causes of outsourced project failure.

Get Involved

There's a broad misconception that it's possible to somehow extract the work from an outsourced project team without getting involved in the day-to-day management of the individual team members and their tasks. The conventional wisdom goes something like this: you're paying the vendor to handle all of the management overhead, so they should also be able to handle any personnel management problems that arise. This might work in some instances, but in other cases, it leads to a client who is unhappy with the vendor, and to a vendor who does not really interact with the client.

In fact, that very management overhead at the vendor can be a major source of problems on your project. For example, an in-house development team in an organization can standardize on a single language and platform; a vendor, on the other hand, must be ready to take on a broad range of technologies for many different clients, most of which will not have any application whatsoever to your project. To accomplish this, the vendor has an incentive to keep all of the programmers on the team cross-trained in multiple technologies. One way to do this is to make sure that each programmer is only assigned to any one project for a short period of time, in order to expose him to many technologies. This means that long-term engagements can be difficult to set up: many of the people on your project will see that by staying on your team for a long time, they are falling behind on the technologies that allow them to advance within the vendor's organization. This does not necessarily work against you, but it certainly does not work to your advantage.

Similarly, most good outsourcing vendors will put effort into cross-training other people in their organization on best practices learned from each client. While this can be good (because it can potentially help them address your needs better), it also means that some of your project team members will be allocated in part to helping other project teams internally at the vendor.

In other words, there are many ways that your needs and the needs of the vendor are not perfectly aligned. This makes sense—you have two different organizations, with different businesses and goals. But this difference introduces distance between the client and the vendor, which can lead to some specific ways that many outsourced projects fail.

The most common response to this—and the most serious mistake that a project manager can make when working with an outsourced project—is to assume that it's the vendor's responsibility to fix every problem that comes up in a way that will guarantee that the software gets built properly. There is very seductive logic here: "I'm paying the bills, and the vendor will lose my business if they don't get this right, so they *have* to take care of everything!" This attitude fails every time. The vendor does not have enough information to build the software properly, and a hands-off project manager who leaves everything to the vendor will find that the software that is delivered does not meet the needs of his organization.

Constantly Communicate Project Goals

The people working on your project have different goals than you do. Many of them may see the tasks that you give them as simply an opportunity to expand their knowledge. Others are completely devoted to the work that you have given them, but they don't necessarily see the context in which you have asked for it; all that they know about the project is what you have told them, and they don't (or can't) have an intuitive understanding of your organization's needs because they don't work there.

What this amounts to is the fact that you are the only person working with the project team who has your organization's needs and goals in mind. As a result, outsourcing teams are much more susceptible to the "Do what I mean, not what I say!" problem. An in-house project team almost always has a grasp on what it is that the organization does; people get an enormous amount of context just from working at an organization. Team members at an outsourcing vendor lack this context, and, unless you work to provide that context for them, that can lead to serious project problems.

For example, programmers who have worked at an accounting company for any length of time will have naturally absorbed some knowledge of accounting. When these programmers are given a task, they will immediately see why the organization needs that task done in terms of that accounting knowledge. They will be much better equipped to fill in the gaps when presented with incomplete requirements.

If the same task is given to a team at an outsourcing vendor, the programmers will not have the same background or knowledge. Even if that vendor has experience with other accounting projects, the team members do not spend each day working at an accounting company, talking to other people who do accounting, or reading the company newsletter about the latest clients. They do not come to the table with the same expectations about the software that an in-house team would.

This is why it is especially important to communicate the goals of your project to your team all the time. You need to personally make sure that the team members understand your organization's needs, and that the tasks they are performing are in line with its goals. Since they are not immersed in your organization's culture, you have to be the ambassador of that culture, so that they are always kept on track. You have to act as a rudder, constantly steering the team toward the goals of the project. That could mean that you need to have daily discussions with someone from the team. You may need to spot-check work from selected team members to make sure you are getting what you think you are asking for.

This can be very difficult and time-consuming, but it is easily the most important thing that you can do to make sure your project does not fail.

Many outsourced projects fail because their project managers fail to understand or do anything to compensate for this situation. They often blame the vendor for not understanding what they are saying. This is frustrating for everyone involved: the project manager feels betrayed by the vendor, while the vendor feels like the client did not adequately communicate his needs or goals. Nobody is happy with a failed project.

But despite how many project managers feel about their projects, in most cases this is not the fault of the vendor. Rather, it's a fact of life due to the way the outsourcing industry is structured. Each vendor has its own business to run, and it's absolutely understandable and expected that they would want to train people and encourage them to grow within their organization. It often falls to the project manager of the outsourced project—in concert with the management team at the vendor—to balance the vendor's needs with the project's goals. This means that you must form a relationship with their management that allows you to deal with that problem and to reach an acceptable compromise.

The more you are able to integrate the outsourced team with your organization, the more context they will have. If you are able to dedicate multiple people at your organization to communicating with the outsourced team, the team stands a better chance of understanding the complexities of your organization's environment, and of ultimately meeting your organization's needs. It doesn't always fall to the project manager alone to communicate the culture, context, and needs of the client organization. The more people you can involve in that process, the better it will be for the outsourced team. If your organization is willing to put in the effort, they can build a sense of teamwork between your organization and the vendor's that would not be possible to build on your own.

Make Sure the Project Is Estimated Well

The further away you get from a task, the easier it seems; the devil is usually in the details. Outsourcing allows you a lot of distance from your projects. For example, if your own team is making estimates, you often expect those estimates to be examined and questioned by senior management. But an outsourcing company does not have the same checks, and also does not have the same implicit trust. In some ways, you're far more likely to distrust them; but you're also much more likely to have little or no visibility into the way they run your project.

Sometimes it's the client's fault that realistic goals are not set for the project. There may be a lack of due diligence on the part of the client contracting the outsourced services—for example, choosing companies based on cost only. Some companies may be cheaper because they don't understand the project being proposed, while some may be cheaper because they just aren't very good. (For some reason, clients don't care what the reason is for a very low price until they see the final product, or lack thereof).

On the other hand, sometimes it's the vendor's fault. Vendors tend to promise things they can't deliver. (This shouldn't be *too* surprising—most software engineers have experienced projects where the promised deadline was unrealistic.) Many vendors are perfectly aware of the myths about outsourcing, and are happy to let you continue to believe them. ("Your project can't fail because there are many people sitting in the wings, just waiting to jump on if the project starts going downhill."*) When you're talking about a software project, it's going to be a long time between when the contract is put in place and the point when you figure out that the project is not progressing—especially if you don't have good checkpoints in place.

One effective way to prevent the vendor from taking on work that the team cannot perform is to understand their capacity from the outset. Ask them to show you the results of a project of similar size. (If they have never taken on a project of similar size, you may want to switch vendors!) Get involved in the estimation process, and make sure that the people who are going to do the work buy into the estimates that the project plan is based on.

Don't be afraid to meet with the vendor's project team and hold your own estimation sessions, once the project team is assembled. It is not uncommon for a vendor to have a separate estimation team that provides estimates when a contract is being negotiated; this team may provide estimates that are sufficient for a contract, but insufficient for planning your own organization's goals. By getting personally involved in the estimation process, you can ensure that your project plan is better grounded in reality.

---

* Remember Brooks' Law: "Adding manpower to a late software project makes it later." (See Chapter 10.)

Management Issues in Outsourced Projects

There are some important ways project management is different for an outsourced project than it is for a project developed in-house. It's not just the relationship with the vendor that's different; it's also the relationship between you, your management at your own company, and your team members. By paying special attention to transparency, information sharing, and communication, you can make sure these relationships lead to a successful project.

Actively Manage Your Project

If you have a relatively small project with well-defined requirements, known acceptance criteria, and a specific deadline—in other words, a fixed amount of work in a fixed period of time—then the project will probably work out fine. The success of a project like this hinges primarily on the technical competence of the programmers and on their ability to work together as a team. This is especially common when an organization that has never developed software before needs a specific piece of software written and does not want to build up its own IT infrastructure.

If you are a project manager at an organization that makes software as part of its core operations, then you are probably not in this situation, and your outsourced projects will probably not be this simple. They are much more likely to involve an open-ended commitment (one that, in some cases, could go on for years). Many organizations that outsource their work do not have a good grasp on their requirements, and often have not put much thought into what they need from the project or the vendor (other than "working software"—which, in practice, is not an easy thing to pin down).

The truth is, many outsourced projects don't go well. What's more, the clients at those projects don't necessarily realize that their projects have started to go bad until they receive a piece of software that does not do what they need it to do. This situation is harder to prevent here than it would be in an in-house project, for several reasons. If you are getting a much cheaper labor cost than you would for your own employees, then you might have a much larger project team than you are used to managing. You might also be used to having a lot of visibility into how your projects are going, because your in-house programmers talk to you routinely and give you (and your users and stakeholders) a lot of status updates.

When you are managing an outsourced project, the status doesn't readily present itself. If you have a good management structure in place, you can trust your delegated managers at the vendor to relay the status to you. However, the most reliable way for you to get a good handle on the status of your project is to collect it yourself. If, for example, you are building a project, you should ask for nightly build reports and unit test results. You should track the lines of code produced on a daily or weekly basis, and you should have access to a defect tracking system with metrics. Numbers like that can give you regular snapshots of the health of the project.

You should know the names of the people on your team. Ask for a CV or resume for each person. Have regular conversations with at least one representative for every project—minimally, you should talk to that person weekly. But if you really want a handle on how your project is going, you, or someone in your team, should talk to someone from the outsourced team every day—the same as you would if they were in your office! (Luckily, with instant messaging, it is very easy to keep in touch with a large team by adding them all to a buddy list and spending time each day shooting messages to them.)

One effective way to make sure that you will get all of the information that you need to run the project is to set up a communications plan with the team lead at the vendor. Make it clear from the outset of the project exactly what information you need them to gather for you. If you do this, it is very important that you only ask them to gather information that will actually be useful to you, and that you use it and review it with them: if you do not use the information that they gather (or if they do not see how it will be useful), then it will just seem like busywork to the team, which is demoralizing and counterproductive.

If you don't make sure that the people at the vendor know why you are asking for this information and what you are using it for, it's very easy to build up an environment of distrust with your outsourcing vendor. The only way to combat that is with transparency. In other words, somebody at the vendor is going to spend half a day each week gathering data for you. Make sure that you respect that time.

The best possible scenario is when you've set up standards that let the people at the vendor monitor themselves. You want the team to be as autonomous as possible, while still being productive and giving you information that you need to monitor the project. Your goal should be to have the team assist you in managing the project without losing control of it. One way that you can do this is by setting up an inspection process where the team can inspect documents and report the results to you (see below). If knowledge that you need to know has been properly transferred, you can write a quiz, and have all of the people on the team take it independently and send you their results. The key is that you must know at all times what the team is doing, and that it's in line with what you want them to do.

Share Information with Your Management

Many senior managers think that software development should be free. They think their internal IS departments are overpaid. Now they're cutting a big check to an outsourcing company, and they expect everything to be smooth and easy; there should be no problems or difficulties whatsoever. If you're the project manager on a project in this environment, you are set up for a thankless job.

When senior managers have unrealistic ideas about outsourcing, a project manager's successes will almost certainly go unrewarded because there is already an expectation that outsourcing is easy. If you do well as the project manager, the credit will go to the outsource company. What's more, in an environment like this, there is little incentive not to fail—if you do, it will be blamed on the outsourcing company. People are already biased against outside organizations handling their business; nobody wants you to waste money, but they won't blame you for somehow being "snowed" into thinking that another company could do as well as your own organization.

On the other hand, many senior managers have a much more realistic view of outsourced projects. They realize that they are difficult to manage, and that they require a lot of work and overhead. In this case, it is even more important that they are kept in the loop; you will need them to support you in case you make any controversial decisions, if you need further funding, or when you need their approval.

Regardless of the attitude of your senior management toward the project, it's always a good idea to keep them informed of everything you are doing. This means that you need to constantly go back to your own senior management and make sure that you still have their buy-in. If your boss thinks that managing an outsourced project is easy, you will have a very difficult time explaining why you spend so much time managing it. You must make sure your organization's managers understand what it is that you and your outsourced team are accomplishing, and how you are dealing with them on a day-to-day basis. You are the bridge between your organization and the vendor; it is your job to bring transparency to the process. Just as you have to focus on constantly steering the vendor team into meeting your organization's goal, you also need to constantly steer your organization's management so that you are always apprised of their goals and they have visibility into how the vendor is meeting those goals.

To provide adequate transparency into the project, you must give status reports to your organization's senior management. Any metrics that you use to track a software project will be useful; you should make them available. Encourage your management to visit the outsourced team and meet with the vendor's management. All of the methods in Chapter 10 for making a project transparent should be applied. In this way, you can make sure that your management can actively get information whenever they need it—and you can help them understand just how difficult the job of managing an outsourced project is.

A large part of establishing an understanding with your managers is sharing the issues that you are resolving, so they understand the effort you are putting into your project—especially when it comes to managing the team. It may seem obvious to your senior managers that the team doesn't work for you, but it's not obvious that this can create its own set of problems. There's a difference between being someone's client and being someone's boss. You don't set the performance goals of the software engineers; it is rare that you even know what they accomplish in their careers.

Build a Relationship with the Vendor's Management

You must have a good relationship with the entire upper management of your vendor organization. You must know who to escalate to if things go wrong, and you need to be able to trust them—and have them trust you as a credible and knowledgeable source of information for your project. You have to partner with the management of your project at the vendor company. They need to understand your goals. And most importantly, they need to understand that when you ask them to change the way they do their work, you are doing it to help them continue making money from your organization.

It is very important that you maintain this positive, cooperative relationship with your vendor's management. This is not always easy. There are times when the vendor has procedures in place that make it more difficult for you to see what's going on in your project, communicate with your team, or do your work in other ways. When this happens, don't just go in and make a bunch of changes. Instead, carefully discuss the problems and reevaluate the procedures that caused them. There is nothing wrong with the vendor having a business to run. Vendors need to keep their employees happy and challenged. Sometimes there are situations in which the vendor's goals are simply different than yours, and you must reach a compromise by being open, honest, and transparent.

One common mistake that many project managers make is to set up a complex or convoluted escalation process. Some vendors come to the table with these escalation procedures prebuilt, inserting a layer that blocks communication between you and your team. A policy that puts an escalation process in place will typically require that a team member first talk to the project lead and then to the manager at the vendor (and often one or two other people) before they are allowed to communicate directly with you. (This time-consuming process is often put in place specifically to bolster the management hierarchy at the vendor.) Often, the escalation procedure resembles the playground game of "telephone," where a message is passed from person to person until it is essentially unrecognizable. This is not a good way to communicate, especially when a problem is serious enough to warrant the involvement of the vendor's senior management (who will not know the specifics of the problem and are therefore more likely to obfuscate it).

Some people are more comfortable with an escalation process in place than without it. Middle managers at a vendor like it, because they can intercept problems that might be potentially embarrassing (such as an incompetent team member). They can better manage the client's perception by only allowing the "good" questions to be asked: for example, they can tweak the questions to make them seem less negative. Many project managers also like the escalation process, because it provides distance (and cover) if the project starts to go wrong. The further they are from the project team, the less culpable they are for its failures—it gives them a sort of "plausible deniability."

There are often good reasons for this. Many outsourcing clients are very hands-off and do not want to be "bothered" with the day-to-day operations at the vendor. Sometimes that makes sense, like when the client has little IT or project management experience. Many clients who have outsourced work honestly can't handle the idea that any mistakes have been made, and, even though that's a completely irrational and unrealistic expectation, they will use it as a reason to start renegotiating or dismantling contracts. These procedures are there to protect the vendor from crazy or irrational clients—and there are an awful lot of those in the outsourcing world!

However, since you are a good project manager and a reasonable person, you can work with the vendor to adjust things so that they work better for everyone involved. If there is a convoluted escalation procedure in place at the vendor, you are perfectly within your rights as a client to modify it or, even better, dismantle it entirely. This is okay, even if that's the "regular way" that clients interact with your particular vendor. The benefit of doing things the "regular way" does not outweigh the increased chance of miscommunication, scope problems, and requirements problems. Provided you take responsibility for your part of the end deliverable, you should be able to work with the team in the way you are most comfortable.

In addition to escalation, there are other procedures at the vendor that might not suit your method of working. Their system for performance reviews might reward your team members for things that are important to the vendor's organization but are not necessarily important to your project. For example, they might be rewarded for years of service at the vendor. It looks great from the vendor's perspective to have a team of "seasoned professionals" (who may have been around for a long time, but may not necessarily be stellar performers). If a vendor can quickly assemble a team of people with many years of experience, they can use this as a sales tool to get more lucrative contracts. Therefore, when they are recruiting potential employees, some vendors might offer a compensation package that rewards years of experience over knowledge. What's more, some vendors work very hard to prevent attrition because it looks worse for clients, and so will work very hard to keep from losing employees who have seniority—even if these employees are not all that great at their jobs.

It's not just hiring and firing practices that might not suit your project. There may also be trouble with the specific ways that vendors reward employees. It is common for vendors to reward employees for seniority with things like increased responsibility and access to new technology. This can be bad for your project: it is very unlikely that you will need to change your team members' responsibilities or switch technologies over the course of your project, which means that you are cutting your team off from what they traditionally expect as a reward for seniority. In other words, if you are developing a piece of software in Visual Basic, the chances are that you will not change to Java over the course of your project. If people on your team feel that they are falling behind in their technical skills, they will look to switch to another project at the vendor.

Look around your own organization: you can probably think of one or two people who have been there a long time, yet are not great employees! There's no reason to think that this isn't also true at the vendor. The bottom line is that a team member with years of experience in IT or seniority at a vendor is not necessarily competent. This means that the less you rely on the vendor's management to assign responsibilities to and reward your team members, the more control you have over your project. The best way to handle this is to set up your own system of rewards. For example, you can offer a bonus based on actual performance rather than seniority. To do this, you need to have a good handle on how well each person does her job—which, once again, means that you need to communicate with them. This works especially well if you personally assign tasks to the team members, rather than relying on the vendor's management to do that for you. This will require that you do your own project planning (see Chapter 2), and that you find ways of objectively measuring the performance of the people on your team.

It's not just processes at the vendor that need to be adjusted for your project. You may need to adjust them in your own organization as well. For example, your organization may have security policies or intellectual property policies that make it more difficult for you to manage your projects. These are problems you would normally never have to think about, but, since you are working with an outside vendor, you may now have to take them into account. Sometimes companies do not have policies in place to share information between the client company and a subcontractor. This slows down the process of creating software and sometimes makes it impossible for the expectations to be met.

Many project managers find it difficult to communicate project priorities to the team. Just as you might be the sole point of contact for your organization, you may be working with a single point of contact in the vendor's company who handles your requests. They may misinterpret you, or never actually understand your goals. Unless you negotiate for it, you may never actually have access to the team.

Build a Relationship with Your Team

You don't have the same kind of relationship with the team that you would with a team in your own organization. As project manager, you do not directly hire the resources assigned to the project. You can veto any team member, but you do not have immediate access to employment history, performance reviews, personnel files, salary information, or other important information you would usually need to make those decisions. If someone does a bad job, your only recourse is to have him moved off of your project. It's likely that he is never even told that there was a problem; he's probably just been told that he's been reassigned. This means that your team could contain people who were removed from other projects in the past due to performance problems and don't know it.

You have to gain the respect of the people you have hired to do your project. The simple fact that you're paying the bill doesn't establish you as the ultimate authority in how the vendor should manage the project. It's your job to establish yourself as a credible partner and to work with the people at the vendor, in order to make sure they meet your goals (and to assure them that you respect theirs!).

It's a common misconception that, because you are paying a contractor, you have more control over the work product. Somehow people assume that by simply writing a big enough check, a vendor will snap to attention and build exactly the software they need. After all, their payment depends on the client's satisfaction, right? So the vendor must be doing everything they need to do in order to satisfy the client. This is an odd attitude: you also pay your employees, and their performance reviews are dependent on your satisfaction as well, but that does not guarantee that all of their projects will succeed. The truth is that outsourcing projects are at least as likely to have problems as in-house projects. And when they do have problems, you have only a few possible recourses. This means that you actually have less control over the performance of individual outsourced team members and their work products than you would with an in-house team.

Being the sole point of contact with the subcontract team is a big change for many project managers. When you are the project manager for an in-house project, your team has access to the entire organization: they can talk to managers, stakeholders, users, etc. This is not the case on outsourced projects, where the vendor must route all communication through the project manager. This introduces many potential pitfalls into your project. The most costly problems involve the project scope and software requirements. If you do not describe the project adequately, you will end up with software that does not meet the needs of your organization. An in-house project team has many more opportunities to catch these problems.

This requires that you pay a lot of attention to your project team members, possibly more than you would to an in-house team. This is paradoxical, as most project managers are more likely to spend time with an in-house team than they would with a team at a vendor. It's not only your job to communicate your company's needs to the team, it's also your job to understand the needs of each team member. For example, if your team member needs clarification—and it is essentially impossible to run a project where a team member does not need clarification!—you are that person's only resource for gathering the information. If you do not provide a communications path from the team to your organization, they will simply make assumptions about any missing or unclear requirements. This will almost certainly lead to a misunderstanding. Sometimes those might be small problems that are easily corrected once the build is delivered. But small problems can snowball into big ones, and that could lead to software that does not do what you expect it to.

One of the hardest parts of working with your project team is correcting problems. Keeping a team motivated when they are not performing as well as you would like them to is difficult enough when they are in-house (see Chapter 10). It is even more difficult to handle this situation in an outsourced environment. Not only is the team in another organization, where you don't have the same access to them, but they also do not have the same goals as you do.

Expecting your project team to give you credibility in reviewing their work is like expecting your car mechanics to listen to your criticisms of how they fix your car. Most of the clients that your team has dealt with in the past have probably been relatively hands-off. The clients have been mostly ignorant of how software is built at their organization, so it's likely that some of your team members have never even been addressed directly by a project manager at a client. Now they're faced with a project manager who is taking the time to evaluate their work in detail. This new attention may not necessarily be welcome at first, especially since you will almost certainly ask them to make changes to how they work.

You need to be aware of the fact that when you are saying something negative, you need to present it with a lot of objective supporting evidence. Over time, you will gain credibility with them. But, at least initially, you will have to prove that you know what you are talking about. You will not be recognized as an authority just because you are paying the bills. This is a reasonable attitude for the team members to take, since it's true of most of their clients. You have to give them good reason to understand that you are different.

The way to build up credibility with your team is to show that your interests are in line with theirs, and that you are often right. It's no coincidence that this is exactly what you need to do with your team in your own organization. The difference is that when you are a project manager of an in-house project, you come to the table already in an authoritative role. With this team, you have a much different role. You have wide authority to modify the team and to add or remove people, but you start out with very little credibility to make technical decisions (although you do have the authority to do so).

It's very important to see this from the team members' point of view. Consider a project in which the project manager is trying to guide the team toward making technical decisions that they are not fully comfortable with. In an in-house situation, if this situation leads to a failed project, the team can stand behind their manager and point to a decision that was made for them. With an outsourced project, the project manager is accountable in his own organization, but the team members are just as accountable in the vendor's organization. If the vendor loses the contract, the team members will be blamed and their careers will be impacted. So it takes some work to get them to trust you—and rightfully so.

It's harder to earn the trust of the vendor team than it is to earn the trust of an in-house team. You are not at the vendor every day, and the team does not know you and does not have the opportunity to get to know you. This is especially difficult when you make an unpopular decision, whether it concerns team responsibilities, technology, specific approaches to problems being solved, or some other decision. Every group in every organization discusses decisions that are made by managers; usually you will be there to defend those decisions if they are misunderstood. However, in an outsourced situation, your decisions have legs. People may attribute motives to your decisions that you did not intend. They may see those decisions as personal rather than professional. And worse, they may not feel comfortable enough talking to you to ask you about them. Team members have spent their careers at the organization learning its particular culture and processes, and the client is suddenly making changes to them. Often, you have not had time to evaluate how your changes will work with the process: this is another barrier to earning the team's trust, and you need to take it into account when working with them. The more open you can be to the team members' perspectives, the more intelligent your decisions will be. (Don't forget that you generally benefit from team members' experiences on past projects!)

You cannot expect to be at the vendor every time your decisions are called into question. This is why your partnership with the management of the vendor's company is so essential. They are your ambassadors to the team, and, if they trust you and understand why you have made your decisions, you can depend on them to smooth out these problems. This is why you need to be transparent with them about your decisions and the reasoning behind those decisions.

Collaborate with the Vendor

If you are the project manager on an outsourced project, your day-to-day work will be similar to what you would do on a project for software being developed in-house. There are, however, some important changes you need to make, in order to work with the vendor. Because it's so easy for the vendor to get lost in the details and lose context, tools and techniques in every phase of the software project must be modified, in order to keep the vendor in the loop and communicate your high-level goals for the product.

Plan and Manage the Project Scope

In an in-house project, you start with the project scope and the set of resources already known to the organization, and use those to estimate the schedule, budget, and due date (using the tools and techniques in Chapters 2 through 4). An outsourced project, on the other hand, is exactly the opposite: you start with a scope and a budget, and the vendor provides an estimate on the number of resources and the time expected to complete the project.

This is one of the main advantages to outsourcing: you have much more flexibility in allocation of resources. You can specify the scope and the expected budget, and ask for an estimate on both the number of resources and the expected time to complete the project. Alternately, you can specify the scope and the deadline, and ask the outsourcing vendor to estimate the number of resources and the project cost. However, in all cases, you will still need to know the scope of the project. Luckily, there is very little difference in defining the scope of an outsourced project and defining one within your organization. The description of the vision and scope document in Chapter 2 can be used in an outsourced context as well.

However, there is one aspect of the project that is known during the planning stage but that is not covered in a typical vision and scope document for an in-house project: *knowledge transfer*. The outsourced vendor will not have prior knowledge of your organization, its products, or its users. It is your responsibility to teach your team about your organization and its goals. This can be done through meetings, documentation, working off-site at the vendor, bringing consultants from the vendor on-site to work with your organization's management and experts, or some combination of these things.

The main advantage to having someone from the vendor come to work at your organization is that it is less disruptive to you. It can be a successful way of transferring information; the person who works with you can act as your advocate within the project team, and she can use her understanding of your needs to keep the project team on track. The disadvantage is that you are depending on that person to collect the information, rather than teaching it yourself. This means that any misunderstanding might not be easily recognized early in the project. Also, each piece of information must first be learned by the vendor's representative and then retaught to all of the other members of the team; that takes time, and it may be less reliable than teaching it yourself.

The most effective way to avoid these problems is by working directly with the vendor's team. (Many vendors are located in the same city as the organizations they work for, but if your team is in another city or country, this could mean spending weeks, or even months, living out of a suitcase!) By going directly to the team, you can be sure that you have communicated your needs effectively. You can verify the team's knowledge in conversation and, if necessary, through a test or quiz. When a project manager works directly with the vendor's team, the knowledge transfer takes less time and there is less chance for misunderstanding.

Your method for knowledge transfer should be decided and covered in the vision and scope document. One effective way to do this is to include the vendor as a project stakeholder. This should make sense: the vendor has clear needs (including knowledge transfer) that must be fulfilled on the project. By adding the vendor as a stakeholder, you ensure that those needs will be considered when planning the project tasks.

Some project managers limit their interaction with the team to a set of milestone reviews during the project. For those managers, deadlines are the only monitoring tools. This is a mistake—the project manager cannot be disconnected from the project like that. It takes time and effort to work with the individual team members to verify that the work is being done properly, and that it meets the standards that your organization needs; if you don't take the time to do this, you can lose control of your project and not even know it. Unfortunately, by default, most outsourcing projects are set up so that the project manager at the client has a very small role in the project, and the contractor is responsible for keeping the team on track.

Success for the project manager and success for the vendor are often two different things. The project manager wants to deliver the software that meets the needs of the stakeholders in the project. The subcontracted team is trying to meet its contractual obligations. If the contract is not written specifically enough, or if the project manager is not able to collaborate with the team and revise its goals when necessary, it is likely that the goals of the project manager and the goals of the subcontracted team will diverge and possibly even be in conflict with one another.

Do Your Own Estimation

The estimation process in Chapter 2 was based on the assumption that the work being estimated would be done by a known project team. That isn't always the case when you work with an outsourced vendor. Once your team is in place, you can use the process outlined in the chapter in much the same way. But when you are negotiating your initial contract, the people who are estimating the effort are most likely not the people who will eventually do the work.

Learn about your resources: ask them about their backgrounds and about what they are capable of, in order to understand who should be assigned to various tasks. Find out who is more senior in your team; adjust expectations, if necessary, based on the new estimates they give you. Remember, even if they don't work for your organizations, these are not just faceless resources—they're people with different capabilities and skill sets. The more effort you put into understanding them, the more likely they will understand your project and its goals, and the more accurate your team's estimates will be.

Once your team has been created, you should work with them; gather the team members together and hold a Wideband Delphi estimation session. (Alternately, use another method to gather estimates from the team—the important thing is that the team uses a repeatable method for estimating the software, and that they agree that the estimates are realistic.) When the team makes the new estimate, use the same materials that were used to create the initial contract. This is a your first chance to see if your original expectations were realistic.

It's important to keep in mind that the original estimate done by the vendor may already have been written into a contract. If the numbers that your team comes up with are different than those written into the contract, you may have a problem with your budget or with your own legal people. You may need to renegotiate the contract, or you may need to add (and pay for) more resources, in order to meet your deadlines. But it's much better to know this at the beginning of the project rather than find out later on, when the work is underway.

One common and very unfortunate pitfall that many people fall into is assuming that all of the estimates from a vendor are padded (just like an in-house project!). Even worse, many project managers assume that the vendors' estimates are chronically underestimated ("They said they only need two weeks for this task, but they'll really take five"). This is a mistake. If you consistently mistrust the estimates coming from the group, the people making those estimates will very quickly catch on and begin to meet your expectations. If your team really does have a problem estimating, that's a problem that should be dealt with and corrected through tracking the schedule variance and other metrics in the same way you would track any employee on your team who has such problems (see Chapter 4).

Maintain Your Own Project Schedule

Giving up control of the schedule is a common mistake. It allows project managers, who are responsible for the ultimate success or failure of their project, to maintain almost no knowledge of how it is progressing or of who is doing what. It is your job to know why things are slipping, and whether or not commitments will be met—and you can't expect to adequately understand the complexities of your project with just a couple of status meetings. You must be an active participant in gathering knowledge about your project. In order to find out how the work is progressing and understand the problems your project is facing—which are necessary in order to make informed suggestions—you need to maintain your own project schedule.

Many project managers take a hands-off approach toward managing their outsourced projects, when they would never take such a risk with projects developed in-house. And it really is a huge risk; it means giving up a lot of control. Organizations of all types stretch the truth to keep their clients happy, and outsourced vendors are no exception. Keeping control of your project means verifying the status and the quality of the work product in the exact same way you would on your in-house project team. Review the work through both formal inspections and informal peer reviews (see the following section) to maintain an active understanding of your project tasks and their progress. But above all, know who is doing what and how far they have progressed.

If your project was done in-house, you would never let anyone keep the schedule for you. The project schedule should be kept and updated by you just as you would keep it in your organization. You should be notified immediately of any slippage, and hold regular schedule reviews as well as event-driven reviews with your outsourced project team. Everything in Chapter 4 applies to your outsourced project team, and it is your responsibility to stay on top of it. If you don't, the team will keep moving forward on their schedule, perhaps toward their own goals, and will continue to bill you for their time, whether or not it meets your needs.

Hold Reviews and Inspections

A review is one of the most important tools a project manager has for knowledge transfer, and it is difficult to overstate the importance of reviews and inspections in an outsourced project.

The more feedback you give, the more the team will understand what you want. One of the most common causes for outsourced project failure is that the project manager does not check the team's work until major milestones are delivered. If the team misunderstands a major work product and it is not inspected until the end of a project phase, the effort for that entire phase could be wasted. Many of the most serious problems that plague outsourced projects can be caught early with inspection and constant collaboration.

Unfortunately, reviews in outsourced projects can be highly time consuming; much more so, in fact, than in an in-house project. In an in-house project, the team is already familiar with that particular organization's standards, and there are usually plenty of examples to work from. The project manager doesn't need to spend nearly as much time making sure that the team understands the work being accomplished. What's more, an in-house team normally understands the mission of the organization and the needs of its users. Many project managers take this for granted, and don't think to communicate these things to the vendor. It requires constant effort and vigilance on the part of the project manager to make sure that the needs are properly understood when moving work outside the organization.

In addition to knowledge transfer, reviews are also important tools for collaboration. It is important to encourage collaboration between the project team members at the vendor and the team members within the organization. When an inspection team is made up of people from both organizations, the only way for them to reach consensus on a work product, in order to approve it, is to collaborate on identifying and fixing the defects in that work product. After the inspection, everyone has a better understanding of the work to be done, as well as of how everyone else thinks about that work.

At the outset of the project, you must figure out which work products need to be inspected. You should add these inspections to the schedule as strategic milestones, to ensure that the vendor is in the loop. However, it will often be too time consuming to inspect every work product that you would in an in-house project, because inspections that span multiple organizations are much more effort-intensive than inspections that only involve people from a single organization. It will take some practice and experimentation before you find the "sweet spot" where you are catching enough defects, encouraging sufficient collaboration, transferring enough knowledge, and, most importantly, giving the proper guidance to your vendor team.

The most direct route for identifying and fixing defects is to have everyone on the inspection team meet in person. However, there are times (such as when an outsourced vendor team is in another country) when this is simply unfeasible. Luckily, there is a highly successful precedent in the software industry of collaboration without face-to-face meetings. Some of the most successful open source projects (such as Linux, Apache, Mozilla, Perl, PostgreSQL, and Subversion) are excellent examples of distributed teams who review each others' work without having face-to-face meetings. Project teams for most large, successful open source projects accomplish this through discussion groups, mailing lists, and other collaboration tools. They also browse log messages from the version control system, and use an automated project monitoring system (see Chapter 7) to keep the team up-to-date on the health of the code. Using these tools, project team members can collaborate on resolving the defects without having to meet face-to-face, but also without requiring enormous effort from the moderator. People collaborating in this way have produced some of the most reliable, defect-free software available at the time of this writing. You can take advantage of this in your own software projects.

Table 11-1 shows an inspection process that has been modified to be used with an outsourced project. This script differs from the one in Chapter 5 in that it does not require an inspection meeting. Instead, the inspectors prepare comments and send them back to the moderator, who consolidates them and works with individual inspectors to identify solutions that they all agree on. This requires much more time than a single inspection meeting because instead of having one single discussion about each defect, the moderator must have many different discussions with individual inspectors regarding each defect. It also requires that the selected moderator have extensive familiarity and expertise with the work product being inspected. This may mean that the project manager must serve as the moderator, but that's not always the case.

TABLE 11-1. Inspection script for multiple organizations

Name	Inspection script for use in multiple organizations
Purpose	To run a moderated inspection (without a meeting) for a team with members in different organizations
Summary	In an inspection, a moderator leads a team of reviewers in reviewing a work product and fixing any defects that are found. The inspectors are from multiple organizations, so they never meet face to face.

Work Products	*Input*
	    Work product being inspected
	Output
	    Inspection log

Entry Criteria	A moderator must be selected, as well as team of 3 to 10 people. A work product must be selected, and each team member has read it individually and identified all wording that must be changed or clarified before he or she will approve the work product. A unique version number has been assigned to the work product.

TABLE 11-1. Inspection script for multiple organizations (continued)

Name	Inspection script for use in multiple organizations
Basic Course of Events	1. *Preparation*. The moderator distributes a printed or electronic version of the work product (with line numbers) to each inspector, along with a checklist to aid in the review. Each inspector reads the work product and identifies any defects that must be resolved, compiles those defects into a single document, and returns it to the moderator.
	2. *Compile the draft inspection log*. Each list of defects returned by each inspector must be compared with the others, in order to identify and combine overlapping defects. The moderator compiles a draft of the inspection log that includes all distinct defects found by inspectors. The log does not yet contain any solutions to those defects.
	3. *Identify conflicts*. The moderator searches for any defects reported by different inspectors that contradict each other. For each set of conflicting defects, the moderator holds a discussion (either in person, via teleconference or video conference, or using a collaboration tool like a mailing list or instant message system) between the inspectors who identified those defects, in order to identify the assumptions behind the defects and resolve them into a single defect. The inspection log is updated to reflect the combined defects.
	4. *Identify solutions*. The moderator uses the same means to meet with individual inspectors, to identify solutions to the defects and add those solutions to the inspection log. If more than one person identified the same defect, they must all be involved in creating the solution. Inspectors may also identify additional defects that were not originally found, as well as their solutions.
	5. *Compile and distribute inspection log*. The moderator compiles all solutions identified in Step 4 into the inspection log. Any defects that were not resolved are left as open issues to be resolved by the author. The moderator sends the final inspection log to all inspectors for confirmation. When the inspectors have confirmed that the log is correct, it is sent to the author of the work product.
	6. *Rework*. The author repairs the defects identified in the inspection meeting.
	7. *Follow-up*. Inspection team members verify that the defects were repaired.
	8. *Approval*. The inspection team approves the work product.
Alternative Paths	1. During Step 5, if one or more team members find errors in the inspection log, the moderator must address those errors before rework can occur. The script returns to Step 2.
Exit Criteria	The work product has been approved.

While not every work product can be inspected, every work product in your project should be reviewed. Use deskchecks to have people in your organization spot-check the work done by vendors. This will help to find errors early on, and it can also generate confidence within your project team. If you are on top of the errors in your project, you can quickly correct problems if things start to go off track. There should be no surprises when delivery time comes.

In addition to inspecting work products, it is important to encourage the team within your organization to mentor their counterparts in the outsource vendor (and vice versa!). The more the two teams learn from each other, the less they will make mistakes or blame one another when things go wrong. The project manager of an outsourced project should try to create a cohesive team for the project that spans both organizations. While your team members may be paid by different organizations, they are all working toward the same goals and should feel comfortable both criticizing and praising each other's work.

Maintain Control of Design and Programming

The challenge of managing the design and programming of an outsourced project is collaborating with your engineering team. Clearly, the programming work is going to be taking place in the vendor's organization; the only question is whether the various aspects of the design take place in your own organization or at the vendor.

There are always design constraints for any piece of software: it may need to work with an existing enterprise infrastructure; you may have legacy code that must be integrated; you or others in your organization may have already decided on a language or platform; there may be user interface or other design standards that are already in place and must be met, etc. Minimally, you must make sure that these are communicated to the vendor.

The easiest way to maintain control over the design of the software is to design it yourself. Sometimes it's easiest to come up with a solution yourself that meets all of your needs, and to provide that as technical direction to the programming team at the vendor. You can do this by writing a technical specification or approach document. If you do this, it's very important that you put checkpoints in place, in order to make sure that the work is really being done according to these documents. The vendor team should inspect the document, and there should be periodic reviews or walkthroughs scheduled throughout the project, in order to verify that the work is being done according to your design.

One of the most common mistakes that project managers make on outsourced projects is to blindly trust that the vendor team fully understands and has properly interpreted all of the design documentation provided. If you do not check in at many points along the way to make sure that your intentions are being properly interpreted, it's very likely that you will end up getting software that technically complies with the specifications but that does not really meet your needs. This is a very frustrating position for a project manager. However, by implementing reviews and inspections (see above), you can avoid this problem.

Once you have put in place controls to ensure that the software design meets your organization's needs, you then need to ensure that the software is being built well. The tools and techniques in Chapter 7 are especially helpful here. Require that the team build unit tests for all code, and that those unit tests are run regularly, with the results of the unit tests published across the teams. Use an automated project monitoring system to create nightly builds and run unit tests, and have the results published across teams. Have in-house software engineers do spot-check code reviews with vendor team members—preferably using code samples that were already reviewed by the vendor team. (To some people, it may seem like a waste of time to review code that has already been reviewed. In fact, it's especially helpful, because it allows your team to both verify that the code is being built properly and to audit the vendor's code review process.) Use automated code analyzers to enforce widely accepted coding best practices that may slip through a code review.

Some project managers may be hesitant to get this involved with the way the vendor team builds the code. It may seem somehow intrusive that you are second-guessing the abilities of the programmers at the vendor. It's important not to fall into this trap. Almost every vendor will welcome this collaboration. It means that you are sharing responsibility for the quality of the code. You are recognizing the challenges that the team developing the product will face, and you are helping them solve those problems. And it means, ultimately, that there will be no surprises: you won't end up with interminable QA cycles. In other words, both the project manager and the vendor should see this as a win-win situation.

Take Responsibility for Quality

You are responsible for the quality of your products, even when you contract the work out. It's easy to forget this. If you are paying a vendor to build a project, it somehow makes it easy to consider quality just another deliverable. It's not—it's a responsibility.

Many times, outside providers will offer "testing" of their products as part of the development estimate. It's not uncommon for this testing to be done not by an independent testing team but by the programmers who wrote it, or by junior members of the programming team with little or no test experience. When this is the case, they generally do not have much test documentation. Do not let this happen to your project. Demand resources allocated exclusively to test activities. Expect to review and inspect all test documentation. Be sure that your test activities are defined in your vision and scope document and, if possible, discussed in your contract.

Just as you would have members of your test team involved in all document inspections in your own organization, schedule your designated test team outside to review all documents and schedule their time researching and writing test plans as well. If you use specific metrics to measure product quality, expect your test team off-site to provide the same data and meet the same standards. Collaborate with them as you would your own team—spot-check the test plans, and test the results to be sure that the testing is being done as you would expect. Defect tracking should be done within your own organization. Test results should be monitored, and redundant tests should be done within your organization to be sure that bugs aren't slipping through.

Don't make decisions that undercut your QA team. When the project has reached its testing phase, there are many points when the project manager has to decide between doing things in less time and doing them thoroughly. As the end date looms closer and closer, it becomes less and less appealing to choose the "thorough" option.

For example, say you have a project 25% through its regression test cycle after a minor bug fix. Everyone expected the test to go well, but instead, a major defect was found. The lead tester at the vendor asks whether they should cut a new build now or if they should finish the regression test. It's possible that there are no more major bugs lurking within the code, and you could potentially cut out 75% of the time it takes to regress the software. Do you do it? If you are taking responsibility for the quality of the product, the answer is "absolutely not": you know that chances you will find another defect when you cut the next build are greater if you haven't completed the current regression test. But it's difficult to make this decision with looming deadlines, clients putting pressure on you, and, most importantly, a compliant vendor willing to cut out work in order to meet your deadline.

It's even harder to keep your commitment to software quality when a small change is made to a product that is already in production and rolled out to clients. It's very tempting to "just make the change" and run a cursory test (for example, testing only the fix itself or smoke testing only a few "core" areas of the software). If you stop to think about it, however, it's even more important to run a full regression test when making even a small change to a product that's already been rolled out. The users already have a good feeling about the software and expect it to keep meeting their needs. It's one thing to deliver a poor quality product from the beginning; it's quite another to replace software that's already working with software that's buggy. There's no easier way to upset your users and make your team look incompetent.

The point is that if you want to release software that will satisfy your users and stakeholders, then your off-site team needs your support, and your commitment to quality must be unwavering. If time is a real constraint, you should use proper planning. People in your organization must review and understand the test approach the vendor will take. Don't ever commit to deadlines that don't include estimates for software testing. (And always assume there will be multiple iterations of testing—it's foolish to assume there will be no defects and the first test will be the last!) If the estimated project plan runs past the deadline, cut the scope—not just the testing. Work with your QA team to identify time-consuming activities that can be automated or made more efficient.

Finally, don't just assume that just because the vendor's organization meets certain certifications or has been assessed (CMM Level 5, ISO 9000, Six Sigma—see Chapter 12), it means that they know better than you do how to run your project. Don't assume that the vendor never cuts corners. A good track record for past projects does not necessarily translate to a similar performance on your project. Even when you are working with a certified vendor, you still need to take responsibility for your portion of the work.

CHAPTER TWELVE

Process Improvement

IF YOU ASK A DOZEN PEOPLE ON A SOFTWARE TEAM to describe how the team should build software, you'll get at least a dozen different answers—and most of those descriptions, if followed, will produce *something*. But what's produced may not be very good: it may not be useful to the users, it may not be of very high quality, and the team may not be comfortable building, delivering, or maintaining it. A software process makes sure that everyone on the team agrees up front on how they will build software, while simultaneously ensuring that the software will be built in a way that works for the team and the organization.

Life Without a Software Process

Many process improvement experts see the world as black and white: there are bad software teams without a formal process, and good teams that have one in place. But the world is not that simple. You should understand exactly what a software process brings to the table, and why having a process is important.

Teams Can Be Effective Without a Formal Process

There are many successful teams that do not spend time looking at the big picture and writing down a software process. In most organizations like this, individual programmers or small teams are responsible for entire projects: they talk with the users and stakeholders to understand what they need from the software, they build the software, and they deliver it to the users. People in this situation get used to the "jack-of-all-trades" role—they do everything themselves, from gathering requirements to designing and building the software to testing and deploying it. This is an effective way to build software: by limiting the number of people involved and making each individual responsible for the entire project, less communication and documentation are required, and there is less overhead and complication for the project.

In addition to the "jack-of-all-trades" situation, there are also "skunk works" programmers who will generally take the initiative and build software that was not necessarily asked for, but that addresses certain users' or clients' needs. This tends to happen when a programmer has a lot of knowledge about the needs of the users, and she can independently identify tasks that are being performed poorly that could be automated with software. When this goes well, the programmer is revered as a genius in the organization: she produced software "under the radar" that was useful to the people in the organization, yet required no work on their part: it was simply delivered, finished, as a wonderful surprise. This is a highly satisfying way for a programmer to work—no pressure, no expectations, and high rewards.

Another way that many teams work effectively is by relying on a development manager who has a very good understanding of the needs of the users and stakeholders. A highly capable manager who is willing to put an enormous amount of effort into design, architecture, and programming can serve as the hub of all software projects, parceling out work to individual programmers and integrating it all back together. As long as this person is capable of keeping everything in his head, the team can keep delivering software. This requires an enormous commitment on the part of the manager, but it is also very satisfying and leads to a lot of respect from others in the organization (not to mention job security).

What all these organizations have in common is that they do not have a formal software process. A *software process* is a set of activities that, if done, will result in software. It's important to recognize that all of the organizations described in the previous few paragraphs do have a software process—it's just not a *formal*, or documented and repeatable, process.

You are already familiar with many of the activities in typical software processes, because they include many of the tools and techniques in the first part of this book! In an organization that has put a lot of effort into a good process improvement program, the process activities will include a wide variety of tasks. These tasks will cover not just programming but also requirements management, project planning, configuration management, quality assurance, and other tasks meant to ensure that the software is of sufficient quality. Making improvements to the process will positively affect the way the team builds software in the future.

It's very important to recognize that teams that do not have a formal process are generally happy! A team that produces successful software projects can point to their successes with pride. The varied work, high visibility, and wide responsibility mean that the programmers are highly respected in the organization. Respected, that is, except when projects fail.

The most common source of failure is that this sort of team does not scale up very easily. While it's true that small projects and small teams can work well without a formal software process, it gets harder and harder to do the work as the scope of the software project gets wider, the team gets bigger, or the users and stakeholders become less available. When a team outgrows an informal process, projects begin to have problems. Programmers who used to produce lots of software find that their projects have started to feel "bogged down." The users are increasingly unhappy and the software is increasingly late. The work just doesn't seem fun anymore. When this happens, many of the "Diagnosing Problems" scenarios in the first part of this book start to look very familiar.

The shift from a happy and productive team to a bogged-down team usually happens because the team has taken on more people, larger projects, or new kinds of work. Suddenly, they have to retain more knowledge about the users' and stakeholders' needs than they can keep in their heads. Some teams find that this happens when they add the fourth (or sixth, or ninth) person to the team; others find that it happens when they try to take on a project that does not resemble any of their previous ones, or when they team people up to work on larger or more complex projects.

One of the most common situations in which a team gets "maxed out" arises when a small programming group with a good track record of building projects for individuals is faced with having to build a project on a larger scale—especially if it is intended to be used by people outside the organization. Previously, the programmers were able to sit down with the people who would be using the software on a day-to-day basis and talk with them about what they needed. Those users would stay involved with the project throughout the entire development phase, giving feedback on prototypes and intermediate builds and helping the programmers learn more about their needs. A programming team used to working in this environment can have trouble building software meant for users outside of the organization. The problem is that the users are no longer available to the programmer whenever input is needed. A programmer used to walking across the office and asking for clarification about a confusing or unclear concept will often have trouble adjusting to a situation in which that input is not readily available.

This problem is compounded when the knowledge needed to define the behavior of the software does not exist anywhere in the organization. Programmers know how to build software; they are not necessarily familiar with the day-to-day business of the people who will use it. This is where the "jack-of-all-trades" can suddenly find himself on shaky ground. He's spent a great deal of time learning about the particular needs of a small number of users; if a new project requires that he understand a completely different set of users, he may have to spend a very long time building up sufficient expertise in this new area.

Lack of Process Maturity Is Not "Immature"

There are many excellent textbooks on the nuts and bolts of software process improvement, but few of them acknowledge the fact that many successful organizations do not have a formal software process. In fact, process improvement experts often talk about process improvement in ways that are actually insulting to software professionals who feel they have done a good job and gone a long way in their careers. They use words such as "immature," "haphazard," "chaotic," and even "childish" to describe the software process of an organization that does not have a formal software process. This is not a useful way to convince people to change the way they do their jobs. (This was a major consideration in choosing "initial" as the label for the first maturity level in the CMM—see the section "The Capability Maturity Model.")

For example, one otherwise excellent book on practical process improvement contains a chapter demonstrating this problem. It compares the key behaviors of a child (moody, unpredictable, inconsistent, living for the moment, thrown into a panic by unexpected setbacks) with the behaviors of a "mature adult" (stable, reliable, consistently capable, plans ahead, copes well with the unexpected). The author uses this comparison to illustrate the difference between an organization with a formal process and one without. This is quite insulting to anyone who works in an organization without a formal process; it's also untrue, since there are plenty of organizations that in no way display those characteristics. Yet some process improvement professionals attempt to change organizations by showing them exactly this sort of "evidence," presumably in hope of shaming the team into adopting the changes they recommend.

Even worse than insulting people into changing is evangelizing to them, but this is exactly what many process improvement experts do. As unlikely as it sounds, process improvement textbooks and articles literally talk in terms of religion, believers, disbelievers, and evangelism. To someone who thinks this way, process improvement is a way of thinking that requires faith; unbelievers cannot be "converted," no matter how much they are cajoled or harangued. It's not surprising that many process improvement efforts fail. People distrust evangelists and suspect they have more of an allegiance to the process than to the organization and the team. Software engineers who are pestered or pressured into "accepting" a new process will not hesitate to abandon it if they are put under any external pressure to do so—especially if they had no input or feedback when it was developed.

This is no way to convince someone to change the way he does his job. But it is, unfortunately, a representative example of the way some people approach process improvement. They treat the programming team as a bunch of immature children who can barely do the work assigned to them. Or they treat the team members as infidels and unbelievers, leading the team to wonder how these religious lunatics got into the office. Then the experts are surprised that the team members—who consider themselves and their past projects successful, even if they weren't perfect—reject this new process improvement effort.

The truth is that programmers love being the "go-to" person. They love having lots of successes, and they love when users can go directly to them without having to bother with documentation and testing in order to get programs written. There is a lot of job satisfaction in doing things this way. And in cases in which the software is all in the same area of the organization's business and repeatedly draws on the same knowledge of the users' needs, a team can be highly successful working like this. If you put yourself in the programmers' shoes, you'll realize that you would need a really good reason before you would be willing to change. (See Chapter 9 for more information on why changes like this often fail, and how to successfully make changes in your organization.)

If Things Are So Great, Why Change?

If there are no complaints about the way the team is building software, then there's no reason to change! If all your organization needs from you is that you assign one or a few programmers per project, and if you can always guarantee that experts, users, and stakeholders will be available to the programmer whenever she needs them, then it might make sense to keep things flexible and variable and change them only as needed.

However, few teams are really in this situation. At some point, most teams will need to grow in size or capability. This can mean taking on more programmers and solving more complex problems. Without a formal process, organizations often run into problems when they try to expand the team or get people to work together on larger projects. For example, the programmer who was working on one project could be needed on another team, or could leave the organization altogether; this makes it difficult to expand the team because they have lost critical knowledge required to build and maintain the software. If there is no formal process in place, there is no guarantee that knowledge was ever written down.

The most serious problems in expanding a team involve communicating the needs of the organization, users, and stakeholders, and setting the expectations of the organization about what will be delivered, when it will be delivered, and how much it will cost. Having a formal process in place ensures that there is consistency between projects, so an expanding team can rely on a library of past estimates, guidelines for working together, and other important tools to help them work. They do not have to keep reinventing the wheel; for every problem that has been solved before in the organization, the solution is available to them.

Expanding the team is not the only place a formal process is useful. It can also help in an organization where experts, users, or stakeholders are no longer readily available to the programmers. This is another area where the formal process can help. It means that requirements gathering activities are planned for from the beginning, and that there is a training program in place to help the users and stakeholders learn to work with the requirements analysts, ensuring that requirements are gathered at the beginning of the project.

Software Process Improvement

Software process improvement is the art and science of changing an organization's software process in order to build better software. In the first part of this book, you learned to diagnose and fix problems for individual projects. When you adopt a specific tool for your project—for example, if you implement inspections on your project team and have them all follow the script in Chapter 5—you are formalizing part of the software process for that project by having the team follow a written description of that activity. Software process improvement is very similar, except that instead of improving one project at a time, you work on improving the entire organization.

The tools and techniques in the first part of this book make up many of the nuts and bolts of software process improvement. But while this book so far has been about making specific improvements to the way software is built on the scale of an individual project, there is another perspective: the high-level organizational perspective. It's very important to diagnose chronic problems your organization is having and address them with specific practices to be adopted for all projects. By stepping back and looking at the software process as a whole, you may be able to plan ahead and anticipate the inefficiencies in the way your team develops software. In doing so, you can avoid problems before they have serious impact on your organization. That is where software process improvement can really help your team excel.

Software process improvement always involves looking at the big picture. This generally means writing down the entire software process as a whole and making sure that it is followed on each project. It involves not just diagnosing specific problems and attacking them individually, but also looking at entire projects and identifying areas that can be improved.

Software process improvement differs from the approach described in the first part of this book. In Part I, you learned how to diagnose individual problems on your projects and use specific tools, techniques, and practices to fix those problems. In much the same way, software process improvement can be evolutionary, allowing you to use iterative cycles to fix individual parts of your organization's lifecycle. But software process improvement differs from the diagnose-and-fix approach, because it requires that you change the culture of your organization to one of continuous process improvement. Software process improvement requires patient and consistent support (in both actions and resources) from your senior managers, in order to be effective. It also requires a broad consensus among the software engineers. If you can gather this kind of support behind a process improvement effort, you can address issues that are beyond the scope of individual projects and dramatically increase the capability of your software organization.

There are specific process improvement tools to help you do this. There are models and certifications that help you assess the state of your organization's process, and that serve as a framework for improving that process. There are also processes and methodologies you can adopt that describe the complete set of activities, roles, and work products needed to build software. By applying these tools, you can give your organization the ability to fix problems before they get serious enough to cause your projects to slow down.

Models and Certifications

To many experts, software process improvement in practice means using a model or certification standard as a guideline for assessing and improving a software organization. Some of the most common models are the Capability Maturity Model, ISO 9000, and Six Sigma. These are not processes in and of themselves. Rather, they are systematic frameworks that were developed for evaluating any software organization (no matter what process is in use), identifying improvements that will increase the ability of the organization to build better software, and certifying that the organization has met an objective standard for capability.

The Capability Maturity Model

The *Capability Maturity Model* (CMM), is a process improvement method developed by the Software Engineering Institute at Carnegie Mellon University. It provides a set of best practices meant to address important aspects of software development: productivity, performance, costs, predictability, and stakeholder satisfaction. The purpose of the CMM is to define the characteristics of a mature, capable process in a way that can be measured and compared to processes at other organizations.

The CMM was developed in coordination with the U.S. Department of Defense (DoD) to help organizations privately improve their own processes. (It was also adopted by the DoD as a way to provide the U.S. military with a consistent method to identify the most capable software contractors. While this has been successful, it has also led to some abuses of the assessment system—see below.) The result was a model (first published in August 1991) that contained five maturity levels, ranging from "Initial" (in which an organization does not apply tools, techniques, and practices consistently across all of its projects) to "Optimizing" (in which a software process was well defined, brought under statistical control using various metrics and measurements, and continually improved based on those metrics).

By the late 1990s, the government and the CMM user community had a great deal of feedback for the SEI team responsible for maintaining the CMM. In response, a project to create the Capability Maturity Model Integration (CMMI) was initiated in order to address these concerns. This new version was released in 2002.

Both the CMM and CMMI are divided into *key process areas* (KPAs) that define specific goals and practices. Each KPA addresses a specific area of software engineering. There are several dozen KPAs, including requirements management, project planning, project monitoring, configuration management, and training. (These areas of improvement should seem familiar by now!)

Each of the five maturity levels of the CMM is represented by its own set of KPAs; for an organization to achieve a specific maturity level, it must implement all of the practices in each of the KPAs for that level. The CMMI also contains five maturity levels; however, some of the focus of the CMMI has been drawn away from maturity levels in favor of implementing specific practices and goals. It does, however, still support a level-based assessment.

The most important part of each KPA is a set of one or more goals that define the "heart and soul" of each KPA. For example, the Project Planning KPA of CMMI v1.1 contains three goals:

Establish Estimates
   Estimates of project planning parameters are established and maintained.

Develop a Project Plan
   A project plan is established and maintained as the basis for managing the project.

Obtain Commitment to the Plan
   Commitments to the project plan are established and maintained.

These are sensible goals that, if met, will lead to a well-planned project; if any of these goals is not met, then the project will have a clear planning problem. The remainder of the KPA lists specific practices that should be performed, in order to meet those goals. For example, the "Establish Estimates" goal is met with specific practices:

Estimate the Scope of the Project
   Establish a top-level work breakdown structure (WBS) to estimate the scope of the project.

Establish Estimates of Work Product and Task Attributes
   Establish and maintain estimates of the attributes of the work products and tasks.

Define Project Life Cycle
   Define the project life cycle phases upon which to scope the planning effort.

Each practice is further defined with subpractices. For example, the "Estimate the Scope of the Project" practice requires that a WBS is developed, work packages are defined in sufficient detail to provide estimates, and work products are identified that will be acquired externally or reused. Again, these are all sensible activities that need to be performed in order to estimate the scope of a project.

Within each practice and subpractice is additional information providing advice and tips for implementation. There are usually lists of typical work products—for example, the subpractice for estimating the scope of a project lists the task descriptions and WBS as work products. However, these are just suggestions. The most important part of the CMM and CMMI is meeting the goals, and the practices are simply an efficient way of meeting those goals.

When an organization begins a process improvement effort based on the CMM or CMMI, a good first step is to set up a *software engineering process group* (SEPG). This is a team of software engineering professionals and/or managers within the organization who are dedicated either part- or full-time to improving the software process. They identify problems and inefficiencies, define the practices needed to address those problems, and implement them in the project teams.

Another important part of the CMM and CMMI is the assessment process. In an assessment, an assessor is brought into the organization. He spends time (typically one week) reviewing the process documentation, interviewing the people on the team, and verifying whether the process is actually carried out on real projects. The result of the assessment is a report that identifies which practices are in place, which practices are missing from key process areas, and the maturity level of the organization.

Assessments are a useful tool that SEPGs can use to identify areas for improvement. However, there is a downside to assessments. There are many organizations that must comply with the CMM or CMMI in order to qualify for certain government programs or to bid on contracts that require a minimum maturity level. Other organizations pursue a maturity level for publicity or public relations purposes. The assessment process assumes that the organization being assessed is honestly representing its practices. A software organization that is intent on getting assessed at a certain level can create reports and work products that will make it appear as if all of the practices have been implemented. This is just like a company that fools an accounting auditor by keeping two sets of books—it may pass the audit through no fault of the auditor.

When the CMM or CMMI is abused, it is no longer an effective way to improve an organization. The practices that are part of the KPAs then simply amount to pushing paper around. Documents that could be useful have simply become bureaucratic forms to be filled out. A project plan is created not to help the team understand and plan the work, but simply to satisfy an organizational policy. When this happens, the team members still face the same problems they have always faced: increasing delays, decreasing quality, overtime, dissatisfaction, and poor software development practices. But now they also get to fill out a bunch of paperwork.

Despite this potential abuse, when the CMM or CMMI is used well, it can be a powerful tool for actually improving the software process and capability of an organization. It contains a wealth of good practices, as well as advice for implementing those practices. When an organization really works toward understanding and fulfilling the goals and implementing the practices, they stand a good chance at truly building better software.

NOTE

The Capability Maturity Model and a great deal of supporting information can be obtained for free from the Software Engineering Institute web site at *http://www.sei.cmu.edu/cmmi/cmmi.html.*

ISO 9000

ISO 9000 is a family of *quality management* standards defined by the International Standards Organization and implemented by over half a million organizations around the world. Quality management refers to the practices performed by an organization in order to fulfill the customer's requirements (and any legal or regulatory requirements). The goal of quality management is to improve customer satisfaction, while at the same time continually improving the performance of the organization.

Every ISO 9000 standard defines a set of minimum "pass or fail" standards that are used to judge whether an organization is in compliance. ISO standards, like the CMM, have a certification process in which an organization's practices are assessed by a third-party assessor who audits the organization's compliance with the quality system, and whether that system is effective. The result of the audit is a set of recommendations for changes to be made, in order to bring the organization into compliance.

ISO 9000 is based on eight core principles:

- Organizations must focus on their customers by understanding current and future customer needs.
- Leaders within the organization must create and maintain an environment in which people can become involved and fulfill the organization's objectives.
- People at all levels are important to the organization.
- Activities and resources are best managed as a process.
- Organizations have many interrelated processes, which must be understood and managed as a system.
- The organization should continually improve its performance.
- Decisions should be well informed and based on real data and information.
- An organization and its suppliers are in a mutually beneficial relationship.

The ISO 9000-3 standard contains a set of guidelines that interprets ISO 9000 so that it can be applied to the development, supply, and maintenance of software. It is divided into sections that define standards for many areas of a software organization, including management practices, the quality system, contracts, document and data control, inspection, training, deployment, process control, and the design and development of the software.

Each of the sections contains standards for the day-to-day work that goes on in the organization. For example, within the software development and design section are standards for software development, software design, design and development planning, organizational and technical interfaces and design review, verification, validation, and change control.

Each of these standards defines specific practices that must be implemented in the organization. For example, the software development requirements require that a project plan be developed. This plan must define the project, list its objectives, contain a project schedule, define the inputs and outputs, identify related plans and projects, identify project risks, and identify assumptions. These requirements should seem familiar: they are all part of the project plan in Chapter 2.

Like the CMM, the ISO standards can be abused by an organization and reduced to bureaucracy and paper pushing. There is a great deal of pressure on many organizations to achieve an ISO 9000 certification at any cost, since they may be ineligible for certain contracts without it. However, when the standards are used properly, they can provide good guidelines to a project manager looking to improve how her organization builds software.

> **NOTE**
>
> Information on ISO 9000 can be found at the International Standards Organization web site. The URL at the time of this writing is *http://www. iso.ch/iso/en/iso9000-14000/iso9000/iso9000index.html*

Six Sigma

Six Sigma is an approach to improving quality in manufacturing and business processes. It was developed at Motorola in the early 1980s, and it has been used successfully at many software organizations. The goal of Six Sigma is to produce a product of consistent quality by statistically measuring the defect rate, improving the processes to eliminate those defects, and then monitoring the improvements. Six Sigma has been used to successfully improve organizations in many industries. While it has a reputation for success in large companies with thousands of employees, Six Sigma can be applied to small project teams as well.

The Greek letter sigma refers to standard deviation—Six Sigma means "six standard deviations from the mean." To achieve this level of quality in a manufacturing process, 99.9997% of all products must be of acceptable quality (or 3.4 defects per million opportunities). It's not hard to get an intuitive grasp on what this means in the real world. According to Jeannine Siviy at the Software Engineering Institute, a Four Sigma level of quality—meaning that we're 99.9% sure—would yield:

- 9 hours of unsafe drinking water a year
- 107 incorrect medical procedures a day
- 200,000 incorrect drug prescriptions a year
- 18,322 pieces of mishandled mail an hour
- 2,000,000 documents lost by the IRS a year
- Two short or long landings at any major airport a day

Variance is an important part of Six Sigma. There is a saying at General Electric, an early adopter and innovator in the Six Sigma world: "Our Customers Feel the Variance, Not the Mean." All processes have some inherent variability. No process, especially not a software process, produces defects at an entirely regular rate. What GE found is that customers can get used to a "noise level" of defects; it's the large changes in quality that will really get their attention. This is where Six Sigma is especially useful. It is the statistical variances that will take a product from one standard deviation into another; the process problems that cause these variances are the ones most likely to be identified and fixed.

The goal of Six Sigma is to think of every aspect of the business as a process that can be improved in a way that can be measured statistically. The main tool for doing this is a five-phase approach called DMAIC (see Table 12-1).

TABLE 12-1. DMAIC: A five-phase approach to Six Sigma

Phase	Description
Define opportunities	Determine customer and core processes. Determine the customer's requirements for the products and services being produced. Map the processes that are being improved. Gain the customer's commitment.
Measure performance	Develop a plan to collect and measure the defect data. Collect data from many sources in the organization and determine the defect rates and other metrics. Compile and display the data.
Analyze opportunity	Analyze and verify the data collected. Determine the root causes for the defects and identify opportunities for improvement. Prioritize the improvement opportunities.
Improve performance	Design creative solutions to improve the processes. Create a problem statement and a solution statement for each problem. Test specific improvements with an experimental approach. Deploy the improvements.
Control performance	Monitor the improvement programs to control them. Develop an ongoing monitoring plan to keep the process on the new course and prevent it from reverting to its previous state. Assess the effectiveness of the improvement. Develop staffing and training incentives to make the improvements permanent.

Six Sigma professionals have a training and certification program called the Black Belt program. The Certified Six Sigma Black Belt is a professional trained to implement Six Sigma in an organization and train others in the Six Sigma principles, systems, and tools. They have a thorough understanding of the DMAIC model and fundamental knowledge of project management.

> **NOTE**
>
> More information on Six Sigma can be found at the iSixSigma web site (*http://www.isixsigma.com*) and the Motorola University web site (*http:// www.motorola.com/motorolauniversity*).

Processes and Methodologies

There are also complete processes that can be adopted by an organization. Unlike models and certifications, these methodologies define the activities to be performed and the roles that people in the organization must fill in their daily work. In many cases, they incorporate many project management practices similar to the ones in this book. But unlike the diagnose-and-fix approach, a methodology provides a complete process that can be adopted all at once by an organization.

Adopting an "off-the-shelf" process or methodology is fundamentally different from using a model or framework for process improvement. Instead of improving the existing software lifecycle, you adopt an entire process that's "tried and true." Unlike the diagnose-and-fix approach, adopting a specific process requires revolutionary, rather than evolutionary or incremental, changes. It is usually much harder to convince people to adopt an entire new process rather than one specific tool or technique. It also requires determined management support to gain acceptance, because it requires a complete change to the entire lifecycle.

Extreme Programming

Extreme Programming (or XP) was developed in the 1990s by Kent Beck when he was working on a project at Chrysler (although its roots stretch back to SmallTalk projects that he and Ward Cunningham worked on at Tektronix in the mid-1980s). It represents one of the fastest growing movements in the software world today, and many of the techniques in this book will seem familiar to people who have worked in an XP environment.

XP consists of a set of rules and practices that govern all areas of software development: planning, designing, coding, and testing. These practices emphasize interaction and collaboration between the engineering team and the stakeholders and users, as well as the ability to respond quickly to changes in order to produce working software. The goal of XP is to lower the cost of change. Uncontrolled changes are the most common cause of software project failure (see Chapter 6); by putting basic XP principles and practices in place, a project team can control the changes.

The specific planning practices employed by XP are intended to be as lightweight and agile as possible, and have a high level of user involvement. XP projects are planned in short iterations using the Planning Game (see Chapter 3) in order to make frequent small releases. The requirements are documented as *user stories*, which are written by the users. Each user story is a brief, three-sentence description of a specific behavior that must be performed by the software. It is much less detailed than a use case or a requirement, and should only contain enough information to allow a developer to create a basic 1, 2, or 3-week estimate. Once 80 or so user stories are created, a *release plan* is built by the developers; they divide the project into 1- to 3-week iterations. An *iteration plan* is developed when each iteration begins. *Project velocity* is a metric that gauges how much work is getting done on the project by comparing the sum of the estimates for the user stories planned in the current iteration with the estimates for the tasks actually performed (similar to variance, in Chapter 4).

The main principle behind XP design is simplicity: a simple design is always more efficient to build than a complex one. Classes and methods should be named consistently; a *metaphor* should be used to help guide developers in creating consistent names. Functionality should never be added before it is scheduled. The developers should "refactor mercilessly"—that is, they should refactor the design and code whenever possible (see Chapter 7).

XP coding employs some familiar practices: test-driven development (see Chapter 7) and pair programming (see Chapter 5). In addition, one important principle in XP coding is that the customer must always be available to the developers. This allows them to get constant feedback and clarifications. Users and stakeholders are an active part of the development team, and the developers have face-to-face communication with them throughout the course of the project. In addition to the user stories, they are responsible for negotiating which user stories are included in each release, giving feedback on the results of each iteration and, most importantly, filling in the details that are missing from the user stories.

Testing in XP consists of unit tests and acceptance tests. All code must have unit tests, and all unit tests must pass before the code can be released. When a bug is found in production, an additional unit test must be written to guard against it in the future. When software is delivered, the customer is responsible for running *acceptance tests* to verify that the user stories are all implemented properly. The customer is responsible for verifying that the acceptance tests are correct—meaning that the unit tests truly verify that the work has been done—and for reviewing the results of the acceptance tests to determine whether the software is ready for release.

Many programmers have turned their struggling development teams around using XP. One of its biggest advantages is that it does not require widespread organizational change, which means that it can be implemented by a small group of programmers without getting managers involved. For a team that does not have any project planning or requirements gathering, working in an XP environment will be an enormous relief. XP is an effective way to promote good social and organizational change by putting good development and project management practices in place. It's no wonder that there are a growing number of professionals who have come to depend on XP for all of their work.

One common misunderstanding is that XP is not a disciplined or well-defined process, and that XP and the CMM and ISO 9000 are all somehow mutually exclusive. In fact, XP projects follow a very specific set of rules and practices. It is possible for a good team that has fully implemented XP to pass a CMM or ISO 9000 assessment.

On reason XP is effective is that it addresses one of the most common problems in software development: the hands-off customer. Just as a hands-off client can cause serious problems in an outsourced project (see Chapter 11), serious project problems can happen when a stakeholder does not act as if he has a real stake in the software. It is very easy for a software project to go off track, and it needs constant direction to keep the scope of the project current with the organization's needs. XP provides an effective solution to this problem by making the stakeholders a part of the development team and requiring them to be involved in the day-to-day work of the project.

There are, however, some important drawbacks to XP. It is not clear that XP can be extended to large teams. Some experts feel that XP is difficult to implement with teams that are larger than about 12 people. (There is some research in this area, and a few researchers have reported success on large teams using a modified version of XP.) Another drawback is that it only works on software projects that can be delivered incrementally, or do not have human users. The original C3 project at Chrysler was a payroll system; it's not clear that XP would work for a different team at Chrysler developing a fuel injection system or anti-lock brake system.

But the most important drawback to XP is that the customer must always be available. There are many environments in which this is a very difficult requirement to meet. The users and stakeholders in most organizations have their own jobs to do, and it would be unreasonable to require that they devote all of their working time to a software project. Requirements elicitation (see Chapter 6) requires specialized skills and people, which often makes it difficult to implement in small organizations, but it is much less demanding of the time of people outside of the engineering team. And once the requirements are written, they can be reviewed for defects. While it's generally not possible to catch every defect before the programming begins, it is possible to find many of them—and it is much faster to fix defects on paper than it is to fix them in software, especially when they are not caught until late in the project.

XP proponents often say that face-to-face communication is superior to written communication, and that XP's reliance on face-to-face meetings and very little documentation frees the process from the "bureaucracy" of requirements documentation. However, reliance on face-to-face communication for detailed requirements introduces its own problems. Defining the behavior of software is a particularly complex and error-prone process. It is very easy for people to reach misunderstandings when talking about software behavior. This is especially risky when a customer has been involved as a project team member since the beginning of the project. The customer's expectations will often evolve along with the project, as a side effect of the influence of the rest of the programming team. The result is that the customer is more likely to accept the software, even if it does not fully meet the needs of the people in the customer's organization who were not on the project team. This sort of tunnel vision is much easier to avoid when the customer keeps his eye on his task and his organization's needs rather than on the details of the project and the developers.

Drawbacks aside, for projects in which the circumstances and team are compatible with XP, it is a very powerful tool. Many project teams across the world have made a huge difference in their projects by adopting some or all of the XP practices.

> **NOTE**
> Additional information about Extreme Programming can be found in *Extreme Programming Explained: Embrace Change* (2nd Edition) by Kent Beck (Addison Wesley, 2004).

Rational Unified Process

There are many complete software processes that are available and ready to be adopted out of the box. Typically, such a process will include a complete set of activities to be performed over the course of the entire software project. These activities usually include scope definition, requirements engineering, architecture, design, programming, and testing activities. One of the most popular off-the-shelf processes is the *Rational Unified Process* (RUP).

The activities of RUP are based around the idea of highly iterative development. After an initial planning phase, the software project enters a cycle of iterations, each of which results in an executable release. Each of the iterations contains distinct activities for planning, requirements specification, analysis and design, implementation, testing, and stakeholder evaluation. The advantage of iteration is that it allows the project team to identify and correct misunderstandings early on in the project, keep the stakeholders up-to-date with deliverables to help them gauge the progress of the project, and distribute the project's workload more evenly over the course of the project.

RUP includes a disciplined approach to requirements management that is based on the idea of managing changes. The requirements in RUP are similar to those in Chapter 6. They include use cases as well as functional and nonfunctional requirements. RUP incorporates software design using the Unified Modeling Language (UML), a visual modeling system for graphically representing the use cases, class model, object interactions, and components of the software.

One core element of RUP is the continuous assessment of the quality of the system. The testing activities involve creating test cases based on the functionality introduced in each iteration. By incorporating testing activities in each iteration, RUP allows the team to identify defects early, and to continuously assess the health of the product. RUP also has a clear change control system to ensure that every change is evaluated; measurements of the rate of software changes are used to assess the status of the project.

One thing that makes RUP unique is that it is a product in addition to a process. RUP is available from Rational Software, a subsidiary of IBM. An organization licenses RUP from Rational Software, which keeps the software up to date and provides regular updates to the process and its documentation.

There are many software packages that go along with RUP. Requirements and use cases are stored, managed, traced, and edited using the RequisitePro software. Rational Rose, a UML editing tool, is used to capture and visually model the software architecture. Other products are used for configuration management (ClearCase), change request management (ClearQuest), test case management (TestManager), performance testing (PerformanceStudio), test automation (Rational Robot), and tools to support other areas of the software process. Each of these products is also available separately, and RUP can be implemented without these tools. Many organizations license RUP as a complete process engineering suite. RUP was also built to be adaptable to the needs of individual organizations; Rational Process Workbench is a tool for customizing and extending RUP to meet your organization's needs.

The support tools in RUP are a strong feature. However, they also present a significant pitfall. Some project managers feel that they can simply buy their way out of a software process problem by buying RUP and distributing it to the team. But while some problems can be solved by adopting a process like RUP out of the box, many project management problems cannot be solved by writing a check. This is why it is often easier to adopt small, piecemeal changes like adopting individual practices, tools, and techniques than it is to force an entire organization to adopt a complete software process immediately. However, if that problem can be overcome, then an out-of-the-box process such as RUP can be a powerful tool for building better software.

> **NOTE**
>
> More information on RUP can be found in *The Rational Unified Process: An Introduction* by Philippe Kruchten (Addison Wesley, 2000).

Moving Forward

There is no single process, framework, or methodology that works all the time. Every organization is different. What's more, organizations are made up of people who need to be convinced that the change really is necessary. While these practices can be very useful as guidelines, the most important part of improving the software process is helping people in your organization understand their role in the development of software.

One reason these process improvement tools have a good chance of successful implementation is that each of them takes into account the basic project management principles introduced in Chapter 1. Whether the process is adopted all at once or good practices are adopted individually, if these principles are followed, then the team will build better software.

This book has been all about specific tools and techniques that, if applied individually, will help a project manager improve the way her organization builds software. Most software organizations will see substantial benefits from a piecemeal approach to building better software. Specific problems can be diagnosed, and individual tools and techniques can be applied to help alleviate those problems. In this way, a project manager can introduce changes directed specifically at the most troublesome problems. But whether you select a piecemeal, diagnose-and-fix approach or have the clout to initiate a full software process improvement effort, solving the problems that affect your projects is within your reach.

Bibliography

Chapter 2. Software Project Planning

Brooks, F. P. *The Mythical Man-Month: Essays on Software Engineering*. Addison Wesley, 1995.

Christensen, D.S. "Value Cost Management Report to Evaluate the Contractor's Estimate at Completion." *Acquisition Review Quarterly* (Summer 1999).

Fleming, Q. W., and J. M. Koppelman. "Earned Value Project Management: A Powerful Tool for Software Projects." *STSC CrossTalk: The Journal of Defense Software Engineering* (July 1998).

Humphrey, W. S. *Managing the Software Process*. Addison Wesley, 1989.

Leffingwell, D., and D. Widrig. *Managing Software Requirements: A Unified Approach*. Addison Wesley, 2000.

Leffingwell, D., and D. Widrig. *Managing Software Requirements: A Use Case Approach*. Addison Wesley, 2003.

Parkinson, C. N. *Parkinson's Law: The Pursuit of Progress*. John Murray, 1958.

Paulk, M. C., B Curtis, M.B. Chrissis, and C.V. Weber. *Capability Maturity Model Registered Trademark Integration (CMMI Superscript SM), Version 1.1: CMMI Superscript SM for Systems Engineering and Software Engineering (CMMI-SE/SW, V1.1: Continuous Representation).* Carnegie Mellon University Software Engineering Institute, 2001.

Paulk, M. C. *The Capability Maturity Model: Guidelines for Improving the Software Process.* Addison Wesley, 1995.

Potter, N. S., and M. E. Sakry. *Making Process Improvement Work: A Concise Action Guide for Software Managers and Practitioners.* Addison Wesley, 2002.

Thayer, R. H. *Software Engineering Project Management.* IEEE Computer Society, 1997.

Wiegers, K. "Saving for a Rainy Day." *The Rational Edge* (April 2002).

Wiegers, K. E. *Software Requirements.* Microsoft Press, 1999.

Wiegers, K. E. *Peer Reviews in Software: A Practical Guide.* Addison Wesley, 2002.

Chapter 3. Estimation

Beck, K. *Extreme Programming Explained: Embrace Change.* Addison Wesley, 2004.

Humphrey, W. S. *A Discipline for Software Engineering.* Addison Wesley, 1995.

Potter, N. S., and M. E. Sakry. *Making Process Improvement Work: A Concise Action Guide for Software Managers and Practitioners.* Addison Wesley, 2002.

Standish Group. *CHAOS: A Recipe for Success.* The Standish Group International, 1999.

Thayer, R. H.. *Software Engineering Project Management.* IEEE Computer Society, 1997.

Wiegers, K. E. "Stop Promising Miracles." *Software Development* (2000).

Chapter 4. Project Schedules

Brooks, F. P. *The Mythical Man-Month: Essays on Software Engineering,* Addison Wesley, 1995.

Christensen, D.S. "Value Cost Management Report to Evaluate the Contractor's Estimate at Completion." *Acquisition Review Quarterly,* Summer 1999.

Fleming, Q. W., and J. M. Koppelman. "Earned Value Project Management: A Powerful Tool for Software Projects." *STSC CrossTalk: The Journal of Defense Software Engineering,* July 1998.

Humphrey, W. S. *Managing the Software Process.* Addison Wesley, 1989.

Leffingwell, D., and D. Widrig. *Managing Software Requirements: A Unified Approach.* Addison Wesley, 2000.

Parkinson, C. N. *Parkinson's Law: The Pursuit of Progress.* John Murray, 1958.

Paulk, M. C., B Curtis, M.B. Chrissis, and C.V. Weber. *Capability Maturity Model Registered Trademark Integration (CMMI Superscript SM), Version 1.1: CMMI Superscript SM for Systems Engineering and Software Engineering (CMMI-SE/SW, V1.1: Continuous Representation)*. Carnegie Mellon University Software Engineering Institute, 2001.

Potter, N. S., and M. E. Sakry. *Making Process Improvement Work: A Concise Action Guide for Software Managers and Practitioners*. Addison Wesley, 2002.

Thayer, R. H. *Software Engineering Project Management*. IEEE Computer Society, 1997.

Wiegers, K. "Saving for a Rainy Day." *The Rational Edge* (April 2002).

Wiegers, K. E: *Software Requirements*. Microsoft Press, 1999.

Wiegers, K. E. *Peer Reviews in Software: A Practical Guide*. Addison Wesley, 2002.

Chapter 5. Reviews

Beck, K. *Extreme Programming Explained: Embrace Change*. Addison Wesley, 2000.

Gilb, T., D. Graham, et al. *Software Inspection*. Addison Wesley, 1993.

Software Engineering Institute. "Software Inspections." *Software Technology Roadmap*. J. Foreman. Carnegie Mellon University Software Engineering Institute, 2004.

Standish Group. CHAOS: A Recipe for Success, The Standish Group International, 1999.

Wiegers, K. E. *Peer Reviews in Software: A Practical Guide*. Addison Wesley, 2002.

Williams, L., R. R. Kessler, et al. "Strengthening the Case for Pair-Programming." *IEEE Software* (July/August 2000).

Chapter 6. Software Requirements

Christel, M., and K. Kang. "Issues in Requirements Elicitation," Software Engineering Institute, Carnegie Mellon University.

Gottesdiener, E. "Top Ten Ways Project Teams Misuse Use Case—and How to Correct Them." *The Rational Edge* (July 2002).

Kulak, D,. and E. Guiney. *Use Cases: Requirements in Context*. Addison Wesley, 2000.

Rumbaugh, J. "Getting Started: Using Use Cases to Capture Requirements." *Journal of Object-Oriented Programming* 7(5) (1994).

Thayer, R. H., M. Dorfman, et al. *Software Requirements Engineering*. Los Alamitos, Calif., IEEE Computer Society Press, 1994.

Wiegers, K. E., *Software Requirements: Practical Techniques for Gathering and Managing Requirements Throughout the Product Development Cycle*. Microsoft Press, 2003.

Chapter 7. Design and Programming

Collins-Sussman, B., B. W. Fitzpatrick, et al. *Version Control with Subversion*. O'Reilly, 2004.

Fowler, M., and K. Beck. *Refactoring: Improving the Design of Existing Code*. Addison Wesley, 1999.

Hunt, A., D. Thomas, et al. *Pragmatic Unit Testing in Java with JUnit*. Pragmatic Bookshelf, 2003.

Chapter 8. Software Testing

Burke, D. "All Circuits are Busy Now: The 1990 AT&T Long Distance Network Collapse," California Polytechnic State University, 1995.

Crosby, P. B. *Quality Is Free: The Art of Making Quality Certain*. McGraw-Hill, 1979.

Grady, R. B., and D. L. Caswell. *Software Metrics: Establishing a Company-Wide Program*. Prentice Hall, 1987.

IEEE Computer Society. IEEE Standard for Software Test Documentation (IEEE Std 829-1998), Software Engineering Technical Committee of the IEEE Computer Society, 1998.

Kaner, C., J. L. Falk, et al. *Testing Computer Software*. Van Nostrand Reinhold, 1993.

Spolsky, J. "Top Five (Wrong) Reasons You Don't Have Testers." *Joel on Software* (April 30, 2000).

Westfall, L., and C. Lohr. Software Metrics, Version 1.2, The Westfall Team, 2000.

Chapter 9. Understanding Change

Cialdini, R. B. *Influence: Science and Practice*. Allyn and Bacon, 2001.

DeMarco, T., and T. R. Lister. *Peopleware: Productive Projects and Teams*. Dorset House, 1999.

Humphrey, W. S. "Justifying a Process Improvement Proposal." SEI Interactive 3(1) (2000).

Standish Group. CHAOS: A Recipe for Success. The Standish Group International, 1999.

Chapter 10. Management and Leadership

Abe, J., K. Sakamura, et al. *An Analysis of Software Project Failure*. Proceedings of 4th International Conference on Software Engineering, IEEE Press, 1979.

Addison, T., and S. Vallabh. *Controlling Software Project Risks—an Empirical Study of Methods Used by Experienced Project Managers*. Proceedings of SAICSIT, 2002.

Balachandra, R., and J. H. Friar. "Factors for Success in R&D Projects and New Product Innovation: A Contextual Framework." *IEEE Transactions on Engineering Management* 44(3) (1997).

Brooks, F. P. *The Mythical Man-month: Essays on Software Engineering.* Addison Wesley, 1995.

Glass, R. L. "Evolving a New Theory of Project Success." *Communications of The ACM* 42(11) (1999).

Jurison, J. "Software Project Management: The Manager's View." *Communications of the Association for Information Systems* 2 (1999).

Klein, G., J. J. Jiang, et al. "Wanted: Project Teams With a Blend of IS Professional Orientations." COMMUNICATIONS OF THE ACM 45(6) (2002).

Kumar, V., A. N. S. Persaud, et al. "To Terminate or Not an Ongoing R&D Project: A Managerial Dilemma." *IEEE Transactions on Engineering Management* 43(3) (1996).

Letters. Software Project Failure Lessons Learned. *Communications of the ACM.* 42 (1999).

Molo kken, K., and M. J orgensen. "A Review of Surveys on Software Effort Estimation." *Journal of Systems and Software* 70(1-2) (2004).

Pinto, J. K., and S. J. Mantel. "The Causes of Project Failure." *IEEE Transactions on Engineering Management* 37(4) (1990).

Thayer, R. H. *Software Engineering Project Management.* IEEE Computer Society, 1997.

Chapter 11. Managing an Outsourced Project

Antonucci, Y. L., and J. J. Tucker III. "IT Outsourcing: Current Trends, Benefits, and Risks." *Information Strategy: The Executive's Journal* 14(2) (1998).

Apte, U. M., M. G. Sobol, et al. "IS Outsourcing Practices in the USA, Japan and Finland: A Comparative Study." *Journal of Information Technology* 12 (1997).

Aubert, B. A., M. Patry, et al. "Managing IT Outsourcing Risk: Lessons Learned." *Cahier du GReSI* 01(11) (2001).

Bhatnagar, S. C., and S. Madon. "The Indian Software Industry: Moving Towards Maturity." *Journal of Information Technology* 12 (1997).

Dibbern, J., T. Goles, et al. "Information Systems Outsourcing: A Survey and Analysis of the Literature." *Database for Advances in Information Systems* 35(4) (2004).

Fielden, T. "Keeping Your IT Partners on a Short Leash." *InfoWorld* 23(7) (2001).

Fowler, A., and B. Jeffs. "Examining Information Systems Outsourcing: A Case Study from the United Kingdom." *Journal of Information Technology* 13 (1998).

Hirschheim, R., A. Heinzl, et al. "Information Systems Outsourcing: Enduring Themes, Emergent Patterns and Future Directions." *European Journal of Information Systems* 12 (2003).

Jennex, M. E., and O. Adelakun. "Success Factors for Offshore Information System Development." *Journal of Information Technology Cases and Applications* 5(3) (2003).

Jones, C. "Evaluating software outsourcing options." *Information Systems Management* 11(4) (1994).

Jones, P. "Information Systems Outsourcing." *Supply Management* 7(24) (2002).

Khalfan, A. "A Case Analysis of Business Process Outsourcing Project Failure Profile and Implementation Problems in a Large Organisation of a Developing Nation." *Business Process Management Journal* 9(6) (2003).

Kyrki, A. Offshore Software Development: From Outsourcing to Partnership?, Lappeenranta University of Technology.

L. P. Baldwin, Z. Irani, et al. "Outsourcing Information Systems: Drawing Lessons from a Banking Case Study." *European Journal of Information Systems* 10 (2001).

Lacity, M. C., and R. A. *Hirschheim. Beyond the Information Systems Outsourcing Bandwagon: The Insourcing Response*. Wiley, 1995.

Lee, J.-N., and Y.-G. Kim. "Understanding Outsourcing Partnership: A Comparison of Three Theoretical Perspectives." *IEEE Transactions on Engineering Management* 52(1) (2005).

Leinfuss, E. "Outsourcers Have Limited Liability." *Computerworld* 26(13) (1992).

Mearian, L. "Merrill Lynch Mixing Outside, In-House Apps." *Computerworld* 36(47) (2002).

Nicholson, B., and S. Sahay. "Some Political and Cultural Issues in the Globalisation of Software Development: Case Experience from Britain and India." *Information and Organization* 11 (2001).

Palvia, S. C. J. "Global Outsourcing of IT and IT Enabled Services: A Framework for Choosing an Outsourcing Coutry." *Journal of Information Technology Cases and Applications* 6(3) (2004).

Power, M., C. Bonifazi, et al. "The ten Outsourcing Traps to Avoid." *The Journal of Business Strategy* 25(2) (2004).

Roy, V., and B. Aubert. "A Resource-Based Analysis of Outsourcing: Evidence from Case Studies." *CIRANO Working Papers* 2001s-23 (2001).

Roy, V., and B. A. Aubert. "A Dream Project Turns Nightmare: How Flawless Software Never Got Implemented." *Cahier du GReSI* 02(05) (2001).

Segalstad, S. H. "How to Use and Misuse a Consultant." *Scientific Computing & Instrumentation* 19(12) (2002).

Soliman, K. S. "A Framework for Global IS Outsourcing by Application Service Providers." *Business Process Management Journal* 9(6) (2003).

Suh, R. "Guaranteeing That Outsourcing Serves Your Business Strategy." *Information Strategy: The Executive's Journal* 8(3) (1992).

Chapter 12. Process Improvement

Beck, K. *Extreme Programming Explained: Embrace Change*. Addison Wesley, 2004.

Deming, W. E. *Out of the Crisis*. Massachusetts Institute of Technology, Center for Advanced Engineering Study, 1986.

Fowler, M., and J. Highsmith. "The Agile Manifesto." *Software Development Magazine* (August 2001).

Humphrey, W. S. Introduction to Process Improvement. Carnegie Mellon University Software Engineering Institute, 1993.

International Standards Organization. *ISO 9000-3 1997 Guidelines in Plain English*, Praxiom Research Group Limited, 2004.

International Standards Organization. Quality Management Principles, International Standards Organization, 2001.

iSixSigma.com. iSixSigma web site retrieved August 10, 2005 from *http://www.isixsigma.com*.

Kruchten, P. *The Rational Unified Process: An Introduction*. Addison Wesley, 2000.

Motorola University. Motorola University web site retrieved August 10, 2005 from *http://www.motorola.com/motorolauniversity*.

Paulk, M. C. *The Capability Maturity Model: Guidelines for Improving the Software Process*. Addison Wesley, 1995.

Paulk, M. C., B Curtis, M.B. Chrissis, and C.V. Weber. *Capability Maturity Model Registered Trademark Integration (CMMI Superscript SM), Version 1.1: CMMI Superscript SM for Systems Engineering and Software Engineering (CMMI-SE/SW, V1.1: Continuous Representation)*. Carnegie Mellon University Software Engineering Institute, 2001.

Phillips, M. CMMI V1.1—Improving and Integrating (presentation). Carnegie Mellon University Software Engineering Institute, 2002.

Rothman, J. "Achieving a Repeatable Process." *Software Development* (June 1998).

Siviy, J. M. Six Sigma & Software Process Improvement. *Software Engineering Measurement & Analysis Initiative*, Carnegie Mellon University Software Engineering Institute, 2002.

SixSigmaTutorial.com. "Six Sigma Tutorial." May 20, 2005 from *http://sixsigmatutorial.com*.

Zahran, S. *Software Process Improvement: Practical Guidelines for Business Success*. Addison Wesley, 1998.

INDEX

Jennifer Greene and **Andrew Stellman** have been building software together since 1998. Andrew comes from a programming background and has managed teams of requirements analysts, designers, and developers. Jennifer has a testing background and has managed teams of architects, developers, and testers. She has led multiple large-scale outsourced projects.

Between the two of them, they have managed every aspect of software development. They formed Stellman & Greene Consulting in 2003, with a focus on project management, software development, management consulting, and software process improvement. They have worked in a wide range of industries, including finance, telecommunications, media, nonprofit, entertainment, natural language processing, science, and academia.

For more information about them and this book, visit *http://www.stellman-greene.com*.

COLOPHON

OUR LOOK IS THE RESULT of reader comments, our own experimentation, and feedback from distribution channels. Distinctive covers complement our distinctive approach to technical topics, breathing personality and life into potentially dry subjects.

Jamie Peppard was the production editor for *Applied Software Project Management*. Chris Downey was the copyeditor, and Ann Atalla proofread the book. Matt Hutchinson and Claire Cloutier provided quality control. Lydia Onofrei provided production assistance. Johnna VanHoose Dinse wrote the index.

MendeDesign designed the cover of this book. Karen Montgomery produced the cover layout with Adobe InDesign CS using the Akzidenz Grotesk and Orator fonts.

Marcia Friedman designed the interior layout. Melanie Wang and Phyllis McKee designed the template. This book was converted by Keith Fahlgren to FrameMaker 5.5.6. The text font is Adobe's Meridien; the heading font is ITC Bailey; and the code font is LucasFont's TheSans Mono Condensed. The illustrations that appear in the book were produced by Robert Romano, Jessamyn Read, and Lesley Borash using Macromedia FreeHand MX and Adobe Photoshop CS.

Better than e-books

Buy *Applied Software Project Management* and
access the digital edition FREE on Safari for 45 days.

Go to www.oreilly.com/go/safarienabled
and type in coupon code AQIY-M73H-7AEU-9RH6-VMZF

Search
thousands of
top tech books

Download
whole chapters

Cut and Paste
code examples

Find
answers fast

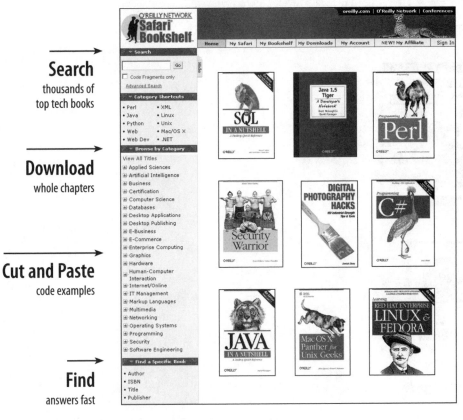

Search Safari! The premier electronic reference
library for programmers and IT professionals.

Related Titles from O'Reilly

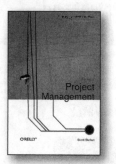

Software Development

The Art of Project Management

Head First Design Patterns

Head First Design Patterns Poster

Essential Business Process Modeling

Essential Service Bus

Practical Development Environments

Prefactoring

UML 2.0 in a Nutshell

O'REILLY®

Our books are available at most retail and online bookstores.

To order direct: 1-800-998-9938 • *order@oreilly.com* • *www.oreilly.com*

Online editions of most O'Reilly titles are available by subscription at *safari.oreilly.com*

Keep in touch with O'Reilly

Download examples from our books

To find example files from a book, go to: *www.oreilly.com/catalog* select the book, and follow the "Examples" link.

Register your O'Reilly books

Register your book at *register.oreilly.com* Why register your books? Once you've registered your O'Reilly books you can:

- Win O'Reilly books, T-shirts or discount coupons in our monthly drawing.
- Get special offers available only to registered O'Reilly customers.
- Get catalogs announcing new books (US and UK only).
- Get email notification of new editions of the O'Reilly books you own.

Join our email lists

Sign up to get topic-specific email announcements of new books and conferences, special offers, and O'Reilly Network technology newsletters at:

elists.oreilly.com

It's easy to customize your free elists subscription so you'll get exactly the O'Reilly news you want.

Get the latest news, tips, and tools

www.oreilly.com

- "Top 100 Sites on the Web"—PC Magazine
- CIO Magazine's Web Business 50 Awards

Our web site contains a library of comprehensive product information (including book excerpts and tables of contents), downloadable software, background articles, interviews with technology leaders, links to relevant sites, book cover art, and more.

Work for O'Reilly

Check out our web site for current employment opportunities:

jobs.oreilly.com

Contact us

O'Reilly Media, Inc.
1005 Gravenstein Hwy North
Sebastopol, CA 95472 USA
Tel: 707-827-7000 or 800-998-9938
    (6am to 5pm PST)
Fax: 707-829-0104

Contact us by email

For answers to problems regarding your order or our products:
order@oreilly.com

To request a copy of our latest catalog:
catalog@oreilly.com

For book content technical questions or corrections: **booktech@oreilly.com**

For educational, library, government, and corporate sales: **corporate@oreilly.com**

To submit new book proposals to our editors and product managers:
proposals@oreilly.com

For information about our international distributors or translation queries:
international@oreilly.com

For information about academic use of O'Reilly books:
adoption@oreilly.com
or visit:
academic.oreilly.com

For a list of our distributors outside of North America check out:
international.oreilly.com/distributors.html

Order a book online

www.oreilly.com/order_new

Our books are available at most retail and online bookstores.
To order direct: 1-800-998-9938 • *order@oreilly.com* • *www.oreilly.com*
Online editions of most O'Reilly titles are available by subscription at *safari.oreilly.com*